Liverpool Studies in European Regional Cultures 7

The Irish Border
History, Politics, Culture

LIVERPOOL STUDIES
IN EUROPEAN REGIONAL CULTURES

OTHER TITLES AVAILABLE IN THIS SERIES

Culture, Tourism and Development: The Case of Ireland edited by
Ullrich Kockel, 1994, ISBN 0–85323–369–1

***Landscape, Heritage and Identity: Case Studies in Irish
Ethnography*** edited by Ullrich Kockel, 1995, ISBN 0–85323–500–7

Watching One's Tongue: Issues in Language Planning edited by
Máiréad Nic Craith, Vol. 4, 1996, ISBN 0–85323–611–9

Watching One's Tongue: Aspects of Romance and Celtic Languages
edited by Máiréad Nic Craith, Vol. 5, 1996, ISBN 0–85323–621–6

THE IRISH BORDER

History, Politics, Culture

edited by

MALCOLM ANDERSON
and **EBERHARD BORT**

*Published on behalf of the
Culture and Economy Research Unit
at the Institute of Irish Studies,
University of Liverpool*

**LIVERPOOL UNIVERSITY PRESS
1999**

First published 1999 by
Liverpool University Press
Senate House
Liverpool
L69 3BX

British Library Cataloguing-in-Publication Data
A British Library CIP Record is available.

ISBN 0–85323–951–7

Printed and bound in the European Union by
The Alden Press in the City of Oxford

Contents

Acknowledgements

This volume is based on papers presented at a conference jointly organised by the International Social Sciences Institute and by Irish Studies at the University of Edinburgh. The conveners were Malcolm Anderson, Eberhard Bort, and Robert Mullally.

For financial support of the colloquium we wish to thank the Justin Arbuthnott Fund for Anglo-Irish Understanding, the Faculty Group of Law and Social Sciences at Edinburgh University, the Department of Celtic/Irish Studies at the University of Edinburgh, and the ESRC (Economic and Social Research Council) through the research project on the internal and external frontiers of the European Union - ESRC R000235602.

The maps on page 67 and page 71 are drawn from T W Moody, F X Martin and F J Byrne, *A New History of Ireland*, Vol IX, part 2, by permission of Oxford University Press; the smaller map on page 67 is after T W Moody and F X Martin, *The Course of Irish History*, by kind permission of J H Andrews; the Boundary Commission maps on pp 88, 91 and 93 are © Crown Copyright, reproduced by permission of the Ordnance Survey of Northern Ireland, permit no.953. These and the maps in Máiread Nic Craith's chapter (pp.178, 190-92) were drawn by Anona Lyons of the Geography Department at the University of Edinburgh.

The contributions by Shane Connaughton and Eugene McCabe are reproduced by kind permission of the authors. Eugene McCabe's 'Borderlands' was first published in *The Irish Times* on 25 February 1995; Shane Connaughton's *A Border Diary* was published by Faber and Faber in 1995.

Borderlands

Eugene McCabe

Midweek I woke, or half-woke, disturbed in the middle of the night. I couldn't find a word. Joint *what* document? I tried the alphabet quickly ... then slowly. No good. I wakened Margôt:

'The document: what's it called?'

'What document?'

'For peace ... the historic one. The two governments.'

Long silence.

'I'm still asleep.'

'I'm sorry ... it's like "makeshift" but not "makeshift". A word with that sort of sound and shape.'

'Framework.'

'Well done ... go back to sleep.'

Framework, makeshift - an unconscious connection? I pray to God my half-asleep, instinctive substitution is wrong and that the now controversial document, or some form of it, becomes a platform for continued dialogue.

This morning I'm looking for a key word or words ... Border, the Border, Borderlands. Mister Noah Webster in his big blue dictionary gives all three:

Border: from the Latin *Bordatura*. The limit of a country. A natural or man-made division between peoples and regions.

The Border: the district on or near the boundary between Scotland and England first established under the Roman Empire.

Borderland: a vague or undetermined situation, condition or place.

* * *

Clearly an obstacle to normal contact and communication, a hindrance, a nuisance, a hostile, unfriendly, defensive thing: Border.

When did it first register with me? Long ago as a child outside Clones and on our way to Corranny, under Carn Rock where my grandfather, John MacMahon, was born in Co Fermanagh. At the corrugated Southern customs post, my father would say: 'The pass, son ... it's in the glove box.' When stamping exit or entry, the Southern customs men would sometimes wink and joke, or maybe come out and talk if it was quiet.

Malcolm Anderson and Eberhard Bort (eds), *The Irish Border: History, Politics, Culture*, Liverpool University Press 1998, 1-5

HM Customs (a more permanent-looking post) had a tendency toward no eye contact and a polite matter of factness: them and us, the other foot, the other side, the Border. Though as a child you couldn't grasp the difference clearly because the first farm in Fermanagh, 'Oatfield', looked very like Drumard in Monaghan ... same trees, crows, fields, outbuildings.

Further on, at Knockballymore, my grandfather once muttered and thumbed: 'They say King Billy slept in there on his way to the Boyne.'

Myth? Probably. I've never checked.

Then Lisnaroe and the Dummy's Lough, followed by Summerhill where, again 'There was a murderer lived hereabouts.' And the jolt of that word 'murderer' against the images created in a child's mind by the word 'Summerhill' - high sun and swallows, the wonder and beauty of blackthorn ditches, deep green meadows, cattle cuddling high on drumlins. Who would murder who and why? It was too frightening and terrible to think about.

At Drumard and Lackey Bridge, it was my mother's turn to speak ... 'This was closed when I was a girl ... the Troubles ... we had to go on to the Priest's Bridge through Clerkin's quarry and yard and on to Corranny that way.' And she might quote again from the article in the *Anglo-Celt* about the MacMahons being driven from the Monaghan lowlands to the poor putty uplands of Fermanagh, and then the bit we all knew by heart: 'And that is why to this day in many's a poor Fermanagh cabin, when you find the name MacMahon, you invariably find an inborn grace and a natural courtesy of manner.'

Years later, at a well-researched lecture about the MacMahons, I listened for an hour with my mother to the tales of intrigue and betrayal, of cattle-raiding and brutality, burnings and drownings, no hint anywhere of inborn grace and natural courtesy of manner.

On the way home she was very quiet. Finally she spoke. 'I'm not sure, dear, that that man had all his facts right.'

History, I agreed, could be dodgy. If you're not there how can you tell, and being there you might tell it differently from the next fellow! Whatever about the brutality or gentility of her distant forbears, as an only child she was very proud of her father and of the high point of his life - as a prosperous republican Glasgow businessman he had the honour (pre-war) of driving de Valera round Loch Lomond. Post-war, his nephew Willie Dunn was offered a knighthood for services to the crown. 'If you take that,' his uncle said, 'I'll never talk to you again.'

The knighthood was refused. So clearly, along with inborn grace and natural courtesy of manner, there was a long memory and a fair dollop of unforgiving pride in my genes. I'd imagine that, generally throughout the country, family mythology, historical mythology, should all be tagged with a health warning: '*Myth can induce a form of madness and zealotry that leads to death.*'

* * *

The haggard field behind our house looks down on Lackey Bridge, a focus for over a decade. American senators have come to take a look, along with *taoisigh*, *tánaistí*, prayer groups, Sinn Féin jazz festivals, a persistent road-opening committee and TV crews from all over Europe.

Early on, a Swiss crowd put me standing and talking against a bollard. Afterwards, over coffee, the director shrugged his leather jacket and said: 'Of course, Ulster is 400 years out of date ... it's the yawn of Europe.' Because what he said was undeniably true, I couldn't mutter about yodelling and cuckoo clocks! A poor bloody squabble, but our own!

Was it four or five years ago that Charlie Haughey stood at Lackey for his telly biog and talked about his 'feelings of deep anger'? Valid enough if you're after grassroots approval, but after 70 years of division, the word sadness would have been more appropriate, because now almost everybody's angry ... Paisley, Trimble and Ken Maginnis roaring into the camera like the brown bull of Cooley. Is the anger part guilt because they've waited and waited year in, year out with murder in both camps every other week and, apart from noisy threats and condemnations, have been unable, apparently, to give a radical lead? A unionist John Hume would have seen the light or dark approaching long ago and made a bold, unpopular move to break the deadlock or risk his political career trying to.

Last winter sometime Marcus (our son) was mid-river at Lackey checking to see if he could risk crossing in his car to save the ten-mile round. When he looked up, Dick Spring - who had refused to be photographed against a bollard which read *Britain, Ireland's torture* - was looking at him. He beckoned the man in the river, questioned him and then, rarest of rare things, listened attentively.

Remember that Russian diplomat who appeared some years ago on the *Late Late*? What had struck him most forcibly about the Irish personality, he said, was: 'Everyone talks, no one listens.' Last year, a Ukrainian called Bogdin Kolitenko came to Fermanagh: a 20-year-old blacksmith, bearded, six feet four. He had left Kiev with the equivalent of £50 and worked his way across Europe. He arrived here wearing American army surplus combat jacket, duds and cap. We tried to explain that wearing such a uniform was unwise in this area. He roared laughing: 'I have nothing else to wear ... they will have to shoot me.' And for six weeks, he walked and cycled up and down from Corranny to Clones, talked with and greeted everyone he met.

Not once was he stopped by another uniform and he often said that he found this Border area the loveliest and most peaceful place he had been since leaving Kiev.

He learned to drink pints, to play the bodhrán (and bought one, the real McCoy, from a West of Ireland maker) and from bits and pieces, he set up a mobile forge for Marcus. Before leaving, his final gesture was to put a piece of scrap steel from a Lackey bollard into his rucksack. 'A reminder,' he said. 'I'll hammer it to Damascus steel and call it Fermanagh steel.'

And the point of this story? If a young stranger can fall in love with our Border country and its people in bad, sad times, how many thousands might come here in the future if the bombs were put away for good and agreement reached?

* * *

At the opening of Monaghan Library in the 1970s, I suggested that this island was small for two Arts Councils, and, though unable to merge, they could and should work together to show the way to rise above the political vacuum and the sectarian nightmare. I went on to say that the day would come when, hopefully, Orange bands would march in Monaghan and elsewhere in the South, not just on the 12th but on St Patrick's Day, as a cultural event we could all relate to without hatred and triumphalism. There was a great deal of wry smiling and head shaking.

I still believe that day will come ... sometime. We have suffered enough in this part of the world from myth and history, from suspicion, from dislike of the unlike that leads to nothing but bloodletting and the gas chambers. And the fact is that for 15 years now, both Arts Councils have worked together to run Annamakerrig, willed by Tyrone Guthrie to promote harmony between both parts of the island.

As Chancellor of Queens, Guthrie once caused great upset by saying publicly: 'How would you feel if the Germans came here in 1940 and stayed for 400 years?' A simplistic, shock-tactical thing to say, but deliberately said. A few days later, a heavyweight delegation came down from Queens and asked him to resign. He said that if he was caught out telling a lie he would resign but not for asking a question intended to help. When comes such another?

The 27 concrete bollards at Lackey Bridge are smashed and, as I write, foundations are being poured for the new bridge. There is a feeling that it will never again be closed. That chapter is finished. Things are returning to normal. Local farmers from both sides and both persuasions haunt Lackey, scavenging for the massive steel spikes and rubble. A huge jackhammer (£17,000 worth) was stolen one night from a Japanese Hymac.

There have been strong words and at least one scuffle. One farmer wiring a digger to load his trailer had the battery blown up in his face and is hospitalised. Others look on: 'There could be no luck with thon stuff ... It was bad news from day one.' I'm not sure it's all that bad. From the scrap steel and rubble of the old bridge - the phoenix of a new framework?

As children we sang the lines of a nineteenth-century poem my mother put to music:

So let the Orange lily be
Thy badge my patriot brother
The everlasting green for me
And we for one another.

Why not? Give it time. Let's talk. Let's hope. And the best of British and Irish luck to us all.

* * *

Addendum (January 1996)

We're into a new year after one year plus of uneasy peace, tiptoing round terror, shadow boxing and swearing on both sides and nobody prepared to hope too loudly lest the whole thing fall apart.

In the early days of Knock Airport before the High Tech arrived, passengers could sometimes look up on the notice board and see opposite 'Time of Arrival' the word 'soon'. Vague but hopeful! And if the question now is asked: 'Has permanent peace arrived?' - we can't yet echo Molly Bloom's great affirmative and say Yes Yes Yes... But what we can do is hope passionately and say quietly to ourselves and maybe to each other: Soon, soon, soon...

From *A Border Diary*

Shane Connaughton

Day 13: Sunday 27 August [1994]

We're along a narrow country road skirting numerous lakes. It's the middle of nowhere. County Cavan *is* nowhereland. You can rattle around empty lanes and roads, rarely meeting a soul. It's the last undiscovered part of Europe. There are over three hundred lakes and three grand rivers - the Erne, the Finn and the Annaghlee. Up in the north-west of the county the longest river in the British isles rises - the Shannon. The spot is known as the Shannon pot. I drove up there into the Cuilcagh Mountains and the only people I met were two Germans in leather shorts flying down on bicycles. It's magnificently lonely. All you have for company are birds and sheep. The views are spectacular, especially in the evening when the sun's going down. The light then is gold and green, the mountainy shadows slender and dark. The leathery Germans were disconcerting. Further down the country they are moving in, building holiday compounds, houses and restaurants. Adrian Dunbar, an actor friend of mine from Enniskillen, says the only weapons we have are the bad winters and the potholes on the roads. He thinks we should be going round *making* potholes, not filling them in. Nothing will deter them, though. They'll come well-wrapped against the cold and, if necessary, on tractors. Potholes won't worry them. The EEC is opening up the country. If the Loyalists and the IRA ever agree to peace, then we're banjaxed. Round here will be full of tourists in no time.

This morning I met a friend in Milltown village. He was delighted we were filming nearby. We were bringing a bit of life to the place. 'We get few tourists round here and most of them are German. The English are supposed to be this and that, and what they did and didn't do to this country. But if you ask me, they are the only ones. They spend money. They love the pubs and the crack. And any fish they catch, they put them back in the water. The Germans don't spend a penny. They even bring their own cornflakes. And the fish they catch, they put them in fridges and smuggle them back home. Look. Look.' We watch a Volkswagen van drive slowly through the village. On the roof is a boat and a canoe. Strapped to the back are bicycles. 'I betcha,' my friend says, 'if we could see the back seat it's packed with cornflake packets.' None the less he gives the van a cheery wave. Fatal that. They'll be back in droves next year.

Malcolm Anderson and Eberhard Bort (eds), *The Irish Border:
History, Politics, Culture*, Liverpool University Press 1998, 7-13

The scene being shot is where Albert [Finney] as the sergeant comes upon what he hopes is a murder. There is a headless 'corpse' in a ditch. Disappointingly for him it turns out to be a grisly accident. The location is a ditch along a thick overgrown hedge near a lake. Between the hedge and the lake are swampy fields of rushes and ragwort. The lake is bottle-green in the cold light and whipped up by a bitter wind. Across the lake on the other side is the remains of the fourteenth-century Drumlane Abbey. The old walls stand in the middle of a cemetery. The light glints off the modern black-marble headstones. Shafts of light come out of the clouds and imprison for a moment a field, a stretch of water, a tree, a herd of cattle. The camera crew stand looking at the light and shadows. Mike Southon, the DOP [Director of Photography], says, 'I can't get over the purity of Ireland. And somehow the people are the same.' 'Yes,' says Ken, the sound man, 'can you imagine a group of English extras being asked to hang around in a field for three days and wait until the crew have been served dinner before they can have any? They'd riot, the bastards.'

'For English extras it's work,' I say. 'For the locals round here it's a day out. Three days at a mock cockfight is three days of fierce excitement.' The women extras love the work. It's not work to them. The best thing of all about it is they don't have to cook dinner. Someone serves them dinner. Most women here cook dinner every single day of their lives. When the women queue up at the catering bus, they beam from ear to ear. I think it's the women who keep the country going. My daughter Tara, who helps out with the casting of extras, is phoned up all the time by women trying to get work for their husbands. The men have not worked for years because there is no work, and what there is is seasonal or casual. For a man to get £40 a day on the film is manna from Heaven. But it's the women who always make the call. Men feel ashamed phoning a slip of a girl for a job standing around and getting paid for it. Men need work. Even if they've land they need extra. The land in Cavan is poor. It can't sustain its people. The young are still emigrating. They abandon their nowhereland for London or Birmingham.

Everywhere we go there are rotting cottages and their overgrown, lost gardens. Windows are boarded, doors are chained. You can feel the damp as you walk past. Where we are today, there is such a cottage just along the road. The place is slowly crumbling into the earth. It overlooks the lake and Drumlane Abbey. Surrounding mature trees are eaten with ivy. Apple trees covered in moss stick out above monster-high nettles. Red apples hang in the morning light. You'd get stung trying to reach them. The house walls are cracking apart. A local man says it belongs to someone working as a porter in a hospital in Cavan. 'It was left to him. By his uncle.' Memory is an old black iron kettle, a cracked blue and white mug. A crow comes out of the chimney. A black, feathery ball of smoke. The wind comes up off the lake and through the hedges, nettles and trees, making a deep, weird noise like it's blowing at an angle into the neck of a big bottle. The outhouses at the rear of the cottage are stone built. But the cold and ivy are prising the stones apart. Through a crack I can see the shafts and skeleton of a cart lying flat on the floor, congealed in the hard mud like a fossil in rock. Hanging on the wall is a horse harness - the britchin, the collar... They are rotten, eaten by age and damp. It takes only a few winters for the decay to devour an empty house.

Along from where we're filming in the other direction is an amazing building. It is a long, low corrugated-iron shed with the hint of a gospel hall about it. It is almost covered to the roof with nettles, ivy and big scars of rust. I get into it through a rotten door at the back. At one end is a tiny stage. The people who stood on it must have touched the roof with their heads. The stage is utterly rotten and ready to fall. The floor of the hall is covered with old fifties television sets and wirelesses. They are all smashed and without their electronic guts. A local entrepreneur used the place after it ended its days as an Orange hall or the meeting-place of some biblical sect or other. Tall, skinny, pale thistles grow up through the TV sets. The sets are piled higher than my head. I can smell the black-and-white fifties and stark days of conspirational prayer on bare floorboards to a God stripped of Romanism and Southern Irish superstition. The place reeks of the severe mercy of the Lord. There are still plenty of gospel halls along the Border - on either side; spiritual fortresses where on Sunday afternoons young men in dark suits pray for deliverance from earthly plots and political dangers. first they meet outside for a chat, then they go inside to pray. It all has a hint of a sunless Alabama. I remember the fifties version - a Bible in one hand, a B-Special rifle in the other.

Coming out of the place I can hear the Angelus bell ring in Milltown. I drive back to Leggykelly and call on Cissi Connolly. She has an apple pie baking in an iron pot on the open fire. It looks scrumptious. We talk about the land, the people. 'Oh,' she says, 'round here we take it or leave it. Here a thing lies where it falls.' Another thing she said was, 'Oh, all the Protestant women were great cooks. The best.'

...

The sky clouds over and the rain squalls down. The drumlins disappear, the country goes dark. Across the lake the abbey becomes invisible. And then, as is typical, one field lights up. It's as if the sun is being held in a giant fist with a little light escaping through the knuckles. This lit field dazzles. Although on the other side of the lake you can easily pick out the brown clumps of rushes. More light escapes and soon the land is gleaming all over, except for one small field hedged by tall trees and dense bushes. This field remains in the dark, as though the giant fist holding the sun has opened, but a thumb still casts a shadow.

The lake is crowded to the edge by reeds and bullrushes. They shiver and part, and out sail two swans. They glide to the middle of the water and, facing each other, neck to neck, remain motionless. Like ballroom dancers awaiting the music.

Day 14: Monday 29 August

Today all the vehicles are parked outside my old primary school: St Brigid's, Killoughter, a mile from Redhills. The school is down the brae from the Catholic chapel and graveyard. The chapel and grave-yard, planted on top of a huge outcrop of rock and whin, dominate the view. As you come along the valley, way above you can see the yew tree by the graveyard gate. It is the only tree that has flourished on that barren hill. From the graveyard the scenery is fantastic. You look right down on top of the trees in the demesne, on the Orange hall along the Cootehill road, on Shannow Wood, on the tiny fields and, in the distance, the mountains. And on to my old school.

School was a penance in my time there: the cane ruled; girls wet the seats with fear; hair was pulled out, ears twisted, flesh and bone punched and beaten. A favourite sermon at Sunday mass was 'spare the rod and spoil the child'. Beating children had official sanction. It wasn't a sin to thump a defenceless girl or boy. Any father who stood up to the system was considered odd. In revenge, the teacher wouldn't teach that parent's children. For that reason, very few complained. Round and about I sometimes hear people say beatings should be brought back into the classroom. It's crazy. It's akin to beating a woman until she loves you.

We eat lunch outside the school gates. The kids are on holiday, but the school is open for painting. I take my courage in my hands and walk into the old classrooms. It's a futile exercise. The old voices aren't there.

...

Every Easter we came to the graveyard to pray at the grave of an IRA man killed in the War of Independence. Beforehand, repub-licans made speeches. It was so exciting up on top of that hill, the six counties in the distance, listening to the fighting talk. We'd be so fired up that if ordered to do so we'd have marched on Stormont with our bows and arrows and catapults. Maud Gonne spoke here one Easter. This rocky cemetery, this wild hill so near Heaven, links death and romance. It's full now. They've opened a new one on the other side of the chapel. That's built on rock, too ...

I drive across the Border and fill up at McCracken's pumps. He's not there, but young McKiernan is. He's got unleaded. The entrance to Clogher market is blocked off by two massive corrugated gates. Why anyone would drive down here to fill up is a mystery. I go into the dilapidated house. It smells of damp.

'Well, Adie, how's the form?'

'I appreciate your business.'

He writes out a receipt. Ken North's name is on the heading. Because of his great weight, he moves very slowly. He writes the receipt on top of the pool table. The slate is visible under the torn baize. He sits back on an old settee. The house is a shambles. It's amazing it's standing at all, having taken the force of at least two bombs. Why do the place up when it could be bombed again any night? Adie's complexion is as pale as the thistle growing up through the television sets in the abandoned gospel hall. Though barren and blasted, life sprouts, clings. McCracken and McKiernan are hardy men struggling to get bread in a world coming down around their ears. Bordermen.

One of the bombs that went off here killed a soldier. He was defusing the bomb which had been placed in a creamery can. When he first looked into the creamery can he thought the job was an easy one. He was too relaxed. The real bomb was right at the bottom. It went off... Locals say that when the soldiers first arrived on the scene they took drink and were merry. So that when the bomb specialist set about his work he was careless. I can't believe this rumour. Rumours run wild along the Border. This shop is a knot in the body politic. Mrs North worked for the RUC, an office job. Therefore the shop is a target. She still works for the RUC, she won't give in - and therefore puts lives in danger, her own included. The IRA won't give in either. Until Mrs North stops working for the police... But she won't stop working for the police. Why should she? So the wheel keeps turning. However the Norths no longer run the place. So I suppose for the moment it's a draw. Political bitterness runs red as blood. How are we going to live in peace? There must be a better way than soldiers, bombs and bigotry.

'Do you think there'll be a ceasefire?' I ask Adie.

'You'd never know. There might... and there mightn't. It's hard to tell. Like the weather.'

The soldier killed defusing the bomb was an Irishman from Limerick. He'd emigrated to England years before, joined the Army ... A hay field, a creamery can - though familiar, rural and homely it can kill you. A creamery can full of milk, awaiting collection, shining in the sun, was once upon a time innocence itself. Now they're full of Semtex or the middle classes buy them in antique shops. And when you think of it a creamery can with its strong slender form and tight-fitting lid is a perfect canister for a bomb. How would you set about defusing one? For a start how would you get that long-lipped lid off and live to tell the tale?

Outside, an Army helicopter flies across the checkpoint near Wattlebridge. At the Finn bridge a man fishes from the parapet. Down below, cattle stand in the water and go in under the bridge. A dragonfly darts out and zips along the river just above the surface. Its gossamer wings sparkle blue and gold.

The other side of the bridge down off the main road is the blasted remains of the Nicholls' shop. It used to be a fine two-storeyed building with sheds. People came from all over the South to purchase goods for smuggling back across the Border. I remember Mrs Nicholl. We came from Redhills to buy butter. The Customs were always trying to catch you, and often did. All they had to do was lie in wait on the Southern side and nab you as you cycled past. The Nicholls were Protestant. Opposite the shop up on the roadside is a smaller house. The McAdams live here. I went to school with Pat. He was a pocket dynamo, very cheery, played football. Needless to say, his nickname was 'Tar'. The McAdams are Catholic. In the seventies a bomb was planted in the Nicholls' shop. One of the young McAdams worked in the shop. He and Mrs Nicholl had time to get out. Rumour said that Mrs Nicholl mentioned the cash register and young McAdam ran back in to get the money. Whatever, the bomb went off and the young boy was killed. His sister who was near by was blinded. Mrs Nicholl, over seventy at the time, was flung twenty yards across a wall, but she lived. The shop was wrecked. Mr and Mrs McAdam were out at bingo that evening. They arrived home to devastation: a dead son, a blind daughter. But they were lucky. Seconds before the bomb went off another daughter and son were in the shop. But they walked off up the road before it exploded. More rumours spread. Someone in the Nicholl family had planted the bomb, because the business was going badly. This rumour was quickly scotched. Next day the IRA claimed responsibility. Why hadn't they given a warning? They did. Unfortunately it was a shop some distance away that got the warning.

Pat McAdam was working in Belfast at the time. At first the RUC notified the wrong man that his brother had been killed. Oddly enough this man's brother was killed later on in the Troubles. Mrs Nicholl is still alive. She's over ninety now. The McAdams, cheery as ever, get on with life. The shop is crumbling back to earth, a ghostly monument to the invisible war.

It's funny the way we talk about a bomb being 'planted'. Like it's a vegetable. Ulster was 'planted' in the seventeenth century. And because of that bombs are 'planted' in the twentieth. The other day someone said to me, 'Make hay whilst the sun shines.' It made me think of Mickey Nann. The secret war is full of secret meanings. Along the Border language is a double-edged sword.

When I return to the graveyard the filming is in full swing. They have laid tracks down for the camera the whole way along the laneway, from the graveyard gate to the chapel road. When Albert sees me coming he gives me a look. Then a wink. I listen to all the English accents: Cockneys, Mancunians, Home Counties ... The English have been in Ireland for 900 years, millions of Irish live in England, yet the gap cannot be bridged. Maybe all this will help.

A grey stone wall surrounds the graveyard. Over the wall the land falls sheer away - all rocks, whins, fluffy thistles. Two calves are at the strand of barbed wire. Stuck to the wire is a sack. The calves eat the sack, pulling at it, ripping it. On a clump of rock a white pony stands, his weight on three legs. He's asleep, the lucky bastard.

I make for home and bed. Going through the village I see a Gaelic football match is in progress. I call on Seamus Kelly and gingerly we walk down the garden backs and watch the match, while leaning over the fence that runs around the pitch. Annagh are playing Drumgoon. Annagh is the parish name. It combines Redhills and Belturbet. It's an under-sixteen match. Seamus shouts at the referee over some crime or other committed by a Drumgoon player. Blow me if the referee doesn't shout back at us: 'What the fuck would you know about it?' At this the two of us bellow after him like lunatics but he runs away down the field keeping up with play.

There's a lad playing for Annagh and he scores six goals. He's blond-headed and built like a young bull.

'Who is he?' I shout to Peter Reilly, who is team mentor.

'Aubrey Shaw. He's a Protestant out of Belturbet.'

Protestants rarely play Gaelic. Each time he pulls on the jersey, I wonder if he realises he's debunking history. Maybe things are changing. At last.

Change and the Irish Border:
An Introduction

Malcolm Anderson and Eberhard Bort

Ireland has proved too small to be divided. Though their country was partitioned politically in 1920, the peoples of Ireland have rarely allowed this to interfere with daily life in practice. Even after seventy-five years of separate statehood they are, by and large, unwilling to regard as their stamping ground anything less than the whole island. During the war years, it is true, the political border assumed reality, and in recent decades the IRA campaign of violence has succeeded in deepening divisions and inhibiting movement. In general, however, the taking of holidays, the pursuit of leisure, and cultural and, increasingly, economic activities, simply ignore the political boundary.

David Harkness[1]

I

David Harkness presents us with one perspective on the Border and it is, in political terms, a soothing and hopeful vision. He is saying that for ordinary people, for most of the time, the Border simply does not matter even though the Border assumes occasionally a rather tiresome political prominence. The alternative perspective is less reassuring - the Border as a fundamental feature of the Irish political landscape which has a determining influence over the nature of the political regimes North and South of it: deeply etched in the political cultures of the population, it is a crucial political instrument in the hands of the authorities in both halves of Ireland, used for both symbolic and practical effect. In the South, the stable democracy, deeply marked by Catholicism and with a party system created by a passionate difference of opinion on whether to accept a peace treaty with Britain which implied partition, is inconceivable without the Border. The northern political system, strongly influenced by militant Protestantism and anchored on an Ulster-British sense of iden-

Malcolm Anderson and Eberhard Bort (eds), *The Irish Border: History, Politics, Culture*, Liverpool University Press 1998, 15-37

tity has, for the past seventy-five years, been focused on maintaining the Border.

On balance, there is no doubt that the Border played a decisive role in shaping the politics of North and South. Considering the changes in the last decade affecting borders in Europe and Ireland, the question now posed is whether it will continue to do so in the future.

The Border as Political Instrument

Two widely separated and nicely balanced examples - Easter 1966 and Easter 1996 - illustrate how the British and Irish governments have used the Border; on the former occasion the Northern Irish government had tried to seal the Irish Border, on the latter the same objective was pursued by the government in Dublin. The contrasting reasons for doing so demonstrate attitudes towards the Border and uses of the Border. In 1966, sixty years after the Dublin Rising, fear was high in Belfast that the fervour with which the South commemorated 1916, would bring with it the danger of an invasion, perhaps a symbolic one, to recapture the 'fourth green field'. At Easter 1996, the Dublin government attempted to secure the Border against British 'mad cow disease' by preventing the smuggling of British beef into the Republic. Commemorations of 1916 - such as there were - were no longer regarded as threatening the North. Very far from it - even staunch Loyalist farmers in the North discovered that their cattle were perfectly sane and 'Irish'!

The additional resources used to prevent smuggling of British beef were impressive; more than 800 extra *gardaí* - overseeing more than 200 crossings - were made available to provide 'an intensified level of control', and smuggled cattle were seized on the border.[2] According to the Minister for Agriculture, Mr Yates, 'Operation Matador', which started in March, cost 'the state £500,000 a week in overtime payments':[3]

> Many of the Border crossings which had opened since the cease-fires now have a Garda presence. Lanes and roads are guarded 24 hours a day by Gardai and fields are monitored by patrols. Cows and calves have been counted in Border fields. Every vehicle going South is checked.[4]

The Irish Minister for Justice, Mrs Owen, announced in the Dáil that 'this extra Border security would add £16 million to the cost of policing the Border'.[5] The Border had never been more closely guarded from the Republic. The estimate by Mrs Owen was on top of the reinforcements sent to the Border earlier that year, when fears of

Loyalist paramilitary retaliations to the IRA's Canary Wharf bomb of 9 February meant returning to 24-hour rosters and additional mobile checkpoints along the Border.[6]

Sealing the Border to prevent smuggling (in both directions) and to counter the disruptive effects of Irish republicanism was, in the longer run, probably bound to fail. But policies designed to reduce the importance of the Border by improved trans-Border co-operation were not, for many years, marked with greater success. In January 1996, when the State Papers of thirty years before were made publicly available, it was disclosed that the Dublin and Belfast governments had achieved greater understanding on cross-Border co-operation by 1968 than had been generally realised.[7] This co-operation subsequently made the operations of the Provisional IRA more difficult but it did not prevent a twenty-five-year armed campaign.

Setting the Agenda in the 1960s

In the light of current cross-Border co-operation, it is striking to see the similarities between what is now being attempted and what was proposed in the 1960s - from common tourism, transport and energy policies to co-operation in education, culture and the arts. Reading these papers underlines the loss of 25 years of potential development which the Lemass-O'Neill meetings might have made possible.

These meetings are worth recalling because they show the limits of political decision and political will in effecting fundamental change in the practical and symbolic significance of the Border. Perhaps the most interesting document released about the meetings is T K Whitaker's account which describes being met at the Border, the drive to Stormont, and the welcome from O'Neill. Lemass is shown genuinely to believe in co-operation - most of the preparatory work and the ideas came from his office. These ideas included the joint promotion of tourism, the abolition of the Border system for private cars, cross-Border exchanges of pupils, teachers and scholarships, cultural co-operation, cost-sharing in the health services, the elimination of wasteful bidding for outside industrial investment (though on this point the Northern Ireland officials seemed sceptical), joint agricultural research, a reduction in tariffs, electricity co-operation including the joint development of nuclear power, and fisheries and game protection.

In hindsight, it is surprising 'how widely the visits were applauded (Ian Paisley was a lonely voice) and the rapidity with which ideas for substantial cross-Border co-operation were put on the table'.[8] Yet, from a Northern point of view, it could also be argued that in terms of prestige and without giving anything away, Northern Ireland's standing had been raised everywhere while Mr Lemass had announced he was meeting 'the Prime Minister of Northern Ireland'. It had never been intended that the Border should be more than a political boundary; the tariff wall had been raised by Eire as a result of the Trade War.[9]

Events elsewhere, however, ensured that most of the proposals were put on hold, some indefinitely. The spiral into political violence resulted in the upgrading of the Border as a security frontier, as the Troubles started in 1968. 'For the Unionist government', Liam O'Dowd and James Corrigan have observed:

> the borderlands were regarded as both the 'frontier' against the nationalist Free State and as an area of questionable allegiance and loyalty. The combination of these factors ensured that the border region had a high security presence especially during periods of ethnic-national violence.[10]

The next two decades changed the political significance of the Border; policing the Border (closing Border crossings, fortified checkpoints, police and security co-operation) became a central issue for British and Irish government collaboration.

Hardening attitudes towards the Border were highlighted by the 'Border Poll' of 1973, a constitutional referendum in the North which, one year after the introduction of direct rule, 'replaced the guarantee of Northern Ireland's position within the UK which resided in the former Stormont Commons and Senate'.[11] The SDLP and the republicans boycotted the poll. The result was as expected; it reflected the separate communities in the North: 58.5 per cent of the total electorate voted, of which 97.8 per cent supported a Northern Ireland as part of the UK; 48.5 per cent abstained. Needless to say that Unionists liked the result, whereas the SDLP commented that 'it proved nothing since everyone knew that there was a Protestant majority in Northern Ireland'.[12] Looking at polls and elections in Northern Ireland, Kevin Toolis, author of *Rebel Hearts: Journeys within the IRA's Soul* (1995), put it in a nutshell:

> Elections within the boundaries of Northern Ireland are sectarian headcounts which confirm the obvious, that there are 850,000 unionists and 640,000 nationalists. The boundaries of the northern state were designed to produce this result.[13]

Europe and the Border

The accession to the European Union of both the UK and Ireland in 1973 did not, in the short term, reverse the trend because it coincided with one of the worst periods of strife in the North - between Bloody Sunday in January 1972 and the failure of the Sunningdale power-sharing executive brought down by the Loyalist workers' strike in 1974. 'The political and security problems of Northern Ireland were far higher on the agenda than EC membership.'[14] An open border 'with no travel restrictions, no language barrier and an interchange-able currency on either side' became less open through intensified policing, and then by the abandonment of currency parity between Punt and Pound in 1979, which created 'a volatile shopping and trading zone along the Border'.[15]

However, a changing external environment has, since 1974, seemed to many the best hope for devaluing the impact of the Border. The Single Market project with its plan to abolish internal border controls on the movement of capital, goods, services and EC citizens 're-focused attention on border regions within the EC'.[16] This stimulated hopes, first voiced by the founder of the SDLP, Gerry Fitt, that the Northern Ireland problem would be submerged in a wider European context. Liam O'Dowd quotes Richard Kearney's

> contention that conflict over the Irish border, and between Britain and Ireland, will be dissolved in a wider European 'constellation of regions.'[17]

'As barriers in Europe fall,' wrote Gemma Hussey in 1995, 'and borders become blurred, the central national question of the Republic of Ireland's relationship with Northern Ireland may be eased.'[18] John Whyte sounded the same note when he argued that 'in a few years' time, one can expect the border between the North and the South in Ireland to mean less in practical terms than it does now'.[19] Assessing the first months of the Peace Process, Mary Holland held 'the hope ... that over a period of time the Border will seem to whither emotionally'.[20]

Yet, all these hopes of a withering away of the significance of the Border in the context of 'Europe 1992' were dismissed by O'Dowd, writing in 1992:

> EC economic integration and moves toward closer European unity certainly have not resolved the violent conflict on the Border nor prevented it becoming an increasingly militarised zone. EC economic integration, the policies of both governments, the activities of the British army and the IRA all seem to point in the same direction, to the consolidation of the

Border as an international boundary. Even the AIA [Anglo-Irish Agreement] and the management of EC and IFI [International Fund for Ireland] development funds have involved the re-affirmation of the administrative integrity and sovereignty of both the UK and Irish (twenty-six county) states. In Ireland, at least, a EC of national states seems a far more substantial reality than the chimera of a federated 'Europe of the Regions'.[21]

The Cease-Fire and the Border

The IRA's declaration of a 'complete cessation of violence' on 31 August 1994 seemed to herald a great leap forward. Dozens of Border roads were immediately reopened, often by local groups who did not wait for official approval. The EU Commission President, Jacques Delors, initiated a £240 million 'peace package' for 1995 to 1997, aimed at the six counties of Northern Ireland and the six Border counties of the Republic, targeting primarily projects generating employment and combating social exclusion. Much of that funding was to be provided through locally-based cross-community and cross-Border partnerships. After 'teething difficulties',[22] money began to flow, and Monika Wulf-Mathies, the EU Commissioner in charge of regional policies, maintained 'that in bringing people together throughout the community to work on specific projects the initiative has already made a significant contribution to building the peace process from the bottom up'.[23] The Washington Investment Conference took place in May 1995, with nearly 1,300 participants, to generate American investment and channel it towards the Irish borderlands, followed in October by a US business development mission consisting of 14 medium-sized American firms, visiting Derry, Strabane, Lifford and Monaghan. A cross-Border investment trust was launched in early November 1995, hoping to raise £40 million.

In December 1995, Dick Spring launched the 'Register of Border Links', commissioned by Co-operation North, documenting 'the extent and nature of existing non-political cross-Border links'.[24] A £29 million loan scheme for small businesses in the Border counties was announced in March 1996, as part of the EU support for the Peace Process, and welcomed by Baroness Denton, the North's Economy Minister:

> This is another welcome example of the friendship offered by Europe to Northern Ireland and the Border counties. Small

firms have a very significant role to play in the economic future of the province.[25]

A speaker for Dick Spring's office echoed these sentiments:

> The Border counties have many structural problems in common with Northern Ireland. It is our intention that this scheme will contribute to the progressive easing of these problems by mobilising the energy and initiative of small businesses.[26]

The 'peace dividend' was clearly shown in trade figures. Northern sales to the Republic rose by 26.4 per cent between January and September 1994 and by 18.5 per cent for the same period in 1995, topping at £454 million. Sales from the Republic to the North increased by 10.3 per cent in 1995, from an increase of 2.4 per cent in the previous year so that, according to the Irish Small and Medium Enterprises' Association, the trade gap between the Republic and Northern Ireland narrowed in 1995. During 1995, unemployment in Northern Ireland had fallen to 11.4 per cent, its lowest level for 14 years; house prices had risen by more than 11 per cent (against a four per cent decline in the UK overall); the number of first-time visits by potential investors had nearly trebled; and the Northern Ireland Economic Council pronounced 'that the province was expecting its best economic prospects for 25 years'.[27]

Tourism revived strongly. The number of people from the Republic visiting Northern Ireland increased significantly after the cease-fire and grew by about 35 per cent in 1995. In 1994, revenue generated by visitors from the Republic was £34 million sterling, an increase of 13 per cent. For the first six months of 1995, the number of visitors to the North rose by 18 per cent. However, the number of tourists - excluding business travellers and people visiting friends and relations - was up by 63 per cent. More people visiting the Republic from abroad now included a visit to the North in their itinerary. A total of 110,000 visitors to the Republic visited Northern Ireland, nearly 30 per cent more than in previous years. Companies handling visiting groups showed massive interest in including Northern Ireland. Car hire companies and tour operators confirmed the Northern Irish Tourist Board's view of the massive increase in travel across the Border by visitors who would never have thought of including Northern Ireland in their Irish holiday before the cease-fire.[28] The Northern Ireland Tourist Board and the Republic's Bord Fáilte in January 1996 decided to co-operate closely, including joint presentations at tourism fairs.[29]

Cultural and educational co-operation was facilitated by the Peace Process. The opening of Lough Derg Heritage Centre by Mary Robinson in November 1995 marked a blossoming of cultural co-operation. Presenting a new television series in September 1995, *Now You're Talking* - a co-production between BBC Northern Ireland and RTE for learners of Irish -, the Irish Minister for Arts, Culture and the Gaeltacht, Michael D Higgins, said the project illustrated the potential for building on 'the deep and continuous cultural links' between North and South. 'In the cultural area,' he explained, 'we have been able to make such progress because a great deal has been there already, that we have done quietly through arts councils and through other bodies, directors of museums and galleries.'[30]

The first cross-Border further and higher education institution was established in autumn 1995: the £1.3 million Rural College, situated close to the Border at Draperstown. Funded mainly by the International Fund for Ireland, the College has strong academic links with Queen's in Belfast, as well as with universities in the Republic and in Britain.[31]

Evidence of Changed Perceptions of the Border

A political initiative, the Peace Process, the IRA's response to it, the close co-operation of the London and Dublin governments, and the political and material encouragement of the EU and the USA seemed to influence attitudes at the grass roots. An *Irish Times/Guardian* poll in February 1996, held after the IRA's Canary Wharf bomb which ended the (more or less) non-violent phase of the Peace Process on 9 February 1996, provides insights on perceptions of the Border at that time. The most important finding was that the Border was 'no longer regarded worth an angry argument, let alone a life'.[32] This view was shared by the overwhelming majority of people living in 'these islands': 89 per cent in the Republic of Ireland, 81 per cent in Britain, and 80 per cent in Northern Ireland.

On the importance of the Border, 17 per cent of those questioned in the North believed that 'the Border matters and people should be prepared to fight for it if necessary'. Twenty-one per cent of Northern Protestants held this view.[33] In the Republic, only seven per cent said they believed the Border mattered and that people should be prepared to fight for it if necessary. While a further 37 per cent said it mattered but was not worth risking any lives for, 44 per cent of respondents said it did not matter and was not worth arguing about.[34]

The poll also showed that the overwhelming majority of voters in the Republic no longer viewed a united Ireland as their preferred option. Thirty per cent favoured it, while 55 per cent of respondents in Northern Ireland would prefer to see Northern Ireland remaining part of the UK. In Britain, 32 per cent of respondents saw an independent Northern Ireland as their preferred option.[35]

The Northern correspondent of the *Irish Times*, Dick Grogan, commented that:

> There is food for thought in the religious breakdown in regard to the minority of people who think 'the Border matters and people should be prepared to fight for it if necessary'.
> Only 17 per cent of the Northern sample, overall, agreed with this, but the breakdown shows that five times more Protestants than Catholics held that view, whereas half of the Protestants and 35 per cent of Catholics felt it was not worth risking any lives for.
> Very significantly, 70 per cent of all Catholics in the sample felt that the North should either remain part of the UK or be linked both to the UK and to the Republic.[36]

'There is,' he concluded, 'apparently, a strong element of overall disillusionment with absolutist political solutions and considerable openness to compromise.'[37] Denis Coughlan saw in the findings of the poll a reflection of 'the reality of EU membership and the declining importance of the Border in economic and symbolic terms'.[38] But changes in perceptions and attitudes were not evenly spread. It is significant that the impulse within the IRA to end the cease-fire seems to have come from the Border area. The men who planted the bomb were, *The Sunday Times* reported, from Monaghan, from 'the cradle of violence in the cross-border Monaghan/South Armagh/ Louth region'.[39] It was mainly from this Border zone that the strongest 'rumblings of discontent' within the 'Republican strongholds' had come and put pressure on the IRA command to end the cease-fire.[40] The *Irish Times* saw 'the greatest strength of support for an increased IRA campaign' after the breakdown of the cease-fire 'among republicans in the Republic and in the border area of south Armagh and Fermanagh'. 'These are,' it stated laconically, 'the republicans least affected by loyalist violence.'[41] Jim Cusack also noted 'a tendency among members of the Tyrone and Armagh brigades of the IRA to act in an autonomous fashion', and that 'the man reputed to hold the actual position of IRA chief-of-staff' was originally from Co Tyrone but 'has been living in Monaghan for almost 20 years'.[42] Catholics in the borderlands, according to A T Q Stewart, were bitterly disappointed about the failure of the Boundary Commission in 1925 to deliver any changes of the Partition border:

> They now felt that they had been let down by the Free State government and were trapped in a unionist state which would always regard them as second-class citizens. More and more of them turned from moderate forms of nationalism to the un-

compromising absolute of republicanism, and this further hardened unionist attitudes.[43]

The Border and Constitutional Proposals

The collapse of the IRA cease-fire put a temporary end to a period of vigorous speculation about constitutional settlements, from the 'Irish dimension' through 'joint authority' or 'joint institutions' to cross-Border bodies as intimated in the Framework Document of February 1995, with executive, harmonising or consultative functions.

The Dublin parties (Fianna Fáil, Fine Gael, Labour Party, Democratic Left and Progressive Democrats) had repeatedly stated that the territorial claim over Northern Ireland could be, in a negotiated settlement, amended to include the prerequisite of con-sent by a Northern majority. At a meeting of the Forum for Peace and Reconciliation in May 1995, the Fianna Fáil leader, Bertie Ahern, explained it thus:

> The principles and immutable political commitments under-lying the changes which we will propose in the Irish con-stitution will remove any jurisdictional or territorial claim of legal right over the territory of Northern Ireland contrary to the wishes of the people of Northern Ireland.[44]

As early as June 1994, the then Taoiseach Albert Reynolds called such constitutional changes a *quid pro quo* for cross-Border insti-tutions with executive powers: 'Institutional links between North and South will have executive powers. That's the type of overall framework we're looking for.'[45]

The Ulster Unionist leader, David Trimble, arguing that Articles 2 and 3 of the Irish Constitution were 'contrary to common sense and to international agreements', invoked the Helsinki Accord (1975) and the Charter of Paris which established the Organisation for Security and Co-operation in Europe (OSCE), demanding respect for the existing boundaries of states.[46] Business contacts, he contended, had 'developed without the stimulus of cross-border institutions bearing a concealed political agenda'.[47] UK Unionist MP Robert McCartney spelt it out even more clearly: 'The erection of political institutions to create a united Ireland by instalments will be utterly rejected.' Yet, in the same speech, he also welcomed 'the creation of friendly and mutually beneficial relations with the Republic of Ireland'.[48] Roy Bradford, a former Minister in the Stormont Cabinet and the 1974 power-sharing Executive, explained the change in Unionist attitudes to cross-Border co-operation in an opinion article for the *Irish Times*:

> I want to assure you, seriously, that during the past year there has been real change in unionist attitudes towards cross-Border bodies.
>
> Where it is clear that such bodies serve a practical purpose, such as the Foyle Fisheries Commission, where both sides derive benefit through increased efficiency or financial savings, then unionists would not only accept but would wholeheartedly operate such a collaboration across the full range of government activity.
>
> There is one proviso, a vital one. They will not at this juncture accept such a body if it has autonomous executive powers. They see that, with justification, as a united Ireland in embryo. Only when trust and confidence have been firmly established between the two traditions could such a step be contemplated.[49]

The status of cross-Border bodies is closely linked with questions of sovereignty and, of course, the old chestnut of self-determination. The IRA's - and Sinn Féin's - position has always been that the 'Irish people as a whole had a right to national self-determination'.[50] Whereas the British government started from the premises 'that the people of Northern Ireland alone have a right to self-determination'.[51] In the Downing Street (Joint) Declaration of 15 December 1993, the British and Irish governments had found a new formula (which was to be reinforced in the Framework Document of 1995):

> The British government agree that it is for the people of the island of Ireland alone, by agreement between the two parts respectively, to exercise their right of self-determination on the basis of consent, freely and concurrently given, North and South, to bring about a united Ireland, if that is their wish.[52]

Despite the safeguard, agreed by the Irish government, that no change was possible against the will of a majority in Northern Ireland, the Ulster Unionist MP Ken Maginnis called the Framework Document a 'dishonourable blueprint for a united Ireland'.[53]

North-South institutions, according to the Framework Document, were to

> promote agreement among the people of the island of Ireland; to carry out on a democratically accountable basis delegated executive, harmonising and consultative functions over a range of designated matters to be agreed; and to serve to acknowledge and reconcile the rights, identities and aspirations of the two major traditions. (para 13b)[54]

Areas to be considered for such co-operation were: agriculture and fisheries; industrial development and economic policy; trade; energy; transport; consumer affairs; health and social welfare; and education.[55]

Downing Street Declaration and Framework Document show in their wording the influence of John Hume, who has always proclaimed that 'it is the people of Ireland who are divided and not the territory' and that 'they can only be brought together by agreement, not by any form of coercion'.[56] Expounding the Framework Document in the Dáil, John Bruton echoed Hume when he hailed the document as 'the beginning of work towards a wholly new form of expression of traditional aspirations, focusing on individuals and communities rather than on territory'.[57]

From a very different point of view Simon Jenkins, an advocate of local democracy and a fierce critic of the 'official' Peace Process, said that a 'real' peace process could be envisaged, taking account of realities on the ground. He referred to the 'steady redrawing of the political map' in Northern Ireland:

> The ethnic cleansing of Ulster west of the Bann has continued. The predominantly Catholic areas, especially the Londonderry conurbation, are virtually parts of the Republic. The border with Donegal hardly exists and Londonderry, on my last visit, felt like a Southern town. From Armagh through Fermanagh to Londonderry lies a sickle of nationalism, a *cordon sanitaire* between Protestant Ulster and the Irish Republic. Northern Ireland is being normalised by peace and its local democracy reflects that normalcy. This is more important than a dozen round-table conferences.
>
> There is no reason for this process not to develop. There is no reason for nationalist and Unionist councils, perhaps after judicious amalgamation, to be denied more discretion over housing, schools, transport and industry. There is no reason why the existing links forged with the South by Londonderry and other nationalist councils should not grow on their own. The border is now politically permeable. Northern Ireland could be a test-bed for bottom-up democratic politics in healing the wounds of divided societies.[58]

'The outright warfare in the border areas since 1969,' the historian A T Q Stewart wrote in *The Narrow Ground*:

> has inevitably suggested the possibility of redrawing it, and Northern Ireland would doubtless now be glad to give up the area of south Armagh around Crossmaglen and perhaps the western parts of Derry.[59]

The Future

In an introductory overview of developments concerning the Border, a range of crucial unpredictable factors have to be considered. Those include the determination and ability of the Provisional IRA to continue its campaign of violence, the restraint or otherwise of the Protestant paramilitaries, the effects of changes of governments and the impact of unforeseen incidents. But the European Union dimension is likely to be a constant factor. Notwithstanding the well-informed scepticism of Liam O'Dowd, European funding for cross-Border projects has the potential to have a lasting effect by helping to decentralise decision-making processes from Dublin, London and Belfast to the Borderlands. But there are other issues which could create tension and harden the Border. Ireland may wish (and be able) to join EMU (European Monetary Union) whilst the UK remains hesitant and negative. Even more direct in the effect on the Border are potential differences about the Schengen arrangements for lifting internal EU border controls. The UK (government and opposition) has firmly and repeatedly ruled out acceding to the Schengen Conventions. Ireland would be disposed to join, but cannot unless the UK joins; it would not only disrupt the common travel zone in existence since Partition, but also erect an EU external frontier at the Northern Irish Border with increased security and identity checks. In general, the UK debate about opting out of EU arrangements provokes unease in Ireland. The Peace Process would be even more complicated, Joe Carroll commented, if the Republic had to 're-erect economic and social legislation borders because Britain opts out of its EU obligations'.[60]

Both current tensions and speculation about the future undermine David Harkness's view of the minimal role of the Irish Border, quoted at the beginning of this introduction. Indeed, he represents a view from the North. Few Southerners have regarded the North as anything other than 'a place apart' (in Dervla Murphy's famous phrase).[61] 'The average Southerner,' Tim Pat Coogan noted, 'does not go North either for holidays or day excursions.'[62] None the less, in defence of Harkness, it may be argued that in sports,[63] literature, theatre, music and many other fields (trade unions, scholarly and professional associations, and other organisations), the Border often seems negligible as a barrier.[64] In focusing on the Border, one should not become obsessed by it.

II

How, then, is this volume situated in Border-related literature? It is the first book-length treatment of the Irish Border and related themes since Heslinga's controversial *The Irish Border as a Cultural Divide* (1962; 3rd ed. 1979). However, there has appeared, more recently, an issue of *The Irish Review*,[65] which discussed boundary and identity questions in the context of post-colonial theories and frameworks of regionalism;[66] and Liam O'Dowd's study *Whither the Irish Border?*[67]

Heslinga took a geographer's view of the Border, unlike the political, historical, cultural and literary perspectives found in this volume. He established a link between Ireland's sea and land boundaries: 'if the idea of a sea boundary had not arisen, there would not have been a land boundary.'[68] In other words, had there been no nationalist movement which assumed that the natural boundary was the sea, there would be no Border. This Border, he argues:

> shows some conformity to the frontiers of one of the most important kingdoms of Gaelic Ireland, *i.e.* that of the O'Neills of Tyrone who for centuries claimed to be kings of Ulster and who remained virtually independent from Dublin till the end of the sixteenth century. The present land boundary also approximates to the southern frontier of the pre-Gaelic kingdom of Ulster, which was for some time strengthened by what is today known as the Black Pig's Dyke.[69]

Heslinga concludes that both separation and partition have their roots in the Reformation and Counter-Reformation: 'both sections of the Irish Border, the sea and the land boundary, are in the last resort religious frontiers.'[70] The problem of Northern Ireland, for Heslinga, is that the majority of the population have close cultural links with Scotland and scarcely any with the rest of Ireland. The Scottish connection has recently been re-emphasised by two publications, Graham Walker's *Intimate Strangers*,[71] and *Scotland & Ulster*, a symposium edited by Ian S Wood.[72]

The emphasis on the cultural realm is most clearly to be seen in the publications of the Cultural Traditions Group[73] and a volume called *Culture and Politics in Northern Ireland*,[74] as well as in the cultural policies of groups like 'Field Day' and the writings of Brian Friel and Seamus Heaney, imaginatively crossing frontiers and thus echoing the credo of Claudio Magris, derived from his personal experience of central European frontiers:

> I take the view that literature is, among other things, a journey towards discrediting this myth of the other side, towards grasping that everyone finds himself now on this side now on the other - that Everyman, as in a medieval mystery play, is the Other.[75]

One problem raised by the cultural perspective, as John Whyte points out in his classic text, *Interpreting Northern Ireland*,[76] is that if religion and culture partition Ireland into two territories, the dividing line does not coincide with the Border. It is in this respect, as well as in the relationship between the land and sea boundary, that Heslinga is questionable. E Estyn Evans, though he concurs with Heslinga in stating that it was 'the peninsula in the north-east that has repeatedly and most conspicuously demonstrated its separate identity among the regions of Ireland',[77] also points out other, more complex, tensions between north and south and east and west:

> On economic grounds the term 'the Two Irelands' is often taken to refer to east and west rather than north and south, and in Cromwell's time it seemed that the Six Counties to be separated from the rest of Ireland were to be those of Connacht and Clare.[78]

Duncan Morrow put the Irish Border in the context of ethnic conflicts in the wake of the collapse of European empires,[79] building on Frank Wright's influential comparative study on ethnicity and conflict in Northern Ireland.[80] An anthropological analysis of the 'symbolic dimension of the Irish Border' is offered by Thomas Wilson.[81]

Clare O'Halloran, in *Partition and the Limits of Nationalism*, laid her finger on the point that Irish nationalists, however prolific in denouncing the Border, were short of ideas about how to resolve the problem; Partition was, mainly, 'an irritation'.[82] Writing in 1987, O'Halloran could open her study with the statement that 'the lack of prominence given to partition in the Treaty debate has been matched by the minimal attention accorded it by historians'.[83] Yet, at least one of the historians she quotes as having given the impact of Partition 'only passing consideration',[84] has meanwhile corrected that impression: Tom Garvin published his study *1922: The Birth of a Nation* in 1996, citing Partition as one 'cause of the stability of early Irish democracy'.[85] 'It seems to have been tacitly accepted by Dublin,' Garvin writes, 'that Northern Ireland was too big for them to handle.'[86]

'When all Ireland lay under British rule,' Sarah Nelson has written, 'Unionists could feel both British and Irish.'[87] That changed with Partition. Arthur Aughey views Partition as 'both failure *and* success' for Unionism, as it left southern Unionists, and particularly those of Cavan, Donegal and Monaghan, outside the Union and generally weakened the cause of British unionism.[88] The separate paths of North and South after Partition, from a Unionist point of view, are characterised by Aughey thus:

> For Unionists like Craigavon, the settlement of the 1920s had divided Ireland effectively into zones of majoritarian democracy. The southern parliament embodied Catholic majoritarianism (which it defined as Irish) and the northern parliament embodied Protestant majoritarianism (which it defined as British).[89]

Only O'Neill meeting Lemass in the 1960s 'was a tentative step towards changing those assumptions on both sides'.[90] Progressive claims for closer co-operation between North and South and the all-Ireland perspective of nationalists, Aughey sees countered, after the failure of Stormont 'as a "bulwark" of the Union', by increasing Unionist emphasis on the integration of Northern Ireland within a multi-national UK, as embodied in the Campaign for Equal Citizenship in the 1980s.[91]

A specific argument on the fringes of Unionism has been repartition of Northern Ireland. Yet, as McGarry and O'Leary have shown, it 'has been canvassed as a solution only by academics prepared to think the unthinkable',[92] particularly by Liam Kennedy in *Two Ulsters: A Case for Repartition* (1986) and 'Repartition'.[93] Tom Wilson has drawn 'contingency plans for the border [which] should be kept ready as a shot in the locker which could be used if required'.[94] Arguing the dangers of demographic developments, which, 'with the existing border, may ultimately bring about a Catholic majority',[95] he wants to keep the option of repartition. Following A T Q Stewart's position,[96] he contends:

> By transferring the area west of the river Foyle together with Fermanagh, West Tyrone and Newry, the proportion of Catholics in Northern Ireland could be reduced from the current figure of about two-fifths to about one-fifth. The change in the sectarian composition would be still greater if, as would seem likely, movements of population in both directions were to take place in response to the change in the frontier.[97]

Yet, because of the chances of that 'demographic pressure', he foresees resistance from the Republic to such a re-drawing of the Border:

Although, in principle, the nationalists should be glad to gain these fragments of 'Hibernia Irredenta', they would not easily be reconciled to losing the chance of having the whole of Northern Ireland voted into the South by a Catholic majority.[98]

But, he argues, the 'famous Article 2 of the Republic's Constitution would then become a boomerang', as 'the Republic could hardly refuse to accept these areas which are already held to be - as of right - part of the national territory'.[99]

Repartition, however, has one serious drawback. Even Liam Kennedy's most radical solution, with West Belfast as a Southern Irish exclave, would leave new minorities:

> The major problem with the option of partition when applied to Northern Ireland is that the population there is so interspersed that any attempt to redraw the border will leave a substantial minority of Protestants in the section ceded to the Irish Republic.[100]

Yet, McGarry and O'Leary, advocates of a consociational, power-sharing model for Northern Ireland,[101] recommend repartition as 'the most benign of drastic default options if more desirable strategies should fail'.[102] The scenario, obviously showing strains of exasperation on the authors' side, goes like this:

> Clarification of the choice between partition and power-sharing, through the threat of partition, just might produce a consociational settlement. Focusing people's attentions on the consequences of the former might persuade them of the merits of the latter.[103]

Thus, McGarry and O'Leary, said to be close to the thinking of the Social Democratic and Labour Party (SDLP) in their approach, come from the opposite end to the problem of repartition than Kennedy or Wilson.

The spectrum of unionist thinking ranges from clinging to the *status quo* to full integration into the UK on the one side, and an, if needs be, repartitioned, independent Ulster.

In the vein of studies closer to the nationalist view, Liam de Paor's classic *Divided Ulster*[104] - in the eyes of Conor Cruise O'Brien representing 'an Irish Republican point of view'[105] - and Dervla Murphy's exploration in the form of a travel book, *A Place Apart*,[106] have been among the most influential books of a plethora of Troubles literature. In his recent study, *Unfinished Business*, Liam de Paor devotes a full chapter to 'The Border', noting Ulster's pre-Partition, even pre-Plantation difference; but he concentrates on the history after 1969, when 'the Border took on a new character.'[107] In de Paor's verdict, '"Alienation" sums up the Border'. It is an 'area of high stress', where 'serious interdenominational strife began, two hundred years ago', 'a war zone of a kind in the past twenty years'.[108] If *Unfinished Business* can be seen as an update of *Divided Ulster*, then *A Place Apart* found its sequel in Colm Tóibín's *Bad Blood*, describing the impressions on a walk from Derry to Newry in the wake of the Anglo-Irish agreement.[109]

Richard Kearney (*Across the Frontiers, Post Nationalist Ireland*),[110] John Hume (*Personal Views*)[111] and Roy Foster (*Modern Ireland*, 'Varieties of Irishness')[112] look at the Border area in the light of the Single Market and European regionalism. Hume asserts

> that the Single Market will have an important impact on the border as we know it in Ireland. It will allow the border to ebb substantially from economic life on the island. It also provides a context that will require and should inspire policy programs and administrative instruments that will be cross-border and all-Ireland in scope. This in itself cannot remove the political division. But it will allow the real essence of that division to be addressed rather than be distorted and deepened by economic, social, and administrative divergences and rivalries.[113]

And Kearney, champion of a federal Europe of regions - post-modern, post-nationalist and post-sovereign - contends that 'the most likely model of regional democracy to succeeded in Ireland, at the present historical juncture, is one brought about within the context of an integrated Europe of equal regions':[114]

> The emerging Europe has a unique opportunity to be truly democratic by fostering notions of sovereignty that are in-clusive rather than absolute, shared rather than insular, disseminated rather than closed in upon some bureaucratic centre. Northern Ireland could be a testing ground.[115]

Kearney and Wilson, as well as John Hume, end on an optimistic note:

> It is the struggle between one nation-state, represented by the army, and an aspirant to another, represented by the IRA, which for the moment ensures that the border at Newry is the only Check-point Charlie remaining in the new Europe. It is fondly to be hoped that, like the traffic that informally bypasses it, history, too, will shortly pass it by.[116]

> Borders are gone all over Europe, including in fact the Irish
> border. No border means free movement of goods, people and
> services. The activity that will arise from this will consistently
> break down the real border in Ireland, which is in the hearts
> and minds of our people.[117]

This is an encouraging vision of a 'Europe without frontiers' having a
beneficial effect upon the situation in Ireland. Yet, after the
breakdown of the IRA cease-fire, more pessimistic perspectives seem
to be the order of the day.

A fully independent Ulster, in nationalist eyes, is nearly as far
removed from their thinking as full integration into the UK. The goal
of the 'pan-nationalist consensus' is a united Ireland, but compromise could mean any constitutional arrangement with a strong
all-Ireland, Border-transcending component.

III

When looking at the Irish Border, we are talking about, in Liam
O'Dowd's definition, eight hundred thousand people living in the
borderlands and affected by the Border, 16 per cent of the island's
population:

> The Southern side accounts for 10% of the population of the
> Republic and 22% of its Protestant population. The Northern
> side accounts for 28% of Northern Ireland's population and
> 43% of its Catholic population. This diversity, the contested
> nature of the boundary, and the impact of EC developments,
> make the Border area a good place to start looking for clues to
> the prospects of regions and regionalism in the new Europe.[118]

'Looking for clues' for future developments is one of the tasks the
authors of the present volume have set themselves. The book is
based on papers presented at a Conference on 'Chance and the Irish
Border' at the International Social Sciences Institute of the University
of Edinburgh, which brought together different disciplines and
different perspectives in order to assess the changing role and perception of the Border. This Conference was part of an on-going
research project at the International Social Sciences Institute on
frontiers in Europe.[119]

Paul Arthur, in a broad political analysis, places the North-South
and British-Irish relationships firmly in their international setting,
explaining the development of a 'polycentric' nationalism and

pointing out the opportunities offered by interdependency rather than insistence on antiquated models of self-determination and sovereignty.

Ged Martin goes back to the roots (and archives) to offer a history of the origins of Partition, including the findings of the ill-fated Boundary Commission of the 1920s; and Ian S Wood, writing about the disastrous IRA Border Campaign, brings us up to the early 1960s.

Etain Tannam takes a closer look at the changing cross-Border relationship in the light of European regional policies in the 1980s and 1990s; whereas Steve Bruce, the leading expert on Ulster Unionism, gives a more pessimistic assessment of an enduring Unionist attitude towards the Border.

Ulli Kockel brings us, in a long historical view, back to a revised reading of the peculiar Scots-Ulster link as proposed by authors such as, among others, Ian Adamson, Michael Hall, M W Heslinga and E Estyn Evans.

The final three chapters are dedicated to matters of culture and identity. 'As the formation of new versions of life in Northern Ireland takes place,' an optimistic Minister Michael D Higgins said in 1994:

> the older status of the [Irish] language - as opposed to its present status - will be asserted. It will be seen as something that is part of the *préamhacha*, or the roots of the society, rather than belonging to any particular version of political events.[120]

The different language policies north and south of the Border, and their (non-)effects, are the focus of Máiréad Nic Craith's chapter, which indeed emphasises the Irish language as crossing rather than reinforcing the political Border.

Owen Dudley Edwards immersed himself in the literature of the eighteenth and nineteenth centuries to trace the shaping of a frontiers or Border mentality in Ireland, whereas Eberhard Bort follows the development of Border politics and the perception of the Border from Partition to the present, as expressed in twentieth-century Irish literature, particularly in what he defines as coming close to a sub-genre of Irish drama: the Irish Border play.

At the conference, we were privileged to have in Eugene McCabe and Shane Connaughton two distinguished writers from the Irish Borderlands present, who introduced the conference theme by reading from their works. We preface this volume with two pieces by these writers - an essay of high journalism reflecting the immediate sexperience of the Peace Process in the Borders, and an excerpt from a diary kept during the filming in the Borders (at the time the first IRA cease-fire was called) of his autobiographical novel set there.

Notes

1   David Harkness, *Ireland in the Twentieth Century: Divided Island*, London: Macmillan, 1996, p.115.

2   Carmel Robinson, 'Border beef vigil costs £400,000 a week', in *The Irish Times*, 10 June 1996.

3   Sean MacConnell, 'Sealing Border against BSE costs £1/2 million a week in overtime', in *The Irish Times*, 24 April 1996.

4   Carmel Robinson, *art. cit.*

5   *Ibid.*

6   There had been no substantial reductions of the three Garda divisions covering the Border during the cease-fires, 'as some senior officers remain[ed] concerned about the resumption of violence'. *The Irish Times*, 12 June 1995. It took a whole year into the cease-fires before checkpoints along the Tyrone-Donegal and Derry-Donegal Border were removed. *The Irish Times*, 11 October 1995.

7   According to a file inadvertently released to the National Archives - Uinsionn Mac Dubhghaill, 'Papers reveal secret links with O'Neill cabinet', in *The Irish Times*, 2 January 1996.

8   Maurice Manning, 'State Paper: excitement of the first Lemass and O'Neill meeting captured', in *The Irish Times*, 2 January 1996.

9   Eamon Phoenix, 'O'Neill Lemass meeting caused unease', in *The Irish Times*, 3 January 1996.

10   Liam O'Dowd and James Corrigan's interestingly titled 'Securing the Irish border in a Europe without frontiers', in Liam O'Dowd and Thomas M Wilson (eds), *Borders, Nations and States*, Aldershot: Avebury, 1996, pp.117-33; p.120.

11   See W D Flackes, *Northern Ireland - A Political Directory, 1968-1983*, London: BBC/Ariel Books, 1983, pp.47-48.

12   *Ibid.*, p.48.

13   Kevin Toolis, 'Prevarication that pushed IRA to war', in *Scotland on Sunday*, 11 February 1996.

14   Brigid Laffan, 'Managing Europe', in Neil Collins (ed.), *Political Issues in Ireland Today*, Manchester: Manchester University Press, 1994, pp.40-54; p.45. For the wider European context of cross-Border co-operation see also Brigid Laffan, *Co-operation and Integration in Europe*, London: Routledge, 1992.

15   Liam O'Dowd, 'What is a Region?: The Case of the Irish Borderlands', in Proinseas Ó Drisceoil (ed.), *Culture in Ireland - Regions: Identity and Power* (Proceedings of the Cultures of Ireland Group Conference), Belfast: Institute of Irish Studies/Queen's University, 1993, pp.91-101; pp.94-95.

16   *Ibid.*, p.93.

17   *Ibid.*

18   Gemma Hussey, *Ireland Today: Anatomy of a Changing State*, London: Penguin, 1995, p.236.

19   John Whyte, 'Dynamics of social and political change in Northern Ireland', in Dermot Keogh and Michael H Haltzel (eds), *Northern Ireland and the Politics of Reconciliation*, Cambridge: Cambridge University Press, 1993, pp.103-16; p.116.

20   Interview with Mary Holland, in *The Irish Times*, 1 March 1995.

21   O'Dowd, *art. cit.*, p.96. See also Liam O'Dowd, *Whither the Irish Border? Sovereignty, Democracy and Economic Integration in Ireland*, Belfast: Centre for Research and Documentation, 1994; and Liam O'Dowd, J

Corrigan and T Moore, 'Borders, National Sovereignty and European Integration', in *International Journal of Urban and Regional Research*, Vol.19, No.2 (1995), pp.272-85.

22 Patrick Smyth, 'Future of special EU aid package for NI in doubt', in *The Irish Times*, 17 February 1997.

23 *Ibid.;* for an assessment of the European Union's impact for Northern Ireland, see also Paul Hainsworth, 'Northern Ireland and the European Union', in Arthur Aughey and Duncan Morrow (eds), *Northern Ireland Politics*, London and New York: Longman, 1996, pp.129-38. See also Etain Tannam's contribution in this volume, and her related treatments, 'EU Regional Policy and the Irish/Northern Irish Cross-Border Administrative Relationship', in *Regional & Federal Studies*, Vol.5, No.1 (Spring 1995), pp.67-93, and 'The European Union and Business Cross-Border Co-operation: The Case of Northern Ireland and the Republic of Ireland', in *Irish Political Studies*, Vol.11 (1996), pp.103-29.

24 *The Irish Times*, 7 December 1995.

25 Suzanne Breen, '£29m aid package to benefit NI and Border counties', in *The Irish Times*, 5 March 1996.

26 *Ibid.*

27 John Ivison, 'Northern Ireland still in business', in *The Scotsman*, 29 February 1996.

28 Michael Foley, 'Significant increase of visitors to North', in *The Irish Times*, 4 October 1995.

29 Harvey Elliott, 'Ireland unites on tourism front', in *The Times*, 15 February 1996. The IRA's London bombings had an immediate effect on the tourist trade. Inquiries for the first third of 1996 fell by 40,000, compared with the previous year. Yet the number of people seeking information about holidays in the North was still 23 per cent higher than in pre-cease-fire 1994. 'North's tourism hit by London bombs', in *The Irish Times*, 27 May 1996.

30 Quoted in Uinsionn Mac Dubhghaill, 'BBC, RTE new Irish series', in *The Irish Times*, 7 September 1995.

31 Noel McAdam, 'College crosses Irish divide', in *Times Higher Education Supplement*, 10 November 1995.

32 Mary Holland, 'IRA and politicians told loud and clear to get on with the peace process', in *The Irish Times*, 28 February 1996.

33 *Ibid.*

34 Frank Millar, 'British public show most optimism on the peace process', in *The Irish Times*, 28 February 1996.

35 See Geraldine Kennedy, 'Majorities in Ireland and Britain say process can be saved', in *The Irish Times*, 28 February 1996.

36 Dick Grogan, 'Poll results highlight extent of Northern scepticism', in *The Irish Times*, 28 February 1996.

37 *Ibid.*

38 Denis Coughlan, 'Thirst for peace and willingness to compromise indicated in Southern views', in *The Irish Times*, 28 February 1996.

39 David Leppard, Liam Clarke and Peter Millar, 'The dirty coup', in *The Sunday Times*, 18 February 1996.

40 See Denis Campbell and John O'Farrell, 'Back with a bloody vengeance', in *Scotland on Sunday*, 11 February 1996.

41 Jim Cusack, 'IRA may not want Sinn Féin talks', in *The Irish Times*, 5 June 1996.

42 *Ibid.*

43   A T Q Stewart, *The Narrow Ground: Patterns of Ulster History*, London:
     Faber and Faber, 1977, p.176.
44   Quoted in Paul Bew and Gordon Gillespie, *The Northern Ireland Peace
     Process 1993-1996*, London: Serif, 1996, p.100. Ahern's formulation
     closely resembles the one used in the Framework Documents of
     February 1995. (See Bew and Gillespie, p.84).
45   *Ibid.*, p.56.
46   Gerry Moriarty, 'Trimble again deplores Articles', in *The Irish Times*, 10
     October 1995.
47   'Mr Trimble and Economics' (Leading article), *The Irish Times*, 11 May
     1996.
48   Quoted in Suzanne Breen, 'McCartney wants Unionist parties to agree
     platform of principles', in *The Irish Times*, 22 May 1996.
49   Roy Bradford, 'Straws in the wind show signs of hope and change', in
     The Irish Times, 3 January 1996.
50   Bew and Gillespie, *The Northern Ireland Peace Process*, p.19.
51   *Ibid.*, p.20.
52   *Ibid.*, p.33.
53   *Ibid.*, p.85.
54   *Ibid.*, p.84.
55   See also Kevin Boyle and Tom Hadden, *Northern Ireland: The Choice*,
     Harmondsworth: Penguin Books, 1994, pp.186-90.
56   John Hume, 'Europe can offer Northern Ireland a blueprint for peace', in
     The European, 24 August 1995.
57   Quoted in Bew and Gillespie, p.85.
58   Simon Jenkins, 'Ulster's real peacemakers', in *The Times*, 3 February
     1996.
59   A T Q Stewart, *The Narrow Ground: Patterns of Ulster History*, London:
     Faber and Faber, 1977, p.172.
60   Joe Carroll, 'Danger signals for Ireland in EU future', in *The Irish Times*,
5   December 1995.
61   Dervla Murphy, *A Place Apart*, London: John Murray, 1978.
62   Tim Pat Coogan, *Ireland Since the Rising*, London: Pall Mall Press, 1966,
     p.284.
63   With the major exception of soccer, which 'followed the boundaries
     established by partition'. See Alan Bairner, 'The Arts and Sport', in
     Arthur Aughey and Duncan Morrow (eds), *Northern Ireland Politics*,
     London and New York: Longman, pp.181-89, p.187.
64   J H Whyte, 'The Permeability of the UK-Irish Border: a Preliminary
     Reconnaissance', in *Administration* 31, 3 (1983), pp.300-315.
65   *The Irish Review*, 'Defining Borders: Colony-City-Region', No.16,
     Autumn/Winter 1994.
66   Especially Colin Graham, "Liminal Spaces': Post-Colonial Theories and
     Irish Culture', in *The Irish Review*, No.16, 1994, pp. 29-43.
67   Liam O'Dowd, *Whither the Irish Border? Sovereignty, Democracy and
     Economic Integration in Ireland*, Belfast: Centre for Research and
     Documentation, 1994.
68   M W Heslinga, *The Irish Border as a Cultural Divide*, Assen: Van
     Gorcum, 1979, p.10.
69   *Ibid.*, pp.138-139. Ian Adamson, in *The Identity of Ulster: The Land, the
     Language and the People* (Bangor: Pretani Press, 1982), calls it 'the
     ancient frontier between Ulster and the rest of Ireland evidenced also in
     the structure known as the Black Pig's Dyke'. (p.74).

70   *Ibid.*, p.204.

71   Graham Walker, *Intimate Strangers: Political and Cultural Interaction
     between Scotland and Ulster in Modern Times*, Edinburgh: John Donald,
     1995.

72   Ian S Wood (ed.), *Scotland and Ulster*, Edinburgh: The Mercat Press,
     1994.

73   For example, Proinsias O Drisceoil (ed), *Culture in Ireland: Regions:
     Identity and Power*, Belfast: Institute of Irish Studies/Queen's
     University, 1993; on the Cultural Traditions Group see Alan Bairner,
     'The Arts and Sport', in Arthur Aughey and Duncan Morrow (eds),
     Northern Ireland Politics, London and New York: Longman, pp.181-89,
     particularly p.184.

74   Eamonn Hughes (ed), *Culture and Politics in Northern Ireland, 1960-
     1990*, Milton Keynes: Open University Press, 1991.

75   Claudio Magris 'Who is on the Other Side? Considerations about
     Frontiers', in Christopher MacLehose (ed), *Frontiers* (Leopard III),
     London: Harvill, 1994, pp.8-25; p.9.

76   J H Whyte, *Interpreting Northern Ireland*, Oxford: Clarendon Press, 1991.

77   E Estyn Evans, *The Personality of Ireland*, Belfast: Blackstaff, (rev. ed.),
     1981, p.26.

78   *Ibid.*, p.77.

79   Duncan Morrow, 'Games between Frontiers: Northern Ireland as Ethnic
     Frontier', in Jürgen Elvert (ed), *Nordirland in Geschichte und
     Gegenwart/Northern Ireland - Past and Present*, Stuttgart: Franz Steiner
     Verlag, 1994, pp.334-53.

80   Frank Wright, *Northern Ireland: A Comparative Analysis*, Dublin: Gill
     and Macmillan, 1987; see especially chapters 1 and 2, 'The Ethnic
     Frontier and the Metropolis' and 'National Conflict on the Ethnic
     Frontier'.

81   Thomas Wilson, 'Symbolic Dimensions to the Irish Border', in Hastings
     Donnan and Thomas Wilson (eds), *Anthropological Perspectives on
     Frontiers*, Lanham, Maryland: University Press of America, 1994.

82   D George Boyce, 'Past and Present Revisionism and the Northern
     Ireland Troubles', in D George Boyce and Alan O'Day, *The Making of
     Modern Irish History: Revisionism and the Revisionist Controversy*,
     London: Routledge, 1996, pp.216-38; p.226.

83   Clare O'Halloran, *Partition and the Limits of Nationalism: An Ideology
     under Stress*, Dublin: Gill and Macmillan, 1987, p.xi.

84   *Ibid.*

85   Tom Garvin, *1922: The Birth of Irish Democracy*, Dublin: Gill and
     Macmillan, 1996, p.24.

86   *Ibid.*, p.185. For the immediate economic (non)effects of the
     establishment of the Border see D S Johnson, 'Partition and Cross-
     Border Trade in the 1920s', in Peter Roebuck (ed), *Plantation to
     Partition: Essays in Ulster History in Honour of J L McCracken*, Belfast:
     Blackstaff, 1981, pp.229-46.

87   Sarah Nelson, *Ulster's Uncertain Defenders*, Belfast: Appletree Press,
     1984, p.30.

88   Arthur Aughey, 'Unionism', in A Aughey and Duncan Morrow
     (eds), *Northern Ireland Politics*, London and New York: Longman, 1996,
     pp.31-38; particularly pp.31-32.

89   *Ibid.*, p.35.

90   *Ibid.*

91   *Ibid.*, p.36. See also A Aughey, *Under Siege: Ulster Unionism and the
     Anglo-Irish Agreement*, Belfast: Blackstaff, 1989, particularly Chapter 5,

'The Case for Integration'; and John Wilson Foster (ed), *The Idea of the Union: Statements and Critiques in Support of the Union of Great Britain and Northern Ireland*, Vancouver: Belcouver Press, 1995.

92   Brendan O'Leary and John McGarry, *The Politics of Antagonism: Understanding Northern Ireland*, London: Athlone Press, 1993, p.286.

93   In John McGarry and Brendan O'Leary (eds), *The Future of Northern Ireland*, Oxford: Clarendon Press, 1990, pp.137-61.

94   Tom Wilson, *Ulster: Conflict and Consent*, Oxford: Blackwell, 1989, p.254.

95   *Ibid.*

96   See note 56.

97   Wilson, *Ulster: Conflict and Consent*, p.254.

98   *Ibid.*

99   *Ibid.*

100 John McGarry and Brendan O'Leary, 'Conclusion', in McGarry and O'Leary (eds), *The Future of Northern Ireland*, p.271.

101 John McGarry and Brendan O'Leary, *Explaining Northern Ireland*, Oxford: Blackwell, 1995, pp.209-10; see also their 'Glossary of Key Concepts', in McGarry and O'Leary (eds), *The Future of Northern Ireland*, p.xv.

102 McGarry and O'Leary, 'Conclusion', p.273.

103 *Ibid.* p.300.

104 Liam de Paor, *Divided Ulster*, Harmondsworth: Penguin, 1970.

105 Conor Cruise O'Brien, *States of Ireland*, Frogmore, St Albans: Panther, 1974, p.131.

106 Dervla Murphy, *A Place Apart*, London: John Murray, 1978.

107 Liam de Paor, *Unfinished Business: Ireland Today and Tomorrow*, London: Hutchinson Radius, 1990, pp.59, 66.

108 *Ibid.*, pp.68-70.

109 Colm Tóibín, *Bad Blood: A Walk along the Irish Border* (1987), London: Vintage, 1994.

110 R Kearney (ed), *Across the Frontiers*, Dublin: Wolfhound, 1988; *Post Nationalist Ireland: Politics, Culture, Philosophy*, London: Routledge, 1996.

111 John Hume, *Personal Views: Politics, Peace and Reconciliation in Ireland*, Enfield: Roberts Rinehart Publishers, 1996.

112 R Foster, *Modern Ireland,*, London: Allen Lane, 1988; R Foster, 'Varieties of Irishness', in M Crozier (ed), *Cultural Traditions in Northern Ireland*, Belfast: Institute of Irish Studies, 1989.

113 John Hume, 'A new Ireland in a new Europe', in D Keogh and M H Haltzel (eds), *Northern Ireland and the Politics of Reconciliation*, Cambridge: Cambridge University Press, 1993, pp.226-33, pp.231-32. See also J Hume, *Personal Views*, p.115. For an assessment of the controversial approaches to cross-Border regionalism see Paul Bew and Elizabeth Meehan, 'Regions and Borders: Controversies in Northern Ireland about the European Union', in *Journal of European Public Policy*, Vol.1, No.1 (1994), pp.95-113.

114 Richard Kearney, 'Ireland and the Europe of Regions', in Rüdiger Imhof (ed.), *A&E: Ireland: Literature, Culture, Politics*, Heidelberg: C Winter, 1994, pp.133-45, p.140.

115 Richard Kearney and Robin Wilson, 'Northern Ireland's Future as a European Region', in *The Irish Review*, No.15 (Spring 1994), pp.51-69; p.54.

116 *Ibid.*, p.65.

117 Hume, *Personal Views*, p.47.
118 O'Dowd, 'What is a Region?: The Case of the Irish Borderlands.', p.97.
119 For a general introduction to the study of frontiers, see Malcolm
     Anderson, *Frontiers: Territory and State Formation in the Modern World*,
     Cambridge: Polity Press, 1996; also Malcolm Anderson and Eberhard
     Bort (eds), *The Frontiers of Europe*, London: Pinter, 1998; M Anderson, E
     Bort (eds), *Boundaries and Identities: The Eastern Frontier of the
     European Union*, Edinburgh: ISSI, 1996; and M Anderson and E Bort
     (eds), *Schengen and EU Enlargement: Security and Operation at the
     Eastern Frontier of the European Union*, Edinburgh: ISSI, 1997
120 Quoted in Uinsionn Mac Dubhghaill, 'Breaking down barriers to Irish
     language in the North', in *The Irish Times*, 8 October 1994.

Anglo-Irish Relations in the New Dispensation: Towards a Post-Nationalist Framework?

Paul Arthur

... it is necessary to distinguish 'nation' from 'territory' and 'state'. Nationalism has often locked all three into a deadly trinity ... The recognition by many countries of dual nationality acknowledges the possibility of the severance of the link between nation and territory.[1]

The history of theorising about nationalism displays two dramatic faults. One is the tendency to treat the subject in a one-nation or one-state frame of reference: so that each nationalism has to be understood, in effect, mainly with reference to 'its own' ethnic, economic or other basis - rather than by comparison with the 'general historical process'. The second (and obviously related) tendency is to take nationalist ideology far too literally and seriously.[2]

In 1969 the Northern Ireland problem was, in the words of the Downing Street *Joint Declaration* (of 19 August), simply a matter of domestic jurisdiction. A quarter of a century later, it is treated as a problem which concerns the archipelago and which would be solved in the context of the new international system. Assistance from the international community - moral, symbolic, economic and political - would not be spurned. The approach based on purely internal initiatives had run its course and, in the words of a more recent *Joint Declaration* (that of 15 December 1993), the 'role of the British Government will be to encourage, facilitate and enable the achievement of such agreement...', an agreement which 'will embrace the totality of relationships.' Anglo-Irish relations was now the context in which the Northern Ireland problem was to be solved. Here was a recognition that nothing

in the North-South-Britain relationship fits into any known model of relationships between states, and it has been a mistake made by politicians in all three areas to try to find solutions which are based on standard international models that find no relevant application in this unique situation.[3]

Malcolm Anderson and Eberhard Bort (eds), *The Irish Border: History, Politics, Culture*, Liverpool University Press 1998, 41-55

In short, too much attention has been paid to the dreary steeples of Fermanagh and Tyrone; whereas external factors - such as the diminishing Atlanticism in British foreign policy, two decades of common membership of what is now the EU, and the influence of diasporan intervention - has not been given proper obeisance. This chapter will give greater weight to these factors and suggest that an effort is now being made to sever the link between nation and territory. We need to be aware of both the endogenous and exogenous by placing them in terms of the management of the international system. That suggests that the Northern Ireland problem has ceased being simply within Britain's 'sphere of responsibility' and entered the realms of a 'functional regime':

> Basically, functional regimes 'unbundle' the package of rights inherent in territorial sovereignty. Functionalism has therefore sometimes been advocated as an alternative organisational principle for international life. Functional regimes, it was hoped, would not only downgrade the importance of national boundaries but could, through the expansion of transboundary co-operative networks, lead to 'peace in parts'.[4]

Before we pursue these wider issues, it may be helpful to examine the evolving London/Belfast relationship as witnessed in the contradictory messages sent out in the respective Joint Declarations of 1969 and 1993. In 1969, the Union appeared secure, albeit under some strain with a Labour government in office. Unionism had overcome similar frissons in the past; and by 1970, with the installation of a Conservative and Unionist government in London, all seemed right with the world. That certainly lasted less than two years, with the prorogation of Stormont and the *imposition* of direct rule in March 1972. The conditional nature of the relationship was underlined further with the experiment (and subsequent collapse) of power sharing by May 1974. It was to be one of four attempts at seeking an internal settlement of the problem over the next decade. All failed, and in the meantime the British and Irish governments had switched their attention to tackling the problem jointly.

The Dual Polity and the External Support System

In his study of the politics of territoriality within the United Kingdom, Jim Bulpitt writes of the Dual Polity: 'a structure of territorial politics in which Centre and periphery had relatively little to do with each other;' and in which 'until recently the Centre sought not to govern the United Kingdom, but to manage it.'[5] That was a position which held until the late 1960s when there was an unfortunate confluence (from the Centre's point of view) of the rise of Scottish and Welsh nationalism, and the outbreak of serious conflict within Northern Ireland. The Centre's response differed in respect of mainland Britain and Northern Ireland. In the former, greater sensitivity towards the periphery, and the well-worn track of a Royal Commission on the Constitution, was followed. The latter presented altogether more intractable problems, as government lurched between conciliation and coercion. All three cases entailed much closer governance and, in 1972, Northern Ireland was to 'enjoy' the same privileges as Scotland and Wales, with the creation of a territorial ministry and a secretary of state for Northern Ireland for the first time in its existence. In addition, all three illustrated the elasticity of the concept of the United Kingdom and of 'British history':

> ... the term 'British history' has been used here to express the need for something that shall include both the attempt to incorporate Ireland within English or British political structures, and the reactions against that attempt and its consequences. The history of Irish nationality is as much a part of 'British history' in this sense as is the history of Union and Empire, and 'British' history thus denotes the historiography of no single nation but of a problematic and uncompleted experiment in the creation and interaction of several nations. At this point 'British history' becomes independent of Anglo-Irish union and will continue as long as there are a number of nations inhabiting the 'Atlantic archipelago', But 'British history' does not stop there; it extends itself into oceanic, American and global dimensions.[6]

Pocock's essay is particularly apt in this context, with its emphasis on that 'problematic and uncompleted experiment in the creation and interaction of several nations'. It suggests that the unity of the Kingdom may not be irreversible and that boundaries may be permeable. Moreover, it has the merit of imposing a proper perspective through his sense of scale, of time, of geo-politics and of the dynamism of state and ethnic relationships. It also touches on the endogenous and exogenous.

At this stage, we can return to Bulpitt who draws on the latter relationship. He suggests that

> in terms of a Centre's management of its domestic environment it will attempt to construct what can be labelled an external support system, that is to say it will attempt to minimise the impact of external forces on domestic politics, or ensure that

these forces are favourable to the maintenance of domestic tranquillity.[7]

That has a direct bearing on the conduct of the Northern Ireland problem since 1972. It is not our purpose to examine policy making in detail since the imposition of direct rule, rather to highlight the landmarks along the way - a White Paper of March 1973; the Sunningdale Agreement (December 1973); the Anglo-Irish process of the early 1980s culminating in the signing of the Anglo-Irish Agreement of November 1985; the Joint Declaration of December 1993, and the Framework Documents of February 1995. What they all had in common was an 'Irish dimension' and an implication somehow that the constitutional status of Northern Ireland was in question. We shall see, too, that a feature of the period was a growing interest of successive US administrations in the question.

In his study of the Dual Polity, Bulpitt acknowledges the collapse of its external support system with its implications especially for Unionism:

> ... the Unionist elite could not afford to lose disputes with the United Kingdom Centre. As a result it was very reluctant to initiate conflict situations, and above all to publicise them ... the Ulster Unionists were ideal collaborators: stable, quiescent, efficient and yet fundamentally weak in their relationships with the Centre.[8]

The introduction of the Irish dimension was a sharp reminder of this potential weakness; and, in that respect, Bulpitt's next sentence is important: 'The Northern Ireland model was sustained by the Centre's indifference, not by peripheral strength.'[9]

Indifference became impossible to sustain with the rise of the civil rights campaign in the late 1960s. That movement had borrowed heavily from examples elsewhere, including Martin Luther King's struggle in the United States. It coincided, too, with changes in the international system - a more assertive Commonwealth unwilling to accept unilateral British decisions;[10] an acceptance that the world had grown more interdependent, highlighted by British and Irish entry into the EEC; and in the gradual diminution of the Anglo-American special relationship. Perhaps the most striking example of the collapse of the external support system has been the degree to which the Northern Ireland question has become an 'intermistic' issue in Congressional politics, culminating in the Clinton administration's role in the current peace process. Intermestic issues

> straddle the domestic and foreign sectors and are symptomatic of an increasing interdependence between America and the

dynamic on the political track, with a firmer determination from both governments and the establishment of an International Body to provide an independent assessment of the decommissioning issue. Significantly, the body was headed by former Senator George Mitchell, a close confidant of the President. His team was completed by Canadian General John de Chastelain and a former Prime Minister of Finland, Harri Holkeri. Again, one is struck by the degree to which the Northern Ireland question has been internationalised and is no longer seen as solely a matter for the United Kingdom government. The United States, in particular, has become a major player.

Anglo-Irish-American Relationships

'Special relationships' are fashionable. In his triumphant sweep across Britain and Ireland, President Clinton invoked the Anglo-American relationship when he addressed both Houses of Parliament. As we saw above, he might have encountered some degree of scepticism. Earlier in 1995, there had been no common approach to Northern Ireland. Those in his audience with longer memories would have been hard pushed to disagree with the survey of the post-war literature which concluded that in some of its aspects (such as intelligence and nuclear matters):

> the relationship remains special in quality ... Yet it is no longer special in importance either to America or to the world at large. That is the difference between the 1980s and the 1940s.[14]

A swift appraisal of the range of issues in which the United Kingdom was bypassed by the United States - from the abrupt end of Lend Lease to the Reykjavik summit of 1986 - is indicative of its diminishing influence.

In a sceptical piece in the *Guardian* (22 February 1993), Hugo Young pays obeisance to continuing British influence but believes that 'it has been, and in its non-fictive aspect continues to be, the curse of post-war Britain. Its effect has been actively bad.' Foremost among its defects has been 'the refusal to join the Common Market when it started.' Here was another example of the burden of Britain's imperial past - the myth of its unique position between Atlanticism and Europeanism, encapsulated in the phrase 'special relationship'. But it was not unique in its capacity for myth-making. Taoiseach Charles Haughey told Speaker Jim Wright on Capitol Hill on St Patrick's Day 1987 that 'there are no two countries anywhere in the world which have such a special relationship as ours.' And it was the government's Discussion Paper of October 1972 which stated: 'The geographical and historical facts of life oblige us to recognise the special relationship that exists between the component parts of the British Isles.' In the meantime, the more powerful states in Europe, such as Germany, were establishing their own special relations with the United States.

It needs to be remembered that, unlike Ireland, the United Kingdom entered the EEC in an unemotional frame of mind. Its first attempt had been vetoed by President de Gaulle because

> in his view, Britain would constitute a Trojan horse for the United States, on the one hand impeding Western Europe's emergence as a unified entity under French leadership and, on the other, leading ultimately to an Atlantic community under American 'hegemony'.[15]

By the time of Irish and British accession, global economic conditions had deteriorated:

> ... the first stage of the Community's development coincided with the optimism and the burgeoning prosperity of the 1960s. Britain's accession, by contrast, came just as the boom was about to end with the first oil shock, and its first year of membership coincided with the worst recession since the 1930s.[16]

It has to be remembered, too, - borrowing an expression from Tony Crosland when he addressed the European Parliament in 1977 - that the Community represented Britain's first permanent engagement on the continent of Europe since the Reformation. Unlike its other alliances, the EEC was the only international organisation of which it was not a founder member. Tugendhat describes its dilemma succinctly:

> In a nutshell, Britain was turning away from a set of assumptions and policies that had failed, towards an experiment that seemed to be succeeding, in the hope that it would yield political influence and economic growth that could not be obtained by other means.[17]

In short, her external support system was collapsing and that was to have implications for the Northern Ireland question.

Contrast that attitude with that which pertained in Ireland. Given its diminutive size and humble position in world affairs, Ireland worked on a more modest plane. Until 1939, the Irish were obsessed with sovereignty issues (especially in relation to the United Kingdom) but that 'was undermined by the lack of adequate universal defence and economic self-sufficiency, and by the enormous continuing dependence upon British trade.'[18] These inadequacies were exposed during the war; and the post-war period seemed to confirm that the Irish 'had managed to maintain a basic freedom of decision and action' by remaining aloof from organisations like the Atlantic Pact, but 'to some extent the Irish were again allowed this freedom because neither the United States nor Britain considered Irish participation in the new defence arrangements to be crucial.'[19] Similarly, entry into the EEC was not so much the action of an independent actor, but rather a stark choice between the perils of autarky and the opportunity to make economic progress.

In his first major policy statement as Minister for Foreign Affairs, Garrett FitzGerald told the Dail (9 May 1973) that it was time to formulate new general guidelines for future foreign policy because of the movement 'towards greater interdependence in the world economy;' the 'evolving situation in Northern Ireland;' and 'the accession to membership of the European Communities.' All three factors were important and interlinked. Irish public opinion was strongly in favour of membership because it expected to benefit from the Common Agricultural Policy and from European regional development funds. It is conceivable, too, that 'Europe' has had an emollient effect on the problem:

> Since 1972 Britain has never made the defence of the union between Britain and Northern Ireland a touchstone of national strength in a way, for example, that it elevated the Falklands/ Malvinas in 1982 ... in the last analysis Britain has behaved towards the Irish Republic as another member of the EEC to which it might accord a recognition of the kind it expects itself.[20]

Finally, it is conceivable that the Irish Republic entered the Community in a more realistic frame of mind than the United Kingdom in that it was more conscious of 'the emergence of a global economic system which stretches beyond the control of any single state.'[21] In a White Paper of January 1972, *The Accession of Ireland to the European Communities*, the Department of Foreign Affairs drew the distinction between independence and sovereignty. The latter was defined as 'the freedom to take autonomous decisions and actions in domestic and foreign affairs.' It accepted that 'as a very small country, independent but with little or no capacity to influence events abroad that significantly affect us,' Ireland enjoyed very little effective economic sovereignty:

> For most countries other than the major powers, the real freedom, as distinct from the nominal right, to take national

action and pursue policies in the economic and trading sectors is circumscribed to a very great extent by the complex nature of international, economic and trading relationships ... our vital interests may be affected by the policies and actions of other larger countries and groups of countries. This gravely restricts our capacity to exercise the right of freedom of action and thus represents a very real limitation on our national sovereignty.

The Irish were recognising the reality of the permeability of boundaries and frontiers which come as 'no surprise to those whose independence and identity have been deeply affected by the hegemonic reach of empires.'[22]

J J Lee has interpreted the Foreign Affairs position as accepting that the

national interest was the only valid criterion in policy formulation. Everything else, even sovereignty, which was merely a means towards serving the national interest, must be subordinated to that decisive consideration.[23]

Other member states of the EEC had already 'accepted the limitations involved in their national interests are best served by membership.'[24] The United Kingdom's problem was that it never came to terms politically and psychologically with the pooling of sovereignty. It was to have an enormous effect on the debate within the Commons, especially after John Major succeeded Margaret Thatcher as Prime Minister, and it was to cast a deep fissure on domestic politics and introduce a strain of rabid (English) nationalism into that debate.

Another player began to take action in the autumn of 1994 when the EU Commission created a special Task Force to look into further ways in which it could give practical assistance to Northern Ireland and the border counties to assist in the peace process. It produced the 'Delors package' (also known as the Peace and Reconciliation Programme) which would run for five years, with a budget of 300 million ECUs for the first three years, and financing for the final two years to be subject to review. It was yet another indication of the enhanced role played by 'Europe' in seeking out a solution.

Towards a 'Polycentric' Irish Nationalism

Inherent in nationalism is a recognition of the existence of others. It is the way in which the national group treats these others that distinguishes polycentric nationalism, which respects the other and sees each nation as enriching a common civilisation, from ethnocentric nationalism, which sees one's own nation as superior to all others and seeks domination.[25]

One politician who had paid particular attention to developments in Europe and to the Irish-American diaspora was John Hume, the leader of the SDLP and Member of the European Parliament. In a series of articles he highlighted the influence which the United States and Europe could bring to bear on the Northern Ireland problem. In 1979, for example, he wrote a prescient article - 'Northern Ireland: A British Problem' - for *Foreign Affairs* in which he invoked American assistance as a prestigious third party.

In a collection of essays centred around a conference organised by the Woodrow Wilson Center in 1990, he wrote of 'A new Ireland in a new Europe,' a Europe which recognised that

> the democratic nation-state is no longer a sufficient political entity to allow people to have adequate control over the economic and technological forces that affect people's opportunities and circumstances ... The issue is to maximise the real sovereignty of the peoples of Europe rather than ossify our democratic development around limited notions of national sovereignty that only give space to multinational vested interest.[26]

This was a theme which Hume had pursued ever since he had become an MEP after the first direct elections to the European Parliament in 1979, and one which he would have addressed to Sinn Féin during and after the SDLP/Sinn Féin talks which ran from March to September 1988. Sinn Féin had not contested the 1979 elections but its candidate in 1984, Danny Morrison, argued that he would use the European Parliament to attack the British presence in Northern Ireland and to highlight instances of British injustice and repression. He failed to be elected in 1984, and again in 1989 when he had advised negotiated withdrawal from membership because it had been a 'disaster' for Ireland. Yet less than three years later, Sinn Féin believed that the

> political and economic transformation of Europe provides a golden opportunity for Ireland to finally resolve its British problem and embark on a process of economic and political reunification and transformation to the benefit of all its people.[27]

We do not have to agree with the rhetoric, but simply note the sea change in attitude. One explanation lies in a republican audit which recognised that after 25 years of a war of attrition the IRA had not won but nor had they lost: their supporters were weary and their opponents in the British political establishment indicated that they were ready to discuss a settlement which would bring Sinn Féin in out of the cold and allow them to sue for a 'new Ireland'. Another explanation lies in Sinn Féin's removal from being a narrow sect and its willingness to engage in dialogue with political opponents. This enabled it to build up a nationalist consensus with the SDLP, the Irish government and Irish-America. As a result, it has lifted its eyes above the parapet and scanned distant horizons. It was this larger vision which allowed it to move from the narrow sectarian ground of conspirational physical force nationalism. It may have recognised at last that nationalism 'is no longer a major vector of historical development'[28] and that

> '[t]he nation' today is visibly in the process of losing an important part of its old functions, namely that of constituting a territorially bounded 'national economy' which formed a building block in the larger 'world economy', at least in the developed regions of the globe. Since World War II, but especially since the 1960s, the role of 'national economies' has been undermined or even brought into question by the major transformations in the international division of labour, whose basic units are transnational or multi-national enterprises of all sizes, and by the corresponding development of international centres and networks of economic transaction which are, for practical purposes, outside the control of state governments.[29]

The process begun with the Anglo-Irish Agreement of 1985 had helped to unbundle the properties of 'nation', 'state' and 'territory', and had enabled some of the antagonists to examine the conflict anew. The internationalising of the Anglo-Irish problem had blurred distinctions about boundaries and shibboleths about state sovereignty. Wilsonian national self-determination has seen its day. In its place, interdependency offered a new way forward. 'People' rather than 'territory', 'means' rather than 'ends' - these were to be the beacons for the way ahead.

Notes

1   Vincent Geoghegan, 'Socialism, national identities and post-nationalist citizenship', in *Irish Political Studies*, 9 (1994), p.71.

2   Tom Nairn, *The Break-up of Britain: Crisis and Neonationalism*, London:Verso, 1977, p.93.

3   Fine Gael, *Ireland: Our Future Together*, Dublin: Fine Gael, 1979, p.36.

4   Emil Kratochwil, 'Of Systems, Boundaries and Territoriality: An Enquiry into the Formation of the State System', in *World Politics*, 39,1 (1986), pp.48-49.

5   Jim Bulpitt, *Territory and Power in the United Kingdom: An Interpretation*, Manchester: Manchester University Press, 1983, p.238.

6   J G A Pocock, 'The Limits and Divisions of British History: In Search of the Unknown Subject', in *American Historical Review*, 87,2 (1982), p.318.

7   Bulpitt, *op. cit.*, p.59.

8   *Ibid.*, p.146

9   *Ibid.*

10 David Low, *Eclipse of Empire*, Cambridge: Cambridge University Press, 1991, *passim.*

11 Richard Maidment and Anthony McGrew, *The American Political Process*, London: Sage/Open University, 1986, p.135.

12 Cmnd 5259.

13 Tim Pat Coogan, *The Troubles: Ireland's Ordeal 1966-1995 and the Search for Peace*, London: Hutchinson, 1995, p.351.

14 David Reynolds, 'Re-thinking Anglo-American Relations' in *International Affairs*, 65,1 (1988-89), pp.89-111.

15 Robert S Jordan and Werner J Feld, *Europe in the Balance: The Changing Context of European International Politics*, London: Faber, 1986, p.114.

16 Christopher Tugendhat, *Making Sense of Europe*, London: Viking, 1986, p.117

17 *Ibid.*, p.119.

18 Trevor Salmon, *Unneutral Ireland: An Ambivalent and Unique Security Policy*, Oxford: Clarendon, 1989, p.105.

19 *Ibid.*, p.171.

20 Frank Wright, *Northern Ireland: A Comparative Analysis*, Dublin: Gill and Macmillan, 1987, p.222.

21 David Held, ed., *Prospects for Democracy* (A special issue of *Political Studies*), 1992, p.32

22 *Ibid.*, p.22.

23 J J Lee, *Ireland 1912-1985*, Cambridge: Cambridge University Press, 1989, pp.463-464.

24 *Ibid.*

25 Yael Tamir, 'The Enigma of Nationalism', in *World Politics*, 47 (1995), p.430.

26 John Hume, 'A new Ireland in a new Europe', in D Keogh and M H Haltzel, eds., *Northern Ireland and the Politics of Reconciliation*, Cambridge: Cambridge University Press., 1993, pp.226-33; p.227.

27 Sinn Féin, *Towards a Lasting Peace in Ireland*, Dublin: Sinn Féin, 1992, p.15.

28 Eric Hobsbawm, *Nations and Nationalism since 1780*, Cambridge: Cambridge University Press, 1990, p. 163.

29 *Ibid.*, pp.173-174.

The Origins of Partition

Ged Martin

I

In 1922, Austen Chamberlain privately admitted that the partition of Ireland 'was a compromise, and like all compromises, is illogical and indefensible'.[1] Partition, the encapsulation of the 'narrow ground' of Ulster,[2] emerged in the form which underlies Irish politics today during a narrow moment in time, essentially packed into eight years between 1912 and 1920, with a five-year epilogue which ended with the division of Ireland enshrined, however illogical the dividing line, with the collapse of the Boundary Commission in 1925. Laffan is surely correct to assert that in 1911, 'Irishmen of all political opinions would have been amazed if they could have foreseen the division of Ireland into two separate states'.[3] However, in a longer context, it may be argued that it was the growth of Belfast that determined not just the outcome but the actual boundary line, so shaping the fate of the 'muddy byways'[4] of Fermanagh and Tyrone, as well as the more marginal Protestant minorities of North Monaghan and East Donegal. It is almost impossible to discuss the origins of Partition without noting the familiar paradox that the Ulster Protestants, who most doggedly opposed Home Rule, were the only people to end up with devolved government within the United Kingdom.[5] Perhaps it is more significant to note that the Northern State as created in the early 1920s was a nineteenth-century answer that proved inadequate to tackle twentieth-century problems.[6]

II

Rebutting O'Connell's demand for Repeal in 1833, Macaulay challenged him 'to find a reason for having a parliament at Dublin which will not be just as good for having another Parliament at Londonderry.'[7] Partition was for long primarily a debating point, used to undermine the case for devolution in Ireland. The perennially impracticable Auberon Herbert was indeed rare in espous-

Malcolm Anderson and Eberhard Bort (eds.), *The Irish Border:
History, Politics, Culture*, Liverpool University Press 1998, 57-111

ing it as a positive way forward on the eve of the first Home Rule crisis:

> Peace grows as often out of disunion as union. It has followed from the separation of Belgium and Holland, and it will follow from the separation of a part of Ulster from the rest of Ireland, at all events for a season, until the time comes when the grass has grown over old graves and the passions buried in them.[8]

Herbert's prediction was quickly undercut by the riots which plagued Belfast throughout 1886, with a death-toll of 32 demonstrating that Ulster's divisions were capable of creating graves enough to continue the passions of disunion.[9]

The first Home Rule bill split the Liberal party when Joseph Chamberlain included a separate assembly for Ulster in what Labouchere called his 'ultimatumest of ultimatums' to Gladstone.[10] In moving the Home Rule bill, Gladstone had made a nod to the possibility 'that Ulster itself, or, perhaps with more appearance of reason, a portion of Ulster, should be excluded' but - like his Liberal successors in 1912-14 - he insisted that any such concession should only be made after the principle of Home Rule had been agreed.[11] Since the 1886 Home Rule bill was defeated on its second reading, partitionist speculation did not enter the realm of the practical in 1886, while the expected veto of the House of Lords in 1893 similarly obviated any need to draw detailed lines on the map.

Outside Ulster, few seem to have taken the issue very seriously. Parnell breezily refused to give up a single Irishman.[12] Henry Pelling has suggested that the Ulster issue was an electoral factor in some British constituencies, but the actual evidence for this is obscure.[13] *Punch* regarded the idea of a Northern Protestant army imposing its own political 'orangement' as a joke, an exception to its habitual equation of Irish absurdity with Catholicism. It carried a map of the North of Ireland - perhaps the first cartographic illustration of Partition in the British press - and named it the 'Orange Free State', a deft allusion to another discontented Calvinist frontier people in uneasy relationship with the Empire.[14] There is some irony in the fact that the only sustained attempt to delimit the eventual boundary between the Irish Free State and its Orange twin was the work of a former town clerk of Johannesburg.

The map in *Punch* also bore a more pertinent and less light-hearted slogan, 'Ulster Vires'. The pun on the legal phrase, *ultra vires*, captured a strand of Ulster thinking which O'Farrell has traced as early as the disestablishment of the Irish Church, that the position of Irish Protestants within the United Kingdom was a fundamental part of the constitution which no parliament could alter.[15] The argument was caught by Lord Randolph Churchill, who had not long before held that 'Ulsteria is not so much an argument as a disease', when he told a packed meeting in the Ulster Hall that 'no change so gigantic' as Home Rule 'could be accompanied by the mere passing of a law' even if parliament 'was so recreant from all its high duties' as to pass Gladstone's bill. He was soon to abbreviate his message: 'Ulster will fight, Ulster will be right'.[16] Such sentiments did not mean that British politicians considered Partition to be a serious option at the time of the first Home Rule crisis. Even Joseph Chamberlain had conceded that 'the Ulster people cannot be allowed to say they will remain as they are whilst a system of self-government is given to the rest of Ireland'.[17] Yet it is arguable that Ulster resistance in 1912 to 'the present conspiracy to set up a Home Rule Parliament in Ireland'[18] was no more than an earthquake along the fault line opened in 1886. As early as 1896, Thomas MacKnight was warning 'that there are two antagonistic populations, two different nations on Irish soil' and that 'common citizenship between the two sections of the Irish people' was impossible.[19] British observers found it hard to imagine how Ulster might have a constitutional status if it were severed from the rest of Ireland. Over a year after a Liberal backbencher, T C R Agar-Robartes, had proposed in 1912 to retain the four Protestant-majority north-eastern counties, Antrim, Armagh, Derry and Down, under direct Westminster rule, *Punch* published a map suggesting that spoil taken from a canal from Newry to Derry be used to fill in the North Channel.[20]

Controversy over Home Rule ran in parallel with a more decorous debate on the merits of a federal constitution for the United Kingdom. Joseph Chamberlain had believed in 1885 that Home Rule could only be secured through 'the adoption of the American Constitution', with local legislatures for England, Scotland, Wales, Ulster and the three southern provinces combined.[21] Carson in 1917 conceded that 'a system of Federation for the whole United Kingdom' could offer special status for Ulster.[22] Two 'Round Table' episodes helped establish federal contexts within which Ulster solutions might be sought. The first Round Table was an attempt to re-establish the unity of the Liberal party in 1887 by taking the Canadian provinces 'as an *analogue*' for Irish Home Rule. Already divided by mutual distrust, the principal negotiators treated the Canadian model in two opposed ways. For Harcourt and Morley, Westminster would be Ottawa and a parliament on College Green would be a subordinate Ontario: Harcourt was subsequently able to score some savage points by quoting from section 92 of the British North America Act, which enumerates provincial powers, to argue that Chamberlain had been prepared to concede wide authority to a Home Rule parliament. Chamberlain, however, appears to have approached the Canadian model in a slightly different sense, as a means by which the special needs of Ulster might be protected, presumably in the way that the provincial structure had recognised the distinct culture of Quebec.[23]

Hovering around the Third Home Rule bill was a different Round Table movement, which aimed at imperial federation. Round Tablers had access to leading politicians and influential publications and their ideas permeated constitutional debate. They failed to overcome the intractable obstacles to constitutional change, not the least of them being the inertia of the existing constitution. Attempts to divide England into regions faltered in the face of derisive references to the restoration of the Heptarchy, while enthusiasm for Home Rule was more muted in Wales and Scotland: Bonar Law doubted whether his home city of Glasgow would defer to a parliament in Edinburgh.[24] Fundamentally, the Round Tablers were looking not within the United Kingdom but without, seeking a means reconstructing the core of Empire to pave the way for an imperial federation. Such a scheme would incidentally make it possible, as one federalist dismissively put it, to 'give N.E. Ulster a little show of its own'.[25] In a curious way, the grandiose vision of an imperial congress was to spawn the tiny pastiche of Stormont.

Leaders of all parties were agreed in dismissing the Agar-Robartes plan to exempt North-East Ulster from Home Rule, although it was notable that Liberals and Nationalists refused to contemplate the division of Ireland, while Carson objected to the exclusion of Fermanagh and Tyrone from Ulster.[26] In 1912, Partition was urged less for any merits of its own but rather as a tactic to block Home Rule. Indeed, a recent change in the rules of the political game made it difficult for either side to contemplate compromise. The 1911 Parliament Act had abolished the untrammelled veto of the House of Lords, used so effectively to crush Home Rule in 1893, substituting instead the power of delay: the Commons could over-ride Lords opposition by passing identical legislation in three consecutive sessions. Thus the Home Rule bill of 1912 would become law, over the objections of the Lords, in 1914, but only then would it become possible to carry amending legislation, since any previous unilateral concession by the Commons would effectively convert the bill into an entirely new piece of legislation.[27] Hence the logic, if not the judgement, behind Bonar Law's denunciation of Asquith's Liberal government as 'a Revolutionary Committee which has seized upon despotic power by fraud'. Deprived of their ultimate power to control the political process through their dominance of the House of Lords, the Unionist [Conservative] opposition fell back on violence of language, such as Bonar Law's statement that there was 'no length of resistance to which Ulster can go in which I shall not be prepared to support them'.[28] The terms of the Parliament Act helped ensure that the Home Rule debate was argued in intemperate terms. This, in turn, fostered among nationalists - especially Sinn Féiners such as de

Valera - a dangerously inverted view of cause and effect, which held that 'the whole Ulster difficulty was artificial, nursed and indeed created by Britain in her own interest in order to create trouble and division in Ireland'.[29]

None the less, some attempts to explore and signal the terms of an eventual settlement were made between 1912 and 1914. The final stages of the crisis, between March and August 1914, are remembered as a time when the British government seemed to lose control of the Irish situation, in the face of gun-running and the reluctance of its own officer corps to confront Northern preparations for insurrection. On the face of it, the Buckingham Palace conference of July 1914 was a failure, and the Irish issue was eclipsed only by the outbreak of European War - and then but temporarily. In fact, the Buckingham Palace talks marked the last point at which Ulster leaders made a constructive if hard-headed attempt to defend their own position while being prepared to accept some form of all-Ireland settlement: they were to be absent from the Treaty negotiations in 1921, and might as well not have taken part in the Convention of 1917. Because the Buckingham Palace talks took place behind closed doors, they proved to be fertile in ideas, most of them impractical but some of them offering clues to the origins of subsequent policies put forward in the very different circumstances of the War.[30]

Carson's motion in January 1913 to exclude the whole of Ulster from the operation of Home Rule hardly represented a compromise, but it did reflect an increasing recognition that the Ulstermen might not achieve their prime objective, the scuppering of any form of devolution.[31] On the government side, the 'county option' seemed the best way to secure Home Rule without civil war.[32] Sir Horace Plunkett's suggestion that Ulster should be placed under a Dublin parliament with the right to vote itself out after ten years was quickly overtaken by Redmond's proposal to allow 'any county in Ulster, by plebiscite, to vote itself temporarily out of the jurisdiction of the Irish parliament'.[33] By March 1914, Redmond had reluctantly accepted the county option, provided that exclusion was limited to a non-renewable period of three years. He was quickly forced to double this, a concession which Carson memorably dismissed as 'sentence of death, with a stay of execution for six years'.[34]

As Dennis Gwynn pointed out, the British government's proposals of March 1914 were very different from the settlement which emerged in 1920.[35] Only the four north-eastern counties would have been exempt from the operation of Home Rule. It was assumed that Tyrone and Fermanagh would vote themselves into the jurisdiction of a Dublin parliament, but the Liberals refused Redmond's demand for Derry City and Newry, parliamentary boroughs with Home Rule MPs, to vote as separate units. Moreover, exclusion was to be temporary. The only hope the Ulster Unionists might have of preventing their automatic inclusion in an all-Ireland settlement lay in the fact that the six-year stay of execution would see at least two United Kingdom general elections, with the possibility that their Conservative allies might be returned to office. Of course, once a Dublin parliament was in being, Westminster could do little more than tinker with Home Rule.[36]

In 1914, any proposal for a separate Northern legislature would have seemed no more than a legitimatisation of Carson's threatened provisional government. Excluded counties would remain under the direct rule of Westminster. However, there had also been proposals to give Ulster some form of collective political personality by which it might safeguard its interests under a Dublin parliament. Known as 'Home Rule within Home Rule', these ideas had been generally discarded by early 1914, but they would recur in the 1920 Government of Ireland Act. Thus, paradoxically, the road to Stormont lay through all-Ireland Home Rule.

Because it was exploratory in intention and inconclusive in outcome, the Buckingham Palace conference does not readily lend itself to summary. Tentatively, however, it may be concluded that the notion of plebiscites by counties was in effect superseded by general if reluctant recognition that it would be necessary to exclude a north-eastern block, either of the Six Counties or some adjusted area based upon them.[37] This subtle shift of emphasis was disguised by the insoluble and acrimonious issue of boundaries, which will be considered later, but the transition from individual malcontent counties to a single embryo province had occurred prior to the outbreak of war. (De Valera, however, continued to preach temporary exclusion on a county basis even at the time of the Treaty.)[38]

Home Rule was suspended for the duration of the war as soon as it became law in September 1914, but within two years, the issue was back on the agenda, with Six Counties Partition now an integral part of the solution. Even Asquith recognised that the Easter Rising had discredited the existing system of government in Ireland in its entirety. Moreover, the War was going badly: American support for the Allies was to be vital, and American opinion was inflamed by Irish wrongs. Hence Home Rule, for so long denounced as a threat to the unity of the Empire, was now crucial to its survival. Partition, originally a device to block Home Rule, had become a means of facilitating its immediate implementation. Both Carson and Redmond put their respective leaderships on the line to force their followers to accept the Six County unit. 'One of Carson's chief difficulties was to make men grasp the significance of the fact that Home Rule was now actually established by Act of Parliament.'[39] The most that Unionists could hope for was modification of its terms.

Unionists in Cavan, Monaghan and Donegal reluctantly accepted that 'the existence of the Empire was at stake' and consigned them-

AN ORANGEMENT IN BLACK AND YELLOW.

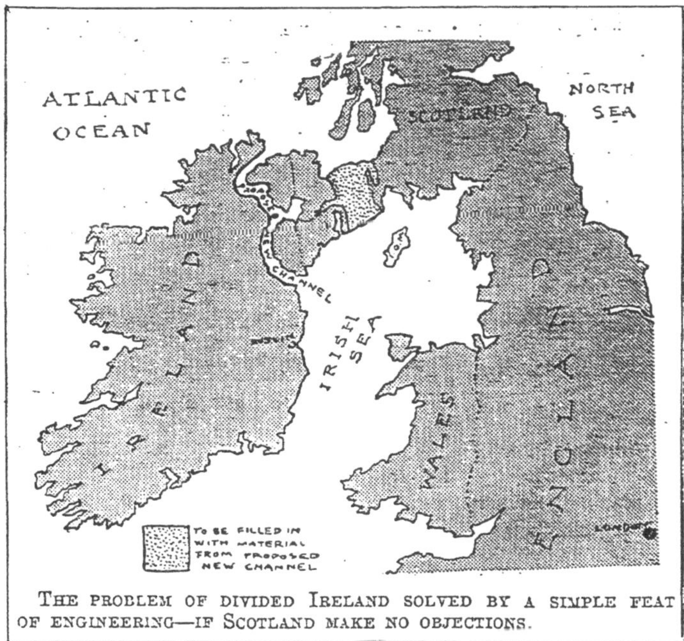

THE PROBLEM OF DIVIDED IRELAND SOLVED BY A SIMPLE FEAT
OF ENGINEERING—IF SCOTLAND MAKE NO OBJECTIONS.

PUNCH 1886 (top) / 1913 (bottom)

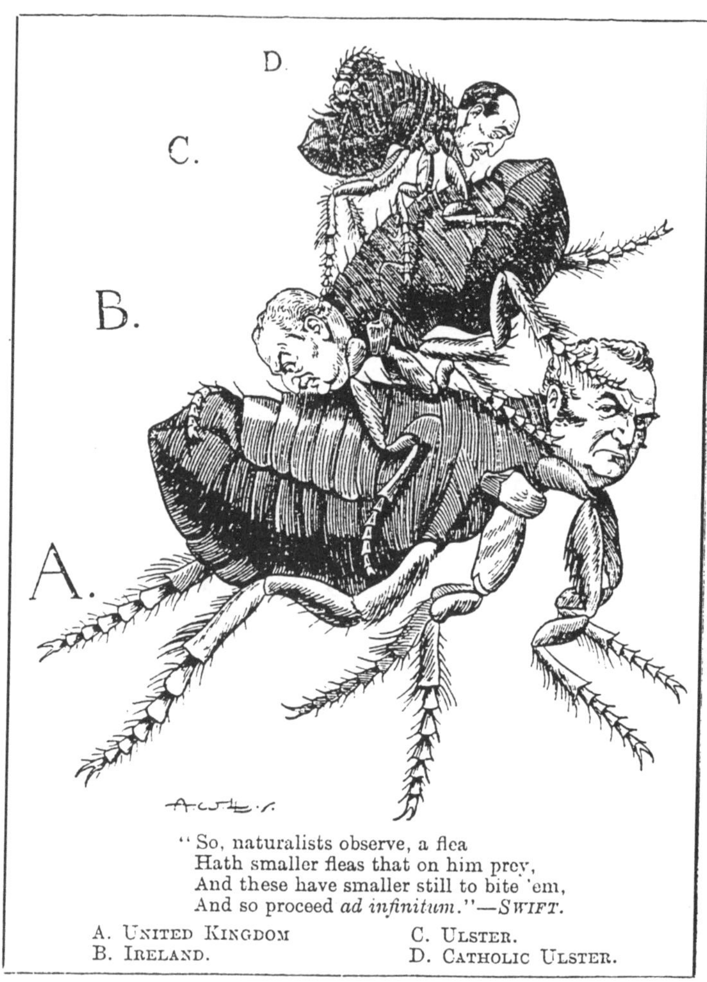

Ulster and the British Identity
Punch (November 1913)

A is *Punch*'s representation of England, John Bull
B is John Redmond, C Sir Edward Carson.
Note that, in 1913, there was no easily identifiable
face to represent Catholic Ulster.

selves to a Dublin parliament.[40] By making the Three Counties the symbolic battle-ground - rather than Tyrone and Fermanagh - the Ulster Unionists appeared to have won the dispute over territory, but Redmond seemed victorious in the longer-term with an assurance from Lloyd George that exclusion would be a temporary war-time expedient. However, the formation of a coalition government a year earlier meant that Asquith and Lloyd George were no longer in full control of events. Faced with a cabinet revolt from Unionist ministers, they conceded the permanent exclusion of the Six Counties, and Redmond duly denounced the offer of truncated Home Rule.[41]

Through the smoke of parliamentary battle, Carson in July 1916 had publicly asked Redmond to shake hands with him on the floor of the Commons. The gesture was rebuffed, but from then on, there would be few opportunities even for the request to be made.[42] It was not merely that the old-style Nationalists were in the process of being swept away by Sinn Féin, which did not even contest a by-election until February 1917. The republican challenge certainly left the Redmondites with increasingly little freedom of manoeuvre, as shown by their withdrawal from Westminster in April 1918. However, it was not possible to foresee the extent of their slaughter in the 1918 general election, and it is hard to avoid the conclusion that even then, they were, like the Asquithians, the victims of Lloyd George's rush to the polls in the hour of victory. Perhaps more significant was the widening breach between Northern and Southern Unionists, which became apparent during the Irish Convention of 1917-18, when one of the Ulstermen described 'the Southern Unionist lot' as 'a cowardly crew & stupid to boot'.[43] In 1914, the Irish factions had been unable to agree. By 1918, they were unable even to talk. This put an end to any hope that an Irish settlement might emerge by consensus, or even with constructive input from any party, North or South. Any post-war attempt at an Irish settlement would have to be the product of a British initiative, and by 1919 British proposals would be a stab in the Irish gloom.

It is important to underline the point that although Partition had become increasingly likely by 1916, there was no suggestion of a separate Northern legislature. An Ulster parliament would please neither those who wanted to remain with Westminster nor those who held to the 'seamless garment' view of Irish unity, while the notion of provincial councils, which had never managed to supplant Home Rule, was now totally out of the running. Moreover, the leader of the Ulster Protestants remained a Dublin Unionist, still conscious of the need for a settlement that would eventually encompass the whole island.[44]

In March 1917, as a member of Lloyd George's war cabinet, Carson drafted 'a sensible and sincere attempt at a solution',[45] a scheme for a Consultative Assembly of Ireland, to be composed of representatives from a Home Rule parliament in Dublin and Ulster's Westminster MPs. As with 'Home Rule within Home Rule', the Ulster representatives would have a veto over the extension of any Dublin legislation on the excluded counties, but where there was practical agreement, all-Ireland harmonisation might be achieved by Order in Council. Carson even envisaged that the Consultative Assembly might be a step towards the unification of the whole island. It would be preferable, he argued, for a local party system to emerge within a predominantly Catholic Southern legislature rather than have an Ulster delegation forming a discordant Unionist bloc from the outset.[46]

In May 1917, Lloyd George seemed to be on the point of adopting Carson's scheme. Certainly he briefed C P Scott, evidently with the aim of winning the support of the *Manchester Guardian*. The government was prepared to introduce Home Rule in the Twenty Six Counties immediately, with a 'clean-cut' of the Six Counties for a provisional period of up to five years. There would be a 'Council for all Ireland', composed of 'the 16 members of the excluded counties' and 'a similar number to be appointed by the Dublin Parliament', with 'power to apply to the whole of Ireland any legislation within the competence of the Dublin Parliament on which both sides are agreed'.[47]

Dillon, aware that in Ireland 'the demand now was for Dominion Home Rule and partition in any shape was scouted', dismissed the Council scheme as 'irrelevant and mere "trimmings"'. Redmond was also emphatic in rejecting the idea. 'His view was that the proper method of accommodation with Ulster was to include it under the operation of the Home Rule Act and then to give Ulster a majority in the Senate. So far as he was concerned they might have the whole Senate.' When Scott pointed out that 'the Senate would have no veto on Finance, which was the matter about which Ulster was most afraid', Redmond replied that he was ready to consider that concession as well. 'There was almost nothing he would not concede for the sake of conciliation and unity.' Redmond was also prepared to consider a Canadian-style federal system, with subordinate assemblies for Ulster 'and Munster too if she wanted it'.[48] Consequently, when on 16 May 1917 Lloyd George publicly offered the Irish leaders the choice of immediate Home Rule, in which Partition would be balanced by a Council of Ireland, or a Convention representing 'all leading interests, classes, creeds and phases of thought in Ireland', the balance of response favoured talk rather than action.[49]

Carson's sardonic dismissal of the Convention as a means to allow the 'clever Irish' to solve the problem which had eluded the 'stupid English!' was an indication of developing friction with his British allies. In January 1918 he resigned from the War Cabinet to resume his political freedom.[50] Paradoxically, this move increased his power to shape an Irish settlement. In 1917, Lloyd George had feared that the loss of Carson would break up the coalition, which at that time retained a substantial following of Liberal MPs.[51] The 1918 general election left Lloyd George overwhelmingly reliant upon Unionist support, and Unionist attitudes to Ireland would be shaped by Carson.

Not surprisingly, the policy announced by the British government in December 1919, which became the 1920 Government of Ireland Act, drew on the proposals Carson had made and Lloyd George had briefly embraced in 1917. For the first time, it was proposed to establish parliaments in both the North and South of Ireland, linked by a Council of Ireland in which both were to be represented equally. This was a scheme which did not seem to stem from the situation of 1919, for it offered Nationalist Ireland far less than was now demanded, and Ulster far more than it had ever sought. It has been pointed out that the prime minister's attention was focused on post-war foreign policy, although the Government of Ireland Act brings to mind Dangerfield's comment that Lloyd George had a penchant for compromise solutions that 'had everything to recommend them but substance'.[52] In any case, although Lloyd George insisted that he was still 'a Gladstonian Home Ruler and wished to keep Ireland as an integral part of the United Kingdom', he was also aware that 'Carson, if he chose, could blow the Bill sky high'.[53]

While the Government of Ireland Act might not succeed in getting Ireland out of British politics, it did offer a way of reducing the impact of Irish politicians at Westminster by cutting the number of Irish MPs to forty. This could only be equitable if Home Rule took effect in both parts of Ireland. Throughout 1920, the increasingly unstable state of Ireland demonstrated the inadequacy of the slowly-progressing legislation, which did not reach the statute book until December. However, just as the pre-war Liberal government had declined to compromise with the House of Lords until its own solution had the force of law, so the post-war coalition refused to make concessions to republican insurgency until it had laid down its own framework for a settlement. Indeed, the more obvious the barriers to the implantation of Home Rule in the South, the more essential it became to make Home Rule work in the North. Furthermore, the proposals of December 1919 had envisaged at least the possibility of a nine-county Ulster, which would in due course vote itself into an all-Ireland parliament.

Reluctantly, Carson decided not to blow the Bill sky-high. The choice facing the Ulster Unionists in 1920 was simply one between parliaments in Belfast and Dublin. As Carson said, if he blocked the 1920 Bill, 'I bring automatically into force the Act of 1914', suspended for the duration of the War. This would box him into a corner in which he would have to invoke the Covenant and call the Ulster Protestants to arms. 'For what? For the six counties that are offered in a Bill which I could have got without fighting at all. No one but a lunatic would undertake such a performance.'[54] As Charles Craig, brother of the North's first prime minister, put it, 'we prefer to have a Parliament although we do not want one of our own'. An Ulster parliament would mean that 'above all the paraphernalia of Government' would be established, thus making it harder for any future combination of Westminster parties - especially the rising threat of Labour - to drive Ulster out of the United Kingdom.[55] Thus a Northern parliament, intended as one of the twin pillars of an all-Ireland Home Rule settlement, was embraced, if reluctantly, by Ulster Protestants as the latest means of maintaining their position within the United Kingdom. In the event, the Southern parliament barely flickered into life, and the Council of Ireland remained a 'fleshless and bloodless skeleton'.[56] Partition has come to be associated with the Treaty signed on 6 December 1921. It is certainly true that the Treaty went through the motions of including Northern Ireland within the Irish Free State while offering it a provision to opt out - which the Northern parliament was formally to activate on 7 December 1922, twenty-four hours after the enactment of the Free State constitution.[57] However, Partition had been completed well before the conclusion of either the Treaty or the Free State to which it gave birth. Indeed, it was at the opening of the Northern parliament in June 1921 that George V appealed for peace in Ireland, a gesture that is usually seen as a landmark in the path to a truce.[58] While communal violence reached appalling levels in Belfast and Derry, the north-east of Ireland was largely spared from the War of Independence during the crucial months when the Northern government was starting to function. The 1920 Act created the Northern Ireland state. The Anglo-Irish War gave it the opportunity to establish its control. By grim and bizarre logic, sectarian anarchy made it all the more necessary not simply to defend but to control the Protestant population.[59]

The negotiations leading to the Treaty have been much described and carefully analysed.[60] It is simplest here to offer a distinction between the central question - the relationship of nationalist Ireland to the United Kingdom - and the most controversial issue, Partition. Realising their military weakness and potential political divisions on the main question, the Irish delegates were ready to manoeuvre to throw responsibility for a break-down on the Ulster problem. There was a combination of realism and romance in this approach: in preliminary talks, Lloyd George's secretary had noted with exasperation that it was 'almost impossible to make any of them admit the reality of the Ulster difficulty' in the face of their belief that 'if we left

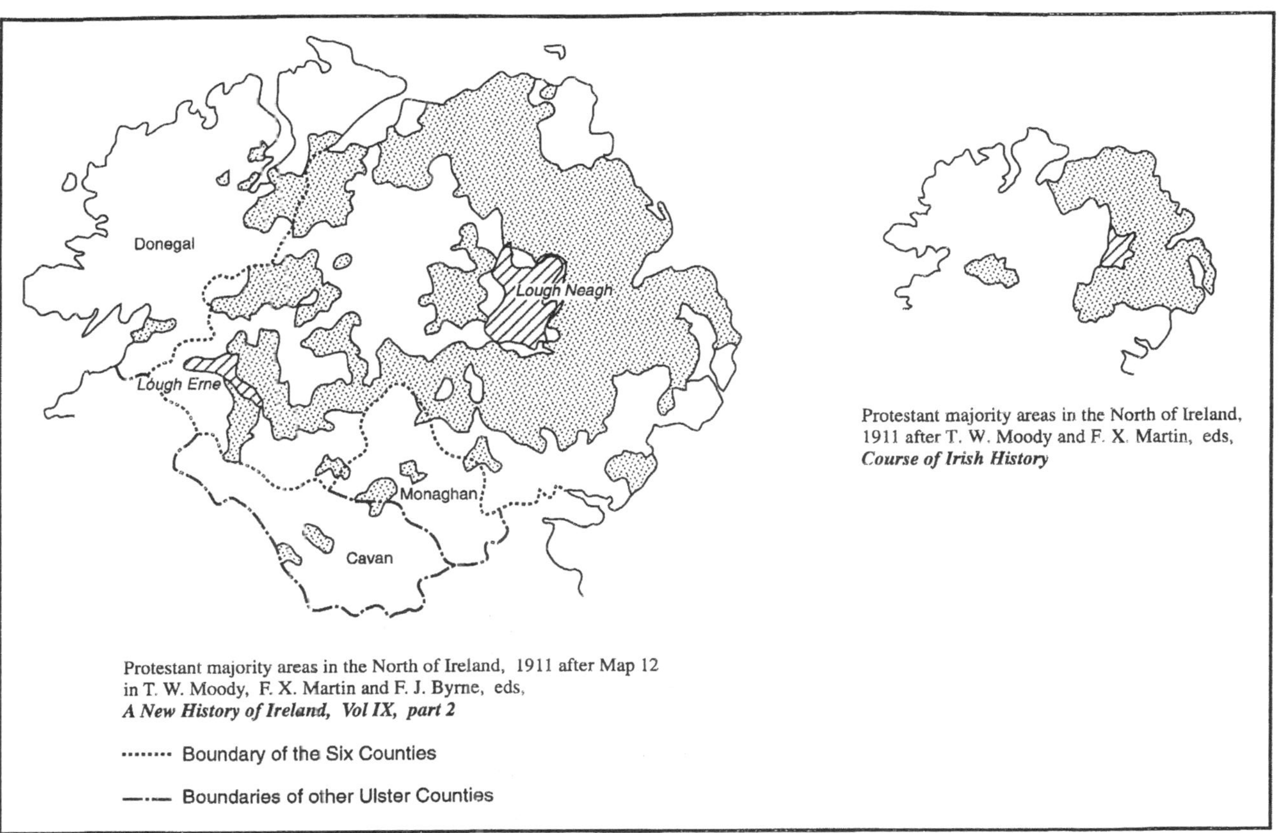

Donegal
Lough Neagh
Lough Erne
Monaghan
Cavan
Protestant majority areas in the North of Ireland, 1911 after T. W. Moody and F. X. Martin, eds, Course of Irish History
Protestant majority areas in the North of Ireland, 1911 after Map 12 in T. W. Moody, F. X. Martin and F. J. Byrne, eds, A New History of Ireland, Vol IX, part 2
.... Boundary of the Six Counties
—·— Boundaries of other Ulster Counties

Irishmen alone they would quickly settle their squabbles'.[61] For Lloyd George, it was tactically preferable that any sticking point should be on an imperial principle rather than a local difficulty.' If the Conference was to fail it would suit him best that it should fail on Sinn Féin rather than on Ulster.'[62] The Treaty negotiations gave Nationalists and Unionists little opportunity for internal squabbles: Ulster was a brooding presence but Craig was not at the table. When on the evening of 5 December 1921, Lloyd George gave the Irish delegation an ultimatum to sign, he improved on the moment with a characteristically dramatic gesture. Producing two versions of a letter to Craig, one reporting a settlement, the other the resumption of hostilities, he announced that a special train was ready at Euston to take one of them to Belfast.[63]

The device by which the British evaded a breakdown over Ulster was the offer of a Boundary Commission. Allowance should be made for the pressures on the two delegations to reach a settlement, but even so, it is hard to avoid the conclusion that the Irish were out-manoeuvred. By agreeing to a Boundary Commission, Arthur Griffith was recognising that there was and would be a Border. Furthermore, by accepting Lloyd George's plea not to attack the Boundary Commission proposal while the government fended off attacks from its own Unionist allies, Griffith went a long way to accepting that Ulster's fate would depend on the interplay of British political parties. In the circumstances, there is almost an element of charity in Lee's verdict that 'Griffith merely reflected the immaturity of nationalist thinking about Ulster in allowing himself to be deluded'.[64]

More generally, both Griffith and Collins talked themselves into believing that a Boundary Commission would transfer extensive Nationalist areas from the jurisdiction of the Northern parliament and so force a truncated 'Ulster' into all-Ireland union. This was an attractive prospect, and British ministers did nothing to discourage it: in their defence it might be pointed out that the prominence of Irish issues in British politics never seemed to have generated much awareness of Irish geography. The Irish leaders were at fault in failing to secure specific commitments in Article 12 of the Treaty, which simply provided for the Border to be adjusted 'in accordance with the wishes of the inhabitants, so far as may be compatible with economic and geographical conditions'[65] by a tribunal whose members were to be selected one each by North and South, plus a British appointee as chairman. The British insisted on an annexe to the Treaty listing their requirements for defence facilities, but the Irish lacked the diplomatic experience to demand more precise definition of the criteria for determining the Border, such as had been included in the continental peace treaties. 'The casualness of the drafting faithfully reflected the casualness of Sinn Féin thinking on the Ulster question.'[66] Perhaps they did not care to travel too far down the road of admitting that Partition was a fixed fact.

Perhaps, in the last resort, they did not care about the North. J J Walsh, a habitually outspoken Deputy from Cork, later explained that he had voted for the Treaty because he recognised that the Sinn Féin revolution

> was a partial one only.... I came to the conclusion that if we included the 3/4 million West British cuthroats [sic] that had dominated the Country and claimed they owned 2/3 of it, they would again influence our national policy. The Irish language and all that pertained to it would go by the board.... and everything we have fought for through 800 years would be smashed to atoms and swallowed up in the British Empire.[67]

Acceptance of Partition

> would at least give us a chance to re-establish our own language, games and culture, and enable us to bide our time, no matter how long, in removing partition by the removal of the partitionists.[68]

'The most remarkable feature of the debates...', say two of de Valera's most sympathetic biographers, 'was the lack of emphasis on the partition clauses of the Treaty.'[69]

Even de Valera, in his Document No. 2, substantially accepted Partition as the status quo. His comments on 'North-East Ulster' formed an addendum - in effect, an afterthought - to the main document. Even his disavowal of 'force or coercion ... upon any part of the Province of Ulster' was not so much a recognition of reality as an attempt at denial, intended to 'eliminate the Ulster question' from the 'fight between Ireland and England'.[70] Sympathetic biographers have suggested that this was a tactical mistake. 'A probing attack on the Ulster clauses of the Treaty might well have revealed their weaknesses and might conceivably have made an issue on which the whole agreement could have been defeated.'[71] Yet to defeat the paper provisions of the Treaty would hardly have removed the real obstacle. 'What was the use of talking big phrases about not agreeing to the partition of our country[?]' Collins challenged. 'Surely we recognise the North-East corner does exist'. As O'Higgins later remarked, it was 'all very well' to denounce Craig as 'a disloyal citizen of the Irish Republic' but it was unlikely that 'the statement caused serious worry, inconvenience, or loss of sleep to Sir James Craig'.[72]

If it was intended to present the Boundary Commission as a stick to beat the North, Craig's pained protest that there was 'no precedent in the history of the British Empire for taking any territory from an established Government without its sanction' made the right noises.[73] However, any prospect that Ulster might offer a field where the two sides in the Treaty debate could unite for the common aim of defending the territorial integrity of Ireland was short-lived. Collins and Craig agreed in January 1922 to deal direct over the Border and other matters. In a further and equally fruitless agreement in March 1922 they declared that 'peace is today declared' but it was only the diversion of IRA activity into the southern Civil War that brought 'comparative peace' to the North in the summer of 1922, with Collins confirming that there was 'no question of forcing Ulster into union'.[74] By the time the Boundary Commission was created in 1925, there was little expectation that it would bring about the major surgery that Collins and Griffith had naively envisaged four years earlier.

The failure of the Boundary Commission coincided with de Valera's attempts to re-position himself to enter Free State politics. Since this required an awkward modification of his previous rejection of the Oath, he 'decided that the partition card was the one to play'.[75] The Northern government unwittingly assisted his political repackaging by sentencing him to a month's solitary confinement in Belfast Prison after he defied an exclusion order to speak in Derry, an episode which gave him the opportunity to refuse to recognise a court which was 'the creature of a foreign power'.[76] Recent scholarship, from the nationalist tradition, has not only been harsh on the 'fraudulent evasions' underpinning Sinn Féin attitudes to the North, but implies that de Valera took care to ensure that Partition remained the inviolate blemish in a Treaty settlement which he otherwise redesigned point by point to his own blue print. In 1952, he refused to consider the harmlessly symbolic representation of Northern nationalists in the Seanad - confirmation that Articles 2 and 3 of the 1937 Constitution were partitionist rather than irredentist, and that no active steps were contemplated for 'the re-integration of the national territory'. Although complaining that he 'resented' criticisms that he had done nothing to end Partition, on returning to office in 1957, he put an end to studies of the practical aspects of reunification begun by the Inter-Party Government.[77]

'We know Ulster cannot live without South Ireland', Collins had said in 1921.[78] Benign voices in the Free State held that the North would come to see that reunification was a matter of self-interest. W T Cosgrave assured a correspondent in 1925 that 'we do not want to force unity upon them, and we do not want them a minute sooner than when they are convinced that it is in their own interests as in the interests of Ireland.'[79] Unluckily, there were other voices. 'Let the grass grow on the streets of Belfast', Séan MacEntee told a public meeting in Dublin in 1929. 'The people who built up Belfast were not Irish but English and Scottish and they would not be Irish until the

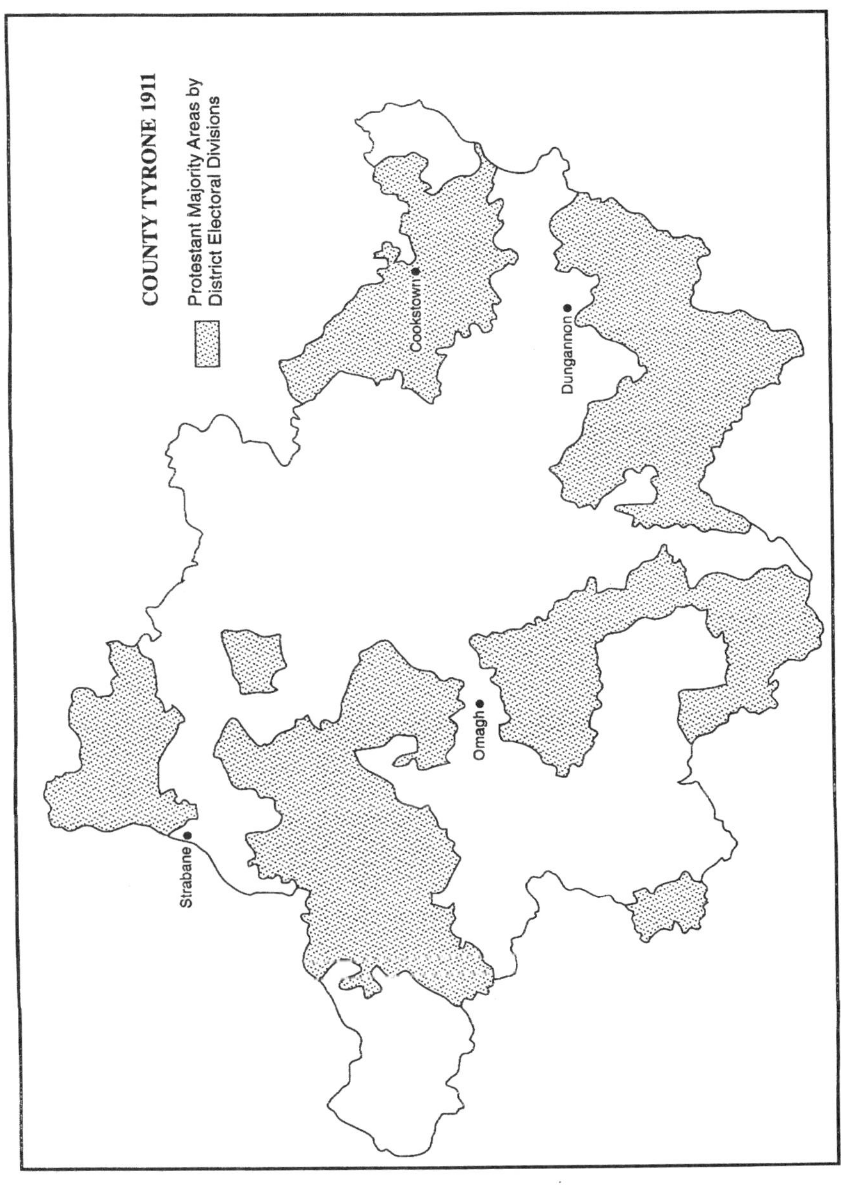
COUNTY TYRONE 1911
Protestant Majority Areas by
District Electoral Divisions
Cookstown
Dungannon
Omagh
Strabane

people of the South showed them they were stronger than they.'[80] It was a short step from MacEntee's espousal of aggressive competition to J J Walsh's aim of 'eliminating the British in this Country by the most ruthless means ... In my view this extermination is the one and only way of ending partition, and all alternative proposals are moonshine.'[81] Ulster Protestants could be forgiven their selectivity in heeding voices from the South.

III

'Ten years count as nothing in a bloodstained quarrel of this kind', Lloyd George commented in February 1914.[82] So far as Partition is concerned, the decade that followed the tentative and derided Agar-Robartes proposal of 1912 counted for a great deal. It was not simply that Partition moved from impractical nostrum to irremovable fact, but that it developed from temporary exclusion by county to permanent devolution within a wholly new 'Statutory Ulster'. Much Irish history for this period is written on the tunnel principle, which regards the First World War as an irritating intrusion that delayed Irish solutions and is therefore best kept at arm's length in scholarly analysis. Hence explanations of the coming of Partition sometimes convey an air of bewildered narrative. Partition needs to be examined within a longer span of time and a wider context of events.

It is three-quarters of a century since the Government of Ireland Act enshrined Partition, and this may remind us that a similar span of time separates the Troubles from the Famine. Various structural changes between 1845 and 1920 were partitionist in their drift, if not necessarily in their intention. One was the gradual solution of land problems. In the Famine era, the nine northern counties had resembled Connacht almost as much as Leinster in their pattern of land-holding: only four per cent of Ulster farms were larger than thirty acres, compared with three percent in Connacht but thirteen in Leinster.[83] The 'League of North and South' of the 1850s was more symbolic than actual: Ulster Tenant Righters were unable to win a single seat in parliament, and most of them abandoned the movement as it became the 'Pope's Brass Band'.[84] However, notwithstanding the Monaghan Orangemen who harvested Captain Boycott's crops, the Land League agitation did shake Protestant solidarity in the early 1880s, especially since it was in the interests of the Parnellites to prove that even in Ulster, customary protection for tenants was inadequate.[85] After 1883, land courts took rent out of Ulster politics, and land purchase completed the process: by 1913, 69 per cent of Ulster farmers owned their holdings, a higher percentage than in the other three provinces.[86] Kindness may not have killed Home Rule, but it did unwittingly divide and rule. Few Nationalists had matched Edward Saunderson in outrage at the Financial Commission's findings in 1896 that Ireland was over-taxed. By 1912, the beginnings of a British welfare state - such as old-age pensions, which were entirely funded by the taxpayer - reversed the cash-flow, and Ulstermen were far more alarmed at the thought of taxation by Dublin.[87]

The other major long-term development was the rise of Belfast and the urbanisation of the Lagan valley. In 1833, Macaulay had located a Northern parliament in Derry. As late as 1845, in planning a Queen's College for Ulster, Peel had thought it necessary to insist that it should not be located in the episcopalian capital, Armagh.[88] In 1821, two per cent of Ulster's population lived in Belfast. By 1911, the proportion was a quarter.[89] It is, however, an over-simplification to attribute the growth of Belfast simply to a general phenomenon called 'industrialisation'. Industrial growth in nineteenth-century Belfast was a whole series of dynamic innovations. As is conventionally stated, these tied the city more closely to the United Kingdom or even world economy than to the rest of Ireland, although Belfast was to have a considerable impact on the demography of its hinterland. Certainly, the success of Belfast underpinned an ideology of Protestant enterprise: the Belfast Chamber of Commerce was Weberian before Weber.

Linen was the pace-making industry until the 1860s.[90] Although originally the product of the retreat from cotton-manufacturing to specialisation in a locally grown staple, by the time of the Crimean War the linen industry felt the loss of imported Russian flax. The industry required cheap, semi-skilled labour and its growth was accompanied by a steady rise in the Catholic percentage of the city's workforce, which trebled in half a century to peak at 34 per cent in 1861, in that mid-century period of 'The Age of Riots'.[91] Shipbuilding followed, almost by chance, and was substantially developed by outsiders, such as the Yorkshireman Edward Harland, the German Gustav Wolff and the Canadian-born William Pirrie. Harland had been trying to establish a shipyard on the Mersey when he was offered the option of buying a bankrupt yard in Belfast, and he was ruthlessly prepared to import strike-breakers from the Clyde when local workers resisted his anti-smoking and wage-cutting style of management. Wolff's family connection with the Liverpool-based Bibby Line was another external stroke of luck which helped the yard in its early years: one important contract was secured during a game of billiards.[92]

Linen and ship-building were not entirely unrelated. Jointly, they enabled Belfast to move into rope-manufacturing. The linen industry had encouraged the manufacture of textile machinery, which probably provided some of the skills on which Harland and Wolff drew when they moved into marine engineering after 1880, enabling them not simply to construct hulls but to produce and fit entire ships in an integrated system of production. Aggressive marketing by Pirrie was accompanied by constant innovation, and within half a century of building their first iron steamers, Harland and Wolff were able to turn out liners like ocean greyhounds, long, slim, twin-screwed and turbine-propelled. Symbolic of this constant innovation was the fact that by 1907, Harland and Wolff were starting to build oil tankers. Nor did they have a monopoly on Belfast entrepreneurship. Workman Clark, the now forgotten 'Wee Yard', also specialised, in smaller passenger vessels, frozen meat cargo ships and banana boats.[93] Moreover, as a fast-growing metropolis, Belfast fed upon its own success, its population encouraging the development of brewing, distilling, milling and (notwithstanding Harland's disapproval) tobacco, while commercial strength was reflected also in a local banking sector.

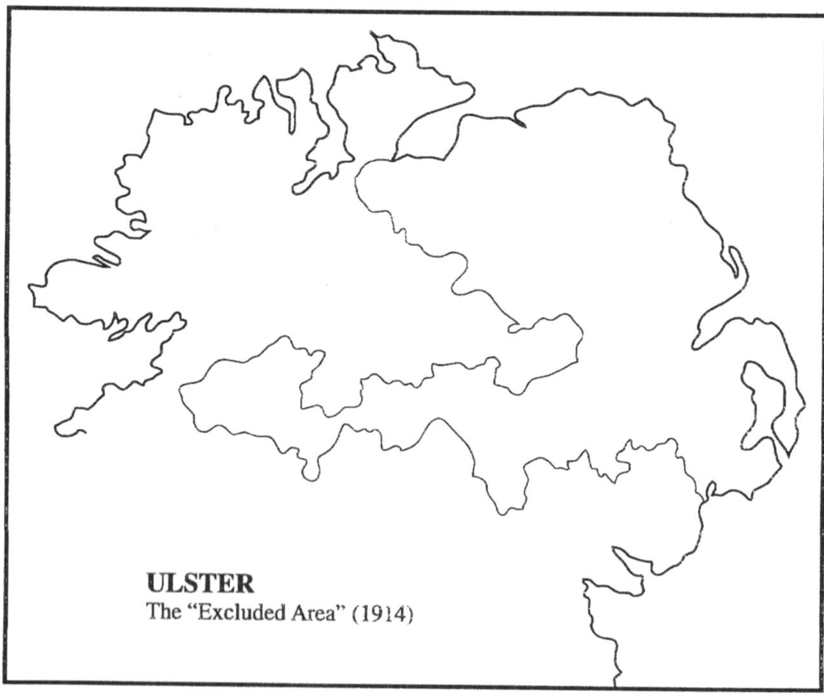

The pace and nature of the growth of Belfast can be seen as a major influence on both the fact and shaping of Partition. In 1861, fifty per cent of the population of the nine counties of Ulster were Catholics. By 1911, this had fallen to 44 per cent.[94] It was Belfast that made the difference, for Belfast provided a local focus for migration, and one in which the increasing need for skilled labour operated to favour Protestants over Catholics. Belfast trebled in size between 1861 and 1911, but the Catholic share of its population dropped by ten per cent to less than a quarter. Thus on the eve of the Partition decade, Belfast had become a Protestant stronghold with its economic interests which it felt to be incompatible with the rest of Ireland. Had Home Rule come in 1886, Pirrie was prepared to move the shipyard to the Mersey.[95]

Although Partition was intended to defend Ulster entrepreneurship from the debilitating grip of Irish nationalism, the longer-term retrospect of the late twentieth century cannot help but note that the massive burst of innovatory growth that created the Belfast economic miracle in the three-quarters of a century before Partition seemed to run dry thereafter. Workman Clark closed in 1935, and the Big Yard only survived thanks to government help and reliance on defence contracts, which had not figured in its order books prior to the First World War. One new industry, aircraft manufacture, came to Belfast for 'the basic reason ... that it made economic sense', but strategy and subsidy played their part.[96] Belfast's nineteenth-century boom had been founded on its proximity to the British mainland. Its only major twentieth-century industrial innovation stemmed partly (but mistakenly, as the city's ordeal in 1941 was to demonstrate) from a desire to move Short Brothers' production out of easy range of the bomber. If Partition belongs to a particular moment in time in Irish history, it was even more specifically the by-product of what now seems a transient flowering of Belfast.

Thus a relatively brief period of rocketing growth had by 1912 placed Belfast in a position to lead a Protestant province - but on its own terms, which were not necessarily those of other Ulster Unionists. Historical emphasis on the Protestant-Catholic confrontation underlying Partition obscures the extent to which the rise of Belfast represented a shift of power within the Protestant community towards the Presbyterians who were heavily concentrated in Antrim and Down, the immediate vicinity of Belfast. In 1911, over 95 per cent of Irish Presbyterians lived in Ulster, almost 90 per cent of them in the future Six Counties. By contrast, 43 per cent of adherents of the Church of Ireland lived in what would become the Free State. The City and County of Dublin contained twice as many Episcopalians as the three Ulster Border counties, and the Church of Ireland claimed a larger share of the population of County Dublin than of Antrim, Derry and Tyrone, as well as being proportionately more numerous in Kildare and Wicklow than in Cavan, Donegal and Monaghan. The Church of Ireland population in Cork was larger than the entire Protestant community in Fermanagh.[97] Few Presbyterians shared the lingering inclination among Episcopalians to go down in an all-Ireland shipwreck.

The Ulster Unionist Council, supported by the Orange Order, presented a common political front between adherents of the Church of Ireland and the Presbyterians, and a beleaguered minority had every incentive to suppress internal tensions. None the less, tensions did exist, even if the Northern garrison mentality rarely gave opportunity for their expression.[98] The 1919 East Antrim by-election was one such occasion, when an Independent Unionist, George Hanna, who was a Belfast solicitor, defeated the official candidate, Major W Agnew Moore of Ballygally Castle, Larne.[99] There was a symbolism in the replacement of Edward Carson, the former MP for Trinity, in 1921 by James Craig, product of the Presbyterian Merchiston Castle School in Edinburgh.[100]

Underlying denominational tensions may help to explain Belfast suspicion of Southern Unionism, but there can be little doubt that the Six County unit was essentially a Belfast Partition, both in its policy origins and in its territorial scope. The unsentimental dumping of the Three Counties (Cavan, Monaghan and Donegal) was Belfast-inspired, as was the insistence on keeping Derry and Newry while all but cutting them off from the surrounding countryside. It was a Belfast MP, Thomas Moles, who most bluntly expressed Belfast priorities in 1916. 'In a sinking ship, with life-boats sufficient for only two-thirds of the ship's company, were all to condemn themselves to death because all could not be saved?'[101] That such a sentiment could come from a representative of the city that had built the *Titanic* is a revealing example of the absence of sentimentality in Belfast priorities.

Well before 1912, there were Partitionist straws in the Irish tempest. While insisting that there was 'no desire for a separate Ulster, nor part of Ulster', MacKnight warned in 1896 that the determination of Unionist leaders that they would never desert their brethren in the South was not shared 'by the commercial classes of Belfast and the North of Ireland'.[102] The formation of the Ulster Unionist Council in 1904-05 was an indication of lack of confidence in the wider Unionist coalition after Balfour's government had seemed unduly sympathetic to Irish devolution. One reason argued for establishing a local organisation was that it was necessary to maintain an active alliance with Protestant working men to prevent them from defecting to labour and socialist politics - a reflection of the North's distinctiveness. The Ulster Solemn League and Covenant of 1912 revealed just how wide that gap had already become. It was significant, too, that it drew upon a Presbyterian tradition of resistance to government.[103]

While individual Northern Protestants took an antiquarian interest in traditional culture, the Gaelic revival had little appeal for Ulstermen. They were Sinn Féiners in the sense of relying on themselves alone, but few were attracted either to the Irish language or its increasing politicisation as a Nationalist tool and symbol: the convention of 1892 was the last occasion that Ulster Unionists displayed the 1798 slogan, 'Erin-go-brágh'.[104] North and South were increasingly out of sympathy at least partly because they had always been out of touch. In 1911 in County Cork, for instance, only one person in 300 had been born in the Ulster counties, and some of these may well have been RIC (Royal Irish Constabulary) personnel or bank clerks whose employment cut them off from the local community. Tim Healy expressed the voice of Cork when he said in 1914 that he had only once visited Belfast, 'and they were the most unhappy twenty- four hours I ever spent'.[105]

The separation of Queen's University from the new National University of Ireland in 1908 was a harbinger of Partition. Removing the Belfast college from what James Craig called the 'Nationalist University of Ireland' enabled the Liberal government to find a way of appeasing the demand for Catholic control of higher education, a scheme which the Ulster Unionists were alone in resisting. Once Queen's was severed from its former partners, the only possible solution was to turn it into a separate university, despite local protests that the new institution had so few students that it would be not even provincial but parochial. Substitute 'parliament' for 'university', and the controversy of 1908 looks remarkably like a dress rehearsal for the Government of Ireland Act.[106]

Northern Protestant hostility to the campaign for a Catholic University in Ireland coincided with a heightened sectarian temperature arising from the papal decree *Ne Temere* in 1907 and its attack on mixed marriages. By 1912, there was little doubt that 'Protestant' was coming to mean Unionist, just as 'Catholic' was a synonym for Nationalist, an absolute equation which made it possible to take census tables for religious affiliation as a basis for territorial division.[107] A few exceptions lingered until the eve of the War. As late as 1913, 400 Protestants attended an anti-Carsonite rally in Ballymoney, home of the celebrated Reverend J B Armour who had so inconveniently pointed out that Home Rule embodied a Presbyterian principle of self-government.[108] Some Protestants may have been willing to vote for Home Rule Liberal candidates if not for out-and-out Nationalists: a Liberal captured Derry City at a by-election in January 1913, polling 2,699 votes, 321 more than a Protestant Nationalist, Shane Leslie, had received two years earlier.[109] Cardinal Logue's mediation between Sinn Féin and the Nationalists to ensure a common front in Ulster at the 1918 general election was probably the last straw. By the time of the Troubles, the

Protestant Home Ruler survived only as a bugbear or debating point, depending on point of view. 'The Ulster Protestant Home Ruler still exists, though small in numbers,' Unionist organiser Dawson Bates wrote in 1919 as he tried to limit the damage done by the revolt in East Antrim, adding darkly: 'but they can make a lot of mischief'.[110] During the Treaty negotiations, Arthur Griffith claimed - with some exaggeration - to have received a substantial Protestant vote in East Cavan.[111]

If by 1912, medium-term influences may be discerned which made Partition possible, it is easy enough to identify two short-term factors in the decade after 1912 which may seem to have brought it about: the First World War and the upheaval in British and Irish party systems. Both deserve attention, yet in the last resort neither did more than underline the fact that the Irish situation was already intractable before 1914. Churchill's purple passage on the post-war world is well-known: 'as the deluge subsides and the waters fall short we see the dreary steeples of Fermanagh and Tyrone emerging once again'.[112] Perhaps tunnel historians are right. Maybe the War did no more than delay the inevitable, and nothing could affect the 'integrity' of the Irish quarrel?

Energetic nationalist mythology ensures that the second decade of the twentieth century is dominated by the events in Dublin at Easter 1916. This emphasis distorts the picture in two respects. It obscures the inconvenient fact that the Rising was intended to be an all-Ireland affair which, with a few exceptions, failed to get off the ground.[113] More important, it also overlooks the fact that for every Irish man or woman who turned out to fight in Easter Week, there were about one hundred others who served in the British forces during the First World War. Even allowing for the fact that Ulster Protestants formed a disproportionate part of the Ireland's war effort,[114] by 1918 far more Catholic Irishmen had fought for the king than for the republic. Somewhere between Mount Street Bridge and the Somme, they slipped from memory, discarded by the needs of rival mythologies of sacrifice. 'The story has an epilogue,' are the opening words of the final chapter of A T Q Stewart's *The Ulster Crisis*, 'which everyone in Ulster knows.'[115] There is a wealth of meaning in those last five words, for they implicitly define 'Ulster' in Protestant terms, and carry the implication that nobody beyond that 'Ulster' knows, or cares. The epilogue was the battle of the Somme in July 1916, and in particular the assault by the 36th (Ulster) Division on Thiepval Wood. The 36th Division had been largely recruited from the Ulster Volunteer Force: their UVF units were even included in the official casualty lists. In two days, 1,850 men were killed and 2,700 wounded. Thiepval became the Northern Protestant counterpart to the blood sacrifice of Easter 1916. Although some of the heaviest casualties on the Somme fell on a unit largely composed of men from Cavan and Monaghan, counties that had been dumped two weeks earlier, Ulster Protestants came to regard Partition as something they had won in 'a Belfast riot on top of Mount Vesuvius'.[116] As Carson put it in 1918, 'the Ulster people, who have suffered severely in the loss of their men at the Front, will regard it as an act of treachery if ... Ulster is put under a Home Rule Parliament'.[117] It was unnecessary even to spell out the argument: what did it matter that Catholics outnumbered Protestants by five thousand in Derry City? If republicans could invoke Ireland's dead generations to justify their rebellion in 1916, then Ulster Unionists were entitled at least by implication to count their own dead on the Somme to hold on to the disputed areas of the province they claimed as their own. This may not be entirely logical, but there is no reason why a community in mass trauma should be expected to be logical.[118] At the very least, it meant that the cavalier attitude that Unionists had taken to inconvenient Catholic majorities before the War could now be wrapped in an aura of sacrifice rather than selfish superiority.

The War also brought about shifts in the party structures on both sides of the Irish Sea. Only one politician on either side was close to the centre of most of the major events between 1912 and 1925, and Winston Churchill was proof of Shakespeare's dictum that one man in his time plays many parts.[119] Between 1912 and 1914, the Liberal-Nationalist alliance was able to set the political agenda, even if Ulster and the Lords constituted a considerable block on its achievement. From 1915 to 1922, coalitions sustained by the British Unionist party held office, but under Liberal prime ministers. Thus Ulster Protestants were still forced to respond to policy initiatives shaped by nominally committed Home Rulers. As late as the Treaty talks, by which time Lloyd George was a prisoner of his Tory allies, he was still toying with the idea of a nine-county Ulster, which Unionists well knew threatened their control of the North.[120] Indeed, one result of the coalitions was a weakening of Ulster confidence in their British allies who, as one suspicious Unionist put it in 1916, seemed to be 'Asquixiated' by political office.[121] Thus although the Conservatives under Baldwin were securely in office in 1925 when the Boundary Commission was allowed to collapse, there was no longer the passionate union of hearts that Bonar Law had voiced in the heady days of 1912-14.

Similarly, the upheaval in southern Irish politics may be more apparent than real in relation to Partition. Carson and Redmond had engaged in occasional bouts of pre-War amiability, but these had not led them to agreement. Sinn Féin was weak in Ulster, and its 1918 electoral pact with the Nationalists further reduced the Northern voice within its ranks. The laughter which greeted the reading of Carson's name at the roll-call for the first Dáil and the subsequent episode of the 'Belfast Boycott' demonstrated the extent to which the north-east was regarded as external to the true Ireland, however much republican rhetoric might insist on the indivisibility of the thirty-two counties. The blood sacrifice of 1916 might have created a republican agenda for Catholic Ireland, but when they turned to Ulster, the new leaders remained stuck in pre-War expedients of temporary exclusion and county option.

The rapid rise of Sinn Féin helped divide Northern Catholics from their southern co-religionists. Joseph Devlin held West Belfast against a nominal challenge from de Valera in 1918 and was able to begin the process of leading Nationalists into the Northern parliament in 1925, while anti-Treaty forces in the South were still moving towards the political arena.[122] It was unfortunate that the Northern Nationalists were never able to make up for the seven-year gap in which they had been ignored in all negotiations for a settlement, their own exclusionist stance enabling the new Northern State to form its institutions without the constructive opposition which had been the philosophical core of the old parliamentary party. If old-style Nationalists had sought consolation for their impotence, they might have found it in the weakness of Ulster republicans. During the Civil War, IRA units in the North supported the anti-Treaty side. A Belfast commander, Joseph McKelvey, was one of four hostages shot by the Free State in retaliation for the murder of pro-Treaty Deputy Seán Hales in 1922. It would be straining for effect to claim that the execution symbolised the extent to which the North had become expendable, but it is perhaps significant that the names of Liam Mellowes and Rory O'Connor are far better remembered than that of McKelvey.[123]

Writing of the failure of the Boundary Commission in 1925, MacDonagh suggests that 'Protestant Ulster ... would yet again have found a way around statutes and parliamentary majorities, whatever happened'.[124] His remark recalls Bonar Law's warning at the start of the Partition decade that 'there are things stronger than Parliamentary majorities'.[125] Among these, we may conclude, would have been the fourteen million rounds of ammunition which the Craig cabinet agreed to purchase in the event of an unfavourable report from the Boundary Commission.[126] It may be that analysis of the minutiae of party politics is ultimately pointless: the most that it can tell us is how the inevitability of Partition came to be accepted, since in essence the solution dictated itself. In that, the 'blessed refusal' of Sinn Féiners to take the oath as members of parliament in 1918[127] meant that the intractable steeples of Ulster reality could be seen in sharper focus thanks to the subsiding deluge of Irish Nationalism at Westminster. 'It is not we who are dividing Ireland', Austen Chamberlain protested in 1920, '... not we who made party coincide with the religious differences'.[128] Politics did not determine the fact of the Border. The most that politics might settle was the line that it would follow.

IV

In 1914, the Speaker of the House of Commons, James Lowther, asked Carson for a definition of terms: 'what do you mean by Ulster and what would Redmond mean by Ulster?'[129] Nationalists could appeal to Ireland's sea-girt, immutable limits. Ulster lacked such dramatic precision, and the result was a disparity between geographical and mental boundaries. Hence Pakenham's insightful comment that Ulster was not so much 'an area or a people ... as a strange abstract factor in tactics'.[130] De Valera was not far wrong in arguing that the idea of Ulster as 'an Irish province with fixed, well-defined historical boundaries, within which there is a solid, homogeneous, political or religious block' was 'a thing of the mind only', although it was curious that someone for whom abstractions had such power could draw the conclusion that this made it 'non-existent in the world of reality'.[131] The elusive quality of this Ulster identity was too much for Lowther's 'bluff unimaginative English sense' as he showed when he tried to break the deadlock over Tyrone in 1914 by asking: 'When each of two people say they must have the whole, why not cut it in half?' Such an approach assumed an equality of participants that they could not recognise themselves. Both sides would go no further than reluctantly to allow unassimilable minorities to contract out of the space which constituted their identity. The problem was that the building blocks of identity in Ireland, provinces, counties, baronies, administrative districts, electoral divisions, parishes and even townlands, were simultaneously rigid and imprecise.[132]

In the 1960s, as Southern opinion began to confront the reality of two Irelands, there was a tendency to argue that Ulster had always been in some way different, shaped by 'its own geographical personality'.[133] Yet to single out Ulster (whatever 'Ulster' might mean) in this way was a well-meaning fallacy, for Ireland is a patchwork of equally distinct areas, each with a unique geographical personality. Parnell's description of County Monaghan as the 'remote north' was probably a joke,[134] but it was mental rather than physical distance that made the joke possible: after all, Carrickmacross is within fifty miles of Dublin.

In the last resort, what made Ulster 'different' - both in definition and degree - was neither its drumlins nor its proximity to Scotland, but its Protestantism. MacDonagh has pointed not simply to a strong manifestation of an 'Ulster Protestant sense of territorality' from the early nineteenth century, but to the equally remarkable fact that it was accepted by their opponents. O'Connellites talked of extending the Repeal campaign even into predominantly Catholic Monaghan in terms more suited to an invasion of enemy territory, so that 'a set of county limits' were taken 'as designating some sort of sovereignty'.[135] MacDonagh suggests that Northern Protestants drew a parallel between Ulster and Scotland: 'more than a province, less than a state, it constituted at least a people'.[136] But did it?

As late as 1861, Catholics actually constituted a majority of the nine counties of Ulster, with 50.5 per cent of the population.[137] By 1911, nine-county Ulster was 56.3 per cent Protestant, still not a secure majority in the eyes of Northern Unionists. 'They are apparently afraid that a big entire Ulster would gravitate towards a United Ireland', Asquith noted in 1914.[138] 'We quite frankly admit that we cannot hold the nine counties', Charles Craig explained in 1920.[139] Unionists in the three excluded counties, Cavan, Monaghan and Donegal, made an eloquent plea in 1920 for the larger unit as a basis for balanced government: 'The ideal position would be to have a fairly strong Nationalist minority in the North and a fairly strong Unionist minority in the South. If this ideal position cannot at present be effected in the South it can and should be in the North'.[140] From the safety of North Antrim, Ronald McNeill looked at the same picture through darker lenses: 'the inexorable index of statistics demonstrated that, although Unionists were in a majority when geographical Ulster was considered as a unit, yet the distribution of population made it certain that a separate Parliament for the whole Province would have a precarious existence'.[141] By opting to guarantee Protestant security within the Six Counties, Unionists ensured that minority communities in both parts of Ireland would become hostages rather than participants.

In 1914, Dillon had 'urged that the Unionists should be challenged to say what they meant by Ulster' since 'they could not give any practicable definition'.[142] The ideal of a Protestant province conflicted with the reality of the constituent counties, for no Ulster county was homogeneous in terms of religion. Antrim (79.5 per cent Protestant in 1911), Belfast City (75.9 per cent) and Down (68.4 per cent) formed the core of the Protestant North-East, but each of these contained substantial Catholic enclaves: Nationalist Down began only twenty five miles south of Belfast. The counties of Derry (58.5 per cent) and Armagh (54.7 per cent) were more mixed. Cavan (18.5 per cent), Donegal (21.1 per cent) and Monaghan (25.3 per cent) were eventually abandoned as hopeless cases, although local concentrations gave parts of East Donegal and North Monaghan an Orange hue. The crucial problem of Partition was to be found in the buffer zone between the Protestant heartland and the sacrificial borderland.

Protestants made up 44.6 per cent of the population of Tyrone, and 43.8 per cent of Fermanagh and Derry City.[143]

Irish county boundaries had clearly never been designed to become customs barriers: Derry, Newry, Strabane, Clones and Enniskillen all lay close to what became the Border. As Three Counties Unionists pointed out, 'Monaghan runs up to a point ... into the very heart of the Province', although they were less convincing in claiming that 'Cavan and Monaghan form a natural boundary' to the south.[144] At the time of Partition, J R Fisher had argued for a 'solid ethnographic and strategic frontier to the South ... from the end of Lough Erne to Bessbrook or thereabouts', which would 'take in a fair share of the people we want and leave out those we don't want'.[145] By the time Fisher served on the Boundary Commission in 1925, it was too late for such major surgery.

Donegal, on the western flank of the Six Counties, was a particular challenge. Protestants dominated an agricultural enclave between Derry City and Lough Swilly, and the farming country around Donegal town, but the rest of the county was Catholic and poor, with much of the population still speaking Irish. Fermanagh extended to within four miles of the Atlantic, leaving Donegal with only one road link to the rest of the Free State. It was - and remains - a county almost totally devoid of towns, looking to Derry and Strabane for local centres. Fisher hoped that the North would take on Donegal, if only to defend itself against charges of selfishly discarding problem areas. 'We *ought* to bear *our* share of the burden of congestion and misery ... and a hostile 'Afghanistan' on our north-west frontier would be placed in safe keeping.'[146] In July 1914, Carson impatiently demanded: 'let us have done with county limits, as if men in one county are going to abandon men in another county just because there may be a majority here or a majority there.'[147] For Donegal, however, any transfer would have to be all or nothing, for Partition on sectarian lines would have shattered it into rocky fragments.

Behind Carson's dismissal of county lines lay the fractured topography and fractious history of Ulster. 'By and large religious maps and contour maps coincided, their colours reversed,' Laffan has remarked; 'brown hills represented green catholics, green valleys represented orange protestants.'[148] It was precisely because county boundaries often followed rivers that Partition was such cruel surgery, even for the victors. Those who sought, between 1912 and 1925, to define 'Ulster' tried to work from the bottom up but precision did not make for clarity. An authority on Local Studies in Northern Ireland has remarked of the concept of a 'sense of place' that 'it is much easier to accept than it is to keep redefining it'.[149] The building blocks of local identity took many different forms, and could be organised for different ends. Traditionally, Ireland was divided into townlands, which were variously grouped into parishes and baronies, and then into counties. Thomas Sexton in 1886 had warned that 'the Catholic population so interpenetrates every portion of Ulster that even if you have a parliament in every parish, you would still have a minority in each.'[150] 'If ... they took the barony as the unit then there would be found predominantly Catholic baronies in every county,' Dillon explained in 1914. 'The puzzle was really insoluble.'[151] Townlands were the smallest building blocks of all, but the Boundary Commission dismissed them as having 'no uniformity as regards area or population, and many of them are very small, and have very few inhabitants, while some have none at all.' Examined in detailed corridors close to the Border, they formed an unhelpful patchwork. The Donegal townland of Fearn, 819 acres and 60 Protestants, was the only totally uncomplicated unit available for transfer.[152]

Nineteenth-century administration had created a new form of building block, the District Electoral Division (DED), which became the basic unit for the tabulation of census information. At the next level were urban and rural districts, which combined into Poor Law Unions, sometimes crossing county lines. After 1885, a new element of classification was introduced when Irish counties were divided into single-member constituencies. Because of its central position in the census and its apparent relation to locality, the DED seemed the basic building block, but it was far from perfect. Although roughly comparable in area, DEDs varied a great deal in population, especially in the disputed counties of Fermanagh and Tyrone. In Fermanagh, they ranged from Rosslea, with a population of 2,158, to Mallybreen, where 143 people just turned the scales to the nationalist column at 51 per cent. In Tyrone, the smallest DED, Carryglass, had barely one-tenth of the population of the largest, Tullyniskane. On the census map, Tullyniskane formed part of a narrow nationalist corridor through east Tyrone, but it contained enough Protestants to form three units the size of Carryglass.[153]

Because populations were so inextricably mixed at very local levels, even the most detailed denominational maps of Ulster are unwittingly misleading.[154] In 1914, British ministers argued that Poor Law Unions 'gave truer geographical and religious boundaries' and 'afford a good basis of give & take'. They were disappointed when 'both Irish lots would have none of it',[155] failing to realise that if the building blocks were flawed, so too would be the edifice constructed from them. This was especially the case in the focus of Partitionist wrangling in 1914, what the despairing Asquith termed 'that most damnable creation of the perverted ingenuity of man - the County of Tyrone'.[156] The Boundary Commission was more restrained. 'Catholic and Protestant districts are mingled in a definite but complicated pattern', with Protestants dominating the low-lying corners and

Catholics the poorer region of the Sperrins in the centre. 'The Catholic blocks are on the whole larger than the Protestant blocks, but the Catholic blocks are in the interior of the county, while the Protestant blocks are mostly near the borders of the county,' itself a complication since Tyrone was 'contiguous to six of the eight remaining counties of the Province of Ulster'. Furthermore, because few Protestants had settled in the poorer upland areas, in both Tyrone and Fermanagh, Catholic majority areas were very Catholic indeed. 'The large Catholic majorities concentrated in these areas have the effect of disguising the real position as to the distribution of population in ... other districts'.[157]

Even on a local scale within Tyrone, administrative divisions did not correspond to local concentrations of Protestants. There were five clusters of DEDs with Protestant majorities, including one of sixteen in the west of the county and another of fourteen in the south-east. Yet only one of the eleven local authorities within the county, the tiny Cookstown Urban District, had a Protestant majority. There were Catholic majorities in all the Poor Law Unions, and in three of the four parliamentary constituencies. In 1911, a Protestant in the Clogher DED might simultaneously feel secure as part of a local majority of 0.39 per cent (or four out of 1,038), challenged within the Rural District of the same name by constituting a minority by 1.6 per cent (220 out of 13,744), reassured by the comradeship of a 2.4 per cent majority in the South Tyrone parliamentary constituency (786 out of 32,656) but threatened within the county as a whole where Protestants were outnumbered by 10.76 per cent (15,365 out of 142,665). The core of the problem was caught in Asquith's comment that the division of Tyrone was 'a matter which to English eyes seems inconceivably small, & to Irish eyes immeasurably big'.[158]

There were mitigating factors which help explain the Protestant belief that numbers alone should not determine their fate. Prior to 1918, the United Kingdom did not have adult male suffrage, let alone accord the vote to women. In 1910, the Irish electorate was only 36 per cent of the size it became after the franchise was extended in 1918. Citizenship, in the form of the vote, was still something to be earned. This was not a factor which altered the political complexion of Tyrone, since Home Rulers held three of the four seats in December 1910. However, two of them were highly marginal, and Catholic illiteracy rates, at 15.8 per cent for the whole county, were more than double those of Protestants. The kernel of Protestant objection to Home Rule was that it was 'maintained by ignorance and pandering to superstition'.[159] In fact, Catholics were in a majority among the literate population in each of the three Home Rule constituencies - but in three rural districts in which they had narrow numerical majorities, they fell behind Protestants in the literacy stakes. It was considerations such as these which explain Carson's blunt objection in 1914 to the proposal for a plebiscite in Tyrone: 'But they will vote themselves in'.[160]

In the event, the unit on which Partition was based became a hybrid of counties and parliamentary constituencies. This was largely a product of the transition from temporary exclusion under Westminster to the creation of a Northern statelet. In 1914, Asquith floated the suggestion of an excluded area consisting of Antrim, Belfast City, the city and county of Derry, North, East and West Down, North and Mid Armagh, South Tyrone and North Fermanagh.[161] There were plenty of objections to this proposal, which would have placed the western shore of Lough Neagh under Dublin rule - North Fermanagh, for instance, actually had a Catholic majority, although it had elected Unionists since 1892 - but it did express the principle that constituencies which had sent Unionist MPs to Westminster could continue to do so for the time being. The definition of Northern Ireland in the Government of Ireland Act as 'the parliamentary counties of Antrim, Armagh, Down, Fermanagh, Londonderry and Tyrone, and the parliamentary boroughs of Belfast and Londonderry' carried forward the assumption of a temporary exclusion, since 'Southern Ireland shall consist of so much of Ireland as is not comprised within the said parliamentary counties and boroughs'.[162] The Treaty also formally placed Northern Ireland within the Free State. One implication of this definition was that foreshores and coastal waters of north-eastern Ireland, which did not form part of any parliamentary constituency, were subject to Dublin jurisdiction. Articles 2 and 3 of the Irish Constitution of 1937 thus reflect British legislative drafting. The delineation of Northern Ireland by a hybrid of counties and constituencies created some spectacular anomalies. South Fermanagh (39 per cent Protestant) was in but East Donegal (40 per cent Protestant) was out. North Monaghan (33 per cent Protestant) was excluded, while South Armagh (32 per cent Protestant) was retained. The abandoned Unionists in Cavan, Monaghan and Donegal found this hard to accept. They accepted that the Three Counties contained Nationalist majorities. 'But so does Derry City, Fermanagh County, Tyrone County, South Armagh, South Down and the Falls Division of Belfast. Yet no one proposes to exclude them.'[163] Nor did anyone seek to include the St. Stephen's Green Division of Dublin, which had returned a Unionist MP in 1918.

V

Although Asquith had been prepared in 1914 to fund 'migration at State expense of Protestants & Catholics into & out of the excluded area',[164] the Treaty promised to shift the Border rather than the people through the device of a Boundary Commission, which met in 1925 under the chairmanship of the South African judge, Richard Feetham. The Free State appointed Eoin MacNeill, a 'wambling professor', in the words of an Ulster critic, who 'should have restricted all his activities to the solution of problems in Gaelic grammar'. When Craig refused to fill the third place, allocated by the Treaty to the North, Ramsay MacDonald's Labour government called the Westminster parliament into special session to pass legislation which permitted the appointment of J R Fisher.[165] Despite the heavy hints of 1921 that it would be a device to undermine Partition, the Commission rejected submissions for an all-Ireland solution by stating that 'its duty ... was to determine a boundary, and not to decide the question whether there should be a boundary or not'. Indeed, Feetham took the narrow view that since he was entrusted with something called Northern Ireland, the result of any revision of boundaries must be 'recognisable as the same provincial entity'.[166]

The Treaty had provided that the Border should be determined 'in accordance with the wishes of the inhabitants, so far as may be compatible with economic and geographic conditions'.[167] Beyond that, the Boundary Commission had to make up its own rules. Feetham interpreted the absence of any provision for plebiscites to mean that 'it was not intended that the Commission should ... rely on the verdicts of bare majorities'. However, the Commission did decide to adopt as its basic building block 'the smallest area which can be fairly entitled, having regard to its size and situation, to be considered separately, and with regard to which separate data are available'. However, individual areas 'cannot be considered alone, but must be examined in relation to conditions in adjacent areas. Overwhelming majorities in surrounding areas which desire a change may, in some cases, be sufficient to justify the disregarding of the wishes of an "island" community which is strongly against a change'. Moreover, it was also 'the duty of the Commission in some cases to override the wishes of inhabitants ... by reason of economic or geographic considerations'. One spectacular example of the discharge of this duty was the case of the Commissioners of the Belfast Water Works, whose interests were taken to outweigh the wishes of the inhabitants of the Mourne Mountains, so ruling out any territorial change in County Down.[168]

The Boundary Commission - Lough Foyle to Lough Erne

Generally, the Commission - or rather Feetham, who wrote its report - relied on two vague concepts, the satisfaction ratio and the market area. The closest it came to defining the former was the explanation of its rejection of the wholesale transfer of Catholic areas of Fermanagh, Tyrone, Derry, Armagh and Down which, it calculated, would 'gratify the wishes of 258,617 persons and be contrary to the wishes of 205,528 others'. Thus, 'in order to achieve the net result of pleasing 53,089 persons, it would be necessary to transfer a total of 464,145 persons, or nearly nine times as many.'[169] Given the intermingling of the two communities, the undefined satisfaction ratio pointed to no more than small and specific transfers. Paradoxically, the revised boundary would have created a very high dissatisfaction ratio. Most Catholic areas along the Northern border and almost all the Protestant districts in the Free State would have remained stranded minorities. In Fermanagh, 71 per cent of the Catholic population of 1911 would have continued to live in Northern Ireland. Over 96 per cent of Monaghan's Protestant minority would have remained in the Free State.

The Commission concluded that the 'market area' of a town generally extended between six and ten miles into the surrounding country. When coupled with the satisfaction ratio, the wish to maintain market areas undivided also pointed to minimal change: within a five-mile radius of Strabane, for instance, there was a Catholic majority among the rural population, but when extended to ten miles the hinterland became Protestant. Although the Commission did speculate that 'the introduction of motor transport' would alter the pattern of retail distribution, overall its economic picture was one of an Ulster in which produce was moved by horse and cart. There was minute examination of the radius of the economic influence of towns as small and as close together as Keady and Newtown Hamilton. In some parts of Tyrone, the Commission treated the Border as little more than a skin to be grafted on to a skeleton of railway branch lines. The North was assured control of rail communications into Fermanagh, while north Donegal retained a station on Free State territory in order to trade with Clones or Dundalk.[170] Overall, the Boundary Commission designed a border for an Ireland that would virtually disappear within half a century.

It is hardly surprising that the Commission gave weight to different arguments as it considered different sections of the Border. 'There was at no time any debate between the members of the commission as to the principles of interpretation', MacNeill reported to the Dáil, with the result that there was 'no definite decision taken which could lead to an application of such principles and to their consistent application ... to different districts affected by the award. The details came before us in a very gradual and a very piecemeal manner.' His opposite number was perfectly happy with this muddled procedure, since it eliminated 'the more extravagant claims', limiting adjustments to 'border townlands for the most part'. Well before the first draft of the report was complete, Fisher was confident that 'no great mischief will be done', and that rectifications could be 'worked out on "fair give and take" lines, even if the "religious" figures involve rather more give than take'.[171]

Examination of the Commission's recommended boundary line shows how its cocktail of criteria combined to limit changes. 'What I should like is that either Derry should be in Donegal, or Donegal should be with the Six Counties,' one witness had said. 'Either would suit me.' All that the Commission would recommend for Derry was the adjustment of 'the customs frontier, now within 3 miles of the city, which interrupts the regular flow of traffic to and from farms in the immediate neighbourhood'. This was to be done by transferring 'such portion of the area of East Donegal adjoining the city as shows uniform Protestant majorities ... without cutting the railway and main road connecting the Peninsula of Inishowen with the rest of the County'.[172] This pushed the Border about two miles to the west.

However, when it came to Strabane, the Commission rejected proposals to move the Border 'a few miles to the west'. A local merchant reported that he supplied the Free State market from depots in its twin village of Lifford, on the Donegal side, which did not require additional staff, 'whereas a depot five miles further from Strabane would require additions to his staff and the cost of his business'. Optimistically, the Commission predicted that 'if the border remains as at present ... Lifford may develop as a commercial and industrial centre for East Donegal'.[173] Strangely, the advantages of having a foot in both camps that determined inaction for Strabane-Lifford did not apply 25 miles to the south-west at Pettigoe. Pettigoe, a real-life Puckoon, was actually divided by the Border and it had suffered in the Troubles. Fortunately, there was a small Protestant block on the Free State side of the line which could be transferred, and the Donegal hill country beyond hardly counted as a market area.[174]

If small concentrations of Free State Protestants could cause such minute consideration of enlarging the North, then inconvenient Nationalist areas on the Six Counties side of the Border surely called for more radical surgery. The Commission was prepared to simplify the line by transferring the bump of Tyrone which protruded into Donegal west of Killeter, although the amputated county would continue to have a Catholic majority. In the heavily Catholic areas of West Fermanagh, however, the Commission moved more cautiously. The core problem here was Lower Lough Erne, and its fringe of Protestant farmers who had invested heavily in drainage and wished to ensure their control over flood prevention. Thus although the Commission proposed to transfer seventy square miles of west

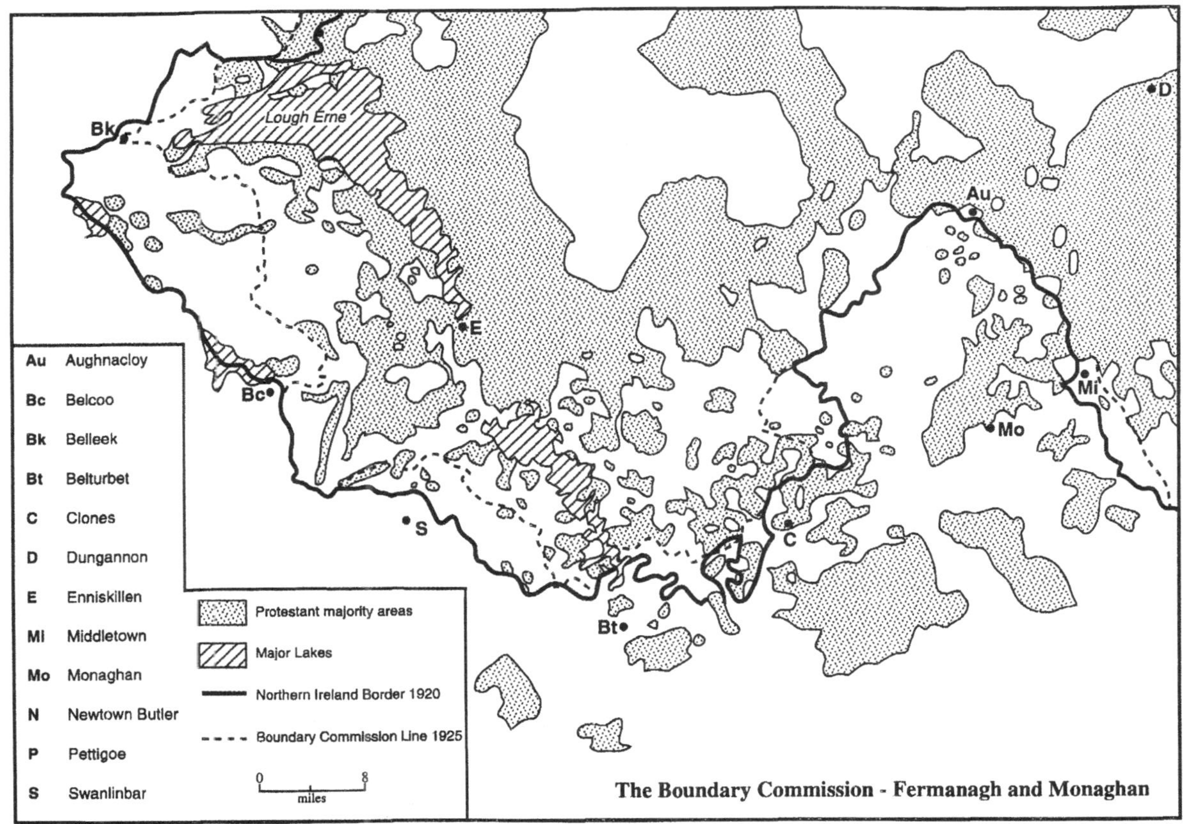
Bk
Lough Erne
Au
D
E
Bc
Mi
Mo
S
C
Bt
Au Aughnacloy
Bc Belcoo
Bk Belleek
Bt Belturbet
C Clones
D Dungannon
E Enniskillen
Mi Middletown
Mo Monaghan
N Newtown Butler
P Pettigoe
S Swanlinbar
Protestant majority areas
Major Lakes
Northern Ireland Border 1920
Boundary Commission Line 1925
0
8
miles
The Boundary Commission - Fermanagh and Monaghan

Fermanagh, a strip from Garrison to Belcoo, its concern to maintain Northern control over watersheds left substantial Catholic majority areas within the Six Counties. The 'outer fringe of Fermanagh' had been one of the sections where Fisher had expected that 'we may have to go pretty deep in places', which seems to confirm that it was Feetham's own caution that determined the Commission's decisions. Perhaps most curious of all was the retention of a small part of Northern territory down river from Lough Erne towards Belleek, coupled with the transfer from the Free State of a three-acre island which was the key to the sluice-gates that regulated lake levels.[175] The transfer perhaps reassured Fermanagh Protestants that they could not be submerged by a nationalist refusal to open the floodgates, but it was absurd to assume that the government in Belfast could operate, let alone defend, installations at the end of a strip of territory only yards wide without the goodwill of their neighbours.

In south Fermanagh, the most obvious anomaly was the Drummully polyp, a Monaghan DED 'practically enclosed' within the North. North and South interlocked like jigsaw pieces, and the Clones to Cavan railway crossed the Border six times in five miles. The Commission sliced most of the area into the Free State. Around Clones the two communities were inextricably mingled, so that only 37 acres containing eight Catholics could be transferred, but further to the north 16 square miles around the village of Rosslea were assigned to the Free State. Transfers in the other direction along this stretch were ruled out since 'the portions of Co Monaghan in which there are Protestant majorities ... are separated from the existing border by districts containing Catholic majorities.'[176]

Further east, the Commission proposed to take a sliver of County Armagh, about eight miles long and two miles wide, which would move the village of Middletown to the Free State but add to the difficulties of equally Catholic Keady, whose merchants had already 'suffered appreciable losses by the interposition of the Customs barrier between the town and an area in Co Monaghan with which trade had been carried on'. The Commission excused itself for leaving Keady not only in the North but closer to the Border by virtually denying that it had 'proper market facilities' at all. Nearby Newtown Hamilton, with half Keady's population, was treated with more consideration, and its Protestant hinterland was to be rounded off by the transfer of an adjoining ten-square-mile block from Monaghan.[177]

All of this set the scene for the Commission's convolutions over Newry. The Commission did make by far its largest recommendation for transfer in south Armagh, both in population (14,676 people in 1911, 13,859 of them Catholics) and in area (84 square miles), a rearrangement which would have transferred Crossmaglen to the

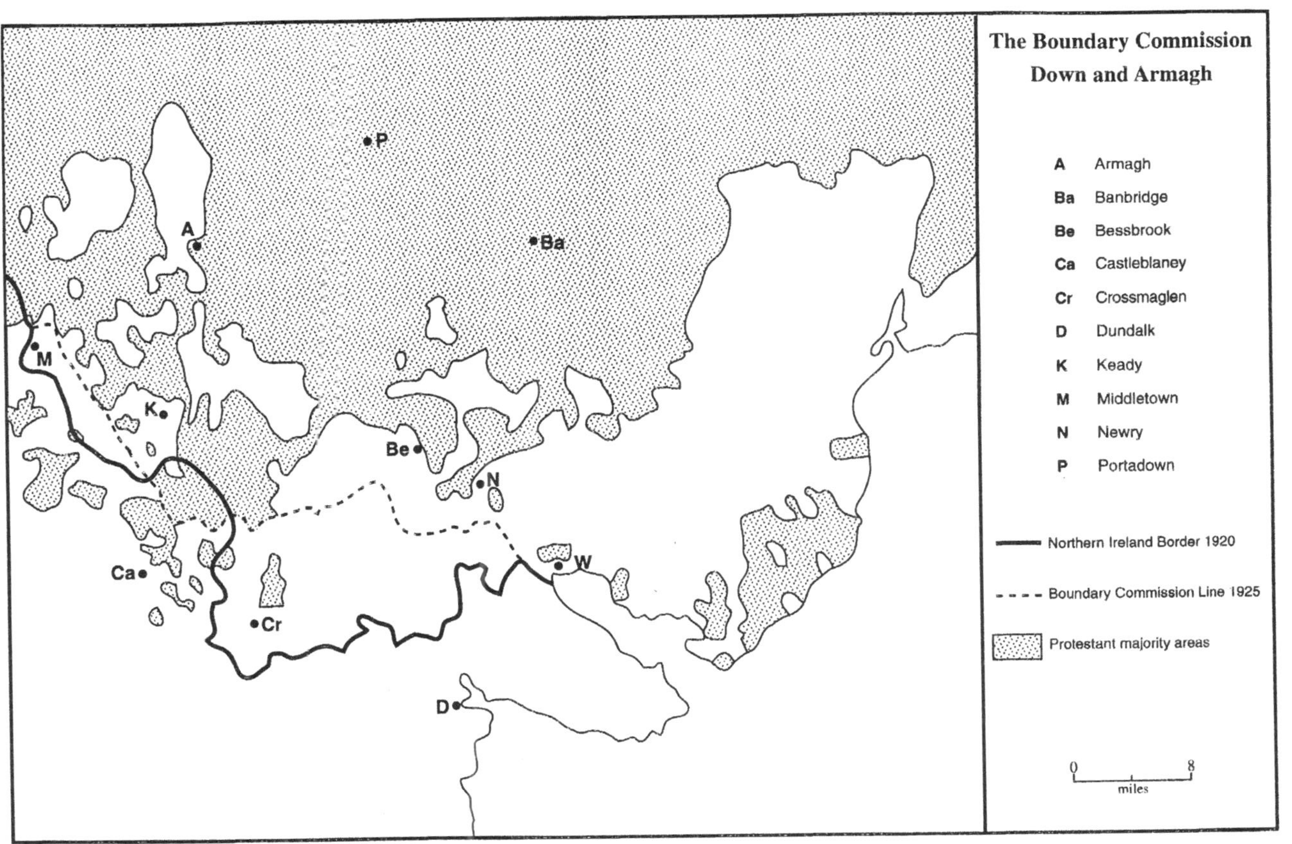

The Boundary Commission
Down and Armagh
A   Armagh
Ba   Banbridge
Be   Bessbrook
Ca   Castleblaney
Cr   Crossmaglen
D   Dundalk
K   Keady
M   Middletown
N   Newry
P   Portadown
Northern Ireland Border 1920
Boundary Commission Line 1925
Protestant majority areas
0   8
miles

Free State. None the less, on census grounds alone the transferred area could have been considerably larger. The problem was that the port town of Newry was a nationalist community located within two miles of the Border and on a frontier between Protestant and Catholic districts. The Commission devoted pages to arguing that proximity to the Border was of little importance since Dundalk limited its market area to the south. On the other hand, to shift the Border north of Newry would sever the town from its hinterland.[178]

The overall effect of the Boundary Commission's recommendations would have been the transfer of 286 square miles to the Free State and 77 square miles to Northern Ireland. Only one in every 25 Northern Irish Catholics would have been placed under Free State rule. The Border itself would have been shortened from 280 miles to 229, perhaps creating the 'stronger and more compact territory' that Fisher had predicted in June 1925, but still double the length of the simple Bundoran-to-Bessbrook line that he had originally supported.

In the event, the Commission never submitted a formal report. A leaked report in the *Morning Post* provoked an outburst of protest from both parts of Ireland, the resignation of MacNeill and the collapse of the Boundary Commission. Its recommendations were not even published until 1969. As the Dominions Secretary, L S Amery, later recalled, 'the only alternative was to leave the boundary where it was, however unsatisfactory from many points of view.'[179]

VI

In some respects, the Northern Ireland state created by Partition was a continuing entity. The challenge facing Craig as first prime minister of Northern Ireland in creating a new administrative structure was immense, but it paled in comparison with the incoming regime in Dublin, which Kevin O'Higgins memorably describes as 'simply eight young men ... amidst the ruins of one administration, with the foundations of another not yet laid, and with wild men screaming through the key-hole.'[180] The North, by contrast, could call on advice from Whitehall and made some efforts to recruit from the collapsing Castle regime in Dublin. Although some members of the new Northern government were out of their political depth, Craig and Lord Londonderry at least had held office at Westminster.

In other respects, the new Northern regime was revolutionary.[181] It had to establish its authority over a wholly new jurisdiction, including a 'West Bank' of obstructive local authorities beyond the

Bann which attempted to continue their relations with the government in Dublin. Craig streamlined his administration from thirty-odd all-Ireland Departments to seven, although this was largely because a 52-seat legislature could only support a small cabinet. Any possibility of the development of strong super-ministries was smothered by the way in which Craig dispensed favours as he travelled around Northern Ireland, like a Tudor monarch on progress. Unfortunately, he lacked the ruthlessness of the Tudors in discarding failed ministers, and the system of government quickly ossified into a minimalist but essentially Protestant apparatus. In the circumstances in which Northern Ireland was established, there was no surprise the new regime should recruit from untrained Protestants when Dublin civil servants and RIC personnel proved insufficient to meet its needs. There is symbolism in the fact that one of the few senior Catholic civil servants was a collateral descendant of Napoleon Bonaparte. More to the point, he went home at weekends to Dublin, and was known to be someone 'whom the Roman Catholics of Ulster would not regard as representing them'.[182] The Nationalist boycott in the formative years of Northern Ireland did nothing to prevent the creation of 'a Protestant Parliament and a Protestant State'.[183]

The scope of the new Northern state was also restricted, and Craig might have done better to have stuck to his demand for full Dominion status. Armour dubbed it 'a form of Home rule that the Devil himself could never have imagined'. In essence, it was a nineteenth-century answer to twentieth-century problems. In the allocation of powers, it was a fossilised temporary expedient, since the Government of Ireland Act had assumed the transfer of broader responsibilities to the still-born Council of Ireland. Craig's cabinet was constrained by the level of revenue it received from London and forced by its own Unionist logic to match services provided on the mainland - a derivative process which discouraged ideological debate within Northern Ireland on the social role of the state. The 74 local authorities across the Six Counties did little to fill the gap. Local government had developed in the Irish rather than British mould, with limited practical aims and high levels of patronage verging on corruption.[184]

Given that most of Craig's cabinet had either served as or would become Presidents of the Belfast Chamber of Commerce, it was unlikely that they would be at the cutting edge of an interventionist State. 'The whole structure and ethos of Ulster Unionism had been based upon a single object - determined opposition to Home Rule - and no constructive philosophy had been developed ... to govern a state they had neither expected nor wanted.'[185] However, even if Northern Ireland governments had sought to pursue activist policies of economic development or social reform, the institutional structure of the new State pointed to parsimony and lack of innovation.

For the Northern State, then, the price of exclusion from an all-Ireland government was that it should be neither fully part of the United Kingdom nor wholly extraneous to it, 'not half-way house, but a lean-to',[186] a shattered fragment of the larger British and Irish State which had broken apart between 1919 and 1922. Remarkably, the underlying fact that the partition of Ireland was also the partition of the United Kingdom did not seem to trouble the people of the larger island. In the decade after 1914, the victorious United Kingdom lost a larger proportion of its territory than did defeated Germany. Yet few in Britain seemed to care. In 1871, statues representing Alsace and Lorraine in the Place de la Concorde in Paris were draped in black, and they remained in mourning until 1919. By contrast, there was no irredentist movement in Britain for the recovery of the south of Ireland. 'The Irish question had been answered for good or ill' and 'faded out of the sphere of British domestic politics.'[187] No doubt the 'Commonwealth' solution of Dominion status helped mask the nature of the retreat, but there remains a sense of almost palpable relief that Ireland was off the British agenda, matched by an equal measure of perplexity when it reappeared half a century later.

Such willing amnesia is striking. If national identities may be defined by religious affiliation, Ulster was the one place in the islands where the three majority cultures of England, Scotland and Ireland were intermingled. Between 1912 and 1914, Ulster Protestants had enjoyed massive support in mainland Britain: even Edward Elgar, one of England's most prominent lay Catholics, came out in support of the Covenant. The crowds welcoming Carson's arrival in Liverpool after the signing of the Covenant were said to have rivalled those who had come to see Crippen.[188] Yet this support did not endure. There was no constituency for Ulster in Britain equivalent to the uncritical and unceasing Irish-American lobby for Nationalist Ireland. Craig got his own way over the abolition of proportional representation in local elections in 1922 by a confrontation threat to resign.[189]

The explanation largely lies outside the scope of this chapter, in the complexity of English nationalism. Deep down, the English found it difficult to accept that anyone else could claim an equal share in the State in which, in Rosebery's phrase, they were the 'predominant partner'. By 1914, a recent study argues, English Conservatives had evolved a 'sense of British identity' which was 'the combination of anglocentrism and the growth of the Empire.' 'The incorporation of any particular non-English element in the Union had come to be seen as a matter of convenience rather than of principle.'[190] Ulster was inconvenient, 'so unreasonable', as Carson sarcastically put it, 'that she values her citizenship in the United Kingdom.'[191]

The Ulster Protestants were fortunate that Bonar Law, New Brunswick by birth but Coleraine by ancestry, was the leader of the Unionist party at the crisis of their fortunes. 'At heart he was an Orangeman and the Orange fanaticism was there,' C P Scott commented in 1921. 'He had brought it with him from Canada.'[192] Perhaps the fundamental English attitude is caught most poignantly in the welcome given to survivors of the 36th Division as they fell back at Thiepval. 'As they came in the artillery-men rushed out ... and shook hands with them, exclaiming "Well done, Paddy! You Irish were splendid!"'[193]

In fact, the Partition of Ireland did have consequences for British politics. The removal of nationalist MPs from Westminster probably fostered the rise of the Labour party, at least by removing one wing of the triple alliance which had enabled the Liberals to remain centre-stage before 1914. Given the subsequent difficulty which Labour has faced in establishing itself as a party of government, and the reformist policies which it has generally pursued when in office, it is open to argument whether British politics or indeed the British people have benefited from its eclipsing of the old Liberal party. It is even arguable that the abandonment of the social problems of the Twenty-Six Counties was a precondition for the United Kingdom welfare state. A British minister in 1938 reported Craig as pointing out that 'if they had been united with the United Kingdom today, they would be costing us a lot of money for unemployment and all sorts of other services.'[194] By and large, British politicians did not rush to embrace comprehensive welfare policies. Faced with the social problems of Catholic Ireland and the fierce conservatism of its Church, they would perhaps have been even less enthusiastic to pledge state support from the cradle to the grave.

If the removal of nationalist Ireland from Westminster had a negative significance which was easy to overlook, the continuing presence of an Ulster delegation retained the potential to influence the fate of governments. Generally, Ulster gave the British Conservatives a net gain of 10 to 12 seats until the alliance was ruptured in 1973, so reducing Labour majorities to single figures in 1950 and 1964. On the other hand, it was the defection of two Ulster nationalist MPs, Gerry Fitt and Frank Maguire, that administered the *coup de grâce* to the Callaghan government in 1979. Nor did the British Conservatives always have reason to welcome the presence at Westminster of their one-time allies. Unionist opposition helped force the resignation of the Heath government after the inconclusive general election of February 1974, and added to the problems of the Major government as its working majority crumbled from 1995.

Partition, thus, was not simply a landmark in the history of Ireland, but a formative event in the development of British politics too.

Partition, then, was a solution dictated by the conjunction within a specific historical moment, the decade 1912-22, of Irish crisis and European war. While the fault lines were deeply embedded in history and religion, the seismic force which brought about the earthquake was generated from the more recent and probably transient rise of the industrial strength and rampant confidence of Belfast and the Lagan valley. Hindsight may conclude that Partition was the worst possible solution for Ireland but, in 1920, it was almost certainly the only feasible expedient. Perhaps, had it been possible to draw boundaries with the same clarity that marked the gulf in identities, Partition might have proved the precondition for the Benelux-style collaboration of two Irelands that Auberon Herbert had predicted in 1886. Unfortunately, neither in principle nor in detail has Partition justified Austen Chamberlain's belief in 1920 that 'the only hope of union in Ireland is to recognize her present division.'[195] A major reason for this was that Partition created not two, but one-and-a-half Irelands, in which the North East would not move to full independence from Britain but never achieved entire equality within the United Kingdom. In the event, Partition did no more than buy a half-century of time which was squandered, and thus it has emerged again in the past thirty years to sit immovably and insolubly as the central issue in the relationship between Ireland and Britain.

Notes

This paper draws on a number of sources, which are cited in short form as indicated here. Two basic studies are Denis Gwynn, *The History of Partition, 1912-1925*, Dublin: Brown and Nolan, 1950 (cited as Gwynn) and Michael Laffan, *The Partition of Ireland 1911-1925*, Dundalk: Dublin Historical Association, 1983 (cited as Laffan). Although neither contains a map, both are extensively documented, and Gwynn drew upon his research into the private papers of John Redmond. For Redmond's principal antagonist, see *The Life of Lord Carson*, 3 vols, London: Gollancz, 1932-36, Vol. 1 by Edward Marjoribanks, Vols 2 and 3 by Ian Colvin (cited as *Carson*). Jonathan Bardon, *A History of Ulster*, Belfast: Blackstaff, 1992 (cited as Bardon) is massively informative.

The student of Partition must follow gratefully in the footsteps of Patrick Buckland, especially his *Irish Unionism*: Vol 2, *Ulster Unionism and the Origins of Northern Ireland 1886-1922*, Dublin: Gill and Macmillan, 1973 (cited as Buckland, *Ulster Unionism*); *The Factory of Grievances: Devolved Government in Northern Ireland 1921-39*, Dublin: Gill and Macmillan, 1979 (cited as Buckland, *Factory*); *A History of Northern Ireland*, Dublin: Gill and

Macmillan, 1981 (cited as Buckland, *History*), *James Craig: Lord Craigavon*, Dublin: Gill and Macmillan, 1981 (cited as Buckland, *Craig*), and his edited *Irish Unionism 1885-1923*, Belfast: HMSO, 1973 (cited as Buckland, ed., *Documents*).

Geoffrey J Hand edited the *Report of the Irish Boundary Commission*, Shannon: Irish Academic Press, 1925 (cited as *BC*).

[1]　Quoted in D G Boyce, 'British conservative opinion, the Ulster question, and the partition of Ireland, 1912-1921', in *Irish Historical Studies*, Vol. XVII (1970), p.104.

[2]　A T Q Stewart, *The Narrow Ground: The Roots of Conflict in Ulster*, rev. ed., London: Faber, 1989, is a brilliant exploration of Ulster mentalities.

[3]　Laffan, p.1.

[4]　Quoted in Randolph S Churchill, *Winston S. Churchill:*Vol.2, *The Young Statesman 1901-1914*, London: Heinemann, 1967, p.506. Churchill had visited Belfast in 1912 to speak in favour of Home Rule. Unionists denounced him for disloyalty to his father and the meeting had to be held in the open air in West Belfast, where it rained. This experience probably explains Churchill's often-quoted connection between Ulster and mud. *Ibid.*, pp.461-68.

[5]　Carson predicted in March 1920: 'It may turn out that the only part of Ireland which will have a Parliament is the part which never asked for it.' *Carson*, Vol.3, p.386.

[6]　See Buckland, *Factory* and *History*; Bardon, chs 11-14 and David Harkness, *Northern Ireland Since 1920*, Dublin: Helicon, 1983.

[7]　Quoted in Stewart, *Narrow Ground*, p.165. Thomas MacKnight noted with some bitterness in 1896 that Gladstone, first elected to parliament in 1832, had probably heard Macaulay's speech. Thomas MacKnight, *Ulster As It Is*, 2 vols, London: Macmillan and Co, 1896, Vol.2, p.144. The name of Northern Ireland's second city is itself a symbol of Ulster divisions. This paper conforms to the usage of the Apprentice Boys: Derry.

[8]　*The Times*, 30 December 1885. Auberon Herbert was a republican, agnostic and vegetarian with an interest in psychic research. He was also the brother of Lord Carnarvon, Lord Lieutenant of Ireland at the time and a rare Conservative supporter of Home Rule.

[9]　I Budge and C O'Leary, *Belfast: Approach to Crisis. A Study of Belfast Politics 1613-1970*, London: Macmillan, 1973, pp.87-91; Buckland, *Ulster Unionism*, p.38; Bardon, pp.381-382.

[10]　J L Hammond, *Gladstone and the Irish Nation* , London: Longmans, 1938, p.491; A L Thorold, *The Life of Henry Labouchere*, London: Constable, 1913, p.303.

[11]　Quoted in Hammond, *Gladstone and the Irish Nation*, pp.516-17.

[12]　Quoted in F S L Lyons, *Charles Stewart Parnell*, London: Collins, 1978 ed., p.351. Although Parnell knew little of Ulster, he had northern ancestors. The family of his American mother, the Stewarts, were Scotch-Irish Presbyterians. Through his great-grandmother, Charlotte Brooke, he was distantly related to Lord Brookeborough.

[13]　Henry Pelling, *Social Geography of British Elections 1885-1910*, London: Macmillan, 1967, pp.369,400,409.

[14]　*Punch*, 12 June 1886. The Boers had established their independence in a short war against Britain in 1881. Parnell had used South African issues in 1877 at the height of the obstruction campaign.

[15]　Patrick O'Farrell, *Ireland's English Question: Anglo-Irish Relations 1534-1970*, London: Batsford, 1971, pp.249-50.

16   R F Foster, *Lord Randolph Churchill: A Political Life*, Oxford: Clarendon, 1988 ed., p.134 and his 'To the Northern Counties Station: Lord Randolph Churchill and the Prelude to the Orange Card', in F S L Lyons and R A J Hawkins, eds, *Ireland Under the Union: Varieties of Tension*, Oxford: Clarendon, 1980, pp.237-88. For his Belfast speech, see Winston S Churchill, *Lord Randolph Churchill*, rev. ed., London: Heinemann, 1 951, pp.448-50. MacKnight thought it 'monstrous' that 'a majority of the House of Commons, no matter how chosen or how small, has a right to deprive any portion of the Queen's subjects in the United Kingdom of their inherited privilege as British citizens to remain under the direct control of the Parliament at Westminster'. MacKnight, *Ulster As It Is*, Vol.2, p.379.

17   Quoted in Michael Hurst, *Joseph Chamberlain and Liberal Reunion: The Round Table Conference of 1887*, London: Routledge and Kegan Paul, 1970, p.393.

18   Ulster Solemn League and Covenant, 1912, facsimile in Buckland, *Documents*, p.224, also quoted in A T Q Stewart, *The Ulster Crisis: Resistance to Home Rule 1912-14*, London: Faber, 1967, p.62.

19   MacKnight, *Ulster As It Is*, Vol.2, p.379.

20   *Punch*, 12 June 1886, p.280.

21   Quoted in Thorold, *Labouchere*, p.272.

22   Quoted in John Kendle, *Ireland and the Federal Solution: The Debate over the United Kingdom Constitution, 1870-1921*, Kingston and Montreal: McGill - Queen's University Press, 1989, p.191. This contradicted his opinion of 1912, *Carson*, Vol.2, p.164.

23   Hurst, *Joseph Chamberlain and Liberal Reunion*, pp.207,390-91. Curiously, in December 1886, Chamberlain drew the analogy that ' Ireland was a Province - as Nova Scotia is a province of Canada'. *Ibid.*, p.145. Nova Scotia at the time was attempting to secede from the Dominion.

24   Kendle, *Ireland and the Federal Solution*, p.174.

25   Quoted in *ibid.*, p.156.

26   Laffan, p.33.

27   Roy Jenkins, *Mr Balfour's Poodle* London: Collins, 1954; E A Smith, *The House of Lords in British Politics and Society 1815-1911*, London,: Longman, 1992, pp.178-183. 'The Home Rule Bill has been caught in the Parliament Act', F E Smith explained in February 1914. 'It either has to become law in its existing form or it has got to be changed by consent.' Quoted in Lord Birkenhead, *F.E.: The Life of F.E. Smith First Earl of Birkenhead*, London: Eyre and Spottiswoode, 1959, p.233.

28   Bonar Law's Blenheim speech, July 1912, quoted Robert Blake, *The Unknown Prime Minister: The Life and Times of Andrew Bonar Law 1858-1923*, London: Eyre and Spottiswoode, 1955, p.130. The speech is quoted in slightly different versions in Carson, Vol.2, p.129, and Gwynn, p.46.

29   De Valera's view, as reported by Smuts, July 1921. T Wilson, ed., *The Political Diaries of C P Scott 1911-1928*, London: Collins, p.397 cited as *Scott Diaries*. Cf. O'Farrell, *Ireland's English Question*, pp.246-247, and, generally, John Bowman, *De Valera and the Ulster Question 1917-1973*, Oxford: Clarendon, 1982..

30   Laffan, chapter 2.

31   Gwynn, pp.52-54; Carson, Vol.2, pp.166-69.

32   Laffan, p.45. Asquith favoured plebiscites 'not in Ulster alone but all over Ireland' to discover whether Protestant minorities were really so opposed to Home Rule as Unionists claimed. E David, ed., *Inside Asquith's Cabinet: From the Diaries of Charles Hobhouse*, London: J Murray, 1977, p.162.

33   Gwynn, p. 93. Liberal leaders had considered county plebiscites in 1887. Hurst, *Joseph Chamberlain and Liberal Reunion*, p.210.

34   Quoted in Carson, Vol.2, p.298, and cf. Gwynn, pp.93-101; Laffan, pp.37-38.

35   Gwynn, p.102.

36   As Carson put it in 1919, 'you cannot knock Parliaments up and down as you do a ball'. Quoted in Laffan, p.64.

37   Gwynn, pp.108,125.

38   Bowman, *De Valera and the Ulster Question*, pp.55-56. Devlin and Dillon were still arguing for county option in 1917, Scott *Diaries*, p.285. George V had favoured a referendum of the excluded area in 1913, to take place after a five or ten year period of exclusion. By March 1914, the king favoured 'a recurring plebiscite every 3 years, which ... would keep the whole place in a condition of chronic ferment'. H Nicolson, *King George V: His Life and Reign* , London: Constable, 1952, p.228; Michael and Eleanor Brock, eds, *H H Asquith: Letters to Venetia Stanley*, Oxford: Oxford University Press, 1982, p.56 (cited as *Asquith Letters*).

39   Laffan, pp.50-55; Ronald McNeill, *Ulster's Stand for Union* London: John Murray, 1922, p.247.

40   Buckland, ed., *Documents* , p.413, quoting *Ulster and Home Rule. No Partition of Ulster* 1920, issued by Unionists from Cavan, Donegal and Monaghan. See also McNeill, *Ulster's Stand for Union*, pp.248-49.

41   Gwynn, pp.132-157.

42   *Carson*, ii, pp.178-179. D. Gwynn, *Life of John Redmond* London: Harrap, 1932, p. 522, denounced the handshake offer as a stunt.

43   Buckland, ed., *Documents*, p.423, and quoted, Bardon, p. 458. For the Convention, R B McDowell, *The Irish Convention 1917-18* London: Routledge, Kegan and Paul, 1970.

44   G Dangerfield, *The Damnable Question: A Study in Anglo-Irish Relations*, London: Little, Brown, 1977, pp.70,81.

45   McDowell, *Irish Convention*, p.72.

46   *Carson*, Vol.3, pp.243-46.

47   *Scott Diaries*, pp. 282-83. The Council was to operate on a 'double majority' basis, requiring majorities in each delegation. McDowell, *Irish Convention*, p.76.

48   *Scott Diaries*, pp.285,289-90.

49   McDowell, *Irish Convention*, pp.76-80. As with more recent attempts to secure an internal political settlement, the size of the Convention became an issue. 'Each twenty men you add more than doubles the danger of disagreement', a Catholic bishop advised. D Gwynn, *Life of Redmond*, p.558, and cf. Carson, Vol.3, p.292.

50   Carson, Vol.3, pp.291,308-11.

51   *Scott Diaries*, p.283.

52   Dangerfield, *Damnable Question*, p.225. 'The Bill has not a single friend in either hemisphere, outside Downing Street', said the southern Unionist *Irish Times*, quoted in Dorothy Macardle, *The Irish Republic: a Documented Chronicle of the Anglo-Irish Conflict and the Partitioning of Ireland, with a Detailed Account of the Period 1916-23* London: Gollancz, 1937, 1968 ed. London: Corgi, pp.311-12. For the political constraints on the government, see generally K O Morgan, *Consensus and Disunity: The Lloyd George Coalition Government 1918-1922*, Oxford: Clarendon, 1979.

53   Quoted in Dangerfield, *Damnable Question*, p.320; *Scott Diaries*, pp.382-383.

54   Quoted in *Carson*, Vol.3, pp.384-385.

55 Quoted in Buckland, *Craig*, p.41. A Report of the Ulster Unionist Council in 1936 endorsed the argument. 'Had we refused to accept a Parliament for Northern Ireland and remained at Westminster, there can be but little doubt that now we would either be inside the Free State or fighting desperately against incorporation. Northern Ireland without a Parliament of her own would be standing temptation to certain British politicians to make another bid for a final settlement with Irish Republicans.' Quoted in Nicholas Mansergh, *The Irish Question 1840-1921*, London: Allen and Unwin, 1965, p.214. As Mansergh notes, the construction of Stormont between 1928 and 1932 was intended to symbolise the permanence of the institution. *Ibid.*, p.215, and cf. Bardon, p.513.

56 Asquith's description, in Mansergh, *Irish Question*, p.212.

57 J M Curran, *The Birth of the Irish Free State 1921-1923*, Mobile, Alabama: University of Alabama Press, 1980, p.263.

58 Nicolson, *King George V*, pp.348-354. Some unlikely historians have regarded the king's speech as effective in itself. Compare A J P Taylor, *English History 1914-1945*, Oxford: Clarendon, 1965, p.157; John A Murphy, *Ireland in the Twentieth Century* Dublin: Macmillan, 1975, p.25; and Macardle, *Irish Republic*, pp.427-28, with Charles Townshend, *The British Campaign in Ireland 1919-1921: The Development of Political and Military Policies*, Oxford: Oxford University Press, 1975, p.191 and F S L Lyons, *Ireland Since the Famine*, London: Fontana, 1973 ed., pp.426-27. An appeal by a king opening a partitionist parliament in Belfast can hardly in itself have appealed to Irish republicans. Smuts, who drafted the king's speech, showed a confused subtlety in his subsequent pleas to de Valera to engage in talks, insisting that the Government of Ireland Act 'was not a partition, but merely that Ulster, which had always proved the obstacle, is now out of the way'. Therefore, de Valera should 'cease talking or troubling about Ulster partition, accept what has been done and talk to the British Government about South Ireland'. W K Hancock, *Smuts*: Vol.2, *The Fields of Force 1919-1950*, Cambridge: Cambridge University Press, 1968, pp.51-57.

59 Buckland, *History*, pp.37-38; J McColgan, *British Policy and the Irish Administration, 1920-22*, London: Allen and Unwin, 1983, chapter 3, which calls the Government of Ireland Act 'the blueprint for partition'.

60 Frank Pakenham Earl of Longford, *Peace by Ordeal* 2nd ed., Cork: Mercier Press, 1951; Curran, *Birth of the Irish Free State*; Sheila Lawlor, *Britain and Ireland 1914-23* Dublin: Gill and Macmillan, 1983. For a more recent summary, see J J Lee, *Ireland 1912-1985: Politics and Society*, Cambridge: Cambridge University Press, 1989, pp.47-55.

61 Quoted in Bardon, p.482.

62 *Scott Diaries*, p.407. Lloyd George told the cabinet that 'men will die for Throne and Empire. I do not know who will die for Tyrone and Fermanagh.' Presumably the pun was more effective in a Welsh accent. Quoted in Laffan, p.78.

63 Pakenham, *Peace by Ordeal*, p.298. It was the measure of the exhaustion of the Irish delegation that they failed to point out (a) that there was no urgency about notifying Craig and (b) that they had demanded Craig's adherence to the terms before signing the Treaty themselves. *Ibid.*, pp.287-88.

64 Lee, *Ireland*, pp.52-53.

65 For the Treaty, see A Mitchell and P O Snodaigh, eds, *Irish Political Documents 1916-1949*, Dublin: Irish Academic Press, 1985, pp.116-121; Curran, *op. cit.*, pp.284-88.

66 Lee, *Ireland*, p.141, and cf. Curran, *Birth of the Irish Free State*, p.134.

67   Cork Archives Institute, CAI/U385, statement by J J Walsh, 1948. Walsh
     had demanded 'a full and clear definition' of de Valera's Ulster policy in
     August 1921, with predictable lack of success. Bowman, *De Valera and
     the Ulster Question*, pp.54-56.

68   *Ibid.*

69   Lord Longford and T P O'Neill, *Eamon De Valera*, Boston: Houghton,
     Mifflin and Co, 1971 ed., p.179.

70   Quoted in T P Coogan, *De Valera: Long Fellow, Long Shadow*, London:
     Hutchinson, 1993, p.290; *ibid.*, pp.743-47 for Document no. 2, also in
     Macardle, *Irish Republic*, pp.886-91.

71   Longford and O'Neill, *De Valera*, p.180, but cf. Bowman, *De Valera and
     the Ulster Question*, pp.64-69.

72   Quoted in Coogan, *De Valera*, pp.292-293; T de Vere White, *Kevin
     O'Higgins*, London: Methuen, 1948, Tralee: Anvil, 1966, p.195. Cf. Lee,
     Ireland, p.53 on 'self-deception'.

73   Quoted in Buckland, *Craig*, p.72.

74   Buckland, *History*, pp.44-48.

75   Lee, *Ireland*, p.151; J J Lee and G O Tuathaigh, *The Age of De Valera*,
     Dublin: ward River Press, 1982, pp.96-99; Bowman, *De Valera and the
     Ulster Question*, chapter 3.

76   Macardle, *Irish Republic*, p.801, Coogan, *De Valera*, p.375.

77   Lee, *Ireland*, p.141; Lee and O Tuathaigh, *Age of De Valera*, pp.98-99,
     Coogan, *De Valera*, pp.643-645.

78   Quoted in Mitchell and O Snodaigh, eds, *Irish Political Documents*,
     p.104.

79   Cork Archives Institute, CAI/U280, Liam T MacCosgair to Richardson
     Evans, 18 June 1925.

80   Quoted in Coogan, *De Valera*, p.421.

81   See note 67.

82   Quoted in Gwynn, p.91.

83   Ruth Dudley Edwards, *An Atlas of Irish History*, 2nd ed., London:
     Methuen, 1973, map 54b, p.181.

84   J H Whyte, *The Independent Irish Party 1850-9*, Oxford: Oxford
     University Press, 1958, pp.158-60.

85   R W Kirkpatrick, 'Origins and development of the land war in Mid-
     Ulster, 1879-1885', in Lyons and Hawkins, eds, *Ireland Under the Union*,
     pp.201-36.

86   L Kennedy, 'The rural economy', in L Kennedy and P Ollerenshaw, eds,
     An Economic History of Ulster, 1820-1940, Manchester: Manchester
     University Press, 1985, pp.42,60 cited as *Economic History*. Land issues
     lingered on in Antrim until the 1920s, in alliance with Liberals and
     Nationalists, Bardon, p.440; Buckland, *Factory*, p.224.

87   Lyons, *Ireland Since the Famine*, pp.212-13; Bardon, p.425.

88   For Macaulay, see note 2; N Gash, *Sir Robert Peel: The Life of Sir Robert
     Peel after 1830*, London: Longman, 1972, pp.479-80. For the choice
     between Armagh and Belfast in 1845, see T W Moody and J C Beckett,
     Queen's, Belfast 1845-1949: The History of a University, 2 vols, London:
     Faber and Faber, 1959, i, pp.30-32.

89   L A Clarkson, 'Population change and urbanisation 1821-1911', in
     Economic History, p.138.

90   See, generally, P Ollerenshaw, 'Industry, 1820-1914', in *Economic
     History*, pp.62-108.

91   *Economic History*, pp.153-55; Budge and O'Leary, *Belfast*, chapter 3.

92   Bardon, p.335; J J Lee, *The Modernisation of Irish Society 1848-1918*, Dublin: Gill and Macmillan, 1973, p.91; *Economic History*, p.91. The Cork ship-building industry remained innovative into the 1860s, which suggests that the advantages of Belfast lay in proximity to coal and iron supplies. A Bielenberg, *Cork'sIndustrial Revolution 1780-1880: Development or Decline?*, Cork: Cork University Press, 1991, pp.92. *Economic History*, pp.87-96.

93   *Economic History*, pp.87-96.

94   *Ibid.*, p.137.

95   Bardon, p.404. 'Look at Belfast and be a Repealer if you can,' Presbyterian minister Henry Cooke had challenged in 1841. Quoted in R F Foster, *Modern Ireland 1600-1972*, London: Allen Lane, 1988, p.303.

96   D S Johnson, 'The Northern Ireland economy, 1914-1939', in *Economic History*, pp.184-223, esp. p.201; Buckland, *Factory*, p.125.

97   Buckland, *History*, pp.2-3; T Keane, 'Demographic trends', in M Hurley, ed., *Irish Anglicanism*, Dublin: Allen Figgis, 1970, pp.169-70.

98   Bardon, p.440. Buckland, *Factory*, p.49, downplays the role of the Orange Order in Unionist resistance 1911-1914.

99   Buckland, ed., *Documents*, pp.428-36.

100   Craig arrived as a schoolboy in Edinburgh in 1882, probably the year in which James Connolly left the city.

101   Gwynn, p.190. The lifeboat metaphor had been thrown at the Ulster Unionists in 1912 by the Solicitor-General, Sir John Simon, at the time when he had been conducting the enquiry into the loss of the *Titanic*. The ship's lifeboats were insufficient to save all its passengers. *Carson*, Vol.2, pp.119-20.

102   MacKnight, *Ulster As It Is*, Vol.2, p.383.

103   Buckland, ed., *Documents*, pp.202-03. Ulster exiles in Edinburgh signed on the tomb in Greyfriars used for the original Covenant in 1638. *Carson*, Vol.2, p. 151.

104   Bardon, p.422, and see illustration facing p.135 of P Gibbons, *The Origins of Ulster Unionism*, Manchester: Manchester University Press, 1975. A Union Jack decorated with 'Cead mile failte' was displayed at Colchester, Essex, in 1908 as part of a Unionist campaign in Britain: Buckland, *Ulster Unionism*, p.71. 'Celtic' became an optional matriculation subject for Queen's University, Belfast, in 1908 thanks to the votes of non-Irish staff: Moody and Beckett, *Queen's, Belfast*, Vol.1, pp.418-19.

105   Quoted in Laffan, p.16.

106   Moody and Beckett, *Queen's, Belfast*, Vol.1, pp.381-89 For Craig, see John A Murphy, *The College: A History of Queen's/University College Cork, 1845-1995*, Cork: Cork University Press, 1995, p.182. The emergence of a Belfast university was complicated by the desire of Queen's College staff to elude the dominance of Dublin, originally threatened in the form of Protestant Trinity College.

107   Lee, *Ireland*, p.11; M Harris, *The Catholic Church and the Foundation of the Northern Irish State*, Cork, 1993, esp. pp.14-17. In 1919, the Catholic Bishop of Down and Connor estimated that there were seventy mixed marriages each year in the Belfast area: *ibid.*, p.38. The Boundary Commission accepted as a working principle an equation between 'Protestants' and 'Unionists', 'Catholics' and 'Nationalists', although one of its members, J R Fisher, privately believed that Nationalists might be transferred to the Free State 'against their will'. *BC*, pp.68-70; St John Ervine, *Craigavon: Ulsterman*, London: Allen and Unwin, 1949, p.499.

108   Bardon, p.440.

109 For the Derry City by-election, Buckland, *Ulster Unionism*, pp.32-34. The
remarkable 95 per cent turn-out included one voter who had fought in
the American Civil War.

110 Quoted in Buckland, ed., *Documents*, p.435. For Cardinal Logue, Harris,
Catholic Church and the Foundation of the Northern Irish State, pp.70-71.

111 Griffith had defeated a Nationalist in a seat in which no Unionist
candidate had appeared since 1892. Griffith's ability to analyse his
support was limited by the fact that he was in Gloucester Prison at the
time of the election. He may have had a personal reason for his claim:
his grandfather had been born a Protestant in nearby County
Monaghan.

112 Quoted in Randolph S Churchill and Martin Gilbert, *Winston S.
Churchill*: Vol.4, *1917-1922*, London: Heinemann, 1975, p.692 and Lee,
Ireland, p.46. Like the 'muddy byways', Churchill's reference to the
'dreary steeples' hangs over Tyrone and Fermanagh. Alistair Rowan,
North West Ulster The Buildings of Ireland, Harmondsworth: Penguin,
1979, contains much to refute the slur.

113 Muddled orders and heavy rain aborted the rising in Tyrone: Bardon,
pp.442-43.

114 Lee, *Ireland*, pp.22-23; Bardon, p.461. 'In the whole conduct of the war
you can find no difference between the North-East of Ulster and any
part of Great Britain.' *Carson*, Vol.3, p.381.

115 Stewart, *Ulster Crisis*, p.237.

116 Bardon, p.455.

117 *Carson*, Vol.3, p.326.

118 D S Johnson estimates the Ulster death toll to be equal to one eighth of
the males aged 18 to 40 at the 1911 census. *Economic History*, p.184.

119 Laffan, p.104. Craig may also be regarded as a continuous participant,
but by definition not at the centre of events.

120 Pakenham, *Peace by Ordeal*, p.161n, oddly presents the nine-county
option as offering 'a sporting chance' to both Nationalists and Unionists.

121 Quoted in Buckland, ed., *Documents*, p.120.

122 Bardon, p.510.

123 It is generally assumed that the hostages were chosen because they
represented the four provinces. M Hopkinson, *Green Against Green: The
Irish Civil War*, Dublin: St Martin's Press, 1988, p.191. Two of the
most comprehensive histories of modern Ireland mention only
Mellowes and O'Connor. Lyons, *Ireland Since the Famine*, p.467; Lee,
Ireland, p.66.

124 Oliver MacDonagh, *Ireland: The Union and its Aftermath*, London: Allen
and Unwin, 1977, p.118.

125 Quoted in Blake, *Unknown Prime Minister*, p.130.

126 Bardon, p.506.

127 Balfour, quoted in Laffan, p.64.

128 Quoted in Mansergh, *The Irish Question*, p.211. Some support may be
drawn for Chamberlain's plea from the subsequent division of India
into two successor states. The 1935 Government of India Act, like the
Home Rule Bill of 1912, revealed the extent of the religious divide. The
British, forced on to the defensive by a combination of external war and
internal nationalist challenge, undoubtedly saw the Muslim minority,
like the Ulster Protestants, as allies. As in Ireland, Partition emerged
within little more than a decade. The Muslim leader, M A Jinnah,
resembled Carson: he was a lawyer, he pursued his career in Bombay,
remote from the Punjab which became the core of Pakistan, and he was
inflexible in negotiations. There are of course differences between

Ireland and India. The Muslims did not seek a continuing link with Britain. Pakistan was based on two distinct blocks of Muslim-majority territory as if Northern Ireland had included North Wexford and East Wicklow. While both partitions were accompanied by bloodshed, in Ireland there were no large-scale transfers of refugee populations. See, generally, T G Fraser, *Partition in Ireland, India and Palestine: Theory and Practice*, London: Macmillan, 1984 and B N Pandey, *The Break-up of British India*, London: Macmillan, 1969.

[129] Quoted in *Carson*, Vol.3, p.409.

[130] Pakenham, *Peace by Ordeal*, p.109, and cf. Lee, *Ireland*, p.45, for the disparity between mental and geographical boundaries. McNeill, *Ulster's Stand for Union*, p. vii, explained that he used the term 'not in the geographical, but the political meaning'.

[131] Quoted in Bowman, *De Valera and the Ulster Question*, p.8.

[132] *Asquith Letters*, p.109. For a study of Protestant and Catholic worlds in 'Ballybeg', a West Ulster community in the present Troubles, see R Harris, *Prejudice and Tolerance in Ulster*, Manchester: Manchester University Press, 1986 ed.

[133] J H Andrews, 'A geographer's view of Irish history', in T W Moody and F X Martin, eds, *The Course of Irish History*, Cork: Mercier Press,1967, pp.27-28. See also the long historical perspective of a Dutch geographer, M W Heslinga, *The Irish Border as a Cultural Divide: A Contribution to the Study of Regionalism in the British Isles*, 2nd ed., Assen: van Gorcum, 1971.

[134] Lyons, *Charles Stewart Parnell*, p.249.

[135] O MacDonagh, *States of Mind: A Study of Anglo-Irish Conflict 1780-1980*, London: Allen and Unwin, 1983, pp.18-20.

[136] MacDonagh, *Ireland: The Union and its Aftermath*, p.18. For a criticism of the view that Ulster contains 'two distinct cultures', see R H Buchanan, 'The Planter and the Gael: cultural dimensions of the Northern Ireland problem', in F W Boal and J N H Douglas, eds, *Integration and Division: Geographical Perspectives on the Northern Ireland Problem*, London: Academic Press, 1982, pp.49-73.

[137] *Economic History*, p.155.

[138] *Asquith Letters*, p.97.

[139] Quoted in Mansergh, *The Irish Question*, p.210.

[140] Buckland, ed., *Documents*, p.416.

[141] McNeill, *Ulster's Stand for Union*, p.279. A further reason for dumping the Three Counties lay in the fear that labour militancy would divide the Belfast Protestant working class from the Unionist leadership. See A Morgan, *Labour and Partition: The Belfast Working Class 1905-23*, London: Pluto Press, 1991. St John Ervine threatened in 1949 that Ulstermen would soon be forced 'to rescue our three lost counties from the Eirean morass'. Ervine, *Craigavon*, p.482.

[142] *Scott Diaries*, p.82.

[143] Buckland, *History*, p.3.

[144] Buckland, ed., *Documents*, p.415. Ulster county limits were drawn in the early 17th century, and generally followed earlier boundaries. R Gillespie, *Colonial Ulster:The Settlement of East Ulster 1600-1641*, Cork: Cork University Press, 1985, p.19; T W Moody, F X Martin and J H Byrne, eds, *New History of Ireland*, Vol.9, Oxford: Clarendon, 1984, pp.43,109.

[145] Quoted in Ervine, *Craigavon*, pp.481-482.

[146] *Ibid.* Of 61 East Donegal submissions to the Boundary Commission, 54 stressed the inconvenience of the customs barrier. *BC*, p.72.

[147] *Carson*, Vol.2, p.402. Craig was probably closer to the Northern mentality in his dismissal in 1929 of the joint constituency of Fermanagh and Tyrone, created under proportional representation, as 'a little bit un-Ulster'. 'Counties in Ulster like to be counties'. Quoted in Buckland, *Factory*, p.242.

[148] Laffan, p.5.

[149] Brian Turner in M Crozier, ed., *Cultural Traditions in Northern Ireland*, Belfast: Institute of Irish Studies//Queen's University, 1989, pp.110-13; p.111.

[150] Quoted in Bardon, p.405.

[151] *Scott Diaries*, pp.82-83. For Ulster baronies, see R Dudley Edwards, *An Atlas of Irish History*, p.16.

[152] *BC*, pp.64,99.

[153] 1911 census figures are taken from *British Parliamentary Papers*, 1912-13, Vol.CXVI.

[154] Compare the maps in *New History of Ireland*, Vol.9, p.81 and Moody and Martin, eds, *Course of Irish History*, p.29. Although the detail varies, the overall picture for 1911 resembles that of 1766, as mapped by P Robinson, in Boal and Douglas, eds, *Integration and Division*, p.43. For the subsequent erosion of Protestants in West Ulster, see map in K Boyle and T Hadden, *Ireland: A Positive Proposal*, London: Penguin, 1985, p.36, and cf. Lee, *Ireland*, p.681.

[155] David, ed., *Inside Asquith's Cabinet*, p.175; *Asquith Letters*, p.109. The Boundary Commission concluded that Poor Law Unions had no economic unity. *BC*, p.63.

[156] *Asquith Letters*, p.109.

[157] *BC*, pp.93,95,91,78. In 1911, the adjoining Tyrone DEDs of Coagh and Munterevlin were 77.3 per cent and 8.4 per cent Protestant respectively.

[158] *Asquith Letters*, p.109.

[159] Quoted in Laffan, p.19. MacKnight in 1896 had reported the story of a woman in Tipperary burnt by a mob as a suspected witch 'only a short time ago'. MacKnight, *Ulster As It Is*, Vol.2, p.393.

[160] David, ed, *Inside Asquith's Cabinet*, p.176. In 1917, the cabinet briefly considered county plebiscites with a weighted 55 per cent majority. McDowell, *Irish Convention*, pp.74-75.

[161] Gwynn, p.127. and cf. *Asquith Letters*, p.105.

[162] Mitchell and O Snodaigh, eds, *Irish Political Documents*, p.91. The Act refers throughout to 'Northern Ireland', avoiding the term 'Province'.

[163] Buckland, ed, *Documents*, p.416, and cf. Lee, *Ireland*, p.45.

[164] *Asquith Letters*, p.105. Carson's description of the Six-County unit in 1916 as 'a refuge and haven for any man that felt himself to be ill-treated elsewhere' also suggests an expectation that Partition would be accompanied by internal migration. It is significant that the Boundary Commission felt able to rely on the 1911 census figures 'as showing with approximate accuracy the proportionate numbers of Catholics and Protestants in the different districts'. *Carson*, Vol.3, p.169; *BC*, p.31.

[165] Ervine, *Craigavon*, p.500, and Lee, *Ireland*, pp.145-48, discuss MacNeill's role. G J Hand's 'Introduction' to *BC*, pp.vii-xxii, is an excellent account of the working of the Commission. See also Bardon, pp.505-09.

[166] *BC*, pp.72,49,66. The latter view was strongly held by Amery. De Vere White, *Kevin O'Higgins*, pp.248-49.

[167] Mitchell and O Snodaigh, eds, *Irish Political Documents*, p.119 Article 12.

[168] *BC*, pp.59,68,51,67,56. A small island in Carlingford Lough was to be transferred from County Down to the Free State. *BC*, p.139.

169 *BC*, p.78.

170 *BC*, pp.73,94,121-22, 113, 148-49. Four RIC Special Constables had been killed in an ambush at Clones station in 1922 while travelling to Enniskillen by the southern route. This incident probably explains the emphasis on retaining the alternative Clogher Valley railway within the North. Fisher had originally expected to make concessions at Aughnacloy. One of the Clones ambush party was later arrested after accidentally crossing the Border. Bardon, p.447; Buckland, *Factory*, pp.195,207; Ervine, *Craigavon*, p.500.

171 Quoted in M Tierney, *Eoin MacNeill: Scholar and Man of Action*, Oxford: Clarendon, 1980, p.345; Ervine, *Craigavon*, pp.499-500.

172 *BC*, pp.73,88.

173 *BC*, pp.95-96. Lifford has not justified these hopes.

174 *Ibid.*, pp.104-05, and cf. Curran, *Birth of the Irish Free State*, pp.197-99.

175 *BC*, pp.99-107. Quoted in Ervine, *Craigavon*, p.500.

176 *BC*, pp.101,106-10,112-13. Like Pettigoe, Rosslea had suffered from communal violence, but as far back as 1883. Buckland, *Ulster Unionism*, p.3.

177 *BC*, pp.116, 118-22,138.

178 *Ibid.*, pp.132-38.

179 Ervine, *Craigavon*, p.500, and cf. Bardon, p.508. For the *Morning Post* map, see Hand in *BC*, pp.xviii-xix. For Amery, see de Vere White, *Kevin O'Higgins*, p.249. The arguments against re-partition as a 'solution' for the Northern Ireland problem are summarised by Boyle and Hadden, *Ireland: A Positive Proposal*, pp.34-37.

180 De Vere White, *Kevin O'Higgins*, p.83.

181 This section draws on Buckland, *Factory*, chapter 1, and Harkness, *Northern Ireland Since 1920*, chspters 2-3.

182 Bardon, p.497; Buckland, *Factory*, p.249.

183 Quoted in Bardon, p.532. Craig's statement, in 1932, was made against the background of De Valera's rise to power in the South. One other post-1921 partitionist influence may be mentioned. In 1924, the BBC opened a relay station in Northern Ireland, 2BE which meant, according to Craig, that Belfast was the second city in the British empire. Radio Eireann began broadcasting in Dublin in 1926, but did not achieve wide coverage until the opening of its Athlone transmitter in 1932, intended to broadcast the Eucharistic Congress of 1932. Radio Eireann broadcast the angelus as a time signal and was used to some effect by De Valera. Unionists regarded it as a source of anti-British propaganda and sought to block programme sharing with the BBC in the North. Ervine, *Craigavon*, p.493; R Cathcart, 'Broadcasting - The early decades', in B Farrell, ed, *Communication and Community in Ireland*, Dublin: Mercier Press/RTE, 1984, pp.39-50.

184 Buckland, *Factory*, chapters 1-2. For Armour, see Bardon, p.514.

185 Buckland, *Factory*, p.5.

186 R J Lawrence, *The Government of Northern Ireland: Public Finances and Public Services*, Oxford: Clarendon, 1965, p.61. The point may be underlined by noting the difficulties in applying 'borderlands' analysis in Ireland. Except in Nationalist areas, there has been little sense of cross-Border community, and even in these cases, the sense of community dates from before the imposition of a dividing line. European integrationist policies may in time create elements of common economic interests and political culture, but thus far Border areas have produced few major politicians of influence in either part of Ireland. James Dillon (Monaghan) had a relatively successful record both as

minister and party leader, and was isolated in his support for the Allies in World War II. John Hume (Derry) and Seamus Mallon (Newry-Armagh) have been imaginative, but of necessity confined to opposition. The failure of the Border region to become a borderlands is best symbolised through its two most notable political products: Lord Brookeborough (Fermanagh) and Neil Blaney (Donegal). Cf. L McKinsey and V Konrad, *Borderlands Reflections: The United States and Canada*, Orono, Maine: Borderlands, 1989.

187 Taylor, *English History*, p.236, and R Rhodes James, *The British Revolution*, Vol.2, *British Politics, 1880-1939* London: Hamilton, 1977, p.169. The Irish Free State was not a comfortable Dominion. D W Harkness, *The Restless Dominion: The Irish Free State and the British Commonwealth of Nations, 1921-1931*, London: Macmillan, 1969.

188 Stewart, *Ulster Crisis*, pp.135,66.

189 Bardon, pp.499-501; Buckland, *Factory*, pp.272-275.

190 John Turner, 'Letting go: the Conservative party and the end of the Union with Ireland', in A Grant and K J Stringer, eds, *Uniting the Kingdom?: The Making of British History* London: Routledge, 1995, p.274.

191 *Carson*, Vol.3, p.386.

192 *Scott Diaries*, p.403.

193 *Carson*, Vol.3, p.184.

194 Quoted in D MacMahon, *Republicans and Imperialists: Anglo-Irish Relations in the 1930s*, New Haven: Yale University Press, 1984, p.210.

195 Quoted in Mansergh, *The Irish Question*, p.211.

The IRA's Border Campaign, 1956-1962

Ian S Wood

It was on a dreary New Year's day as the shades of night came down
When a lorry-load of volunteers approached a border town.
There were men from Dublin and from Cork, Fermanagh and Tyrone
But their leader was a Limerick man, Sean South of Garryowen.

This verse and the song from which it is taken, once popular with the choral element amongst Glasgow Celtic supporters, commemorates an IRA raid across the border into Northern Ireland on 1 January, 1957. The target was the Royal Ulster Constabulary (RUC) barracks in the small village of Brookeborough but the attack Fáiled, costing the lives of two members of the raiding party.

One of these was Sean South, twenty-seven years old at the time of his death and a clerical officer in government service in Limerick. He had served for a time in the Irish army reserve force, and the photograph of him most commonly used shows him in his uniform. He appears to have been a young man of disciplined habits and ascetic lifestyle, a keen student of Gaelic and a devout Catholic. He was influenced also by a local Limerick branch of Maria Duce, an organisation formed in 1945 by Father Denis Fahey of the Holy Ghost Fathers.[1] Maria Duce was overtly anti-Semitic in its ideas, and South himself in 1949 contributed letters to the *Limerick Leader* under his own name, denouncing sinister Judaic-Masonic influences he claimed were warping and corrupting the minds and morals of Irish youth, especially through the medium of Hollywood films.

South's funeral in Limerick was nonetheless a major event, and thousands of people paid their respects to his coffin at every point of its roundabout route from the Border where the RUC handed it over, to its arrival in his hometown. In Dublin, the hearse halted in Parnell Square for a group of priests to say the Rosary to which a large crowd responded,[2] and town and county councils throughout the Republic sent messages of sympathy to South's parents; nearly all the messages were voted for unanimously.

The other volunteer killed with South was nineteen-year-old Fergal O'Hanlon from Monaghan, and he too, of course, figures in another famous Republican song, Dominic Behan's 'The Patriot Game'. Like South, he was a Gaelic speaker, a keen Gaelic footballer

Malcolm Anderson and Eberhard Bort (eds.), *The Irish Border: History, Politics, Culture*, Liverpool University Press 1998, 113-25

and a youthful recruit to the IRA in his native county with its tradition of Republican activism. For many years after his demise, O'Hanlon's mother talked of his death as something exemplary and sacrificial and regarded any compromise on Republican aims as a betrayal of it.[3]

What happened at Brookeborough was that South's unit had planned to explode a landmine against the barracks wall under covering fire from their lorry. The mine Fáiled to explode and South's Bren gun had insufficient ammunition to match the fire directed at him and his men from the RUC inside the barracks. A ferocious fire-fight left South and O'Hanlon severely wounded. Semi-conscious and losing blood rapidly, they were driven at speed along minor roads to some farm buildings a mile or two away, but still on the Northern Ireland side of the Border, where they were left by the rest of the unit who made good their escape.

Years later, Maria McGuire, the young languages graduate of University College, Dublin, who made the world's headlines by her decision to join the Provisional IRA and to tour Europe's capitals seeking to buy arms for it, became close to David O'Connell, another participant in the Brookeborough raid. She recalled how he took her to Monaghan town to see a memorial there to O'Hanlon, who had been a close friend. He told her of his anguish at having to abandon him and South and of his fear at the time that the RUC would arrive to finish them off.[4] RUC officers did, in fact, arrive on the scene, and O'Connell heard a burst of firing at the byre where his comrades had been left. The likelihood is, however, that the RUC were taking no chances over entering the building and that South and O'Hanlon had already died from shock and loss of blood.[5]

O'Connell died in January 1991. He had been seriously wounded in an IRA operation, and spent eleven of his fifty years in prison for his part in the Republican cause.[6] Vincent Conlon, who drove the lorry used in the Brookeborough attack, has also died recently, in his case in June 1995. His funeral was attended by a large crowd in his hometown of Monaghan.[7]

Bungled and futile though the Brookeborough raid had been, it earned South and O'Hanlon their place in the pantheon of Republicanism's fallen heroes, and many Irish people clearly saw their sacrifice as something purer than the compromises and deals of their country's politics. It had also been intended as the centrepiece of an IRA Border offensive launched three weeks earlier on 11 December, which continued into 1962 and claimed the lives of twelve IRA members and six RUC officers. It brought back internment of Republicans on both sides of the Border and the mobilisation of 13,000 RUC 'B-Special' reservists by the Stormont government. The campaign also cost Stormont nearly £1 million in payment for damages, £10 million for increasing policing, and loss of capital investment in the province which is hard to quantify.[8]

Operations by the IRA began on the night of 11-12 December with a momentum which there were not the resources to maintain, around 150 volunteers attacking targets at ten different points along the border. Custom posts, bridges, transmitters and RUC and British army installations were all hit and for a time the RUC withdrew its night patrols in County Fermanagh, but this was mainly to re-group them and to strengthen the defence of its stations and barracks, like the one at Brookeborough.[9]

Bernadette McAliskey, as she is now, had some vivid memories of this period, living as she did at Cookstown in County Tyrone:

At that time it was quite common to hear the sirens beginning to wail at night, up and down, up and down, as it must have been for air raid alerts during the war. As soon as the sirens started, doors in our neighbourhood opened and our neighbours would appear, pulling on their heavy overcoats and shouldering their Sten guns. Most of the Protestant men in our district were B-men, or Specials - members of the civilian militia in Northern Ireland which was formed to fight the IRA. So, while some of my friends' daddies were disappearing into their houses to lie low, other people's daddies were setting out armed after them. At times like these the tragic division in Northern Ireland split even wider to set the Protestant working class against the Catholic working class, while the Church and the Catholic middle class Nationalists threw up their hands in horror at the freedom fighters and stood solidly behind the Government. The B-men were pretty busy in those days: not in Cookstown itself but beyond it on the way to South Derry where the land is poorer and the people, naturally enough, more Republican.[10]

The writer's father had died in August 1956, before the start of the Border campaign, and may, it can be inferred from her reminiscences, have had some earlier involvement in the IRA:

Just outside Cookstown and lying between it and Omagh, there is an expanse of useless bog land known as the Black Bog. Invariably the IRA seemed to head for it, and none of them was ever caught there. Yet there was no cover: the Black Bog is like heath. If a man were to run across it he could easily be seen. Perhaps they had a dug-out in it, or perhaps they lay flat in the bog for a whole day; but for whatever reasons, though the authorities put searchlights on it by night and sent helicopters over it by day, the Black Bog never gave up an IRA man. From our front bedroom window we could see, between two houses opposite, the beam of the searchlights travelling over the bog, and my mother used to stand there on alarm nights, looking across at the bog, and she would say: 'At least they'll never get your father now.' And even if we didn't know quite what she meant, we could guess.[11]

Big claims were made for the IRA's initial attacks, not least in *Pravda*, which in its 29 December 1956 issue disputed British dismissals of them as isolated actions without popular support. It saw the Border raids of that month as part of a much bigger picture: 'Irish patriots,' it declared, 'cannot agree with Britain transforming the Six Counties into one of its military bases in the Atlantic Pact.'[12]

The Republican movement itself was later to make equally large claims for what the first Border attacks achieved: 'Morale in our guerrilla columns was high and the campaign was fast developing into a national effort,' declared a Sinn Fein speaker at the 1964 commemoration rally at Wolfe Tone's grave at Bodenstown. This, of course, was more than two years after the campaign had been abandoned, and he went on, predictably, to blame the Dublin government:

It was they alone who forced the halting of the campaign in a shameless episode of treasonable collaboration and national apostasy for which they must one day answer to the nation that has been so unfortunate to have such traitors and time-servers in its midst.[13]

The Irish government's reaction was indeed one important factor in the outcome of the Border campaign but it is important, first of all, to consider the background to the IRA's decision to revert to armed action against Partition. Serious tension within its leadership had developed out of the Fáilure of the organisation's bombing campaign against British targets launched early in 1939. This was abandoned, as were operations within Northern Ireland for much of the war, but not before internment by both the Northern Ireland and Dublin authorities had put several hundred Republicans into captivity. Others were killed by the RUC, were executed, or died on hunger strike like Sean McCaughey from Auchnacloy in County Tyrone. When his death took place in Portlaoise prison in May 1946, his tongue was described as being shrunk 'to the size of a threepenny bit', and prior to his hunger strike he had survived four years' solitary confinement, two of them clothed only in a blanket. His funeral in Dublin produced an impressive turnout of mourners.[14]

The period after this, however, saw a significant revival of both political and military Republicanism, partly as a result of the release of activists who had spent the war years in internment camps, but also because of the way in which Partition and the national question returned to the centre of the Irish political stage. In February 1948, the Dail elections were notable for the role played in them by the Anti-Partition League which had been set up by Nationalist Stormont MPs and senators in a series of rallies held in sympathetic areas of Northern Ireland early in 1946. Its leadership was mainly provided by Catholic professional men and those in business in a small way, but it had some support from the clergy and made an impact with registration campaigns to maximise the Nationalist vote.[15]

It also sought support from the Irish nation as a whole, and in the Dail elections it sent a questionnaire to all parties and asked voters 'to support no party which does not pledge itself to give active and open support as a Government to the work of the Anti-Partition League ... including the giving of reasonable financial support and publicity.'[16] It also sent out circulars calling for meetings between whichever government might be elected and the League's executive 'to discuss what approach should be made to the British government on Partition.'[17] De Valera was willing to listen to the League but insisted throughout the election that his own Fianna Fáil party was still best placed to achieve a thirty-two county republic.

He and his party, of course, lost the 1948 election, in part because of the impact of a new Republican political movement. This was Clann Na Phoblachta, led by Sean MacBride, a lawyer and former IRA Chief of Staff, who believed the time had come to challenge the existing parties with a programme that was socially radical and which would keep Irish unification at the centre of its agenda. The claim has been made that the IRA directly supported the Clann's formation,[18] and it drew much of its support from anti-Treaty Republicans as well as from those who had been active in 1934 in the Republican Congress. Dissident Fianna Fáil members also joined it, and after two by-election victories in 1947, it had become a real threat to Fianna Fáil.

The Clann also emulated the First Dail with its demand that Northern Ireland MPs representing nationalist areas had the right to sit in the Dublin parliament. Its emergence at this time was perhaps the most dramatic break within the ranks of Republicanism since the founding of Fianna Fáil in 1926, and it was instrumental in ending that party's sixteen-year hold on power. The 1948 election gave the Clann ten seats in the Dail and thus the right to ministerial representation in a shaky coalition with Fine Gael and Labour.

MacBride, as External Affairs Minister, was able to persuade the coalition to pass the 1949 Republic of Ireland Act. This was really just a change of name, since the new Republic's territorial jurisdiction remained the same as that of the Free State, and its constitution was still that drafted by de Valera in 1937. Nonetheless, the political initiative had been skilfully seized from a leader and a party who, despite sixteen years in power, had not moved on from rhetoric to the active declaration of a republic. Ulster Unionist reaction was predictably enraged and in response, the Attlee government in London presented to Parliament legislation underlining Northern Ireland's continued membership of the United Kingdom until the Stormont Parliament decided otherwise.

This in turn brought a barrage of protest in the newly-proclaimed Republic. The coalition in Dublin had already formed an all-party anti-Partition group known as the Mansion House Committee. Fianna Fáil joined, though de Valera had little enthusiasm for any anti-Partition campaign which he did not himself control. His preference was for the larger stage provided by speaking tours of Britain, Australia, New Zealand and the United States, which he had embarked upon after losing office the previous year. To American audiences in particular, he addressed some of his most eloquent attacks on Partition.

Defending his country's neutrality in World War II before a Detroit audience in March 1948, the Fianna Fáil leader declared: 'Our territory was still occupied by Britain, and the injustice continued. You cannot ask a small nation to fight with you for justice when you are inflicting an injustice on that small nation.'[19] To a Boston audience, he likened partition to the brutalities of Soviet rule in Eastern Europe:

> If what is happening in partitioned Ireland today were being done in Eastern Europe by Russia, the people by whom it was being done would be entitled to ask assistance, and many who talk of democracy now would cry out against the injustice.[20]

The British Labour government's 1949 Act, strengthening - as it seemed to do - Britain's veto on Irish unity by transferring it to the custody of the Ulster Unionists themselves, added to the passion of de Valera's oratory, and the *Irish Press* newspaper which he controlled gave sustained coverage to his views. Yet, when he returned to power at the head of Fianna Fáil in the 1951 Dail elections, de Valera offered little more than ritual speeches on the national question, while the Mansion House anti-Partition committee was allowed to languish. Northern nationalists got little in return for their continued representations to Fianna Fáil on the matter of Partition, though at every Ard Fheis or conference, the party carried token resolutions condemning it, something it went on doing after once more losing office to Fine Gael in the election of 1954.[21]

Stagnant and ritualistic though Irish politics had been in the post-war period, there had been enough sustained rhetoric and propaganda on the issue of Partition to fuel expectations which, if not met, could lead to renewed violence, and the Republican movement was indeed re-grouping as its wartime internees were released, and began to return to political activism. Sinn Fein re-formed itself as a party, and the *United Irishman* was launched to support it. At the 1949 Bodenstown commemoration, a resolution was read out re-committing Sinn Fein and the IRA to expelling what was described as the 'invader' from Irish soil. The resolution went on to declare that '... to that end the policy is to prosecute a successful military campaign against the British forces of occupation in the Six Counties.' It was later re-worded to make it clear that such a campaign would exclude any hostile acts against the forces of the Dublin government and, in 1954, the Army Council of the IRA issued this as a Standing Order.[22]

In June 1951, the Army Council sanctioned a series of operations against army bases in Northern Ireland and mainland Britain, primarily to seize weapons and ammunition that could be used in a later and more sustained campaign. Some of these raids were carried out with a panache which captured the headlines, notably that on the R.E.M.E. depot at Arborfield, Berkshire, in August 1955, when the camp guard unit was easily surprised and overpowered, and 82,000 rounds of ammunition acquired, only for it to be quickly retrieved by the police as the raiding party dispersed.[23] Other raids earned heavy sentences for Cathal Goulding and Sean MacStiofan, who would later be key figures in the 1969 split within the IRA.

Republican activists and IRA members paid close attention in these years to the E.O.K.A. terror campaign by Greek Cypriots against British rule on their island. The *United Irishman* ran articles on the struggle there and indeed was still doing so as late as September 1971.[24] There was a big enough Greek Cypriot community in London for contact to be made with it, and the IRA had plans both to use E.O.K.A. expertise in guerrilla war and to help some of its members escape from British prisons. These were aborted by the conclusion of the 1959 London agreement giving Cyprus independence but not union with Greece.[25]

As almost always, the IRA was divided within itself about how best to develop its military strategy, and in November 1956, to coincide with Remembrance Day, a dozen attacks were launched along the Northern Ireland Border over a distance of a hundred-and-fifty miles. These were the work of a breakaway group led by Joe Christie, a maverick figure within the movement who had already been expelled by the IRA's Army Council. Christie, a product of a Christian Brothers schooling and a law degree at University College, Dublin, had been influenced by the E.O.K.A. campaign in Cyprus and favoured the bombing within Northern Ireland of dancehalls, pubs and cafes patronised by British soldiers, but found no support for this during his group's short-lived campaign.[26]

The original Army Council plan for a northern offensive incorporated, it would appear, plans to attack not just the Border but RUC stations within Belfast itself. However, in mid-November 1956, Patrick Doyle, a long-serving Belfast IRA man, was arrested there by police and was found to have on his person plans and letters relating to the forthcoming campaign, including attacks in Belfast. As a result, the Army Council abandoned the idea of operations there. All along, there had been doubts over this, based on fears of a likely Loyalist backlash against vulnerable nationalist areas of the city, and on doubts as to the IRA's ability to defend them.[27] Thus, the offensive launched on the night of 11-12 December was, from the start, essentially a Border campaign.

De Valera had for some time feared just such a decision by the IRA and had made a series of speeches, as well as writing *Irish Press* articles warning against it.[28] This fear was not rooted in pacifism but in practicability and the huge problems which would result from any imposed incorporation of the Northern counties. 'If you brought about the unity of this country by force,' he declared, 'you are condemning the government and parliament of this country to govern that area by police methods.'[29] He went on to argue that the methods needed to hold such an Ulster would be no different to those which the Ulster Unionist regime had resorted to after Partition in 1920.

The IRA, not for the first time, misunderstood and misjudged de Valera. Their leaders clung to 'the illusion that their simple promise to remain quiescent in the South would be sufficient surety'[30] for the Dublin authorities to ignore them. The power of this illusion led them to seek a secret meeting with de Valera in 1956, which some Fianna Fáil members of the Dail arranged, so that they might persuade him either to support or at least connive at a Border campaign.

> De Valera gave them not the slightest encouragement. He was indeed extremely forthright with them and impressed upon them his belief, often stated publicly, that partition could not be solved by force of arms. Their movement, he said, was bound to Fáil; it would cause great suffering without any visible weakening of partition.[31]

This was de Valera the pragmatist speaking, but his audience was made up of those already determined, in the words of Dominic Behan's song, to be 'part of the patriot game', whatever it might cost them.

Once the initial IRA attacks on the Border were launched, de Valera was quick to call upon John Costello, the Fine Gael Prime Minister, for firm legal measures against the IRA. This was politically dangerous for him, given his coalition's dependence upon Clann Na Phoblachta votes, and indeed it broke up on this issue, forcing another election which was held in March 1957. Sinn Fein candidates, despite their party's pledge not to enter the Dail, won four seats there and nearly 70,000 votes, proof of a significant measure of perhaps ambivalent support for the IRA, heightened by the powerful emotions generated by the recent funerals of Sean South and Fergal O'Hanlon.

De Valera, in his last general election as leader of his party, conducted a campaign little different in content from many others in which he had claimed that Fianna Fáil was keeper of the Irish people's conscience on the national question and Partition, yet to be trusted in power precisely because it would never countenance reckless force to bring about unification of the 'national territory'. Unionist newspapers in Northern Ireland in fact welcomed his victory in this election because, in contrast to his predecessor's response to the border emergency, he would be 'master in his own house.'[32]

This indeed proved to be the case, with the new government in Dublin acting promptly to restore to the statute book the Offences Against the State Act. By the end of 1957, a hundred Republicans had been arrested and held without trial under the authority of de Valera's government, while two hundred more were interned in Northern Ireland under the Stormont government's Special Powers legislation. The application of such measures on both sides of the Border is often cited, as one reason amongst others, for the failure of the IRA campaign.

Dr Conor Cruise O'Brien takes that view in a recent book in which he argues that both de Valera and Sean Lemass, who succeeded him in 1959, believed that, by its attacks along the Border, the IRA was simply usurping the right of a legitimate and democratic state to wage war. This view, he argues, was put into reverse by the weakness of the Lynch government in 1969 and 1970 when it allowed the IRA, especially its breakaway Provisional wing, to appear to be doing what the Irish state secretly and in reality wanted to do itself.[33]

The IRA campaign became increasingly sporadic as limited manpower was committed to attacks on mainly isolated RUC stations and off-duty officers. Every operation had to be judged against the vastly superior firepower which the forces of the state could deploy in its defence. These forces were also able to call on 4,000 full-time RUC officers and its B-Special reserve force of more than 13,000 men, as well as British army units based in the province which could be called out in support. Against this balance of strength, every IRA casualty mattered, so it was a disaster for the campaign when a four-man unit, recruited from both sides of the Border, was annihilated by the premature explosion of a landmine which it had been making ready in November 1957 to transport just a short distance into Northern Ireland from Edentubber in County Louth.[34]

Disputes within the IRA leadership about the continuing conduct of the campaign became an open secret as its minimal impact upon British and Stormont governments became apparent. Sean Cronin, who had returned to Ireland from a successful career as a journalist in the United States and had risen rapidly within the IRA to the point where he was responsible for much of the training for and preparation of the Border campaign, resigned from the movement in 1959 after an Army Convention had heard serious allegations against him. These included a charge of Communist sympathies which was never substantiated, but others left with him as the campaign lost whatever momentum it had ever had.[35]

The abandonment of the border campaign was announced by a re-constituted Army Council on 26 February 1962. Arms and equipment were to be dumped and active service volunteers to be stood down. One factor behind the decision was given special emphasis and that was the attitude of the Irish public 'whose minds have been deliberately distracted from the supreme issue facing the Irish people - the unity and freedom of Ireland'.[36] The way was now cleared for the ascendancy of a Dublin leadership dominated by Cathal Goulding and Roy Johnston, whose Marxist analysis of the Irish question and 'stages history', based on the need for Republicans to base their strategy on support for civil rights in Northern Ireland and broad-based campaigns on class issues in the Irish Republic by the mid-1960s, seemed to exclude any resumption of armed struggle in the immediate future.[37]

The ending of the Border campaign, it has been argued, encouraged a reformist element within Ulster Unionism to support Captain Terence O'Neill when he became Prime Minister in 1963 and embarked upon the hazardous exercise of seeking to give the Stormont state a more liberal image and to seek, too, a closer relationship with Dublin. Much has been made of the fact that this 'new departure' in Unionist politics would not have happened when it did if there had been significant support for the IRA within the province's Nationalist areas. Its absence has been described as:

> ... a declaration, by an overwhelming majority of the Catholic population of Ulster, that it was now prepared to forget the old hostilities and explore the possibility of peaceful co-operation within the partitioned state of Northern Ireland.[38]

That such a claim could be made was merely a reflection of the IRA's decision to limit its attacks between 1956 and 1962 to targets on the Border. Had their attacks provoked large-scale Loyalist reprisals against Nationalist areas in Belfast or Londonderry as well as ill-judged operations by the RUC and army, it is not hard to imagine the population identifying itself with the IRA as its protectors, as was to happen in 1970 and 1971.

Sam Thompson's play, *Over the Bridge*, written in 1960 for the Belfast Group Theatre amidst great controversy, was a chilling reminder to audiences of what just one IRA bomb could do to relations between Catholic and Protestant shipyard workers. Too much should not be read into the Fáilure of Northern Ireland's Nationalist communities to support or react to a campaign by the IRA which had very little impact upon them.

Even before the launching of the IRA's campaign, some Ulster Protestants, less elegant of speech and social style than Captain O'Neill and his supporters, were already voicing their fears of the Nationalist minority's growing support for Republicanism. In the May 1955 Westminster elections, Sinn Fein polled strongly in Northern Ireland, partly because the Nationalist party withdrew from any contests. The total Sinn Fein vote was over 150,000, the strongest expression of anti-Partitionist feeling in many years, and more than enough to alarm Dr Ian Paisley, a young Free Presbyterian preacher who was starting to make a name for himself.

Prior to the start of the IRA's first Border attacks in 1956, Paisley was among those invited to a special meeting at the Ulster Unionist party's offices in Belfast's Glengall Street. Many Loyalists who were to become major figures in the 1960s and 1970s also attended, and the meeting's declared purpose was to organise the defence of Protestant areas against anticipated IRA activity, as the old Ulster Protestant Association had done after Partition in 1920, often in its case by sending assassination squads into Catholic areas. The new body decided to call itself Ulster Protestant Action, and the first year of its existence was much taken up with the discussion of vigilante patrols, street barricades and drawing up lists of IRA suspects both in Belfast and in rural areas.[39]

Even though no IRA threat materialised in Belfast, and despite it becoming clear that its operations were being limited to the Border, Ulster Protestant Action remained in being. Factory and workplace branches were formed, including one by Paisley in the city's Ravenhill area under his own very direct control. Their concerns became increasingly the defence of 'Bible Protestantism' and Protestant interests where jobs and housing were concerned. As Paisley came to dominate Ulster Protestant Action, he received his first convictions for public order offences and, in June 1959, a major riot on the Shankill Road followed a speech in which he had with the more distant but still potent image of the IRA on the Border, and an increasing number of people were starting to listen to him.

> The cloud of infection hangs over the city,
> a quick change of wind and it
> might spill over the leafy suburbs.[41]

In his fine poem, 'Coasters', John Hewitt wrote this of events in 1969, but he could have written it a decade earlier.

By the time of these events which were beginning to set the scene for the Troubles that started in 1969, the IRA's campaign on the Border had lost whatever minimal hopes of success it had ever had. It had begun in January 1957 with two young IRA men clutching their rosaries and bleeding to death from terrible wounds in a lonely cow byre close to the Fermanagh border, and it ended in November 1961, for all practical purposes, with an equally young RUC officer having his head blown off in an ambush near Jonesborough, County Armagh. The IRA's penultimate 'success' prior to that was the seizure of another young constable, Norman Anderson, who had crossed the Border near Roslea, county Fermanagh, to take his girlfriend home late at night. His body was subsequently found on the northern side of the Border with thirty-four bullets drilled into it from close range.[42] The Border campaign was a brutal and futile business but it does have an important relationship to the long ordeal of Northern Ireland which began more than a quarter of a century ago.

Notes

[1] D Keogh, *Twentieth Century Ireland: Nation and State*, Dublin, 1994, p.219; also D Hannigan, 'Spiders Under the Stone', in *Fortnight*, February 1993.

[2] T P Coogan, *Ireland Since the Rising*, London: Pall Mall Press, 1966, p.280-81. For a report on the most recent Sean South commemoration see *An Phoblacht*, 11 January 1996.

[3] T P Coogan, *The IRA*, London: Harper Collins, 1995, p.313.

[4] M McGuire, *To Take Up Arms: A Year in the Provisional IRA*, London, 1973, p.25.

[5] Coogan, *The IRA*, pp.314-15.

[6] *An Phoblacht/Republican News*, 3 January 1991.

[7] *Ibid.*, 15 June 1995.

[8] J Bardon, *A History of Ulster*, Belfast: Blackstaff, 1992, pp.607-608; also Keogh, *op. cit.*, p.229.

[9] C Ryder, *The RUC: A Force Under Fire*, London: Octopus, 1990, p.90.

6   *An Phoblacht/Republican News*, 3 January 1991.

7   *Ibid.*, 15 June 1995.

8   J Bardon, *A History of Ulster*, Belfast: Blackstaff, 1992, pp.607-608; also Keogh, *op. cit.*, p.229.

9   C Ryder, *The RUC: A Force Under Fire*, London: Octopus, 1990, p.90.

10 B Devlin, *The Price of My Soul*, London: André Deutsch, 1969, pp.40-41.

11 *Ibid.*

12 Coogan, *The IRA*, p.305.

13 *United Irishman*, July 1964.

14 *Belfast Graves*, Dublin: National Graves Association, 1985, pp.53-54.

15 B Purdie, *Politics in the Streets: The Origins of the Civil Rights Movement in Northern Ireland*, Belfast: Blackstaff, 1990, pp.38-40.

16 J Bowman, *De Valera and the Ulster Question*, Oxford: Clarendon, 1982, p.205.

17 *Ibid.*

18 C C O'Brien, *Ancestral Voices: Religion and Nationalism in Ireland*, Dublin, 1994, p.134.

19 T P Coogan, *De Valera, Long Fellow, Long Shadow*, London: Hutchinson, 1993, p.639.

20 T Ryle Dwyer, *Eamon de Valera*, Dublin: Gill and Macmillan, 1980, p.132.

21 Bowman, *op. cit.*, pp.280-85.

22 Coogan, *The IRA*, pp.255-57.

23 *Ibid.*, pp.268-270.

24 'The Lessons of Cyprus', *United Irishman*, September 1971.

25 Coogan, *The IRA*, p.271.

26 *Ibid.*, pp.292-296.

27 *Ibid.*, p.302.

28 Bowman, *op. cit.*, p.289

29 *Ibid.*

30 J Bowyer Bell, *The Secret Army: A History of the IRA 1916-1970*, London: Anthonu Blond, 1971, pp.305-07.

31 The Earl of Longford and T P O'Neill, *Eamon de Valera*, London: Hutchinson, 1970, p.444.

32 Bowman, *op. cit.*, p.292.

33 O'Brien, *op. cit.*, p.160.

34 Coogan, *The IRA*, p.315.

35 *Ibid.*, pp.326-27.

36 *Ibid.*, p.329.

37 R Sweetman, *On Our Knees: Ireland 1972*, London, 1972. This has a useful interview by the author with Goulding. See especially pp.137-38 and 141-42.

38 C E B Brett, *Long Shadows Cast Before*, Edinburgh, 1978, pp.130-31.

39 E Moloney and A Pollak, *Paisley*, Dublin: Poolbeg, 1986, pp.78-79.

40 *Ibid.*, pp.83-84.

41 Alan Warner, ed., *The Selected John Hewitt*, Belfast: Blackstaff, 1981, pp.41-43.

42 Coogan, *The IRA*, p.329.

Unionists and the Border

Steve Bruce

Introduction

What do Ulster Unionists think of the Border which separates Northern Ireland from the Republic of Ireland?[1] What do Unionists think of what lies beyond that Border? In this brief essay I will offer some observations drawn primarily from my detailed research on Evangelical Christians[2] and Loyalist paramilitaries.[3] The extent to which either of these groups is representative (in the 'average' sense) of Ulster Unionists is contestable: Aughey certainly believes I have exaggerated the role of religio-ethnic identity in Unionism.[4] My claims for the importance of Evangelicals and gunmen are based not on their being ordinary but on them exemplifying characteristics which exert considerable magnetic pull on Unionists well outside the circles of those people who might sensibly be regarded as belonging to those camps. The gunmen clearly have an importance beyond their numbers by virtue of having guns but they are also symbolically significant because, in however debased a fashion, they represent the bottom line. In previous perilous times, Unionists have had to fight for their rights or have had at least to prepare to so fight. Although most Unionist condemn the particular actions of the present paramilitary organisations, many do so in ways which deliberately do not foreclose on the physical force option.

Similarly the Evangelicals possess an important strand of Unionist history, the influence of which can be seen, not only in the widespread support for Ian Paisley's Democratic Unionist party but also in the religious elements of Orangeism and the presence of leading Evangelicals in the Ulster Unionist party. It is not an accident that when the IRA murdered the MP for South Belfast (the Revd Robert Bradford, an Evangelical Methodist clergyman) in 1981, the seat was contested by the Revd Martin Smyth, an Evangelical Irish Presbyterian clergyman, and the Revd William McCrea, an Evangelical Free Presbyterian clergyman. While most Unionist voters are not themselves born-again Christians, Evangelicalism retains a vital role as an ideology which bridges denominational divisions, has an honourable place in the sacred history of Unionism, gives honourable reasons for being opposed to a united Ireland, and

Malcolm Anderson and Eberhard Bort (eds.), *The Irish Border: History, Politics, Culture*, Liverpool University Press 1998, 127-37

vouchsafes a degree of probity in those politicians who can claim to be motivated by it.[5]

The Ideological Centres

Images are often studies in contrasts. To understand how Unionists see the Border, the edge of their world, it is helpful to know what they see as its centre.

Unionism is not homogeneous. Not all Unionists think or feel the same way. But we can identify two important blocs within unionism: the rural Evangelicals, exemplified by the religious and political followers of Dr Ian Paisley, and the Protestant Loyalist working class, partly represented by the two Loyalist terror organisations: the Ulster Volunteer Force (UVF) and Ulster Defence Association (UDA). Each of these blocs has a geographical centre and in both cases, it is a very long way from the Border.

For the rural Evangelical the centre of the earth is Ballymena. The old Stormont constituency of Bannside is crucial to the recent political history of Northern Ireland. In January 1969, Prime Minister Terence O'Neill, who like most rural Unionist MPs had been returned unopposed for the seat since 1946, was challenged by the young Ian Paisley, who portrayed O'Neill's very tentative proposals for reform as a betrayal of Ulster. Paisley's 'Popular Unionist' party fielded six candidates, most in Belfast. Five were heavily defeated with the Ulster Unionist party candidates getting over 60 per cent of the vote, but in Bannside Paisley took 24 per cent against O'Neill's 29 per cent. A revolt within the Unionist party left O'Neill with a minority administration and he resigned. Paisley took the Stormont seat at the by-election and three months later he won the Westminster parliamentary seat of North Antrim. Since then he has built and sustained a massive personal vote which was barely dented by constituency boundary changes which removed almost a third of his electorate.

When the Popular Unionists were reconstituted as the Democratic Unionist Party, Ballymena was one of the first councils which it controlled. In the 1970s and early 1980s it gained renown as the site for some of the most bitter arguments about the opening of council facilities on the Sabbath.

Rural North Antrim owes its honorific place in Evangelical historiography not just to its recent role as the seat of Paisleyism. It also features in Evangelical accounts of previous times of peril for Evangelical Protestants. The great 1859 religious revival began in Kells, County Antrim, and was spread by rural Evangelicals to Connor, Ballymena, and Rasharkin before it had an impact on

Belfast. In 1912 it proved a strong recruiting ground for Sir Edward Carson's Ulster Volunteer Force.

For working-class Loyalists, the centre of the universe is the Shankill Road, which has such widely recognised status as the heart of the Union that people can just call it 'the Road' and everyone knows where they mean. The modern UVF is firmly rooted in 'the Road'. Augustus 'Gusty' Spence, who formed the 1966 UVF, came from the Shankill and his early recruits were drawn from the neighbouring streets, from the local Orange Lodge and from the West Belfast branch of the Ulster Unionist Party (in which a number of Spence's relatives were active). To this day almost every member of UVF 'brigade staff' has come originally from the Shankill (or from Woodvale, a small area of terraced houses at the west end of the Shankill) and many of the leaders of groups in the peripheral estates around Belfast had grown up on the Shankill before they were decanted to Suffolk, Dundonald, Rathcoole and Carrickfergus.

The same goes for the leadership of the other main Protestant terror group. The UDA was formed from a variety of local groups but had at its core the Shankill Defence Association and the Woodvale Defence Association. From its formation in 1971 until Tommy 'Tucker' Lyttle was arrested in 1987, the UDA's overall leaders all came from the Road. This dominance was slightly disguised by the main offices being on the Newtownards Road in east Belfast, but this was a by-product of a leadership challenge. In 1975, Charles Harding Smith, the main figure in west Belfast and nominally vice-chairman, decided to impose his will on the organisation by placing Andy Tyrie, the UDA's chairman and a resident of Glencairn, one of the Loyalist estates on the western fringe of the city, under 'house arrest'. Smith's men forced the editor of the UDA's magazine out of the Shankill Road offices at gun-point. Tyrie's captors do not seem to have had their hearts in their work and he escaped to east Belfast, where he set up the central office with the east Belfast brigade. Harding Smith was later the victim of two assassination attempts by his own people and left Northern Ireland.

Although there were active UDA units in the Village and Ormeau Road areas of south Belfast, and in east Belfast, almost half of the UDA's killings in the 1970s were the work of a group based on the Shankill. The UDA was organised in brigades: west, south, north and east Belfast, Londonderry, mid-Ulster and South-East Antrim. For most of the 1970s and 1980s, in a pattern which owed something to experience and something to Tyrie's preference for working with people he knew and trusted, five of those seven brigades were led by men who had grown up on the Road. When at the end of the 1980s, the UDA renewed its murder campaign, the majority of killings were the work of a gang based on the lower Shankill Road. In 1995 the Ulster Democratic Party (UDP), the political front for the UDA, opened an office on the Shankill. At the opening ceremony the brigadier of the west Belfast UDA said: 'You know, it's good to be back on the Road. This is where we belong!'

The place of the Shankill in Loyalist iconography (which, like that of Ballymena in rural Evangelical thinking, long predates the present Troubles) is ably illustrated by the following short poem composed by one of the 1966 UVF prisoners:

> I'll tell you a tale of a good old road
> A road that has won renown
> Down thru' the years of blood and tears
> For its Loyalty to the Crown.
> In every fight for our faith and right
> And wherever the Orange Cock crowed
> The first in the field and never to yield
> Were the boys of the Shankill Road.

Not surprisingly, Loyalists from other parts of the Province were never too pleased at what they saw as the arrogance of one small part of Ulster usurping the entire cause, but the fact remains that the imagined centre of Ulster Loyalism is the Shankill Road.

The Border Region

The attitude of Ulster Unionists who live in the greater Belfast area, North Down and North Antrim - that is, most of them - to their co-religionists who live in the Border regions - which in practice means everything west and south of Lough Neagh - is complex: a mix of respect, suspicion and derision.

The respect derives from the recognition that Protestants of the Border counties have suffered disproportionately. It is actually quite difficult accurately to quantify and compare levels of threat.[6] One can compare the grand total of fatalities for different parts of the Province but such figures gloss over variations for different sorts of victims. But then a sense of threat may derive from more than the actuarial reality for 'people like us'. Many of the casualties in Border counties have been British soldiers, not Ulster Protestant farmers. But such attacks are pointed reminders to Border Protestants of their vulnerability. It also seems clear from the reactions to Border murders that they have an effect beyond their numbers. The IRA murdering a Loyalist in Glencairn does not lead to the sectarian geography being re-drawn; the murder of a Protestant young farmer in south Armagh often means the removal of a whole family and further territory passing into Nationalist hands. No part of Northern

Ireland shrugs off its casualties but murders of Protestant men in the Border areas carry an extra emotional charge.

Recently a retired UDA brigadier from north Belfast attended a meeting in an Orange Lodge in Markethill, Armagh. As usual at such events there was a big spread of teas and sandwiches and cakes on a large table. One of his hosts had pointedly lifted up the table cloth and shown him the bullet holes in the table legs: the remaining marks of an IRA attack. The north Belfast UDA man said to me: 'You know, the Prods up here don't know the half of it!' On one occasion a UVF man introduced me to a Loyalist from mid-Ulster and, after he had departed, said, with almost a hint of reverence: 'He works for Henry Brothers!' Henry Brothers is a Magherafelt building firm that has frequently been the target for IRA assassinations because of its willingness to do work for the security forces. There is similar sympathy for the Protestants of Londonderry, who have now almost completely evacuated the part of the city that lies on the western side of the River Foyle.

But this sympathy seems abstract, an acknowledgement that the Border Protestants occupy a particularly honorific place in the community of Ulster Unionists but they are distant kin rather than neighbours and siblings. The retired UDA brigadier told me his Markethill story as though reporting his travels to the Hindu Kush.

Furthermore, the Loyalists of the big city seem fully to share the almost universal disdain that city people have for their country cousins. After the mid-Ulster brigadier of the UDA was arrested on racketeering charges, a once-senior figure from the Shankill Road was brought out of retirement to temporarily take over mid-Ulster. When I asked if there was a particular reason why he had been given the job, the Road man replied to the effect that: 'Well, I've worked down there before. I know these people. They're a bit odd. Very close.'

Sometimes the general disdain becomes focused on the particular accusation that Protestants from the Border areas are prone to disingenuously militant rhetoric. That accusation has been increasingly made in the last two years as the two small parties associated with the Loyalist paramilitaries had gone out of their way to distance themselves from the initial reaction of conservative Unionists to the 1994 IRA cease-fire and subsequent political developments. While the DUP struck the expected position of arguing that London was about to 'sell out' Northern Ireland, the Progressive Unionists and the Ulster Democratic Unionists sought to allay Protestant anxieties and to argue that the proposals in the joint Dublin-London 'Framework for the Future' were not as threatening to Unionist interests as they appeared. As David Ervine of the PUP (Progressive Unionist Party) put it: 'The proposals are as bad as it gets, they are not too bad, and with sound political work, they can be made a lot better.' Naturally this position took some selling (especially to members of the UVF) and PUP spokesmen addressed many meetings around the Province. In early 1996 a PUP spokesman addressed a gathering of UVF men and supporters in Markethill. There was only one vocal dissenter: a man in his late 50s whose son is a Free Presbyterian minister. Challenged to defend his attitude of being willing to talk to anyone, the PUP spokesman asked the dissenter what was his alternative. On being told 'Shoot the rebel scum', the PUP man retorted: 'Are you going to do the shooting or are you going to talk up a storm and then let some other bugger get the ten year gaol stretch?'

In the period since the cease-fire, a lot of media attention has focused on whether the UVF's Belfast-based command and political leadership could restrain the militants of mid-Ulster, whose leader has a reputation for being highly public about his murderous exploits. Though some are pleased that this one person's desire for publicity diverts attention from them, many UVF commanders resent the way in which he claims credit for much of the organisation's activity and implies that his unit is the elite of the UVF. Behind that particular source of friction is a more general source of resentment. One leading UVF man said: 'You know, he keeps giving us all this crap about "the loyal people of Ulster" this and that, which is fine for the punters but he even does it in staff meetings. You don't do that in front of your own people!'

Thus within paramilitary circles, there is considerable sympathy for the circumstances of isolated Protestant communities near the Border but there is also a lot of suspicion that the siege mentality breeds inappropriate and irrational responses and fuels a rhetorical militant bluster.

There are also subtle divisions within the world of Ulster's rural Evangelical Protestants. Those far from the Border tend to be more pietistic and less political. Border Evangelicals tend to be more militant than others in their Unionism, and more attracted either to legitimate outlets for self-defence such as the Ulster Defence Regiment or to illegitimate outlets such as terrorism. To give just one biographical example, Ian Paisley is thought of as being the most militant Unionist politician, but one of his Free Presbyterian ministers in Fermanagh, the Revd Ivan Foster, resigned from the DUP because he thought its policies too liberal. When, in response to the murder of Robert Bradford, Paisley launched his 'Third Force' in 1981, Foster led one of the few units that was at all active: he arranged a number of illegal road blocks and led a few patrols. He now edits *The Burning Bush*, a periodical which offers a combination of evangelical sermons and a commentary, often more ultra-Unionist than the DUP party line, on current events.

It is indicative of the close links between Evangelicalism and militant Unionism that the divisions within Loyalism and within Evangelicalism map on to each other. Non-Border Evangelicals are suspicious of their Border cousins for being too militant, too political; non-Border terrorists are critical of their Border colleagues for being too pious and too fond of the religio-ethnic identity rhetoric. In the 1980s, an Evangelical clergyman from close to the Border, who carried a legal handgun for personal protection, told me: 'When I attend clergy meetings in Belfast and Ballymena, I sometimes take my holster off and slap it on the table. You should see them jump!' The commander of the mid-Ulster UVF is clearly much more in sympathy with the politics of the DUP than with the socialist Unionism of the Progressive Unionist Party.[7]

The Success of Partition

If many Ulster Protestants relate to their co-religionists in the Border areas as though they were foreigners, what are Unionist attitudes to what lies beyond the Border? The simple answer is that most Unionists would like the Irish Republic to disappear and, to all intents and purposes, they manage to ignore it. Partition has been a complete success. Or at least it has been complete.

The division of the country meant that very many social institutions and every government agency (bar the Irish Lighthouses) was split. Only cartographers think that proximity is important. One needs to have a reason to travel to some place or even to notice it. Unlike gravity where the strength of the magnetic pull is a function of mass and proximity, social attraction is more cultural than physical.

This may seem obvious but sometimes the obvious needs drawing out. With Partition, Northern Ireland went from being the north-eastern part of Ireland (which, though its status was contested, was in its entirety British) to being a periphery of the British state with very little contact with the rest of Ireland. The centres of many important institutions and agencies lie to the east - in Britain - and not to the south. Central government is in London. While dramatic politics, the sort of thing they are aware of as 'politics', might force Ulster people to contemplate London and Dublin, mundane day-to-day affairs constantly draw attention to London and the British mainland. A news story about tax changes or movement in the housing market will feature London politicians and a variety of 'human interest' case studies drawn to represent Britain, not Ireland. There will usually be an Ulster angle added but the issues, individuals, places, and accents are British. Similarly in the world of work: far more companies in Northern Ireland are branches of

British firms than are linked to Irish companies. Staff move to and from the British mainland. Likewise in consumption: there are major stores and leisure outlets in Northern Ireland that are branches of Irish companies (Dunnes Stores, for example) but there are many more that are British. Despite considerable regional autonomy, the schools and universities are part of a British education system.

The point need not be laboured. For all that there are common interests that promote liaison north and south, this tends to be at a senior management level; most people in Northern Ireland inhabit a world which is *de facto* British. This background steady state can be modified. Nationalists can consciously select out parts of their world that connect them to the Irish Republic but equally well, and with less effort, Unionists can ignore those and construct a thoroughly British world to inhabit. And most do. They holiday in Scotland rather than Donegal. They watch football matches in Glasgow rather than Dublin.

What makes this selection easy is that the part of Ireland south of the Border has consciously engineered its own distinctiveness. From major changes such as giving a privileged constitutional position to the Irish language and the Irish Catholic Church, and promoting Gaelic sports, to trivial symbolic changes such as re-painting the telephone kiosks and letter boxes from British red to green or cream, the Irish state has worked at making itself different. Of considerable significance to the older generation of Unionists was Irish neutrality during the 1939-45 war. It is perhaps hard for us to think ourselves back into the culture of a world war but it is worth it to overcome the easy assumption that Ulster criticism of Irish neutrality is just another handy stick with which to beat the South. Although conscription was not introduced in Northern Ireland, the entire society and economy were mobilised in support of the war effort. Ulster was an integral part of a country fighting a total war. It should be no surprise that those citizens loyal to the United Kingdom and the Allies felt themselves further divorced from their southern neighbours. That their Northern Catholic neighbours were also part of that total war prevented it becoming a further source of division within Northern Ireland but it reinforced the psychological Border between North and South.

Add in the drastic decline of the Protestant population of the South since Partition. Fewer relatives means even less reason to visit. Add the 1950s IRA campaign, launched from the Republic and targeted mainly on Border areas. Add then the further reluctance to go south once the present Troubles had started.

For most Unionists, the south has not only been a distant country but also a hostile one. Its constitution lays claim to the north, its major political parties constantly re-affirm their republican credentials, its courts refuse to extradite terrorists, and its territory provides a relatively safe haven from which the IRA can launch attacks on northern Protestants. There remain Protestant institutions that straddle the Border: the churches are an obvious example. The Loyal Orange Institution is another. The important point is that, even within these institutions, the components in the Republic are viewed as foreign and exotic or foreign and hostile, but always foreign. Orange Lodges from the south are greeted in much the same way as Lodges from Ghana or the Mohawk Lodge from America.

Europeanisation?

Those commentators who have looked for signs of hope have often claimed to find them in those economic, social and cultural changes described as globalisation or, on a smaller scale, Europeanisation. The idea is that the increasing integration of economies and the gradual erosion of local cultures by globalised mass media should weaken local identities and thus weaken the motive for conflict. There is actually little evidence of this. Being equally pro-European Union has done little to decrease French or German attention to national interests. That their nation-state is part of the European Union has done little to weaken Basque or Catalan desire for greater autonomy. Globalisation has not coincided with a reduction of support for Quebec separatism. There is an interesting topic in the apparent failure of globalisation to undermine local identities but lack of space prevents me exploring it here beyond noting that the particular form of the European Union encourages nation-states to pursue their own interests by making them thoroughly conscious of the costs and rewards of membership.

If being good Europeans has not made the French any less French, how much less effect has the European Union had on those peoples who are not at all sympathetic to the Union's project. As with Unionist criticism of the Irish Republic's neutrality in the last war, an understanding of Unionist views of the European Union requires that we get beyond an initial reaction of supposing that when Ian Paisley denounces the European Union (founded by the Treaty of Rome!) he is trading on paranoia to see that there is actually a rational basis to Ulster Protestant dislike for the institution and its ethos. In fact there are at least three quite rational bases for such opposition.

The first is the most general one that any major change in political demarcations, constitutional arrangements and the distribution of powers will be to the detriment of Ulster Protestants. Once the whole of Ireland was British. Three-quarters of it had to be given away but the Unionist party had a clear majority at Stormont. But that too was taken away. It is hard for Ulster Unionists to see further changes in sovereignty as being anything other than a further weakening of their already precarious position. There is also a second specifically religious objection to Europeanisation. We may dismiss Paisley's view that the European Union is pre-figured in the apocalyptic parts of the Bible and still appreciate the essential truth in his vision of Evangelical Protestantism as a minority religion which - if it is already not too late - is on the verge of being swamped by a global culture which combines secularism and Catholicism. Partly because it is supported by a single institutional structure and partly because it is the majority faith of those European countries least affected by secularisation, religion in Europe, in so far as there is any, is the religion of the Catholic Church. There are very few pockets of Evangelical Protestantism left. Northern Ireland is one of them. Any increase in European integration must logically further weaken that last pocket of true Biblical Christianity.

In addition to those two background considerations there is the more obvious point that Europeanisation is a nationalist project. It is promoted heavily by John Hume who argues that the day of the sovereign nation-state has passed but is heard by Unionists as arguing that the day of the British nation-state being sovereign in Northern Ireland has passed.

Conclusion

Of course, there are Unionists who are familiar with the Irish Republic. Some members of the university-educated middle classes will holiday in the Republic. Some businessman have interests in the South. There is a class of cosmopolitan bureaucrats who are at home in Brussels, Strasbourg, and London and for whom Dublin is not the capital city of a very distant country. But very many Unionists have never crossed the Border, have no contact with the Irish Republic, have only hostile images of the South, and have no desire to do anything which might change those images.[8]

Notes

1   This is the text of a lecture to which source references have been added; hence its tone.

2   See Steve Bruce, *God Save Ulster! The Religion and Politics of Paisleyism* , Oxford: Oxford University Press, 1986: and S Bruce, *The Edge of the Union: the Ulster Loyalist Political Vision*. Oxford: Oxford University Press.,1994.

3   See S Bruce, *The Red Hand: Protestant Paramilitaries in Northern Ireland*. Oxford: Oxford University Press, 1992.

4   See Arthur Aughey, *Under Siege: Ulster Unionism and the Anglo-Irish Agreement*. Belfast: Blackstaff Press, 1989; Aughey's work is part analysis and part polemic. He believes that I under-estimate the importance of a new 'civic' unionism (represented, for example, by Robert McCartney MP for North Down, the Progressive Unionists, and some members of the Ulster Unionist Party), but it is not clear how much of that belief derives from hope that this is the case.

5   I do not hold the view attributed to me by John McGarry and Brendan O'Leary, *Explaining Northern Ireland*, Oxford: Blackwell,1995, that religion acts as an independent causal agent in the conflict in Northern Ireland. Rather I hold a view very similar to the one they now claim as a novel contribution to explaining Northern Ireland: that religion plays a major part in the substance and delineation of ethnic identity.

6   For excellent geographical analyses of the violence, see Russell Murray, 'Political Violence in Northern Ireland 1969-1977', in F W Boal and J N H Douglas (eds), *Integration and Division: Geographical Perspective on the Northern Ireland Problem*. London: Academic Press, 1982, pp. 309-332;) and Michael McKeown, *Two Seven Six Three: An Analysis of Fatalities Attributable to Civil Disturbances in Northern Ireland in the Twenty Years Between July 13, 1969 and July 12, 1989*. Dublin: Murlough Press, 1989.

7   He became involved with the UVF when young but withdrew after a short prison sentence. Before his return to the UVF fold, he was, in the Ulster idiom, 'good living' and acted as an Evangelical lay preacher.

8   One of the other speakers at the seminar, clearly more impressed than me by signs of change, cites the co-operation of some independent Unionist councillors in Derry with the SDLP leadership in the city council, councillors in the Republic, and Irish-American interests as evidence of a new spirit among Unionists. I think it is much more telling that the leading loyalist on the Derry-Boston Fund committee resigned because he was tired of being the 'token Prod' and that almost all Protestants have now moved out of the city side of Derry and relocated on the eastern bank of the Foyle or moved further east to Limavady and Coleraine.

Continuity and Change in the Cross-Border Relationship

Etain Tannam

Introduction

The significance of the Border between Northern Ireland and the Republic of Ireland is potentially affected by membership of the European Union. The meaning of state sovereignty and therefore of Borders would diminsh within a federal Europe. More practically, the EU, by sponsoring cross-Border co-operation in a Single European Market (SEM), would obviously have implications for the Irish/Northern Irish relationship. Thus, the EU is of relevance to the Irish/Northern Irish Border in that it may affect 'attitudes towards and perceptions of frontiers, particularly as instruments of cultural defence'.[1] Moreover, it may cause the development of 'practices of transfrontier co-operation'.[2] In this chapter, it is argued that the EU has increased cross-Border co-operation in certain areas of activity, although there remain obstacles to cross-Border co-operation.[3]

The chapter is divided into three sections. In section one the rationale for increased cross-Border co-operation is examined and the counter-argument that such co-operation will not occur is also proposed. In section two, the response of certain groups to EU initiatives is examined to determine whether cross-Border co-operation has increased. Business, local authority, civil service and political responses to cross-Border co-operation are examined.[4] Finally, in section three, the overall effect of the EU on the cross-Border relationship is discussed.

Malcolm Anderson and Eberhard Bort (eds.), *The Irish Border: History, Politics, Culture*, Liverpool University Press 1998, 139-57

The Rationale For and Against Increased Cross-Border Co-operation

There are two main reasons why cross-Border co-operation might be expected to increase in the period 1988 to 1994: the creation of the Single European Market (SEM), and the reform of EU regional policy in 1988.

The Single European Market

The Single European Act (SEA) included specific policy changes which were particularly relevant to the Irish/Northern Irish cross-Border relationship. The move towards the creation of a Single European Market (SEM) implied a degree of policy harmonisation between EU states and aimed to abolish economic boun-daries between states. The Single European Act's emphasis upon achieving an SEM by 1992 meant that poorer regions of the EU were threatened by the prospect of weakening economic performance, whilst their richer neighbours would benefit from the SEM. As peripheral regions of Europe, both Northern Ireland and the Republic of Ireland were faced by the potential threat of the SEM.[5]

In response to this potential threat, it was argued that businesses in Northern Ireland and the Republic of Ireland should join together to maximise their market and to exchange information on investment oppor-tunities. By increasing cross-Border trade and engaging in joint ventures, businessess on both sides of the Border could at least minimise the threat posed by the SEM and maximise their potential market. Moreover, the potential threat of the SEM was recognised by the EU's attempt to reform EU regional policy in 1988.

1988 Reform of Regional Policy

The negative effect of the SEM on the EU's peripheral regions was recognised by the Commission and EU member states in the 1988 reform of regional policy. A stronger EU regional policy was established to compensate the poorer regions of the EU for the losses they would incur. The Community Support Framework (CSF) Programmes, which were drawn up for the Republic of Ireland and Northern Ireland, and the Special Programmes, were financed largely by the Commission and had clear implications for the cross-Border administrative relationship. Rail and road links were to be financed between the east coast of the Republic and the east of Northern Ireland under the CSF. Similarly, special cross-Border programmes were introduced, which would not simply be back-to-back projects, but which had to be formulated jointly by two state authori-ties.

These programmes had to be overseen by a monitoring committee, which represented sub-national, central and Commission representatives. Consequently, EU money was ear-marked for Irish/Northern Irish co-operative schemes. Northern Irish and Irish policy makers and admini-strators were given the incentive to co-operate with each other if they were to receive EU aid. Overall, under Interreg, the EU-sponsored cross-Border scheme, 58 million Irish pounds was made available for cross-Border schemes with Northern Ireland.[6] Thus, there appeared to be strong eco-nomic incentives for increased cross-Border co-operation between Northern Ireland and the Republic of Ireland. However, it was also argued that in situations of ethnic conflict, economic incentives would have little effect on behaviour.

The Rationale Against Cross-Border Co-operation

The main argument against increased cross-Border co-operation is that in Northern Ireland, such co-operation has been perceived by unionists to be a form of unity 'through the back door'. By lessening the economic significance of the Border, Partition itself would gradually be eroded. Thus, cross-Border co-operation and the EU itself have been opposed by Unionist parties. For example, Ian Paisley stated in 1981 that:

> It is already noticeable how much of the EC's aid is channelled to cross-Border schemes ... The evil genius of political and eco-nomic integration that motivates the Common Market can be seen at work in the Dublin talks.[7]

According to Paul Hainsworth, 'European issues can be manipulated to serve partisan ends, even where the origins of domestic conflict have nothing to do with the Community.'[8]

The situation is described as one of 'partisan linkage' politics. Reactions to the EU and to cross-Border co-operation have conformed closely to nationalist and unionist ideologies. Responses have been entirely predictable. Nationalists have approved of cross-Border co-operation because it does not conflict with their aim of achieving a united Ireland and indeed may complement it. According to this argument, the EU has no effect on cross-Border co-operation, because it is subsumed under the traditional rhetoric of ethnic conflict. In the next sections, the validity of these two sets of arguments is examined, by analysing the response of the Irish and Northern Irish civil services, of business communities and of politicians to the incentives for cross-Border co-operation.

The EC and the Irish/Northern Irish Cross-Border Relationship: 1988-1994

Civil Service Co-operation

For the civil service there is evidence of only limited economic co-operation. There are areas of civil service behaviour where, rather than a common interest existing, there is in fact a conflict of interests between Northern Ireland and the Republic.

The number of cross-Border programmes and the consequent extension of cross-Border meetings between Northern Irish and Irish bureaucrats appears to provide evidence that the EU has had an impact on the cross-Border relationship.[9] Meetings on the newly formed monitor-ing commitees took place three or four times a year.[10] Moreover, particuarly at the time of negotiating cross-Border projects, telephone and other contacts were intense between a key group of civil servants in the Department of Finance in the Republic of Ireland and the Department of Finance and Personnel in Northern Ireland. For example, in 1994, the Ballinamore-Ballyconnell canal crossing the Border was opened, funded by Interreg. Its opening reflected close co-operation between a group of key civil servants on either side of the Border as well as between the tourism promotion bodies on both sides of the Border.

However, these meetings, informal contacts and flag-ship schemes provide the only substantial evidence of the EU's effect. In fact, the significance of the EU is weakened in a number of ways. Compartmentalisation of bureaucratic interests undermines cross-Border co-operation. Moreover, there are economic conflicts of interest between Irish and Northern Irish civil servants. There are political obstacles to cross-Border co-operation, unaffected by the EU. Finally, the level of EU funding for cross-Border programmes is actually quite small and thus less likely to have a significant effect on the bureaucratic relationship.

Compartmentalisation of Bureaucratic Interests

It is perhaps not surprising that there is evidence that not only each department, but each division within each department has its own vested interests and its own priorities. In short, there is a compartmentalisation of interests within the bureaucracies. Often, this compartmentalisation means that there is little co-ordination of cross-Border activities across departments and divisions and that knowledge of EU schemes is limited to specific clusters of civil servants. There is no widespread involvement in cross-Border schemes.

Clearly, there are various monitoring committees operating to administer cross-Border co-operation. However, civil service membership appears to differ on each committee, not merely according to department, but according to each division, or sub-division, of each department. For example, different civil servants work on the Leader scheme and on the Operational Programme for Rural Development and on the IGC Rural Development Steering Committee. This factor in itself is not a cause for concern as regards increasing cross-Border co-operation. There is no reason why compart-mentalisation should impede co-operation. However, the weakness of the administrative system lies in the fact that the effect of the EU on cross-Border civil service co-operation has been confined to those individuals who are directly involved in a specific scheme, i.e. on a handful of people within each relevant department. Thus, compart-mentalisation in this context minimises the breadth of cross-Border administrative co-operation. Perhaps more seriously, there is in fact a conflict of interests in some policy areas rather than common interests.

The Existence of Economic and Political Conflicts of Interests

For many Irish and Northern Irish civil servants, there are no short term benefits perceived to exist from engaging in cross-Border co-operation. In fact, in certain areas of civil service activity, Northern Ireland and the Republic of Ireland are perceived to be rivals, not co-operators.

There are a number of areas where economic conflicts of interest exist between Northern Ireland and the Republic of Ireland. Tourism is a case in point. There have been conflicts between both parts of Ireland over the promotion of tourism. Until the announcement of the 1994 ccasefire, Bord Fáilte (the Irish tourist board) detached itself from any association with Northern Ireland. Bord Fáilte feared that, because of the conflict in Northern Ireland, tourists would not visit that region. If the Republic co-operated in tourism with Northern Ireland, then the Republic would suffer from Northern Ireland's negative image. The Irish Department of Tourism was also keen to increase the number of visitors to the Republic. It feared losing visitors to Northern Ireland.

Yet another example of the existence of conflicting interests between Northern Ireland and the Republic is that of the Irish ports. The ports in Northern Ireland, in particular Larne, compete with those in the Republic, in particular Dublin. During the 1988 negotiations between Irish, Northern Irish and Commission representatives, a major difference revolved around the Commission's desire to invest in one port which would serve the island of Ireland as a whole. Larne was suggested as a suitable investment venture, but the suggestion was much opposed by the Irish delegation, because it feared that its Irish ports would lose customers to Northern Ireland. Similarly, any concentration of EU aid on Dublin port was an anathema to the Northern Irish.

Another area where contrasting priorities are held is in the field of transport. Here there are two main difficulties. The main one related in 1991 to the proposed Dublin-Belfast railway improvement scheme. Originally the Irish government proposed the improvement of the Dublin-Cork rail link, but then suddenly shifted to proposing that the Dublin-Belfast link be improved. The decision to improve this link was eventually announced in 1992 after considerable delay. The problem for the Irish government was not one of an absence of common economic interest with Northern Ireland, as much as a difficulty in choosing between various competing economic and political demands in a climate of economic recession. The scheme itself was too costly, according to the Department of Finance.

The existence of different priorities between Northern Irish and Irish civil services implies that there is no automatic link between specific cross-Border initiatives and spillover to broader cross-Border civil service co-operation. For many civil service departments, there are no perceptible short-term benefits to be derived from cross-Border co-operation.

The EU has not provided adequate financial incentives to overcome the possible losses which would result, for example, from developing Dublin port at the expense of Larne. Long-run efficiency becomes a speculative argument and it is short-term profit and loss which dominate civil servant thought. In the short term, Northern Irish and Irish civil servants perceive there to be losses for their regions in some sectors because of cross-Border co-operation. In these areas, Northern Ireland and the Republic of Ireland are rivals, not co-operators.

There is a general problem that the amount of money available for cross-Border schemes is relatively small to date (see above). Although the EU is vital to the Republic's economy, a small percentage of EC funds received is devoted to cross-Border co-operation. Hence, given that the numbers involved in each scheme are small and that the monetary value of each scheme is also relatively small, the potential for cross-Border co-operation is limited. Indeed, the inadequate amount of money made available for cross-Border co-operation, for the period 1990-1993, was mentioned also by Commission representatives who were interviewed.

Business Communities

In contrast to the case of civil servaice behaviour, business groups provide evidence that EU policy is affecting cross-Border co-operation. Businesses are reacting to the creation of the SEM, perceiving it to be both a threat and an opportunity. The increase in cross-Border co-operation is not visible across all sectors, but it is reflected by the increased frequency of cross-Border conferences and by the initatives of the Confederation of British Industry for Northern Ireland (CBI-NI), the Irish Business Employers Confederation (IBEC) and by the activities of the Chambers of Commerce.

Cross-Border Conferences

Despite the political conditions which on a practical level constrained Northern Irish business cross-Border co-operation, it was clear that the EU had a potential effect on such co-operation. Certain landmarks appeared to show that this potential would be realised: for example, in 1990 a cross-Border conference organised by the Institute of Directors in Northern Ireland.[11] The conference was attended by the then Irish Taoiseach, Charles Haughey. It was the first time that an Irish Taoiseach had crossed the Border in 25 years.

Another example of cross-Border co-operation was a conference held in the Templepatrick Hotel in Northern Ireland entitled 'Selling into the Republic'. Facilities were provided for 60 to 70 company representatives, but to the surprise of the organisers three hundred company representatives attended. Similarly, a conference in Dublin was well attended by business communities from both sides of the Border, many of whom engaged in 'networking' to find suitable partners for business. In particular, architects and engineers sought out Southern companies with the aim of making competitive joint bids for construction contracts abroad.

Apart from conferences on business cross-Border co-operation, prominent members of the Northern Irish and Irish business communities expressed their support for the idea of cross-Border business co-operation. In particular, the chairman of the Ulster Bank, Dr George Quigley, advocated the desirability of an East Corridor from Dublin to Belfast, which would gain from added investment and increased cross-Border co-operation. The East Corridor would then emerge in a sound economic state, ready to face the EU's economic threat and its opportunity. This theme is echoed, if not led, by the Confederation of British Industry for Northern Ireland (CBI-NI), the Irish Business and Employers' Con-federation (IBEC) and the Irish and Northern Irish chambers of commerce.

The CBI-NI, IBEC and the Chambers of Commerce

There are two key developments which appear to indicate a change in business cross-Border relations. First, joint initiatives have been imple-mented by the IBEC and CBI-NI and, second, proposals for increased cross-Border co-operation have been made by the Irish and Northern Irish chambers of commerce. Hence, in a new initiative, a Joint Council of both organisations was established to advance the aim of co-operation.

A joint steering group now operates, consisting of four con-federation members from either side of the Border. The steering group consists of the Director General and Director of IBEC, the Director and Vice-Chairman of the CBI-NI, business representatives from both sides of the Border and two especially hired full-time executives with responsibility for the cross-Border dimension. The steering group meets four times a year and the Joint Council, consisting of all members of the confederations who wish to attend, meets bi-annually. The development of trade is the key priority of the Joint Council initiative.

The chambers of commerce both north and south of the Border concur with the confederations' efforts to increase cross-Border business co-operation. In July 1990, a meeting took place in Dungannon, Northern Ireland, of all the chambers of commerce in the Border regions. These chambers founded the Gap of the North Association. The aims of the Gap of the North Association are to improve business contacts, to enter into discussions with state agencies and industrial promotion bodies and to establish a strategy of business promotion in the Border regions.[12]

Moreover, the Northern Ireland chambers of commerce invited the Republic's chambers to participate in consultations with EU officials in 1991. The chambers of commerce are also responsible for attempts to popularise the idea that Interreg should be extended to cover not simply the Border regions in Ireland, but the whole island of Ireland. The argument put by the chambers is that all of Ireland suffers from the problems of being peripheral to the extent that the Republic as a whole may be considered to be a Border region in itself.

Overall, there is evidence of increased cross-Border co-operation in the business sector. The SEM appears to be a key factor in explaining the confederations' and the chambers' strategy. However, there is also evidence of limitations to cross-Border co-operation in the business sector. However, these examples of increased co-operation are countered by more sceptical arguments about the likelihood and incidence of increased cross-Border co-operation.

The Failure of the SEM to Increase Common Interests between Business Groups

As in the case of the civil service, there are areas where common interests in business are not perceived to exist. It appears that business communities on both sides of the Border do not percieve there to be adequate gains to be made from cross-Border trade. Some interviewees commented that Irish/Northern Irish trade is not of potential benefit, because both markets are relatively small. Indeed, there is little statistical evidence to indicate the existence of increased cross-Border trade (see Table 1).

Thus, there is no increased cross-Border trade for the period 1988 to 1994. However, it is possible that such co-operation will evolve gradually in response to the CBI-NI and IBEC's initiatives. For example, latest figures show an increase in Irish exports to Northern Ireland to £719,721 million in 1994.[13] Similarly, imports from Northern Ireland have in-creased to £535,656 million.[14] However, it is too early to determine whether this increase is part of a trend or is, instead, a once-off response to the cease-fire, announced in the autumn of 1994. The response of Northern Irish political parties to cross-Border co-operation and the EU has been equally ambivalent.

Table 1: Cross-Border trade between Northern Ireland and the Irish Republic

	1987	1988	1989	1990	1991	1992	1993
Exports from NI to the ROI	377,367	391,616	488,989	500,122	496,201	468,168	419,152
Exports from ROI to NI	618,811	757,006	776,126	816,497	789,545	825,053	707,800

Figures calculated in millions of Irish pounds
Source: *Ireland in Europe: A Shared Challenge*, 1992, 40, and
Central Statistics Office, *Statistical Release*, February 1995.

Local Councils and Cross-Border Co-operation

Evidence of local government cross-Border co-operation falls into three categories: special cross-Border committees which provide a structured forum for cross-Border meetings and initiatives, the existence of joint studies and the rhetoric of certain local councillors who were enthusiastic about EU-induced cross-Border co-operation.

Special cross-Border committees have been established in both the Dundalk-Newry area (the East Border Region Committee) and the Donegal-Derry/Londonderry area (the North West Cross-Border Group) to advance the economic development of these economies. Although these committees were established before the EU's recent policy reforms, it appears that these EU policy initiatives have provided greater impetus for each committee's activities. In this way, the EU has increased cross-Border co-operation between local councils.

The North West Region Cross-Border Group comprises Derry/Londonderry city council, Donegal county council and Strabane district council and it has been given impetus by the reform of EU regional policy and by the creation of the SEM. The group aims to work together for the benefit of North West region as a whole. The argument is that as areas on both sides of the Border in the North West face common problems, they should join together to develop a common strategy so as to overcome these economic problems.[15] This logic of co-operation fits neatly with the argument that the EU has created incentives for cross-Border co-operation by not only providing money for such co-operation, but also by increasing the number of common threats and opportunities faced by Northern Ireland and the Republic. In this way, EU policy should provide impetus for the Cross-Border Group's activity.

In 1987, the same year as the signing of the SEA, a North West Study was commissioned by the British and Irish governments to develop a common strategy for the three regions, so as to overcome common problems. The study was partly financed by the Commission and it emphasised the need to build on shared strengths and to overcome peripherality. The study emphasised the need to build on tourism potential, to foster indigenous enterprise and to encourage development. It also emphasised the need to improve infrastructure. Interreg provided funding for the implementation of specific projects outlined in the study.

In April 1993, the North West Region Cross-Border Group office was opened in Derry/Londonderry to implement the recommendations of the North West Study. Again, the office is funded by Interreg. Similarly, the East Border Region Committee has been given fresh impetus by the EU. This committee was established in 1976 and it consists of members of four councils, two from each side of the Border: Newry and Mourne (constituting one council area); and Down (in Northern Ireland), Louth and Monaghan (in the Republic). Although the committee has been in existence longer than the 1987-1992 time span covered by this examination, there is no doubt that the chance to gain regional policy money from the reformed EU structural funds has aided cross-Border activities.

The committee meets every two months and has engaged in tourism studies, which are funded by the EU. Tourism too is at the heart of the joint proposals made to advance the economic welfare of the East Border region. The committees' work also involves the preparation of studies and necessitates joint meetings between councils on either side of the Border. Thus, the establishment of the committees, the resultant cross-Border meetings and the preparation of joint studies forms the core of tangible evidence that the EU has increased levels of local government cross-Border co-operation in the Donegal/Derry/Londonderry and Dundalk/Newry re-gions.

The criticism of the above optimism is that the cross-Border committees have been established in predominantly Nationalist areas. Both Newry and Derry/Londonderry councils have SDLP majorities. It is argued that here is less tangible evidence of cross-Border co-operation in Unionist-dominated areas. This fact would seem to confirm the argument that the EU can have little effect in a deep and bitter ethnic conflict.[16]

However, recent research shows that in fact, whilst some Unionists are likely to be more equivocal in their attitudes to cross-Border co-operation, many are supportive of cross-Border economic initiatives.[17] Thus, when asked if the relationship between Northern Ireland and the Republic of Ireland should be closer, 'the vast majority of Border councillors' agreed.[18] Ulster Unionist (UUP) councillors were evenly divided in their response to this question, whilst a majority of DUP councillors felt that the relationship was 'about right'.[19] Political aspects of co-operation were resisted by Unionist respondents and were thought to hinder increased cross-Border co-operation.[20] However, there was no overwhelming evidence that these councillors opposed economic cross-Border co-operation *per se*. Thus, partisan issue linkage politics is not an accurate description of local responses to cross-Border economic co-operation. Moreover, it is clear that party attitudes to the EU, if not to cross-Border co-operation, are gradually changing.

Political Parties and Cross-Border Co-operation

The Social Democratic and Labour Party (SDLP)

Not surprisingly, the SDLP reacted strongly and positively to the EU's cross-Border initiatives. It increasingly emphasised the potential of a European Union regional policy to advance cross-Border co-operation. In 1991, for example, the SDLP's leader, John Hume, stated that:

> Economic necessity underlines and underpins the idealistic reality of a united Europe ... the nation state has outlived its usefulness.[21]

The SDLP emphasised the desirability of a Europe of the regions, where the concept of nationalism is overrun by a supranational European state of regions. The SDLP pressed for the island of Ireland to be one region within this new Europe.[22] SDLP members also expressed enthusiasm for the East Border Region Committee and the North West Cross-Border Group.

The SDLP's response to the EU in the 1988-94 period is consistent with its political ideology. However, SDLP members argue that the EU is increasingly important not simply for the SDLP, but also for the Ulster Unionist Party (UUP), the Democratic Unionist Party (DUP) and for Sinn Féin.

Sinn Féin

In its 1992 Westminster election manifesto, Sinn Féin stressed that international organisations should be used to whip up international support for the Sinn Féin cause. As regards German unification and the EU, it argued that:

> The stated aim of both processes is to remove artificial barriers and restrictions on the movement of people and goods. German unification is underway. The partition of Ireland ... needs to be addressed in the same way.[23]

Thus, Sinn Féin concluded that 'the political and economic transformation of Europe' is a chance for Ireland to resolve 'its British problem and embark on a process of economic and political reunification...'[24]

In contrast, the 1994 European Parliament election manifesto was far more detailed.[25] In the 1994 manifesto, Sinn Féin was critical of the EU's economic impact and of its lack of democracy. The EU is criticised by Sinn Féin for failing to tackle unemployment, particularly in the Border regions. There is a separate section on the Common Agricultural Policy (CAP) and the need for regional development measures is stressed. Cross-Border development agencies are proposed for the Border areas.

Similarly, the Sinn Féin chairman, Mitchell McLaughlin, has called for a North West development forum and consequently has proposed amendments to local government legislation to make a new local development the agency accountable to local communities.[26] Not surprisingly, support is also given by Sinn Féin for the develop-ment of Ireland as one economic unit to 'exploit the Single European Market and the Structural Funds'.[27]

Support for cross-Border regional developmental agencies, whilst fitting neatly with traditional nationalist ideology, also fits the concept of a Europe of Regions, supported by the SDLP and the European Commission, and represents a modernised Sinn Féin approach to the EU and, hence, to cross-Border co-operation.

The Democratic Unionist Party (DUP)

The DUP's response to the EU's policy initiatives is more ambivalent than that of the SDLP and of Sinn Féin. On the one hand, DUP councillors have expressed a lack of concern about economic cross-Border co-operation, provided there are no political overtones. Economic cross-Border co-operation is not automatically perceived to be a form of 'unity through the backdoor' and the economic benefits to be received from the EU are recognised by UUP and DUP members alike.

Thus, cross-party co-operation occurs. SDLP, UUP and DUP Members of the European Parliament (MEPs) co-operate with the aim of maximising their receipts from the EU. For example, in a meeting with the British Prime Minister, John Major, in the aftermath of the divisive Maastricht Conference, both Hume and Paisley joined together to meet Major to express their discontent at Northern Ireland's exclusion from the new Cohesion Fund which would provide increased regional aid to the EU's poorest states.[28]

Moreover, the fact that Irish and Northern Irish MEPs share a common interest in defending their economies appears to be acknowledged by the fact that UUP, DUP, SDLP and Irish MEPs are members of the EU's Agriculture, Fisheries and Rural Development Committee. The Irish and Northern Irish MEPs work together on European Parliament committees. Informal discussions take place between these MEPs on committee matters.

However, there is also evidence that DUP responses to the EU have changed very little in the 1988-94 period. Although Paisley did sometimes speak on behalf of Northern Irish economic interests, he was by no means consistent in defending those interests. He mixed economic pragmatism with political rhetoric. His political rhetoric indicates that the EU is having a limited effect upon his attitude to cross-Border co-operation and to the EU. For example, in the European Parliament's debate on European Union, in the midst of Irish demands for increased regional aid, Paisley took a loftier angle:

> The true future of the nations in Europe lies in co-operation and not in incorporation. In unity, but not in uniformity. In national sovereignty, not in international submergence and in a family of nations, not in a federation of nations.[29]

The importance of EU regional aid emphasised at this time by Irish MEPs was not mentioned by Paisley. Similarly, in the Maastricht debate, Paisley expressed his opposition to federal union, but he did not mention the importance of EU regional aid to the Northern Irish economy. Thus, it is less likely that the DUP will respond to economic incentives for cross-Border co-operation and more likely that partisan issue linkage will occur.

For example, in the 1994 European Parliament election, partisan issue linkage was strongly evident when Paisley's campaign centred on DUP opposition to the Downing Street declaration of December 1993:

> It is vital the declaration is dealt an overwhelming death
> blow by a massive vote for Ian Paisley in this election.[30]

The central issues were stated at the launch of the DUP campaign as being constitutional issues and security issues.[31] European issues of the Single Market and CAP reform, in contrast, played a minor role.

As regards explicit cross-Border co-operation, Paisley was opposed to any contacts with the Republic of Ireland. Similarly, DUP councillors interviewed expressed opposition to the idea of any joint administrative boards with the Republic of Ireland, even if such boards exercised authority over purely economic areas of activity. For these councillors, business co-operation was acceptable, but a joint board to administer over a particular functional area was construed as being a form of political cross-Border co-operation and, consequently, was deemed to be unthinkable. Thus, overall, the DUP's attitude to the EU and to cross-Border co-operation has not altered significantly in the 1987-94 period.

The Ulster Unionist Party (UUP)

In contrast, the UUP's policy towards the EU has undergone change. The UUP's approach to the EU has changed quite obviously since the Single European Act and, particularly, since the UUP's current MEP, Jim Nicholson, was elected. The pragmatic emphasis on the EU's benefits has been highlighted by Nicholson.

The UUP's perception of the EU's importance is reflected by the fact that there is cross-party co-operation between Nicholson and Hume (as well as Paisley) to receive more aid for Northern Ireland from the Structural Funds. For example, Nicholson and Hume discussed the Northern Irish Structural Funds application informally at various times before the final application was made in summer 1993. Similarly, Nicholson and Hume joined in a delegation of 26 district councils to meet an MEP delegation from the Regional Affairs Committee. Hume and Nicholson had spent a year lobbying for their

European colleagues to meet representatives of the Northern Irish district councils.[32]

In line with this constructive approach towards the EU, the 1994 UUP election campaign centred on European issues. Despite John Taylor's plea to the party to turn the EP elections into a vote against the Republic's constitutional claim[33] and in contrast to the 1989 campaign's emphasis on the protection of national sovereignty, the 1994 campaign emphasised the importance of EU regional aid, transport measures, and agriculture.[34] The UUP pledged to protect Northern Ireland's economic interests, believing 'very strongly that Northern Ireland cannot be any further sidelined within the European context'.[35]

Among the issues emphasised by the UUP in their campaign was the need for local accountability and a voice for Northern Ireland at Council of Ministers meetings. The newly established Committee of the Regions was welcomed as a means by which Northern Ireland would be better represented in Brussels[36] and a regional administration is outlined as a broad UUP aim. Thus, the Paisley strategy of linking the EP elections to the Joint Declaration was resisted. The UUP no longer appears to link European issues to Anglo-Irish/Northern Irish issues. Cross-Border issues are thus less contentious under an EU umbrella. Overall, party responses to cross-Border co-operation have altered, signifying a weakening of partisan issue linkage politics.[37]

Conclusion:
Continuity and Change in the Cross-Border Relationship

The above overview of administrative, business and political reponses to EU incentives for cross-Border co-operation provides a confusing picture of the effect of the EU on Irish/Northern Irish cross-Border co-operation. Civil service cross-Border co-operation has increased in policy pockets, but there are institutional obstacles to more widespread co-operation. Business co-operation appears to have increased in certain ways, although cross-Border trade remains relatively low. As regards party behaviour, SDLP-dominated councils are engaging in co-operation with Irish councils, although there is less cross-Border activity between unionist-dominated councils and adjoining Irish councils. However, there appears to be broad support base for the idea of increasing cross-Border economic co-operation. Moreover, party approaches to the EU have altered, indicating a relaxation of partisan issue linkage politics.

Hence, arguably, the EU does have a role to play in the cross-Border relationship. Whilst there remain obstacles to co-operation, there is evidence that all actors in Northern Ireland respond to economic incentives and hence partisan issue linkage politics does not describe the EU's effect on the cross-Border relationship. Groups in Northern Ireland and in the Republic respond rationally to incentives for cross-Border co-operation and often such co-operation is impeded not by the politics of ethnic conflict, but by the economics of cost-benefit analysis.

Notes

1. Malcolm Anderson, `The Frontiers of the European Union', in Peter–Christian Müller–Graff and Andrzej Stepniak (eds), *Poland and the European Union: Between Association and Membership*, Baden–Baden: Nomos, 1997, pp.205–13; p.206.
2. *Ibid.*
3. The period examined in this chapter is 1988-94. Hence, this chapter does not examine the impact of the special EU peace package, announced in 1995.
4. The following material derives from interviews with civil servants, business people and local councillors, 1991-94. For reasons of confidentiality, I have not quoted these interviewees and have not named them. The arguments made in this chapter are those of the author only.

5   Etain Tannam, `The European Union and Business Cross–Border Co-operation: the Case of Northern Ireland and the Republic of Ireland', in *Irish Political Studies*, Vol 11 (1996), pp.103–29.

6   Etain Tannam, `EU Regional Policy and the Irish/Northern Irish Cross–Border Administrative Relationship', in *Regional and Federal Studies*, Vol.5, No. 1 (Spring 1995), pp.67–93; p.72.

7   Quoted in Paul Hainsworth, `Northern Ireland: a European Role?', in *Journal of Common Market Studies*, Vol. 20, No. 1 (1981), pp.1–17; p.10.

8   Paul Hainsworth, 'The European Election of 1979 in Northern Ireland: Linkage Politics', in *Parliamentary Affairs*, Vol.31, No.4 (1979), pp. 470–81; p.470.

9   Tannam, `EU Regional Policy and the Irish/Northern Irish Cross–Border Administrative Relationship, p.79.

10   *Ibid.*

11   Paul Teague, `Economic and Political Integration between the North and South of Ireland', in *Governance: An International Journal of Public Administration*, Vol. 7, No. 3 (July 1994), pp. 265–83; p.270.

12   Roy Donovan, Speech to CMN Conference `Business Co-operation in Ireland', Jurys Hotel, Dublin, 19 March 1992, p.2.

13   Central Statistics Office, *Statistical Release*, Dublin, March 1996.

14   *Ibid.*

15   North West Region Cross–Border Group, *Final Report*, Donegal: North West Border Group, 1993.

16   Brendan O'Leary, 'Solving Northern Ireland', in *Contemporary Record*, Vol.4, No.2 (1990), p.21.

17   Liam O'Dowd and James Corrigan, 'Buffer Zone or Bridge: Local Responses to Cross–Border Economic Co–operation in the Irish Border Region', in *Administration*, Vol. 42, No. 4 (1995), pp.335–52; p.340.

18   *Ibid.*

19   *Ibid.*

20   *Ibid.*, p.341.

21   John Hume, Speech to SDLP Annual Conference, 1991.

22   *Ibid.*

23   *Ibid.*

24   *Ibid.*

25   Sinn Féin, *Peace in Ireland: A European Issue*, Dublin: Sinn Féin, 1994.

26   *Derry Journal*, 18 March 1993, p.15.

27   *Ibid.*

28   Ian Paisley and John Hume, interview with RTE television, 21 January 1992.

29   Debate of the European Parliament, No.3412/114.

30   *The Irish Times*, 17 May 1994.

31   *Ibid.*

32   *Belfast Telegraph*, 10 February 1994.

33   *Belfast Telegraph*, 18 November 1993.

34   Ulster Unionist Party, *Europe: Making it Work for Ulster*, Belfast: UUP, 1994.

35   *The Irish Times*, 18 May 1994, p.9.

36 Ulster Unionist Party, *Europe: Making it Work for Ulster*, p.7.
37 Etain Tannam, `The European Union and Northern Irish Politics', in
    Ethnic and Racial Studies, Vol. 18, No. 4 (1995), pp.798–817; p.813.

Braveheart and the Irish Border: Ulster-Scottish Connections

Ullrich Kockel

Introduction[1]

As for many of my generation in mainland European countries, my first conscious encounter with Irish Studies, beyond a rather vague awareness of a distinctive literary and musical tradition, was through the primarily sociological examination of the 'Troubles' during my final years in secondary school. Although this taught me a lot about Ireland (and Britain, for that matter), the treatment prescribed by the curriculum, in the spirit of the times, concentrated on civil rights issues and, while not neglecting the historical dimension altogether, left the complexities of history to be unravelled at some future stage.

Nearly twenty years later, I found myself leading an EC-funded study of political culture in regions with contested borders, including Northern Ireland. At the same time, teaching undergraduate courses on Irish culture, I was frequently asked by students why, according to most accounts they had read, Ulster Protestants/ Loyalists appear caught in a 'time warp' (interestingly, nobody has yet asked me that question about the Nationalists). Applying Ernst Bloch's concept of acontemporaneities (*Ungleichzeitigkeiten*)[2] goes some way towards answering such questions, but not far enough, I fear, in this case. Perhaps a key to the problem can be found in a historical perspective that is not based on the common 'island-view', nor indeed on English notions of these islands as a separate continent. This 'island-view' was aptly illustrated by Patrick Hillery who declared in a speech to the UN Security Council in 1969 that the Irish nation was 'an entity which nature and history have made one' political unity of the island 'so self-evident as not to require argument'.[3]

The 'island-view' is rather less persuasive than Irish Nationalist ideology likes to suggest, although its separatist aspirations may be shared by supporters of the Corsican or the Sardinian case; to remain within these islands, the case of Shetland, the Orkneys or even the Isle of Man is far less clear, and, perhaps more importantly, that of the Welsh and Scottish nationalists would collapse completely if the 'island-view' were to be accepted as valid.

Malcolm Anderson and Eberhard Bort (eds.), *The Irish Border: History, Politics, Culture*, Liverpool University Press 1998, 159-73

A major shortcoming of this view of national territory is that it is based on late modern interpretations of salient geographical facts, and on a narrowly retrospective concept of history practically devoid of human agency, driven instead by metaphysical forces. In this essay, I would like to offer some tentative thoughts, based on observations and conversations during field work in both parts of Ireland as well as in Scotland, towards a different historico-geographical perspective. In the process, I shall take certain obscure ideas about Ulster to their speculative conclusion and see where that might lead us.

Ulster Protestant Identity

Recent years have witnessed a deluge of writing, both at the academic and at a more popular level, about the identity (or, indeed, identities) of Ulster Protestants. One aspect of this identity on which virtually all authors agree - whatever their disagreements in other respects - is that Ulster Protestant identity does not have a national foundation, and that, therefore, Loyalists are not nationalists. In his history of Loyalist ideology, Miller argued that while there could be no doubt as to Ulster Protestant determination to remain within a British state, this did not necessarily mean that this determination had its roots in the Loyalists' self-ascription to a British nation. According to Miller, none of the larger 'imagined communities' they could conceivably be part of, Britain, the United Kingdom, 'Ulster', or even Ireland, satisfies for the Loyalists all the criteria associated with a nation in the modern sense.[4]

The resurgence of Loyalist street culture in the 1980s, expressed in parades, murals and the like, is seen by Bell as indicative of a 'crisis of community and identity', and therefore as an essentially regressive aspect of popular culture.[5] Bell's case material is extremely interesting, and his analysis illuminating, but his approach still has much in common with the more or less psychologistic pathologies of the Northern Ireland conflict offered from various quarters. While the cultural resurgence among not only Loyalists, but also Nationalists in Northern Ireland can certainly be regarded as symptomatic of broader societal transformations with interesting parallels across Europe, and as yet another incidence of grassroots reactions against the 'malady of modernity', I have argued elsewhere that it can also be interpreted, somewhat more positively, as reflecting a process of re-negotiating an evidently contradictory framework of ethnic self-ascription, in other words, of seeking to resolve the problem of an apparent 'time warp', noted earlier.[6]

Much of the confusion arises inevitably from the Loyalist practice of calling themselves 'British'. As Miller has pointed out, it does not follow from this ethnic self-ascription that Loyalists identify with any 'British nation', which raises the question, what exactly do they mean by 'British'?[7] Would the designation 'Ukes' - Richard Rose's term - describe their identity rather better, awkward as this label may be? Is there, after all, such a thing as a 'British nation'? And if not, are the Ulster Loyalists 'British' for want of a better term only, or are they, perhaps, the only British people left in these islands?

Enter Braveheart

How does Braveheart come into all this, the Cymric noble who tried to rally the Norman lords of south-east Scotland in defence of a 'nation' created by the Gaels, against their fellow Norman lords from south of the Border, where many held lands for which they had sworn fealty to the Norman king of England? Or so the story goes...

My intention here is not the historical person of Sir William Wallace, nor Mel Gibson's ripping yarn about him. The film, along with such as *Rob Roy* or *Michael Collins*, the colourful commemoration of ethnohistoriographically constructed events produced by the heritage industry, and countless 'historical' publications, whatever their scholarly value, is evidence of the latest cycle of what Köstlin describes as the periodic ethnicisation of European societies during the final years of a century.[8] The Loyalists and Nationalists of Ulster are not alone. Across a narrow stretch of water, in Scotland, ethnicity and nationhood have ac-quired a new political potency. On a visit to East Ulster some years ago, not long after a public opinion poll on the constitutional status of Scotland had produced a figure of some fifty per cent in favour of independence, I noted with interest that a number of murals had been freshly painted, new ones added, all with the same message, summed up in the words displayed in one of them: 'Ulster and Scotland - united we stand' (Fig.1). And I wondered...

In the resurgence of Loyalist popular culture observed by Bell and others,[9] several tendencies can be distinguished, and two of these deserve to be highlighted here: the militant, and the conciliatory. The militant tendency is most visible in the murals, where certain 'Celtic' icons are appropriated, in particular the mythical hero Cú Chullain, who adopts the same pose as 'ancient defender of Ulster against the Irish', depicted on the Newtownards Road in East Belfast (Fig.2), as he does inside the GPO in Dublin's O'Connell

Figure 1   Loyalist Mural in West Belfast

Street, where he signifies the Easter Rising of 1916. On the fringes of this militant tendency, we find Loyalists to whom what lies across the Border is not at all a foreign country but part of their 'home' and 'heritage', a heritage which, from prehistoric stone forts to the Gaelic language, has been usurped by, and must consequently be recovered from, the Nationalists.

The conciliatory tendency also claims Gaelic and, especially, pre-Gaelic Ireland as its home and heritage, but emphasises the potential common ground which this creates, rather than interpreting it wholly antagonistically. Eloquent statements reflecting this tendency can be found in the writings of Ian Adamson and Michael Hall. A significant weakness of Adamson's argument, at least from a reconciliation point of view, is his insistence on the descent of Ulster Unionists from the Cruthin, an ancient people pushed out of Ireland by the Gaels. This idea has also been picked up in literature emanating from a Loyalist paramilitary background, as in the *New Ulster Defender* (Fig.3), a journal declaring itself dedicated to the cause of the LPOWs (Loyalist Prisoners of War).

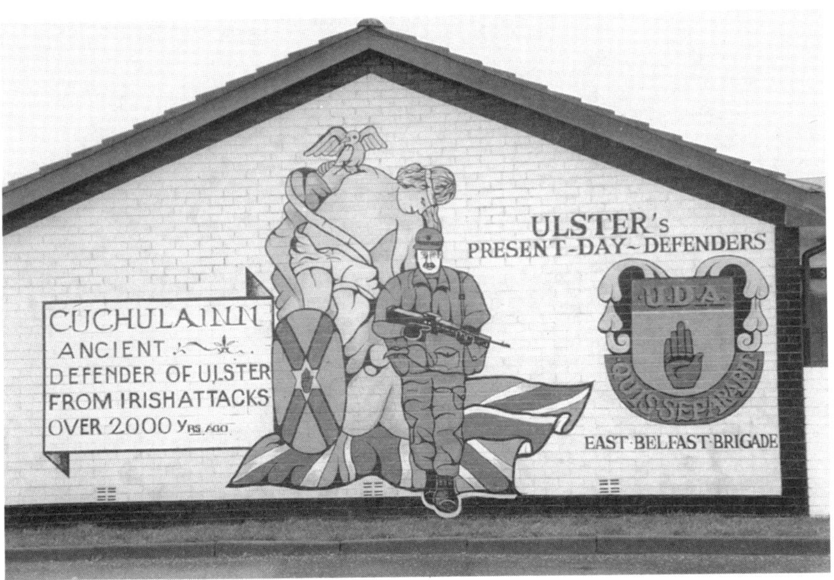

Figure 2   Loyalist Mural in East Belfast

On a partial reading of Adamson, one may well consider this 'we were here first' ideology as sufficient reason to reject the entire argument. But there are pointers here which are too significant in the present context, and neither the militant nor the conciliatory tendency should be readily dismissed for the liberties they take with history. If one followed these tendencies on a conceptual journey back in time, without taking their historiographical claims all too literally, it might just be possible to resolve some of the 'contradictions' in Unionist/Loyalist ideology, and to develop an understanding of their everyday historicity. This is not an attempt to 'understand the misunderstood', nor can it be, in the space of an essay, a full-scale examination of the topic. Rather, what I am trying to do here is to speculate, in outline, how the historico-cultural origins and ambiguities of an apparently split identity may be unravelled, not by reference to some objective foundation for an appropriate identity, which would be impossible to establish, but by looking at the problem through a different lens.

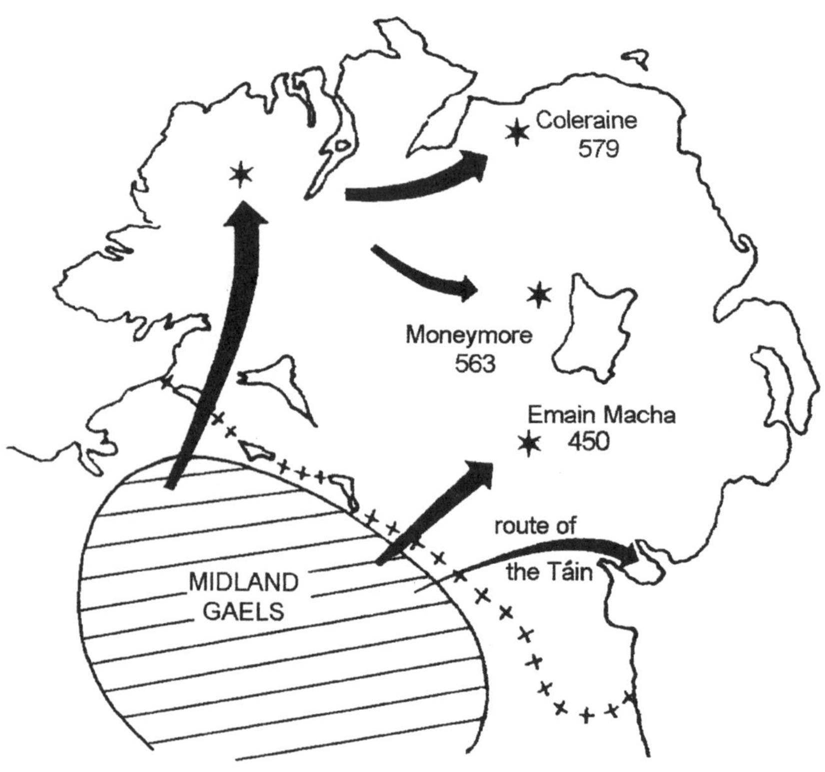

Figure 3 The 'Irish' Attack on 'Ulster' (Anon., 'A sense of belonging can take us beyond the religious divide', *New Ulster Defender*, 1, 6 (13 July 1993)

A Change of Perspective

In his study of *Banal Nationalism*, Billig reminds us that the bounded state is a relative novelty on the political scene.[10] Salewski's two-volume political history of Germany makes the same point more forcefully throughout the first volume, covering the medieval and early modern period up to 1815: the political boundaries of what may be called 'Germany' remained rather vague until the latter half of the eighteenth century, even though the Treaties of Münster and Osnabrück in 1648 had succeeded in carving up the German-speaking lands into moderately defined mini- and micro-territories.[11] Kearney's ingenious and stimulating *History of Four Nations* achieves a chronicle of developments in these islands which takes account of the almost forgotten fact that prior to the various Acts of Union, the only political boundary in this region of Europe that had ever been defined with any degree of clarity was that marked by Hadrian's Wall.[12]

A boundary of sorts between 'Ireland' and 'Britain' has been, rather conveniently, established by nature. The physical fact of the Irish Sea can barely be disputed, although archaeologists tell us that the first human settlers may well have walked across this 'lowland' to Ireland before the area was flooded. However, that does not make the sea as a political boundary any more plausible than lakes, rivers or mountain ranges on the European mainland. To argue otherwise would be a relapse into a crude environmental determinism that belongs squarely with old-style imperialism, regardless of any Left-wing pretences. The protagonists of such an ideology may do well to remember the lesson of the Rock of Rockall affair; those who define the boundaries of political jurisdictions even of island nations seldom accept a mere coast line as the definitive boundary of the state. Indeed, applying the graded system of international sea frontiers, with three-, twelve- and two-hundred-mile zones, one might argue that Britain is an off-shore island lying in Irish waters (or vice versa, which proves the quality and sensibility of the argument). Clearly, the insistence on physical geography alone is a line of thinking about borders which is unlikely to take us very far into serious discourse.

Perhaps we can suspend the material reality of physical geography for a little and, acknowledging that 'nation' and 'territory' are human constructs, speculatively lower the sea level on the Continental Shelf (leaving the English Channel in place as a defensive structure, just in case). We can then picture these islands and the surrounding lowlands as a single land mass comparable to the rest of Europe. Now consider the case of Poland after the Second World War (Fig.4). Over the last two hundred years, Poland has suffered more dramatic changes of national territory than perhaps any other country in Europe, this 'westward shift' being only the most recent realignment. The scale of territories involved in this post-1945 shift readily bears comparison with England, and indeed Britain, and the population 'relocated' in the process numbered in millions.

Why this digression into Central Europe?

Having speculatively lowered the sea level in North-West Europe, we can now see how political territories and their defining boundaries may shift and change over time, irrespective of any lakes, rivers or mountain ranges that remain as 'natural' boundaries. 'Ireland' and 'Britain' are no longer deceptively defined by their re-

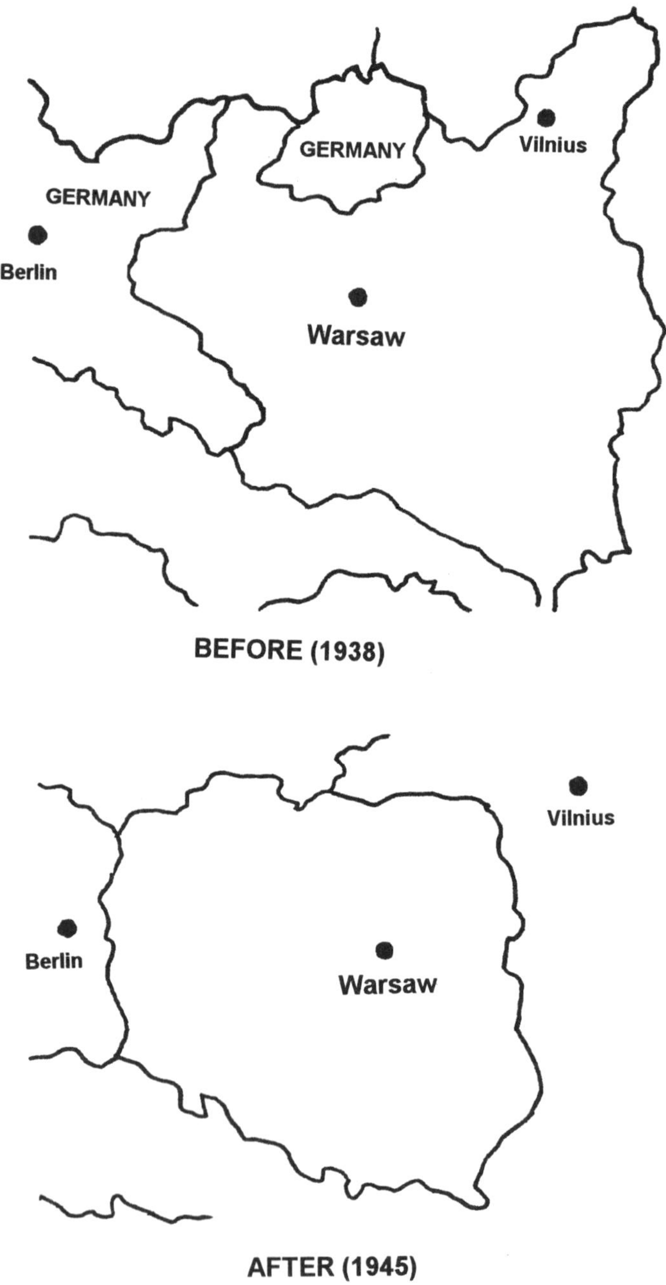

Figure 4   Poland before and after the Second World War

spective coast line, their boundaries become blurred even in the present, let alone in history.

Jackson quotes a text compiled in the early tenth century by the king and bishop of Cashel, Cormac, who wrote that

> [t]he power of the Irish over the Britons was great, and they had divided Britain between them into estates; ... and the Irish lived as much east of the sea as they did in Ireland.[13]

While Cormac's statement may be somewhat exaggerated, there is substantial evidence that the Anglo-Saxons, Danes and Norse were by no means the only people settling in post-Roman Britain. The Irish colonies in Wales and Cornwall became assimilated relatively soon, whereas the successful colonisation of what was to become Scotland - literally 'land of the Irish' - was well under way by the end of the fifth century. Colonists from Ulster formed the Kingdom of Dalriada (Fig.5), which encompassed territories on both sides of the North Channel, and in the ninth century their descendants came to rule as Kings of Scots over the entire territory to the north of the Forth and Clyde, their language and culture displacing that of the native Picts. In the tenth and eleventh centuries, the southern territories of what is now Scotland were added to the realm, and for this period, Jackson suggests that to a significant extent:

> Gaelic must have been spoken for a time not only in, for instance, Aberdeenshire and Kincardineshire and Fife but also as far south as the English border.[14]

Following the Norman invasion, and here Kearney reminds us[15] that the first people to be conquered by the Norman war machine were actually the 'English', by then a mixture of Celts, Romans and sundry North Europeans, Gaelic language and culture were pushed back towards the Highlands and Islands, where, as indeed in Ireland, especially in Ulster, North Connacht and Dublin, a Norse-Gaelic aristocracy rose to power. As the southern and eastern parts of both Scotland and what was now called 'Ireland' came increasingly under the sway of Norman Barons, the Gaelic ascendancy established a firm grip on the northern and western parts of both territories. Throughout the ensuing confrontation between these two very different social and cultural systems, the links across the North Channel remained strong, not least because, as historians rightly point out, transport by ship or boat was infinitely more speedy and comfortable than travel over land in the days before our present rail and road network was developed. The sea-based transport infrastructure of the Gaelic territories was, in fact, a major advantage in their struggle against a largely land-based war machine employing superior military technology and tactics, and a key factor allowing the resistance to hold out for as long as it did. Large polities like those of the MacDonald Lords of the Isles or the O'Neills in Ulster remained effectively beyond the grasp of Norman-dominated jurisdiction for many centuries after the so-called conquest (Fig.6).

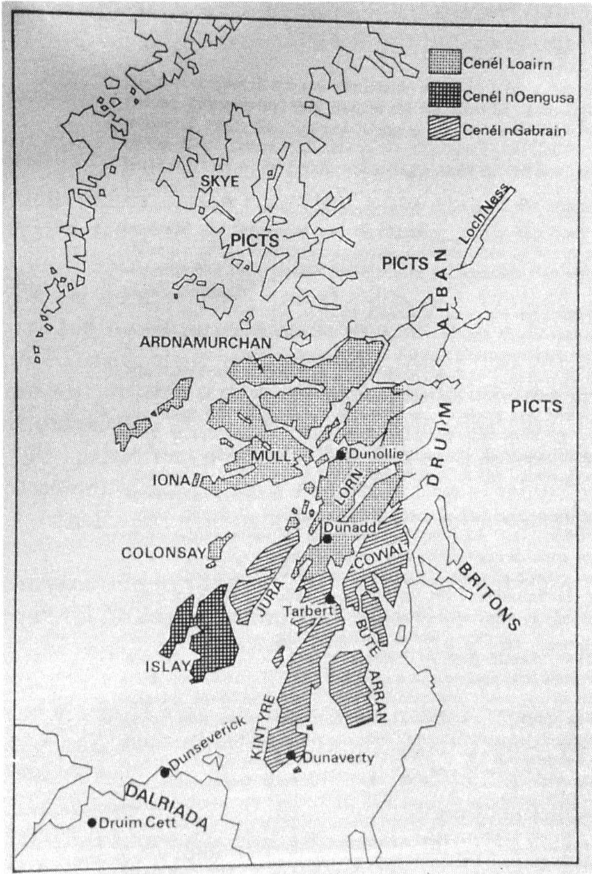

Figure 5   The Irish Kingdom of Dalriada

Quasi in parallel with the Anglo-Saxon conquest of England, there had been a Gaelic conquest of Scotland. And perhaps - research on this period is, unfortunately, far from conclusive - the movement of population associated with colonisation left the 'home' territories in a vulnerable position. Certainly, Anglian and Saxon territories on the mainland were subsequently settled by the Danes from the north and the Wends from the east. Perhaps Ulster, from where Scotland had been colonised, now attracted settlers from the south of Ireland who, in turn, left the southern flank of 'Gaeldom' weakened. This may go some way towards explaining the failure of Irish colonies in

Wales and Cornwall. Just as Anglo-Saxon political territory had moved to the west, with parts in what is now England and parts in what is now North-West Germany (remember, the English Channel, for strategic reasons, was exempt from being drained for this exercise), the Irish political territory can be regarded as having moved to the north, and across the North Channel.

Elisabethan worries about continued Scottish migration into Ulster are understandable, not so much as a Scottish attempt at plantation to parallel English efforts in the southern part of that island, but because it could be seen as providing reinforcements for the Gaelic stronghold across a sea that was still very much connecting, instead of separating both islands. In the wars of the seventeenth and eighteenth centuries, warlords like Alasdair Mac Colla were far from unusual, leading Irish mercenaries under Montrose and dying, tradition has it, near Mallow in the south of Ireland while leading a force of Scottish mercenaries. As late as the nineteenth century, the people of the Highlands and Islands were described by Lowlanders as 'Irish', and their language is known to this day by its Norse name, 'Erse'.

The Gaelic hegemony survived in the north-western parts of these islands, through various alliances, until 1746, and in some areas even beyond that date. In common perception, the battle of Kinsale (1601) marks the end of Gaelic Ireland, and Cromwell's campaign the completion of the conquest, but the last battle of Gaelic Ireland was fought at Culloden in 1746, and the completion of the conquest achieved only by the Highland Clearances.

Viewed from this perspective the 'real', Gaelic Ireland, if the term has any political meaning at all, describes a cultural hegemony which from approximately the fourth century onwards extended its influence from Ulster and, perhaps including the north of Connacht, into and across Scotland, while the southern part of the island, after abortive attempts to colonise southern Britain, came under Norman hegemony from a very early stage. Consequently, cultural aspects such as the by now well-documented interest that Ulster Protestants have historically taken in the Gaelic language become explicable, not as contradictions or 'false consciousness' - an arrogant term in any case - but as in fact perfectly logical in the circumstances.

In the space of an essay, it is impossible to review the details of Scots-English relations in Ireland during the two centuries or so when the final assault on the northern, Gaelic hegemony in these islands took the form of plantation, civil war and religious pogrom. Suffice it to say that throughout the period, relations were less than friendly, and the emigration of Scots from Ulster to the transatlantic colonies in the eighteenth century has long since become the stuff of which myths are woven, and in memory of which heritage centres are built and television series made.

Figure 6   Scotland and Ulster in the late medieval and early
modern period

The major geopolitical fault line in these islands was created by the conflict between a Gaelic 'Ireland' - 'Scotland' meaning nothing other than 'land of the Irish' - and an Anglo-Norman England. From this perspective, Ulster is being defended not against the Gaels as such, but against the (Anglo-) Normans and those Gaelic political interests who collaborate with them. Thus the Irish Border is a crucial part of a North-South divide which cuts across both islands, and the Unionists are holding out against the completion of the Anglo-Norman conquest of the island of Ireland, which is the ultimate hidden agenda of the Nationalist movement. Exactly to whom are the Loyalists loyal, then, and to union with which polity do the Unionists aspire?

Through the Union of the Crowns (1603) and Parliaments (1707), the 'Scots' nation was absorbed into a 'British' nation for which it supplied primary markers of ethnic identity at international level (like Bavaria did for Germany). The test of Unionist ideology would come with greater Scottish autonomy and, perhaps in time, independence. Would this give back to the Unionists the nation they truly belong to? Some indication of whether this speculative argument has any basis at all in everyday life could be gleaned from the reception of the film *Braveheart*, especially in areas of Northern Ireland with a strong Loyalist/Unionist local culture. Contributors to the H-Albion Internet discussion list for British and Irish history noted in 1995/96 that the movie had done exceedingly well in cinemas in East Belfast and other districts whose allegiance to the Crown is not normally in question. But which Crown, one might well ask...

A Nation Once Again, or: The Land o' the Leal

As a more or less distinct ethnic group, the Loyalists/Unionists originate before the rise of 'national' ideologies, and their 'nation' was absorbed in the process of creating a 'Great Britain' for which they supplied significant markers. The Gaelic hegemony never really succeeded in gaining nationhood in the modern sense. In Scotland, a Norman élite took over practically all key positions in the wealthier parts of the land from a very early stage. Thus they created a Norman state whose monarch accidentally inherited the throne of England, a state in which Gaelic culture became ever more marginalised, politically as well as geographically, pushed to the periphery, the Highlands and Islands, where it made its last heroic stance.

In Ireland, too, a Norman élite took over most key positions in the wealthier parts of the land from a very early stage, but here it failed to create a state of its own, perhaps because the territory taken over was much less unified to begin with. And here, too, Gaelic culture became increasingly marginalised, pushed to the periphery of Western Connacht and, especially, Ulster. The present state in the island of Ireland is no more founded on a 'Gaelic' nation than the state in the northern part of Britain which long ago took its name from the Irish. The Gaelic nation has, as yet, no state in these islands. Its people are now scattered far and wide, but their vanguard marches every year to commemorate sundry victories won by a Stuart king. Who knows, some of them may even have toasted Duke Albrecht of Bavaria, back in 1955...

Notes

1   As Eberhard Bort correctly remarked on hearing an earlier version of the essay, this is very much an exercise in 'thinking aloud'. Others who have allowed me to 'bounce off' my ideas about trying to put a different perspective on the Irish situation include Ian Shuttleworth, Mark McGovern and, of course, the participants in the conference which resulted in this volume. That they were prepared to discuss the perspective put foward here does not imply that they would subscribe to it, or any part of it. I am grateful for their questions and critical comments, and hope they will not mind too much that I heeded some and ignored others when putting it all in writing. For a fine example of looking at the history of these islands, and Europe as a whole, through a very different lense, I am greatly indebted to Carl Amery, whose novel *Das Königsprojekt* (München: Piper, 1974) I refer to at the end.

2   See U Kockel, `Mythos und Identität: Der Konflikt im Spiegel der Volkskultur', in J Elvert (ed.), *Nordirland in Geschichte und Gegenwart Northern Ireland: Past and Present*, Stuttgart: Franz Steiner Verlag Wiesbaden, 1994, pp.495–517.

3   Quoted in M Hall, *Ulster's Scottish Connection*, Newtownabbey: Island Publications, 1993, p.7.

4   See D Miller, *Queen's Rebels: Ulster Loyalism in Historical Perspective*, Dublin: Gill and Macmillan, 1978.

5   D Bell, *Acts of Union: Youth Culture and Sectarianism in Northern Ireland*, Basingstoke: Macmillan, 1990.

6   See Kockel, *op. cit.*

7   See Miller, *op. cit.*

8   K Köstlin, `Das ethnographische Paradigma und die Jahrhundert-wenden', in *Ethnologia Europaea*, Vol.24, No.1 (1994) pp.5–20.

9   See Bell, *op. cit.*

10   M Billig, *Banal Nationalism*, London: Sage, 1990.

11   M Salewski, *Deutschland: Eine politische Geschichte. Von den Anfängen bis zur Gegenwart*, Bd. 1: 800–1815, Bd. 2: 1815–1990, München: Beck, 1993.

12 Hugh Kearney, *The British Isles: A History of Four Nations*, Cambridge: Cambridge University Press, 1989; Canto, 1995.
13 K Jackson, 'The Celtic Aftermath in the Islands', in J Raftery (ed.), *The Celts*, Cork and Dublin: Mercier, 1964, pp.73–83; p.75.
14 *Ibid.*, p.79.
15 Kearney, *op.cit.*

Language and the Creation of Boundaries: The Irish Case

Máiréad Nic Craith

Ghosts are cruel,
And ghosts of suicide more cruel still,
To kill a language is to kill one's self[1]

Introduction

The creation of an international border in 1922 resulted in the pursuit of separate policies for Irish in both parts of Ireland. This essay analyses the ideological justification of British and Irish government strategies towards that language. It begins with a consideration of the vibrancy of the language in the nineteenth century and its significance in the quest for separatism. The impact of Partition on the Irish-speaking community in 1922 is then evaluated and the subsequent fortunes of the language, north and south of the border, are addressed. In conclusion, the current vitality of the language is assessed.

Irish in the Nineteenth Century

The census of Ireland is the principal statistical measure of Irish-speaking in the nineteenth century. For a variety of reasons, the figures returned are generally regarded as merely minimalist indicators of the nation's knowledge of Irish. The overall figures and percentages for the censuses 1851-81 are shown in Table 1.

Malcolm Anderson and Eberhard Bort (eds.), *The Irish Border: History, Politics, Culture*, Liverpool University Press 1998, 175-200

Table 1:   Knowledge of Irish as returned in the censuses of 1851-81

Language skills	1851 Number	1861 Number	1871 Number	1881 Number
Irish only	319,602	163,275	103,562	64,167
Irish and English	1,204,684	924,261	714,313	885,765
Total with Irish	1,524,286	1,105,536	817,875	994,932
Total population	6,552,385	5,798,967	5,412,377	5,174,836
Total % with Irish	23.3	19.1	15.1	18.4

Source: See G Fitzgerald, 'Estimates for baronies of minimum level of Irish-speaking amongst successive decennial cohorts: 1771-1781 to 1861-1871', in *Proceedings of the Royal Irish Academy*, Vol 84, C, no. 3, Dublin: Royal Irish Academy, 1984.

These numbers would appear to suggest a rather meagre knowledge of Irish among the general population in the nineteenth century. The reports of school inspectors and various proselytising societies indicate that the actual knowledge of the language was much higher than this.[2] (The apparent rise in the census of 1881 is due to the fact that this was the first census when the language question was actually included on the form rather than appearing as a footnote). There is no doubt however that, overall, many individuals at this time regarded the language as a mark of inferiority rather than a skill to be displayed in public.

Irish and the Quest for Separatism

Some agitators of Irish independence in the nineteenth century viewed the indigenous language as a negative rather than a positive confine. To these individuals, Irish had little symbolic value and was a hindrance to, rather than a component of, the quest for self-determination. Daniel O'Connell, one of the early nineteenth-century proponents of Irish independence, belonged to a strong Irish language tradition. As a child, he was fostered by an Irish-speaking family. English, however, was the language of his home and was to be his preferred medium of communication throughout his lifetime. Of the native language, he wrote:

> I am sufficiently utilitarian not to regret its gradual abandonment. A diversity of tongues is no benefit; it was first imposed on mankind as a curse, at the building of Babel. It would be of vast advantage to mankind if all the inhabitants of the earth spoke the same language. Therefore, although the Irish language is connected with many recollections which twine round the hearts of Irishmen, yet the superior utility of the English tongue as a medium of all modern communication is so great that I can witness without a sigh the gradual disuse of Irish.[3]

Not all politicians in the nineteenth century concurred with this positive view of the anglicisation process. The Young Ireland movement appealed to the language and to the Gaelic past to create a sense of nationality and unity. For them, language was a natural medium within which a nation defined itself. In the associated journal, *The Nation*, Thomas Davis appealed passionately for the restoration of Irish as an important element of national identity.

> A people without a language is only half a nation. A nation should guard its language more than its territories - 'tis a sure barrier, and more important frontier, than fortress or river.[4]

The Gaelic revival at the turn of the century prompted a new interest in the language. The founding of the Gaelic League in 1893 highlighted the cultural significance of Irish. One of the founder members, Dr Douglas Hyde, believed that cultural self-determination was at least as consequential as, if not more important than, political independence. He was anxious to separate the issues of political and linguistic independence and aspired to a non-political Gaelic organisation. This would ensure both Protestant and Catholic participation in the revival movement. Furthermore, it would safeguard the association against the wrath of the British government.

Unfortunately for Hyde, the concept of a non-political organisation was gradually abandoned. The League not only appealed to those who wished for a cultural renaissance. It also attracted many politically active nationalists. At a very early stage, the Irish Republican Brotherhood became involved and, gradually, Protestants became alienated from the whole concept of the revitalisation of Irish. As more political activists joined the Gaelic League, it became increasingly concerned with political rather than linguistic independence. In 1915, 'culture came to the aid of politics' and the organisation declared that the intention of political independence was as important as that of the revival Irish.

> In effect, the extremists confiscated the language, much as they had confiscated Gaelic games. By doing so, they identified the language and the games with a particular political ideology and thereby ensured that anyone who did not share that ideology or who was not willing to pay at least lip service to it would boycott them.[5]

Hyde resigned. Many Leaguers participated in the 1916 rising. Two years later the British government banned the organisation denouncing it as dangerous. Its meetings were declared illegal and those who broke the law by attending such meetings were liable to prosecution in court. Though the British government later retracted their prohibition, this action - in conjunction with that of prosecuting those who gave their names in Irish on official forms and correspondence - augmented the force of Irish as a symbol of separatism. The widespread perception was that speakers of the language were also those who sought political independence from the crown.

Despite the revival efforts of the Gaelic League, Irish continued to decline at the turn of the century. A measure of strength of the language in these years of Gaelic revival can be gauged from the census results of 1891-1911 (see Table 2).

Table 2   Knowledge of Irish as returned in the censuses of 1891-1901

Language ability	1891	1901	1911
Irish	664	620	554
Non Irish	2,805	2,602	2,586
Total population	3,469	3,222	3,140
Irish-speakers as % of total	19.2	19.2	17.6

Source: Statistics Branch, *Census of Population 1926*, Vol. 10, *General Report*. Dublin: Stationery Office, p.129.

There were some regional variations in the knowledge of the language. Table 3 shows the percentages of Irish-speakers in each province as returned in the censuses of 1891, 1901 and 1911. It is interesting to note that the language appears to have been stronger in the province of Ulster than in Leinster before the Border was drawn. A more detailed examination of this last census of Ireland shows that all counties with more than ten per cent Irish-speakers would be located in the new republic.

Table 3   Percentage of the population in each province who could speak Irish 1891-1911

Province	*1891*	*1901*	*1911*
Leinster	1.2	2.3	3.5
Munster	26.2	25.7	22.1
Ulster	5.2	5.9	6.1
Connaught	37.8	38.0	35.5

Source: *Census of Ireland*, 1911: *General Report*, London: HMSO, 1913, p.291.

Table 4   Counties where more than ten per cent of the population had a knowledge of Irish in 1911

Counties	*Percentage of Irish-speakers*
Clare	35.2
Cork	23.8
Donegal	35.2
Galway	54.1
Kerry	38.0
Limerick	10.4
Mayo	46.1
Roscommon	10.8
Sligo	20.1
Waterford	38.4

Irish in Saorstát Éireann

When the Irish Free State (Saorstát Éireann) came officially into existence in 1922, the restoration of Irish was undertaken by its government. Nationalist ideology steered the path which declared Irish as the first national language of the country. In the 1937 Constitution, it was pronounced the first official language of the people. The major aims of the new state were the maintenance of the language in the traditional Gaeltacht areas and the restoration of Irish in anglicised regions.

Some Irish-speakers viewed the restoration of the language as a means of removing the border between North and South. This, of course, was a matter of public debate. One commentator suggested that:

> of all the fallacies of the *Irish Times* and its likes, the most glaring is that the pushing of Irish will tend to stabilise Partition. I know my Ulster as well as any man in Ireland and I say in all sincerity that the surest easy of breaking the barrier between us and the Six Counties would be to make the Free State Irish-speaking. When the Belfast commercial traveller has to learn Irish in order to do busi-ness in Cork or Dublin, he will have learned to respect us at last; and until he does that, he will always be the ignorant bigot that he now is.[6]

For many in the new republic, the Gaeltacht individual was now indispensable as a symbol of Irish identity. This image had undergone numerous revisions prior to Partition. The Gaelic League, despite its promotion of the language, has never achieved the relevance in Irish-speaking areas as it had in anglicised Ireland. Its members were largely urban middle-class individuals who had attempted to reverse the image of the Gaeilgeoir (Irish-speaker) as a backward benign peasant. This was incongruous, however, with the wish to protect the Gaeltacht from the forces of modernisation and to preserve it 'complete with thatched cottages, turf-stacks, donkeys, curraghs and chimney corners'.[7]

The Gaeltacht Commission

Despite an apparent aversion towards internal borders, the Irish government set about the protection of Irish by the appointment of a Gaeltacht commission with specific aims. Firstly, it was to define the meaning and location of the Irish-speaking districts in the Republic. It was also to make recommendations regarding the preservation and en-hancement of the language in these regions. Preliminary meetings were held in March and April and invitations to tender evidence were issued to various bodies. Public sittings were held in Dublin in spring/summer 1925, and evidence was presented by thirty-seven individuals. Commissioners then visited various regions in the country between August and October 1925. All records of such meetings were kept in English. The report noted that 'difficulty was experienced in having oral evidence in Irish taken verbatim, and it was only found practicable to have an English rendering of such recordings in shorthand; accordingly, in respect of oral evidence given in Irish, the English renderings only, are presented.'[8] Consideration was also given to the returns on the census of 1911, and a special enumeration of Irish-speaking and partly Irish-speaking districts was carried out in July and August.

Having considered all the evidence, the commissioners recommended that where 80 per cent or more of the population had a conversational knowledge of the language, it would be regarded as an Irish-speaking district 'regardless of the extent to which English may have an ascendance in daily use under the circumstances of today'. In areas where 25 per cent or more of the population were Irish-speakers, it would be regarded as a 'Partly Irish-Speaking District' They furnished maps defining the Gaeltacht boundaries. They also supplied figures outlining the Irish-speakers in these regions as shown in Tables 5 and 6.

Table 5   Irish-speaking districts in 1925 as defined by the Gaeltacht commission.

County	Number of Irish-speakers	Irish-speakers as per cent of population
Donegal	42,319	88.6
Mayo	21,291	88.0
Galway	46,661	91.6
Clare	2,963	87.8
Kerry	21,890	89.3
Cork	6,877	88.1
Waterford	4,820	77.6
Total	146,821	89.1

Source: Coimisiún na Gaeltachta, *Report*, Dublin: Coimisiún na Gaeltachta, 1926, p.5.

Table 6   Partly Irish-speaking districts in 1925 as defined by the
            Gaeltacht commission.

County	Number of Irish-speakers	Irish-speakers as percentage of population
Donegal	6,921	32.3
Mayo	24,421	38.2
Sligo	879	45.5
Galway county	19,193	44.1
Galway city	5,375	46.9
Clare	13,764	33.7
Kerry	15,587	37.6
Cork	15,635	34.6
Waterford	8,072	33.5
Tipperary	738	59.2
Total	110,585	37.5

Source: Coimisiún na Gaeltachta, *Report*, Dublin: Coimisiún na
Gaeltachta, 1926, p.8.

When one compares these figures with the returns of the census
of 1911, an interesting pattern emerges. In the case of the Irish-
speaking districts, the figures returned in 1926 were considerably
higher than those returned in 1911. In fact, the only region in 1911
which would have qualified as a Gaeltacht lay in Galway. The variation between the two censuses was quite substantial. In the case of
Galway, for example, the 1911 census returned the proportion of
Irish-speakers as 82.4 per cent. In 1925, this had risen to 91.6 per cent.
In the case of Clare, the rise had been from 73.5 to 87.8 per cent.

In the case of the partly Irish-speaking districts, the opposite
pattern emerges. As perhaps could be anticipated, the 1925 figures
are lower than those of 1911. The returns for Waterford had dropped
from 50.9 per cent to 38.2 per cent. In Sligo, the percentage had
decreased from 58.3 to 45.5 per cent. In almost all cases, the decrease
in the proportion of Irish-speakers in these years was considerable -
except in the Tipperary region, where a marginal loss of 0.1 per cent
was noted. The sole exception to this pattern was Galway city where
the proportion of Irish-speakers rose from 37.3 per cent in 1911 to
46.9 per cent in 1925. The commissioners noted the strength of Irish
in this urban region and recommended its location as a unique
'intellectual rallying ground for the language'.

With regard to the status of the language in these regions, it was stated that:

> In prestige, the position of the language in the Gaeltacht is low. The influence of a hostile Government was thrown against it in the past; it was denied as a vehicle of education; it was ignored and repressed in administration. Generally, public representatives, businessmen, church authorities ignored it. The educated were ignorant of it; and they protected their position by affecting to despise it, or often despising it with conviction. Those who spoke it traditionally saw no avenue of advancement open to them or their children without English. Thus, it came to be accepted that the language was destined to pass.[9]

The location of official Gaeltacht borders was frequently reviewed in subsequent years, and in 1956 a Department of the Gaeltacht was established. A Gaeltacht Areas Order identified portions of Cork, Donegal, Galway, Kerry, Mayo and Waterford as official Gaeltacht regions. In 1967, two small communities in County Meath were included within the Gaeltacht boundaries. These families had originally been relocated from Gaeltacht communities in the west of Ireland. In 1974, the Gaeltacht regions in Kerry and Waterford were increased. Further extensions were made to the Gaeltacht regions in Cork and Meath in 1982. Throughout these years, the Gaeltacht regions were regarded as reservoirs for the preservation of the language and symbols of Ireland's cultural identity.

A Deficient Restoration Policy

Outside the Gaeltacht regions, the government adopted a policy of compulsion. Under Cosgrove, Cumann na nGaedheal made Irish compulsory for the public service and the armed forces. It was assumed that these services would soon be agents of an Irish-speaking state. The language was also designated a priority in the education sector and Irish-speaking teachers were introduced at every level. In 1922, a mere 1,107 teachers were qualified to teach through Irish. By 1943, 9,000 teachers were qualified to educate through that language; this represented two-thirds of the teaching force of the country. Financial rewards and other incentives were availed of to promote the language at the level of secondary education. Capitation grants were allocated to schools which operated through Irish. Special increments were awarded to teachers who used Irish as a medium of instruction. Additional marks were offered to students who answered examinations through Irish.

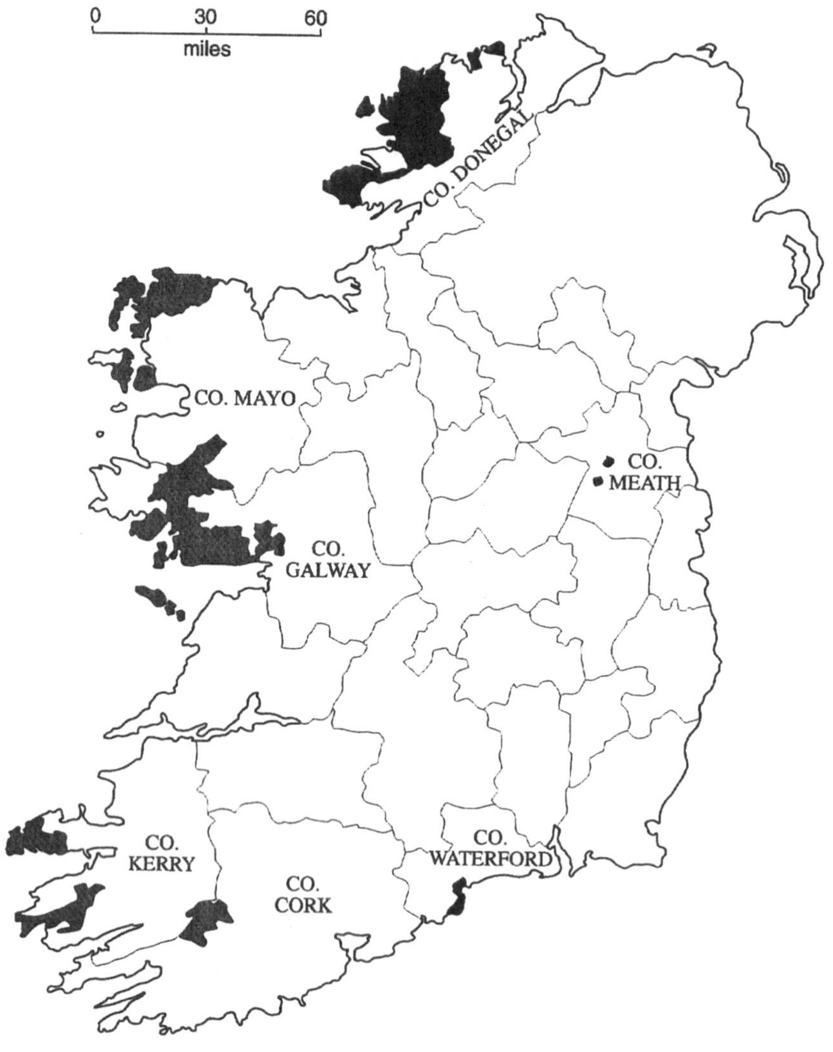

MAP 1:   Gaeltacht Regions of Ireland

Despite the various attempts at the restoration of Irish, the language was never re-activated as a normal means of communication throughout the entire country. Many reasons have been forwarded for this lack of total success. Colmán Ó Huallacháin suggests that the civil war in 1922 was almost as disastrous for the language as the Famine. Proponents of Irish became adversaries. Many leading figures, such as Arthur Griffith, were killed or excluded from the official decision-making process.[10]

The saving of the language was proposed at an individual rather than a societal level. De Valera had suggested that:

> Only one person can save the Irish language and that is the individual citizen ... If they could see the language as Pearse saw it, as the very breath of Irish liberty, they would themselves ensure, without more ado, its survival and its perpetuation.[11]

This assumed a wish of the Irish people to see their language restored as the normal means of communication. Many individuals, however, were unconcerned with a revival of Irish. In *The Colonizer and the Colonized*, Memmi suggests that this cultural schizophrenia, the co-existence of political nationalism and the colonial cringe in Irish people, has its roots in the colonisation process. He notes that this is a common feature in colonised countries whereby the colonised often, in succession or simultaneously, attempts to become different to what he is or to recover all the dimensions which the colonisation process tore away from him. MacSiomóin writes that, given their previous political dependency and material poverty, it was improbable that the native Gael would advance the cause of cultural identity. In summary, he intimates that:

> Irish was appropriated by separatist discourse, and then by the national consciousness, not as a means of effecting a definitive break with our colonised identity, or as the ultimate assertion of a decolonised identity, but as not-English, a symbol among other symbols of national difference. Irish, as symbol, is placed alongside games, dances and music in an equation that ignores the privileged ontological status of language in relation to reality and identity asserted in psycho-linguistic theory and much recent philosophy.[12]

The official designation of Gaeltacht areas has, in retrospect, been perceived as a failed attempt at 'freezing the language borders at a particular point in the geographical recession of the language'.[13] As the individual regions were geographically scattered, a Gaeltacht identity failed to emerge. Akutagawa suggests that the creation of these areas was primarily designed to fulfil the state's cultural objective. These regions would enable the rest of the country to become Irish-speaking. This Akutagawa describes as the 'cultural version of functional regionalism'. State activity in these regions was motivated by the interests of the nation rather that the goals of the region. Government policy, implemented from Dublin, aimed primarily at the maintenance rather than the development of the indigenous industry. In 1969, a Gaeltacht civil rights movement surfaced. This could have stimulated the emergence of a Gaeltacht identity. Their demands were, however, largely ignored. Table 7 illustrates the proportion and percentage of the official Gaeltacht in 1991.

Table 7   Irish-speakers, three years of age and older in the Gaeltacht areas of each county in 1991.

County	No. of Irish-speakers	Percentage with Irish
Cork	2,686	78.0
Donegal	17,574	74.7
Galway county borough	3,923	44.9
Galway	18,331	77.1
Kerry	5,945	76.3
Mayo	7,096	62.2
Meath	600	50.4
Waterford	1,035	79.1
Total	56,469	71.0

Source: Central Statistics Office, *Census 91*, Vol. 7, Irish Language. Dublin: Government of Ireland, 1993, p.54.

The census report of 1986 had noted that of the Gaeltacht areas whose borders remained unchanged between 1981 and 1986, only Galway actually registered an increase in the actual number of Irish-speakers. As the number of non-Irish-speakers here also increased during this period of time, however, the actual proportion of Irish-speakers declined from 80 to 75 per cent. During the five years 1981-86, all Gaeltacht regions had registered a decline in the overall proportion of Irish-speakers.[14] Little had changed when the results of the 1991 census were published. Although the Meath Gaeltacht had registered a marginal increase of 0.3 per cent, every other Gaeltacht had returned a decline in the proportion of speakers of Irish, and the total proportion of Irish-speakers in these regions had declined from 74 to 71 per cent.

Despite a decline in the proportion of Irish-speakers in Gaeltacht regions, elsewhere a rise has been noted. In particular, Census 91 showed that the number of Irish-speakers had increased by 53,129 or 5.1 per cent between 1981 and 1991. Table 8 illustrates the figures and percentages.

Table 8   Number and percentage of Irish-speakers throughout the country, 3 years of age and over, 1926-1991.

Year	Number	Percentage
1926	540,802	19.3
1936	666,601	23.7
1946	588,725	21.2
1961	716,420	27.2
1971	789,429	28.3
1981	1,018,413	31.6
1986	1,042,701	31.1
1991	1,095,830	32.5

Source: *Census 91*, p.17.

Despite the promotion of Irish in schools, many problems mitigated against the success of the language within the system. The state machinery was operated almost entirely through English, and many parents and teachers were unhappy with the prominence of Irish within the state system. This, however, has not inhibited a more recent renewed parental desire for Irish-medium education which has resulted in the establishment of many new schools. The current attention to the language in the media is increasing. At the time of writing, three monthly magazines and one weekly newspaper are published in Irish. One national radio service broadcasts entirely in Irish for 74 hours per week, and *Teilifís na Gaeilge*, the new Irish-language television service, broadcasts for some 21 hours weekly.

Many businesses now recognise the economic potential of Irish. Organisations such as *Gaillimh le Gaeilge* promote the fact that Irish is a cultural resource which is marketable as a tourist attraction.[15] Irish is now visible in the signage of many companies in urban regions. This appreciation of the language at an economic level has had the double beneficial effect of generating income at a local level, while reinforcing respect and esteem for the regional heritage. It is possible, therefore, that the ever-increasing role of Irish in the media and in the spheres of commerce and education will modify and enhance the public perception of the position of the language in society.

Irish in Northern Ireland

In Northern Ireland, the drawing of the Border had ensured a Protestant majority in the new state. Over thirty per cent of the population, however, were Catholic and nationalist. The latter community was largely dominant in the western regions and along the border. There were also some Catholic quarters in Belfast.

Many of these communities also had a knowledge of Irish. The 1911 census had shown that Irish had survived among five per cent or more of the total population in eight regions in the new state. Three of these districts lay totally within the new Northern Ireland state and had over a third of their population Irish-speakers. This Ulster Gaeltacht included the regions of the Sperrins, the Red Bay Gaeltacht in the Glens of Antrim and Rathlin Island off the north coast of Antrim. Furthermore, this new Northern Irish state had three areas along its Border, in which between five and twenty per cent of the population were Irish-speaking. Some twenty per cent of the population of the Strabane area on the Border were also Irish-speakers. In the area around Trillick in south-west Tyrone, about five per cent of the population were Irish-speakers. The overall county figures for the Irish-speaking in Ulster had been increasing with each census.

Table 9 illustrates that there had been a small rise in the percentages speaking Irish in Ulster during these years. In fact this was the only province in Ireland that witnessed a rise in the number of monolingual Irish-speakers in addition to an increase in the number of bilinguals with a knowledge of Irish. The general report noted that with the exceptions of Armagh, Cavan and Donegal, all the county and county borough areas had exhibited an increase in the decennial period in the number of their Irish-speakers.

Table 9   Percentage in each district in Ulster with a knowledge of Irish in the Censuses 1891-1911.

Region	1891	1901	1911
Antrim county	0.4	0.5	1.4
Armagh	2.4	3.6	2.3
Belfast county borough	0.4	1.0	2.0
Cavan county	3.0	5.6	3.3
Donegal	33.4	34.9	35.2
Down	0.3	0.7	1.2
Fermanagh	0.8	1.5	2.5
Londonderry county	1.8	2.4	2.1
Londonderry county borough	1.8	2.4	7.6
Monaghan county	3.3	7.1	7.6
Tyrone	3.9	4.3	5.3

Source: *Census of Ireland*, 1911: *General Report*. London: Her Majesty's Stationery Office, 1913, p.291.

A Unilingual Policy

The creation of a national hegemony commonly involves the promotion of uniformity of language. English was perceived as the appropriate language of citizens of the United Kingdom, and a policy of neglect of Irish ensued. The British government removed the language question from the Northern Ireland census. The magnitude and extent of the Irish-speaking communities could no longer be assessed statistically. Irish-speakers north of the Border were isolated from those in the Republic. Within twelve months, the Gaelic League ceased to function in the south of Ulster. In 1923, the League's organiser for the province had to escape from the Six Counties and subsequently resigned his position. The League was later to re-emerge in the form of *Comhaltas Uladh de Chonradh na Gaeilge*.

In his analysis of the language issue in Northern Ireland, Liam McAndrews pinpoints various episodes throughout the following decades which illustrate the UK government's animosity towards Irish. In August of 1945, for example, Harold Midgley, who was later to become a Minister of Education, made the following attack on the language:

> There are those people who believe they have the supreme and
> heaven sent duty of trying to breathe the breath of life into the
> dry bones of a dead nationalism that can serve no effective
> purpose, and who believe as part of this policy that they ought
> to waste the time and belittle the intelligence of the community
> in trying to revive a language that has no value whatever from
> a world point of view.[16]

Some two weeks later, when the Nationalist MP Eddie McAteer
spoke Irish in Parliament, he was interrupted by Basil Brooke, the
Prime Minister, and S H Hall-Thompson, the Minister of Education,
with shouts of 'no foreign language here'.[17] McAteer was forbidden
to speak further in Parliament in Irish.

More recently, in 1987, when a newly appointed Sinn Féin councillor attempted to use Irish at a meeting of Belfast city council,
Sammy Wilson, an Ulster unionist councillor, immediately called for
a vote. His oft-quoted comment at the time was: 'There'll be no
leprechaun language here'. The vote to continue the council's
unilingual policy was carried by 20 to 13, and the challenging
councillor was prevented from attending the rest of the meeting.

Nationalism, Catholicism and Irish

Symbolically, the language has remained a crucial aspect of their
identity for many of those learning Irish and perhaps the tenacity of
the language is related to both the survival of nationalism and a
recently renewed assertion of ethnic identity. The Catholic community has expanded numerically since the drawing of the Border and
now represents over forty per cent of the population. Nationalism
has become increasingly diverse and intense. Todd and Ruane
suggest that the persistence of nationalism here is related to the
interaction of economic, political and cultural peripherality, unresolved colonial tensions and nationalist ideology. The intensi-
fication of nationalism in recent decades has expressed itself in a
new assertion of ethnic identity, and in some cases in increased
violence. The civil rights struggle in the late 1960s and early 1970s
rekindled a new consciousness about the language. One activist
stated that:

> When the men in the H-Blocks of Long Kesh and the women in
> Armagh prison were stripped of everything, they discovered
> that they could not be stripped of their language. It became a
> means of resistance, of asserting their dignity and identity. In
> the H-Blocks, with no books, no paper, no pens, no pro-
> fessional teachers, young men living in filthy conditions,

frequently beaten, stripped naked ... but unbowed, taught each other Irish by shouting lessons from cell to cell. And as one hunger strike was followed by the other the people outside learned these lessons also and they determined to carry on the cultural struggle, each one from where s/he was.[18]

In his assessment of the importance of Irish, Gerry Adams, in the tradition of the romantic movement, states that language is the means by which we filter our response to the world. It reflects the history, emotions and philosophy of the Irish people for two thousand years. If the language were allowed to die, he believes that the Irish worldview would also be lost. Adams views the language as a natural boundary and suggests that it is 'the "frontier" against our submergence by a West British, shoneen ethos or by a rampant Anglo-American "Rambo" ethos.'[19] He identifies the restoration of Irish as critical to the political struggle for independence:

> Some people talk about 'preserving' the language: it is as if it was something to be kept as an archaic object to be brought out occasionally and to be shown to tourists. It is a notion of 'jam-jar' Irish. My own conviction is that the restoration of our culture must be a crucial part of our political struggle and that the restoration of the Irish language must be a central part of the cultural struggle.[20]

Gerry Adams believes that Irish is incompatible with a Unionist mentality. He says that 'for the Protestant people to embrace the Irish language today would be for them to reject loyalism'.[21] This is a problem addressed by Aodán Mac Póilín who suggests that there is no simple solution to this tension. He says that:

> not all those who claim that the language is equally the heritage of nationalists and unionists have worked out the implications of this principle. This problem arises from the fact that the cultural commitment of many Irish-speakers is inseparable from their political allegiance. Although this is a perfectly justifiable ideological position, it is often accompanied by the unfounded assumption that unionists interested in Irish culture are well on their way to becoming Irish nationalists, an assumption supported by the fact that there are indeed a number of Protestant nationalists who take an interest in Irish. This unresolved conflict between principles which claim to be non-political, and assumptions which are essentially political in their implications is largely unconscious. Unionists, however, are profoundly sensitive to these assumptions and often resentful of them.[22]

Many Unionists and/or Protestants in the North would reject the view of Irish as a political or religious divide. Twenty years ago, at the beginning of the Troubles, a Belfast Orange Lodge had dedicated its new banner with a motto written in the Irish language. The Rev. Martin Smyth, County Grand Master of Belfast, suggested that the banner was printed in Gaelic in order to illustrate the fact that the members sought a return to the 'real significance of Irish history'. After a dinner held to mark the occasion, he suggested that the motto was in a sense a re-affirmation of the Protestant faith.[23] Ian Adamson and Chris McGimpsey, in common with many Protestants, affirm the language as an important element of the Presbyterian tradition.[24]

A more extreme view is held by some Protestants who suggest that the Irish language forms a part of the Protestant linguistic heritage, which was pilfered by Catholics who subsequently attempted to deny this Protestant input. This opinion was expressed in the *Combat* magazine of 25 April 1974:

> The majority of Ulster Protestants equate Gaelic and Irish culture with Roman Catholicism and are of the opinion that no 'good Prod' would have anything to do with such Popish traditions. The truth of the matter is, Ulster Protestants have as much claim, if not more in some cases, to the Gaelic culture as the Roman Catholic population. Someone once said that the Irish language was stolen from the Protestant people by the Papists. It would be more correct to say that the Protestant people gave their culture away to the Roman Catholics.[25]

Generally speaking, the Catholic and/or Republican tradition would reject any intimation that Irish was offered to them by their Protestant counterparts. Many are conscious, however, of the strong Protestant Gaelic tradition and would welcome a greater current Protestant involvement with Irish. The Protestant knowledge of the language is increasing and the *Sunday Times* of 9 May 1993 reported that many working-class Protestants in Belfast were attending language courses, viewing Irish as an important element in breaking down racial sectarianism.

Current Strength of Irish in Northern Ireland

Despite political neglect and linguistic tension, Irish has continued to survive. Kachuk suggests that in recognition of this survival of the language, the British government attempted to re-interpret it in a Northern Ireland context. In this manner, it incorporated it into forms which did not contradict the dominant British culture. In 1990, an Education Reform Order introduced two new courses in all

Northern Irish schools. These were entitled 'Cultural Heritage' and 'Education for Mutual Understanding'. The purpose was twofold:

> an attempt to neutralize the challenge being made by alternative Irish-language activists to British cultural hegemony, the courses were designed to aid in the 'process of incorporation' of the subordinate Irish culture into the Northern Ireland context. In addition, they were intended to act as a resolution mechanism, encouraging an attitude change as a way of ending what the British State perceived as a war between 'two religious communities'.[26]

Table 10   Population with Irish in local government districts in the 1991 census

Local government district	Percentage with Irish	Number with Irish
Antrim	6.5	2,772
Ards	2.3	1,407
Armagh	14.4	7,091
Ballymena	4.4	2,398
Ballymoney	5.3	1,224
Banbridge	5.5	1,774
Belfast	10.9	28,918
Carrickfergus	1.6	493
Castlereagh	2.5	1,472
Coleraine	4.0	1,907
Cookstown	15.8	4,653
Craigavon	9.0	6,397
Derry	16.7	14,999
Down	10.1	5,579
Dungannon	23.2	10,001
Fermanagh	11.6	6,137
Larne	3.64	1,026
Limavady	7.6	2,131
Lisburn	6.08	5,741
Magherafelt	16.8	5,786
Moyle	12.0	1,695
Newry and Mourne	18.9	14,863
Newtownabbey	2.8	2,006
North Down	2.1	1,450
Omagh	15.4	6,697
Strabane	9.9	3,386

In the recent census of 1991, an obligatory language question was re-inserted in the census form and 9.4 per cent of the population stated that they had some skills in the language.[27] A more detailed examination of the figures reveals that in one region, almost a quarter of the population stated that they had a knowledge of the language. The number of Irish-medium schools is gradually increasing and the language is gaining attention in media circles.

Conclusion

The demand for Irish is increasing north and south of the border. Maps 2-4 illustrate the current vitality of Irish in the education system throughout Ireland.

In the Republic of Ireland, many needs have yet to be addressed. At an official level, a language act was never drafted and Irish-speakers are still without a bill of rights. A White Paper in 1965 committed the Irish people to a state of bilingualism rather than monolingualism through Irish. In 1973, the state refused an offer by the European Union to make Irish an official and working language of the Union. Obligations for a knowledge of Irish in the civil service were also removed some two years later. As yet, Irish has no official legal status in Northern Ireland. The fact that Irish-speaking patterns are currently changing both North and South of the Border appears to be only partially influenced by the government policies towards Irish. Public demand is ensuring that the language is gaining an ever-increasing social role.

The centrality of the language to Irish identity in the Republic of Ireland is a question that does not receive much attention in the public arena. For many, the language is valued as a significant symbol of ethnicity. This is not paralleled by the use of the language in the social sphere, and the Gaeltacht borders still represent the reservoirs of Gaelic culture. Some twenty years ago, the Committee on Irish Language Attitude Research found that the average individual placed a considerable emphasis on the symbolic value of the language. He seemed, however, to regard it as a natural divide between the present and the past and lacked any confidence in the future of the language.[28] As in the case of the North, however, there has been a recent reassertion of ethnic identity and this has led to an enhanced use of Irish socially.

Various attempts in Irish history to align political and linguistic borders have failed. In the South, the efforts of the Gaelic Leaguers and members of the new state to ensure an Irish-speaking Twenty-Six Counties were miscalculated. The drawing of borders around

Gaeltacht regions served merely to isolate rather than develop the language. In the North, any endeavour to secure a totally anglicised Six Counties also failed. Despite a policy of neglect, Irish has survived and has gained a new significance socially. The language has refused to recognise political or artificial boundaries. It is now recognised by many as a cultural experience which crosses rather than reinforces the sectarian and political borders.

The following maps (Maps 2-4) are based on information provided in An Roinn Ealaíon, Cultúir agus Gaeltachta, *Treo 2000: Commission to Examine the Role of the Irish Language Voluntary Organisation*, Dublin: Government of Ireland Office, 1997, pp.35-37.

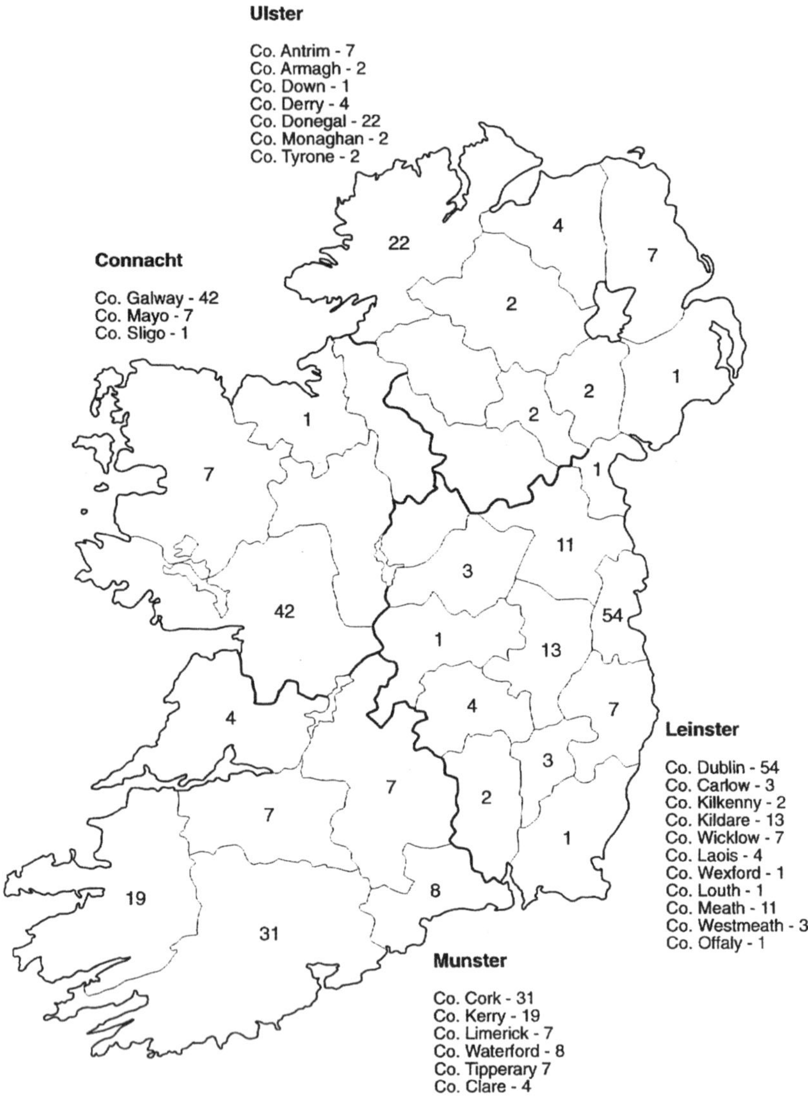

Total: 266 (81 in the Gaeltacht; 185 in the rest of the county)

MAP 2   **Number of Irish-medium playgroups (December 95)**

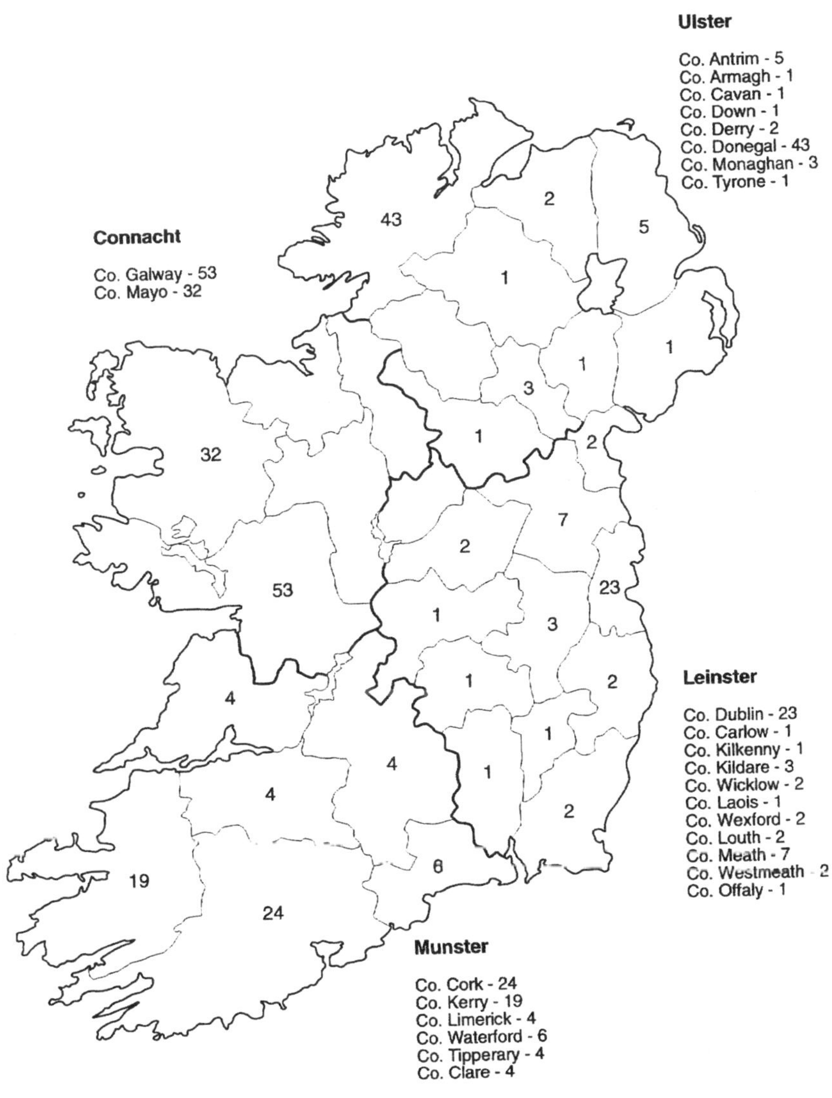

Total: 248 (147 in the Gaeltacht; 101 in the rest of the county)

MAP 3   Number of Irish-medium primary schools 1995/96

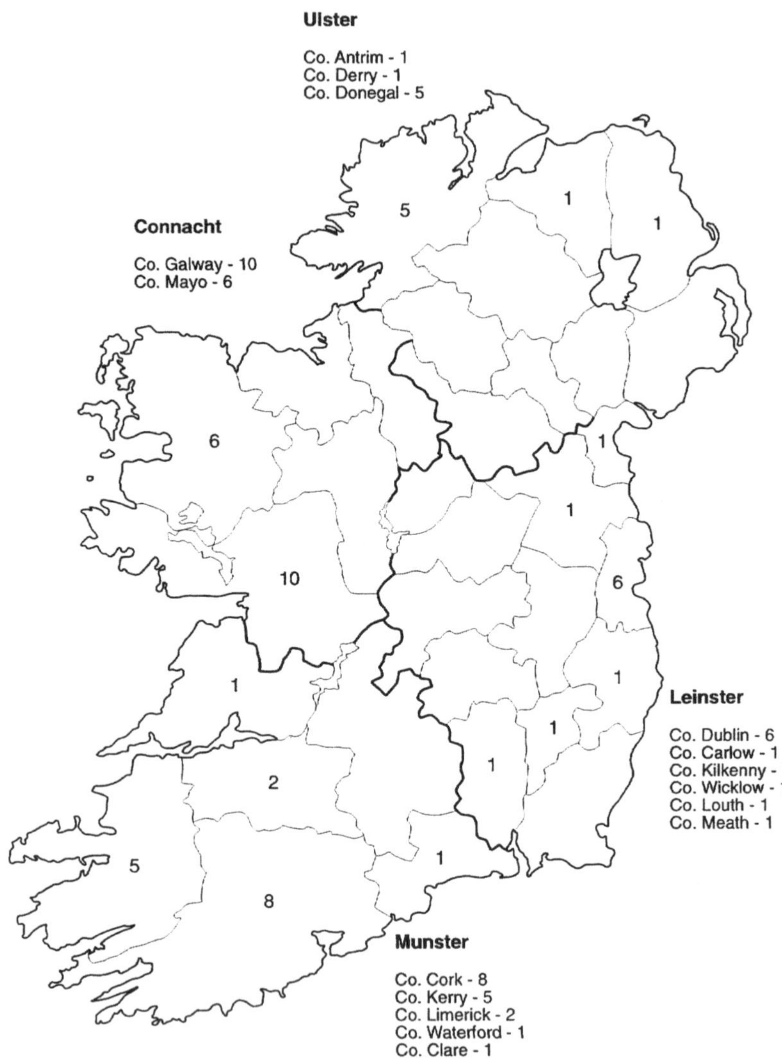

Total: 51 (27 in the Gaeltacht; 24 in the rest of the county)

MAP 4   **Number of Irish-medium post-primary schools 1995/96**

Notes

1   From 'The Frost is Over' by Pearse Hutchinson. Quoted in P Fallon and D Mahon (eds), *The Penguin Book of Contemporary Irish Poetry*, Harmondsworth: Penguin Books, 1990, pp.88-9, p.89.

2   For more information, see M Nic Craith, *Malartú Teanga: An Ghaeilge i gCorcaigh sa Naóú hAois Déag*, Bremen: European Society for Irish Studies, 1993.

3   Quoted in C Chenevix Trench, *The Great Dan: A Biography of Daniel O'Connell*, London, 1986, p.63.

4   Quoted in P H Pearse, *The Murder Machine and Other Essays*, Dublin and Cork: Mercier Press, 1976, p.66.

5   *Ibid.*, p.98.

6   Louis J Walsh in *The Leader*, 2 October 1926, quoted in 'The Problem of the Gaeltacht' in *Fáinne an Lae* supplement, Mí na Nodlag, 1926, p.17.

7   Aodán Mac Póilín, 'Spiritual Beyond the Ways of Men: Images of the Gael', in *The Irish Review*, Autumn/Winter 1994, pp.1-22; p.16.

8   Coimisiún na Gaeltachta, *Report*, Dublin: Coimisiún na Gaeltachta, 1926, p.5.

9   *Ibid.*, p.10.

10   Colmán Ó Huallacháin, *The Irish and Irish: A Sociolinguistic Analysis of the Relationship between a People and their Language*, Dublin: Irish Franciscan Provincial Office, 1994, p.86.

11   Quoted in D. Fennell, *The State of the Nation: Ireland since the Sixties*, Dublin: Ward Press, 1983, p.119.

12   Tomás MacSiomóin, 'The Colonised Mind: Irish Language and Society', in: D Ó Ceallaigh (ed), *Reconsiderations of Irish History and Culture*, Dublin: Léirmheas, 1994, pp.42-71; p.65.

13   M Akutagawa, 'A Linguistic Minority under the Protection of its own Ethnic State: A Case Study in an Irish Gaeltacht', in G MacEoin, A Ahlqvist and D Ó hAodha (eds), *Third International Conference on Minority Languages: Celtic Papers*, Clevedon: Multilingual Matters, pp.125-46, p.131.

14   Central Statistics Office, *Census 86*, Vol. 5, (Irish Language), Dublin: Government Publications Office, p.19.

15   For more information on this organisation see Máire Nic Uidhir, 'Gaillimh le Gaeilge: an Effective Bilingual Movement', in M Nic Craith (ed), *Watching One's Tongue: Issues in Language Planning*, Liverpool: Liverpool University Press, 1996, pp.103-10.

16   *Northern Ireland Parliamentary Debates* 1946, Col. 369.

17   *Ibid.*, 1946, Col. 534.

18   Quoted in Gerry Adams, *Free Ireland: Towards a Lasting Peace*, Dingle: Brandon Press, 1995, pp.143-44.

19   *Ibid.*, p.141.

20   *Ibid.*, p.143.

21   *Ibid.*, p.139.

22   A MacPóilín, 'The Work of the ULTACH Trust in Promoting the Irish Language', in *Ulster Local Studies*, Vol.16, No.2 (Winter 1994), pp.29-37; p.36.

23   See R Ó Glaisne, 'Irish and the Protestant Tradition', in M Hederman and R Kearney (eds), *The Crane Bag Book of Irish Studies*, Dublin: Blackwater Press, 1981, pp.864-75; p.869.

24 For more information, see Roger Blaney, *Presbyterians and the Irish Language*, Belfast: Ulster Historical Foundation, 1996. See also M Nic Craith, 'The Symbolism of Language in Northern Ireland', in U Kockel (ed), *Landscape, Heritage and Identity: Case Studies in Irish Ethnography*, Liverpool: Liverpool University Press, 1995, pp.11-46.

25 Quoted in Ó Glaisne, *art. cit.*, p.870.

26 P Kachuk, 'A Resistance to British Cultural Hegemony: Irish-language Activism in West Belfast', in *Anthropologica*, XXXVI (1994), pp.135-54; p.145.

27 For more information on the current knowledge of Irish in Northern Ireland see M Nic Craith and I Shuttleworth, 'Irish in Northern Ireland: The 1991 Census', in M Nic Craith (ed), *Watching One's Tongue: Aspects of Romance and Celtic Languages*, Liverpool: Liverpool University Press, 1996, pp.163-80.

28 Quoted in Pádraig Ó Riagáin, *Language Maintenance and Language Shift as Strategies of Social Reproduction: Irish in the Corca Dhuibhne Gaeltacht 1926-86*, Dublin: Institiúid Teangeolaíochta Éireann, 1992, p.144.

The Shaping of Border Identities before Partition
Some Clues towards Culture and Society[1]

Owen Dudley Edwards

I

Ulrike Rausch, of the Institute of Canadian Studies at Augsburg, recently drew attention to 'the difference between the *boundary as static end* and the *frontier as dynamic beginning* of the state as a political entity'. It serves to rob us of complacency for the convenience of this book's term 'Border'. She sees the 'creative potential' in 'the process of nation-building' coming from 'the periphery of the new political entity, not the core'[2] and hence associates herself with Frederick Jackson Turner's thesis deriving American democracy and political culture from the frontier. 'The founder of German political geography, Ratzel ... instrumentalized the frontier for the object of state security and growth,' characterising the state 'as a living organism following its nature to expand.' Then 'frontiers grew into defence lines and boundaries.' Since 1945, international law scholarship 'concentrated on the creation of boundaries as stable regimes, their *allocation, delimitation,* and *demarcation* as well as with the settlement of boundary disputes.'

As usual, we Irish think otherwise (in a phrase misremembered and miscontextualised from Bishop Berkeley), 'we' seem to transcend frontier, border or boundary lines: united in nothing else, we agree that everyone is wrong about us. Frau Rausch is open to question from many scholars, particularly Canadians, as to the Turner thesis and its claims for United States uniqueness, and the state's life-dependence on expansion is hardly a tactful diagnosis at this end of the century, but at least it can throw the Irish situation into (faintly comic) relief. The British really created a frontier in Ulster, with the importation of Anglo-Scottish Borderers after the unity of British Crowns in 1603 and the flight of the great Gaelic chieftains from Ulster in 1607. This frontier was later exported in part to America, with the result that the American frontier, as defined in human terms by Turner, would seem an import from Ulster. President Andrew Jackson, born two years after the immigration of his Carrickfergus parents, is taken for a type of the American frontiersman, but

Malcolm Anderson and Eberhard Bort (eds.), *The Irish Border: History, Politics, Culture,* Liverpool University Press 1998, 201-53 happily epitomised the Irish one, being a self-made magnate ably skilled in exploiting democratic sentiment by deployment of mass hostility against central government until he won it himself: he also followed Irish precedent in blessing popular resentment against the aborigines.[3] As Owen Lattimore put it, we need to stand Turner on his head: the frontier did not make the American, the American made the frontier.[4]

The charm of the Rausch version is that when not brutally contradicting it, Irish history seems to take pleasure in living up to it. Ulster was the most primeval part of Ireland until James VI of Scotland and I of England got at it (although Hugh O'Neill's time at Court strengthened his hand in leading the greatest war against the Tudors, and Red Hugh O'Donnell's imprisonment in Dublin Castle seemed to have similar educative effects). The making of a frontier in the Ulster Plantation and its siblings might seem to have ended in the British preservation of a last redoubt of the old Raj, but at the time it asserted the remotest extent of London conquest in these islands. London making its own plantation in Londonderry was the equivalent of carrying the name of William IV's Queen to Adelaide, and that of his Prime Minister to Melbourne, the peripheral maxima from Civilisation's core. Londonderry sounded a symbolic restraint of the hitherto untamed: the 'Derry' part spoke, did anyone know it, of a cult of a Popish saint erected on the memory of some pagan ritual oak.[5] The other Ulster counties make no such concessions, all holding their Gaelic names (as Wicklow, Wexford, Waterford conspicuously failed to do). Only in Donegal does the British metamorphosis assert itself; the name is Gaelic, ominously meaning the fort of the foreigners, but it replaced Tyrconnel, the patrimonial land of the chieftain Conal, counterpart to its great rival and final ally Tyrone. While outwith Northern Ireland today, and sufficiently republican to have given permanent political protection to the disgraced Neil Blaney (Irish democracy's closest link to the Republican paramilitaries), Donegal is a planter county with all of the demographic and aristocratic relics that might be expected. The earldom of Donegal was bestowed on the heir of the architect of the Ulster plantations, Arthur Chichester.

It is not enough to call these Ulster plantations of James's reign the making of the Irish frontier: for Ireland had had her frontiers from the day the Viking hacked out Dublin, and the day the Norman spoke of a Pale.[6] The Reformation brought its religious frontier, and the thin line of English settlers made its frontier on caste and creed, and from time to time in frontier fashion lost defectors to Catholicism or gained defectors to their Protestant ranks. Eighteenth-century penal laws had degraded the Catholics, and driven - especially in Ulster - a new frontier betwixt Protestant and Protestant. 'My mother did often speak to me about Ireland,' observed Andrew Jackson in Boston, 'and the way the rich oppressed the poor in that country':[7] with his unrivalled genius for electorally profitable ambiguity he straddled thereby three Irish frontiers at once. Irish-American Catholics would hear his sympathy at their oppression by Irish Protestantism; Irish Presbyterians would hear his sympathy at their oppression by the Episcopalian Church of Ireland; poor Protestant Episcopalians would hear his sympathy at their oppression by the rich Episcopalians; and rich Irish Episcopalians would not hear him, since they had no need to emigrate.

Quite apart from all of these, there were the frontiers the Scots had made in Antrim as medieval mercenaries, when the Clan Donald virtually turned the North Channel into a family lake. In more modern times, this made for a fighting force in the Glens of Antrim and the Catholicism of Ballycastle and Cushendall north and east of the Protestant strongholds of Ballymoney and Ballymena. The Scots link remains: the first Irish-born Roman Catholic Bishop in Scotland is the present Archbishop of St Andrews and Edinburgh, Keith Patrick O'Brien, whose courage and humanity is transmitted to his flock in the soft lilt of the Antrim glens. And while the frontiers have largely vanished in the other three provinces, Ulster still cultivates hers - on either side of the Border.

As for the Rausch boundaries, they seem mockery indeed. The Republic, at least in theory, has denied the legality of the Partition boundary since de Valera's Constitution of 1937, and in itself has been a stable regime ever since. Its predecessor polity, the Irish Free State, accepted the boundary from 1925 (de Valera in power from 1932 was marking time until his new Constitution), but the regime was far from stable in itself, what with the permanent IRA and, from 1933, the Blueshirt threats to its security. Northern Ireland has regarded the boundary as immutable since 1920, and has never been a stable regime: indeed its permanently ruling Unionist party from 1920 to 1970 justified its exclusion of Catholics from power and first-class citizenship on the plea that Catholics were security risks in a regime too unstable to afford the luxury of trusting them. And Northern Ireland has certainly been unstable since the outbreak of war in 1970.

In any case, a boundary is an unsettling business in Irish political ideology. Parnell's famous remark in his speech of 1885, quoted on his statue in O'Connell Street, Dublin, that 'No man has a right to fix a boundary to the march of a nation: no man has a right to say to his country - thus far shalt thou go and no further' is all the more alarming as an incitement from the greatest Irish constitutional nationalist leader since Daniel O'Connell, and a Protestant. Erskine Childers, seeking to reconquer the pupillage of his Irish nationalist protégés during the Treaty debates in 1921-22, said that in accepting the Treaty they were transgressing Parnell's law.[8] In fact, what

Parnell meant was that he had come to Irish politics with but a tiny handful of like-minded obstructionist MPs alongside him in the Home Rule party in 1875; that he had won enough seats in largely rural southern and western constituencies to make him leader of the party in place of the Tyrone-born Protestant William Shaw in 1880; and that by 1885 he had taken every seat in Ireland save Dublin University's two, and slightly less than half of the Ulster total. On this basis he expected to erode Ulster opposition just as he had overborne that in the southern and eastern cities. But in fact his very success was what set a boundary to the march of his nationalism: Ulster Unionism coalesced between Tories, anti-Home-Rule Liberals, and Orange activists, all three immersed in impassioned mutual hostilities up to that point.[9]

We settle for a Border. It is a sullen word, conceding nothing. It may be horticultural, as herbaceous. It may be psychological, as denoting the proximity of insanity. Or it may indicate a new phase of relationships, uncertain in outcome, as in Graham Greene's unfinished novel *The Other Side of the Border*.[10]

But its most notable use in British literature is in relation to the Anglo-Scottish Border, as Burns, Scott and Hogg remind us. Like the Anglo-Scottish Border, the Irish Border is a line on the map, but a line that marks a historical sense of *mentalités* for centuries before its present definition.

And in the opinion of the present writer, both Borders have the merit of reminding us that neither island has a natural immunity to partition.

II

A colonial culture is one which has no memory. The discontinuities of colonial experience make it almost inevitable that this should be so. A political entity which has been brought into existence by the actions of an external power; a population consisting of the descendants of conquerors, and of slave and indentured labourers, and of dispossessed aboriginals; a language in the courts and schools which has been imported like an item of heavy machinery; a prolongued economic and psychological subservience to a metropolitan centre a great distance away ... One hardly needs to labour the point that such conditions make it extremely difficult for any section of the population to develop a vital, effective belief in the past as a present concern, and in the present as a consequence of the past's concerns.

> The passage of time alone cannot cure the condition; nor a self-assertive nationalism; nor for that matter political independence. However, it mustn't be supposed that the absence of a memory, in the terms defined above, need inhibit the perpetuation of fierce historical enmities. On the contrary. Precisely because the sense of history is so deficient, these enmities tend to be regarded as so many given, unalterable facts of life, phenomena of nature, as little open to human change or question as the growth of leaves in spring or the movement of clouds across the sky. A white South African, for example, feels no need to ask himself how the black man became to be his inferior; he simply knows that the black man *is* inferior.[11]

Dan Jacobson thus begins his introduction to Olive Schreiner's *The Story of an African Farm*. That he is wrong in much of what he says is unimportant; as a South African Jew, son of immigrants, his sense of his own ethnic past was far too concerned with its 6,000-year tradition to make much of the shards of recent historical consciousness among gentiles, whether white or black. But like other great critics such as Samuel Johnson or Edmund Wilson or George Orwell, he is perhaps even more useful when wrong than when right. Like them also, he states hypothesis as fact, and question as answer, but the questions have much to teach us. For instance, we say, or we are told, that we are too aware of history in Ireland, and that it is the cause of the bloodshed in Northern Ireland. But do we realise how very little Irish history was in fact taught in Northern Ireland until relatively recently? The Scotsman James Eadie Todd made it a university subject at Queen's University Belfast in the 1930s.[12] Protestant schools hardly taught it at all until recent times.[13] Protestant children and adults knew that Catholics were inferior, and that this circumstance had been proved by King William III at the Battle of the Boyne;[14] some in the twentieth century and many in the nineteenth century would have known that the need to remind Catholics of their inferiority had existed ever since their insurrection of 1641 had shown they might forget it. A very few sophisticates knew that Presbyterians had in some few cases taken up arms against the government in 1798, and even fewer knew that the first Catholic Church in Belfast had been built with a preponderance of Protestant subscriptions a few years earlier. In general, Irish Protestants in Northern Ireland did need to ask themselves how the Catholics came to be their inferiors; but they seldom required long answers.

The answers would often be different east of the Bann from those given in the future borderlands of south and west Ulster.

The provenance of Border culture has many pitfalls. A very obvious use of song would offer us 'The Londonderry Air', but it has only the faintest Ulster link. The song was taken down in Limavady, east of Londonderry, by Miss Jane Ross, a reliable and frequent transcriber of tunes sung by peasants visiting the town on market day: George Petrie printed it in 1855. It was given words by Alfred Percival Graves, father of Robert, also by Katherine Tynan, and - the most famous ('Danny Boy') version - by Frederic E Weatherly of Somerset. Graves and Tynan were Dublin-born; Weatherly had no Irish connection at all (the supposedly Catholic song's allusion to an 'Ave' is a give-away - an Irish Catholic writer would probably speak of a 'Hail, Mary'). Not even the song may be Ulster. The tune fits no known Irish metre. Dr Noel O'Regan, of Edinburgh, finds it in a Breton mode; the inference is that the song came to Derry harbour from the Breton fishermen ploughing the seas in quest of fish as far as Iceland. A storm-bound Breton singer could easily have transmitted it to Jane Ross's informant, as could an Irish fisherman who had encountered it at sea from the Bretons. The Dublin composer Charles Villiers Stanford included it in his first Irish Rhapsody, and it made its way into certain hymn tunes.[15]

Yet the richness of Borderland society rises up from a native work famous across the world and hardly ever associated with its place of origin: 'Once in Royal David's City'. Its author, Cecil Frances Humphreys (1818-95), would marry a future Bishop of Derry and Archbishop of Armagh, William Alexander (1824-1911) in 1850, but her most famous composition was the fruit of her years as a land-agent's daughter in Strabane. And the carol, while on the surface a prime example of Victorian preachment making Jesus Christ 'our childhood's pattern' ('Christian children all must be / Mild, obedient, good as he'), seems surprisingly aware of its proximity to Popery, although not of its proximity to Paganism. It is remarkably class conscious: 'royal' David contrasts with the 'lowly cattle shed', the 'poor and mean and lowly' among whom our Saviour lived on earth, the 'lowly maiden in whose gentle arms he lay', and 'that poor lowly stable' where we shall not see him 'but in Heaven Set at God's right hand on high'. This cannot be accidental. Any writer, however rudimentary in experience or sensibility, must be alive to the tedium of repetition, and the need for its elimination by polish. In children's writing repetition is present, frequently to assert a *motif* or code, but repetition of adjectives is usually reserved for specific nouns. Here 'lowly' is everywhere. The inference is that Cecil Humphreys stresses Jesus's choice of birth among the untouchables, which in Strabane would have been the Roman Catholics. She was seeking an English audience, but her imagination was fashioned by her surroundings.[16]

The end ('Where like stars his children crowned / All in white shall wait around') may owe something to classical apotheosis of heroes such as Heracles or Perseus, but perhaps can justify itself by the sealing of the foreheads of the just in *Revelation*, vii.3. In any case, pagan inspiration is clearly involuntary here, as it is if present in 'And he leads his children on / To the place where he is gone'. The lost but undead leader still with a future role is famous among European heroes: Charlemagne and Friedrich von Hohenstaufen (Friedrich II in early versions, Friedrich I Barbarossa in later) are not dead but sleeping and will return to lead again. In the British Isles, the classic instance is the greatest of all British kings, Arthur, *Rex Quondam et Futurus*, sleeping in a hillside cave among his warriors and treasure according to Welsh folklore, sleeping in Avalon in much nobler solitude according to the courtlier Normanised versions. There are few Irish equivalents of *Rex Quondam et Futurus* apart from Fionn Mac Cumhaill's slumber, probably copycatted from the Welsh story of Arthur's cave, perhaps later than 'Once in Royal David's City'. A generation of Irish Protestants familiar with that carol conspicuously publicised the most famous Irish lost leader, whose martyrdom was in any case extolled in very Christ-like terms. Isabella Augusta Persse, Lady Gregory, reported the old man repeating 'Tá sé beo' (he is alive), meaning Parnell; Lennox Robinson's play *The Lost Leader* (1918) turned on the possibility; even Yeats's 'Parnell's Funeral' posits a kind of sacramental eating of Parnell's heart to ensure his survival. It is a reminder of the Protestant undertow of Irish political imagery, just as Pearse and de Valera created a political mirror of Catholic sacrifice and its priesthood. 'Protestant' may be too narrow a concept: Yeats seems to be thinking of transubstantiation, and Lady Gregory's story, if true, presumably reported a Catholic old man. And when she wrote it, Cecil Humphreys only thought of herself as Protestant in the Irish political sense: her carol is one of her *Hymns for Little Children* (1848), so High in its Anglicanism that she refused to publish without the *imprimatur* of her spiritual guide, the Rev John Keble of Tractarian celebrity. He agreed, and she sold twenty editions in a few months, the proceeds to support an Ulster school for deaf and dumb children.[17]

Cecil Humphreys organised her collection to illustrate each line of a major prayer. The carol explained the Creed on the conception and birth of Jesus: while the Creed's clause affirming 'The Holy Catholic Church' inspired:

> They were little Jewish children,
> Who within the temple cried,
> 'Honour to the Son of David'
> Standing at our Saviour's side.
> How much more should Christian children
> Know His name, and praise Him too,

> Who of His own Church are members,
> Sons of GOD, and born anew.

The notion that the Christian child must be superior to the little Jews who actually knew and hailed Christ, their fellow-Jew, is as instructive as it is illogical. A Lower-church Protestant might identify more readily with the Jews.[18] But for all of her Catholic sentiments, Cecil Humphreys also showed herself on the Presbyterian Border: 'Maker of Heaven and Earth' prompted another immortal verse:

> All Things Bright and Beautiful
> All Creatures great and small
> All things wide and wonderful
> The LORD GOD made them all.
> The rich man in his castle,
> The poor man at his gate,
> GOD made them, high or lowly,
> And order'd their estate.

Jesus spoke His parable of the rich man and the beggar to show how much God may favour the poor and punish the rich for their failure to alleviate poverty. But Cecil Humphreys seemed much more anxious to give God the credit for their conduct and condition, and her style, for an Anglo-Catholic, had its Calvinistic frontier. She taught her little readers to revere seven Sacraments in place of the Anglican two, to revere Bishops and defer to Priests, yet all the while her incense carried a whiff of Predestination:

> All members of one body vast
> With JESUS for their head,
> And sacraments whereby their souls
> Are born again and fed;
> And Bishops good to order them,
> And priests to train and teach,
> This is the holy Church wherein
> We have our places each.[19]

But Roman Catholics, however lowly, were certainly not outside that Christian church. Her husband's early spiritual charges took them to parish work on the shores of Lough Swilly in Donegal, as well as to Termonamongan, Co Tyrone, and forty years later on her death the Roman Catholic Ellen Haynes was still alive in the latter place to tell of Cecil Alexander's daily visits to dress a cancerous wound over a period of six weeks.[20] She literally took the shawl off her own back to clothe invalids. The question must be asked, how far this refusal to keep charity within sectarian bounds reflected the frontier. She had been brought up initially in Wicklow where her High Anglicanism had ripened in an intense friendship with a girl in the Earl of Wicklow's family who died young.[21] This may have involved enthusiasm for the Young Ireland movement: she is said to have cheered William Smith O'Brien from a place in the Court when he was sentenced to be hanged, drawn and quartered for heading the 1848 insurrection. She might be expected to outgrow that fervour, as the prisoner did, and her husband's career requirements drew her into increasingly Unionist company. She remained a sufficiently devout High Anglican to become almost hysterical at the idea of not receiving the Eucharist when at worship; but learned to refer to Presbyterians as 'Dear, good people! How kind they are to me, how ready to give for Christ's sake! I *do* like them,' in keeping with the growing Union of Protestant hearts in Ulster once the Disestablishment of the Church of Ireland removed their most obvious division and substituted a common fear of the much more numerous Roman Catholics with all sects now on equal terms. Her verse now took on a more obviously Ulster, not to say frontier, resonance, appropriate for the duties of what her contemporary Anthony Trollope termed a she-Bishop. Indeed she so far sank her youthful affections that her 'The Siege of Derry' was metrically scanned and obviously inspired by Macaulay's 'The Battle of Naseby'. 'Naseby', supposedly by a Roundhead Sergeant, alludes to Charles I as 'the Man of Blood', and Cecil Humphreys, if not Cecil Alexander, must have revered him as the King-Martyr but, as Macaulay himself remarked, the Irish frontier turned the highest Tory into the most anti-Catholic Whig in the eighteenth century: her case shows that such transformations were resurrected by the polarisation of Ulster ecclesiastical politics after 1869.[22]

A similar alteration would overtake her husband's second successor in the Archbishopric of Armagh, Charles Fredcrick D'Arcy, whose youthful memories of defending Dublin High Anglican churches against Protestant mobs gave way to leading much larger Protestant mobs - specifically the supporters of the Ulster Covenant against Home Rule in 1912, of which he was the fourth signatory after Sir Edward Carson, Lord Londonderry, and the Moderator of the General Assembly of the Presbyterian Church. D'Arcy, as yet only Bishop of Down and Connor, having thoughtfully provided himself with the supportive opinion of the Ulster-born Law Lord Macnaghten, took his place on the firing-line regardless of its ranking him behind the leader of a faith he had once despised.[23] The change in D'Arcy's case would have come with the frontier experience of his first Bishopric, at Clogher, where in place of the increasingly powerless Protestantism of Dublin, he found a vibrant, zealous people as resolute in Tyrone as the Alexanders had found in Derry. He locked shoulders with the leaders of Protestant society in defence of their order, notable among them the fourth Earl of Erne of Crom Castle, whose low opinion of Home Rule went back to the Parnellites' defiance of his father's Mayo agent in 1880, Captain Charles Cunningham Boycott. So D'Arcy might now stand back to honour the Presbyterian Moderator, and indeed sign an instrument in the Covenant whose very name breathed traditional defiance of Bishop and King. He would not be the first D'Arcy (or Darcy) to discover that Pride may find it necessary to alter its Prejudice.[24]

D'Arcy was perfectly within the spirit which Cecil Alexander had sought to rekindle from the siege mentality of Derry in 1689:

> They were soft words that they spoke, how we need not fear
> their yoke,
> And they pleaded by our homesteads, and by our children
> small,
> And our women fair and tender; but we answer'd 'No
> Surrender!'
> And we called on God Almighty, and we went to man the
> wall.

Yet the growth of her Protestant intransigence preserved a trait of her earlier Muse, its faint flicker of Paganism. Ostensibly the Reformation, as imported into Ulster from the Scottish Borders, had arisen against the compromises made by Catholicism with Paganism (such as the Christmas festival): but Paganism recruited any allies it could find among the warring sects dividing its Christian supplanters. Some Lodges of the Orange Order included pagan ritual, such as 'Riding the Goat': presumably goats were in greater supply on the rural frontier than in the sophistication of Belfast. In the heyday of the Ulster Covenant there was first recorded a street ballad, 'The Old Orange Flute', whose subtlety and charm utterly belies the stereotype liberal or Catholic-nationalist jeer about Orange humourlessness. But the whole song depends on a light-hearted Pagan conceit, and one which moreover parodies the sufferings of Protestant martyrs under Catholic persecution. As in good Pagan tradition, the inanimate object, threatened with blasphemy, becomes animate and rejects such violation of the creed it symbolises:

> So the old flute was doomed and its fate was pathetic,
> 'Twas fasten'd and burned at the stake as heretic,
> While the flames roared round it they heard a strange noise -
> 'Twas the old flute still whistling 'The Protestant boys'.[25]

As many blood-chilled neophyte students of M R James's 'Oh, Whistle, and I'll Come to You, My Lad' can testify, a whistle with supernatural powers is hardly orthodox Protestantism.[26] (Neither, of course, is 'The Protestant Boys', deliberately given a Gaelic air to ridicule Catholics in 1688.)[27]

We don't know the author of the song, but we may be fairly sure that he or she came from the place honoured at its outset:

In the County Tyrone, in the town of Dungannon...

The author felt its mention so essential that it had to be inserted even at the cost of the worst rhyme of the song:

Where many a ruction myself had a hand in.

Such clumsy contrivance has no echo elsewhere in the work. We are very much at the frontier, as the words testify when the ex-Orange convert to Catholicism flees to 'the Province of Connacht'. Connacht thrusts itself between Ulster counties Donegal and Cavan, particularly at Kiltyclogher, Co Leitrim, whose most famous son, Sean McDermott, was busily infiltrating all cultural, athletic, political and gender movements in Dublin with Irish Republican Brotherhood personnel, to roost unobtrusively but infectiously what Carson, Craig, the Moderator and Bishop D'Arcy were signing and their followers were singing. MacDermott's birthplace, poised at the edge of what became the Border in 1920, remained a haven for die-hard Republicans: as late as 1966, his octogenarian sisters were the only next-of-kin of the signatories of the Easter 1916 Proclamation of the Irish Republic to reject Honorary Degrees of the National University of Ireland on behalf of their martyred dead, since to receive them from its Chancellor, Eamon de Valera, for all of his republican piety, was to acquiesce in tacit admission of Irish Partition. In plain language, few citizens of the Republic were seriously interested in Northern Ireland, or in Partition save as an abstract expression of the deplorable. Politicians like de Valera himself used Partition as an excuse to side-step unwelcome proposals. But the view from Kiltyclogher was the frontier view, and Sean MacDermott had known his Ulster, as a tram-conductor and barman in the Belfast of 1902. For the frontier on both sides took itself to the warring labour task force of Belfast. Not that MacDermott emerged with much interest in the labour movement, apart from subsequently seeking to infiltrate it, once he himself had been taken over by that other intransigent frontiersman Tom Clarke, born on the Isle of Wight and come of age in Dungannon en route to HM prisons.[28]

MacDermott was no Pagan (unless there were Pagans to infiltrate) although Patrick Pearse's secretary Desmond Ryan, seeking a sufficient analogy for Tom Clarke, fell instinctively back on Milton's Satan:[29] in fact, Margaret and Rose MacDermott had no doubt as to their brother's Christ-like existence and career, regardless of Christ's lifelong testimony against violence. Yet the whole imagery of Kiltyclogher opens up a pagan experience. Pearse, in search of a Siegfried-like inspiration, latched on to Cu Chulainn, and Oliver Sheppard's statue in the General Post Office, Dublin, commemorates that identification.[30] But Cu Chulainn, Carson-like, came from the south to defend Ulster against the rest of Ireland, at precisely such a place as Kiltyclogher. The idea of defence of a strategic gap by tiny forces against mighty armies long predates recorded Irish history: there is Thermopylae, and there is the legend of Horatius at the Bridge. The wars of William and James interchanged examples. But it seems to persist in an Ulster choice of myths, more than elsewhere.

Many legends of Fionn Mac Cumhaill and the Fianna or Fenians were told up the length and breadth of the country, but Ulster storytellers singled out the tale of the Palace of the Quicken (Rowan) Trees, where a distinguished contingent of the Fianna are imprisoned and faced with imminent death, and they are saved by a defence of a ford made first by Fionn's foster-son and then, on his death, by Fionn's actual son and, when *he* is killed, by the heroic Diarmaid Ó Duibhne, from whom the Campbells of Scotland are supposedly descended. The Campbells became the great Whig clan, and while their Protestant cause throve in Scotland, many came to help Protestantise Ulster. The Fenian inheritance was well known to them: Campbells played a great part in the gathering and preservation of Scottish folklore, and the historian T B Macaulay, evangelist of Anglicisation though he was, habitually alludes to the Campbells as 'Clan Diarmid' with no further explanation (clearly something Every Schoolboy Knows). For all of his English background, he had heard it from his Gaelic-speaking father whose forebears were Presbyterian ministers under the patronage of the Campbells.[31] Although the word 'Fenian' is notoriously a term of almost racist anti-Catholic abuse among Protestant Ulstermen, the Campbells make it clear that many Protestants and Catholics alike could be called Fenians, and the story of the Quicken Trees is one that would fit in perfectly to either the Protestant immigrant tradition or the aboriginal Catholic one.

As the Donegal story has it, a Norse invasion (presumably via the Hebrides) is defeated by the Fianna, the youngest child of the invader king being spared and brought up amongst the Fianna. But the boy forgives nobody and plots revenge. The misanthropic, greedy and shrewd Conán tells Fionn: 'You are doing a foolish thing to keep the son of the King of Lochlann in your company; you must know well the hatred that he bears us; his father and brothers and many friends were slain by the Fenians. ...' So the boy Míogach is sent off to 'build a house' and receive 'the tribute of two districts'. He returns, Fionn fails to identify him, Conán does, and the boy obliges

Fionn to visit his house on the mainland while a welcome is prepared in the boy's other house, on the island. They find the house

> lined with rich silk, and every part was in the noblest colours, in the way that Conán praised it greatly. They put aside their arms, and when all were seated Míogach left them and closed the door behind him. The Fenians sat and waited long.
>
> "Tis a wonder to me,' said Finn, 'that they keep us here all this time without food or drink.'
>
> 'It is on the island they are preparing the dinner,' said Goll, 'when 'tis ready they will bring it.'
>
> 'There is a great wonder,' said a champion from Leinster. 'The fire that gave such a sweet odour when we came has the smell now of bodies in decay, and gives more smoke than we have seen in any place hitherto.'
>
> 'There is a greater wonder still,' said Glas Mac Aonchearda. 'The house planks were of noblest colours when we entered; now they have but one colour, and are fastened with hazel twigs.'
>
> 'Here is a wonder beyond all,' said Faolán. 'The house that had seven doors when we came has no door now but the one, and that on the north side letting in snow and wind. There is a greater wonder than that. Stuffs which we sat on are gone; there is nothing now under us but the earth, and it colder than the snow at daybreak.'
>
> 'We are under sentence,' said Finn, 'to be in the house of one door, called the Quicken Fort, and do you rise and leave the house in haste.'
>
> 'We will,' said Conán, and he started, but could not move from his place.

Fionn then chews his Thumb of Knowledge and learns they are about to be massacred by a foreign army secretly brought into the country:

> 'It is as well for us,' said Finn, at last, 'to have courage in time of death. We have no more to get in this world beyond what has come us already. And do you sound the *dord-fhiann* as mournfully as you can before death.'

The lament in fact alerts their kindred and the trickle of relief begins its quest.

One significant point seems to be that the Fianna are quite unusually united. They are ultimately saved by Diarmaid, who in another story will be forced to abduct Fionn's promised bride, be murderously pursued by Fionn, and ultimately treacherously killed by him. When the prisoners are rescued, the king of the invaders is killed in battle by one of them, Goll Mac Mórna, who had previously killed Fionn's father, and who will subsequently be starved to death while on the run from Fionn. Conán is a figure of fun, while feared for the magic of his bitter tongue, but it was he who prevented the vengeful Míogach from subverting or destroying the Fianna while still in their ranks. Equally, their enemies are united. Míogach was always irreconcilable, and the policy of clemency towards him was definitely a mistake. The anxiety of Fionn, faced with apparently certain death, to protect his foster-son above his own family, and the foster-son's reply, is a peculiarly beautiful expression of spiritual links:

> 'Who is that with you?' asked Finn.
> 'Your foster son, Insin.'
> 'My dear son,' said Finn, 'take my foster child away at once, do not leave him here longer exposed to the foreigners.'
> 'It would be unseemly to treat my foster father thus and leave him bound and I free,' said Insin.
> 'If you are unwilling to leave me,' said Finn, 'go with Fia and defend the ford if you are able till the Fenians come.'

And when Fia has to report Insin's death, although Fionn's life depends on Fia, he will not bless his real son until he is sure he did not permit the foster-son's death in his presence and that he did avenge it on the slayer. (Fia is then killed in his turn, and avenged by Diarmaid.)

The story, with Scots as well as Ulster versions (and Campbells among its transmitters), is chillingly appropriate to both sides of the Ulster divide.[32] Take it from the Catholic viewpoint. Ireland (Ulster, anyway) is invaded, the invaders are withstood, they are not fully eradicated, their remnant brings in a far more dangerous invasion using new weapons, the dangerous new invasion is however hedged around by fair promises that it is simply a form of benevolence, the appearance of benevolence changes by means of the new (magical) weaponry to grim imprisonment. The survival of the prisoners and recovery of their liberty and land depends on inflexible unity of purpose as well as trust in the action of individual guerrilla fighters of slightly uncertain ethics and loyalties. The story may easily be read with the old Norman invasion, the new gunpowder-aided Anglo-Scottish invasion, the propaganda with promises of shares in the plunder of monasteries which dwindled rapidly into land confiscation and dismissal of Catholics to bad land and little patronage - and the need for alliance in which O'Neill must bury the hatchet with, rather than in, O'Donnell, and aid from Spaniards, Papal forces, Munstermen, etc., must be accepted. The subsequent tradition of hope surviving through the careers of highwaymen *aka* reparees *aka* tories would fit in to the successive single championships, and the deaths of Insin and Fia are highly appropriate for the hunting down of such figures. One of the most illustrious, Redmond O'Hanlon, was from our own Border, although the family is Armagh rather than Donegal or Leitrim.

From the immigrant standpoint it is equally applicable. The Fianna are nomads so that a migrant people can identify with them. Ulster Protestantism can take its new country as an extension of its old lands on the Anglo-Scottish borders. It is that country, defined by its Protestant-ism, which is menaced by invaders - Papal troops as reported from the south in the cause of James Fitzmaurice Fitzgerald, Spanish troops in alliance with O'Donnell and O'Neill. Surviving O'Neills, etc., cannot be trusted and will plot the destruction of the Protestants, however benevolently. They have the magic and tricks of Popery with which to do it. Eventually they throw off the mask after fair speaking and supposed benevolence, and the insurrection of 1641 breaks out. Individual figures of somewhat dubious provenance come to the rescue - Oliver Cromwell, William III. Presbyterians and Protestant Episcopalians are forced to ally with and trust one another however much bad blood there may be between them. The story posits a succession of different foreigners, so that the Catholics' ulti-mate dependence on French allies in place of the Spaniards would again fit in. William III was a kind of foster-son, even if his rela-tionship to his uncle and father-in-law James II was a little more than kin and less than kind. And with Diarmaid as the greatest of all the heroes, the story would in any case be very gratifying to Clan Diarmid.

And presumably also to Sean MacDermott.

Curiously enough, Cecil Alexander ultimately took to writing verse in the dialect of the Ulster Scots, although her own ancestors were principally English. One poem, 'The Legend of Stumpie's Brae', was based on a Donegal folk legend, in which an unfortunate was done to death and had his feet removed (whence his name). He informs his murderers (in her poem, which Tennyson is said to have wished he had written):

> 'Ye think ye've laid me snugly here,
>> And none shall know my station;
> But I'll hant ye far, And I'll hant ye near,
> Father and son, wi' terror an' fear,
>> To the nineteenth generation.'

She may be more happily remembered by 'Once in Royal David's City'. But she picked up both the underlying pagan *motif* in Border culture as well as the longevity of Border vendetta.[33]

And like the Fianna amid the Quicken Trees, Stumpy can be Protestant or Catholic, depending on the culture of the avenger who invokes him.

III

> Good boys and girls, who may chance to read it, that time is long ago. Great wars, work, and learning, have passed over the world since then and altered all its fashions. Kings make no seven-day feasts for all comers now. Queens and princesses, however greedy, do not mine for gold. Chairs tell no tales. Wells work no wonders; and there are no such doings on hills and forests, for the fairies dance no more. Some say it was the hum of schools - some think it was the din of factories that frightened them; but nobody has been known to have seen them for many a year, except, it is said, one Hans Christian Andersen, in Denmark, whose tales of the fairies are so good that they must have been heard from themselves.[34]

The Fairy Palace of the Quicken Trees was probably collected in the above form on the borders of Donegal, Leitrim, Tyrone and Derry in the 1870s, although variants go back at least to 1603, and others were still being recounted in Ulster Gaelic well into the present century. Story-telling, like any other form of historical narrative, must be affected, and is often determined, by the pressure of contemporary events. Folklore may be retailored, and sometimes remade, in the light of fashions or orthodoxies prevailing when it is transcribed. Fianna stories given Christian endings are one example of this. Others will be the softening or hardening of ethnic, class, religious or national myths. Henry Glassie singles out folklore on the land struggles and on the famines, but his data have obviously been reshaped in the light of later days:

> The situation was bad: the oppressive environment created by the landlords after the Plantation of Ulster, beginning in 1609. The response was rebellion: the successful campaign of the Land League, beginning in 1879 ... The Land League's Agitation was a peasant revolt that worked ... its mode is comparable to the Civil Rights Movement out of which the current Troubles boiled.[35]

Modern Fermanagh looks back, a Catholic nationalist view eradicating the non-violent preachments of the Land League ('the landlords ... middlemen, agents, and bailiffs ... could be opposed, fought, and justly murdered') and eliding the non-violent Civil Rights campaign of 1969 into the violent sequel which in many respects arose to counteract, not to advance, its work. But whether in 1879, 1969, or more recently, the folklore of the land controversies is harmonised with the new conventions, and if different ethnic or religious groups are more polarised later, they impose their own orthodoxies on their ancestors. The folklore of land struggle on the north-western frontier in Ireland is Protestant as well as Catholic, before 1885, and there are signs that it could be interchangeable, but it will take some patience to shake out its evidence, especially when it may question later norms of political faith. (The tradition of Ulster Protestant radical Francophile republicanism, honouring the men of 1798, is Antrim and Down.)

The claim of Frances Brown[e] (1816-1879) as secondary folklore source is exceptionally high, in that she was blinded by smallpox in infancy and hence depended on hearing; and what she heard in her native Stranorlar, Co Donegal, in her first thirty years survives, however adulterated, in her writings.[36] Of these the masterpiece is *Granny's Wonderful Chair*, in which a chair-cushion (actually an enchanted prince) tells seven stories, which it naturally often turns on metamorphosis. But land continually returns as a subliminal *motif*. In the introductory scene at the unhappy court to be transformed by the stories:

> There was somebody caught every hour stealing the cups, and a multitude of people were always at the gates clamouring for goods and lands, which Queen Wantall had taken from them. The guards continually drove them away, but they came back again, and could be heard plainly in the highest banquet hall; so it was not wonderful that the old king's spirits got uncommonly low that evening after supper.

In the story 'The Christmas Cuckoo':

> ... he had been prime-minister at court, and in high favour, till somebody told the crown-prince that he had spoken disrespectfully concerning the turning out of his royal highness's toes, and the king that he did not lay on taxes enough, whereon the north country lord was turned out of office, and banished to his own estate. There he lived for some weeks in very bad temper. The servants said nothing would please him, and the villagers put on their worst clothes lest he should raise their rents...

The happy opening of 'The Lords of the White and Grey Castles' proclaims:

> There were no lords like them in all the east country for nobleness and bounty. Their tenants lived in peace and plenty...

But they are enchanted, and in their absence their wicked agents or stewards usurp their children's property:

> The lords had thought their stewards faithful, because they served so well under their eyes; but instead of that, both were proud and crafty, and thinking that some evil had happened to their masters, they set themselves to be lords in their room.

Towards the end the cushion is cut open and a white bird emerges:

> It flew over the palace garden and into a wild common, where houses had been before Queen Wantall pulled them down to search for a gold mine, which her majesty never found, though three deep pits were dug to come at it.

And at the happy ending (which is only a happy penultimate: see epigraph):

> The houses and lands which Queen Wantall had taken away were restored to their rightful owners. Everybody got what they most wanted. There were no more clamours without, nor discontents within the palace...

The same undertone permeates other of her fictions, such as *The Nearest Neighbour* (1876), set in Swedish Pomerania under serfdom (*Granny* is placeless), where Mats Smeker, agent of the profligate absentee landlord, is Prussian-born and free:

> His policy was to keep his lord in good humour, and never give him an occasion to visit his estate or look into his own affairs, which Mats managed so as to satisfy his demands, and at the same time to enrich himself.
>
> The two men were greedy of gain. With the one it was to spend on the follies and fashions of the Swedish capital; with the other it was to hoard and hide away in a strong box. But it made both concur in oppressing the poor peasantry, and forget that there was One who would bring every work into judgement, with every secret thing, whether it was good or whether it was evil.

This story keeps up the theme of resentment, reproach and, alternatively, deceptive deference, on the part of tenants or serfs: the blacksmith is in a privileged position, 'there being nobody of his trade within three Swedish miles' and he also being free-born, but his wife's outspoken response to the domineering agent leads to victimisation of their adopted child.[37]

We must allow, as always in modern folklore, for the contribution of book-learning: Frances Browne was blind, but listened voraciously, persuaded or paid many persons - notably a sister maintained as amanuensis - to read to her, and the retentive preservation of folklore would mingle with books. She probably knew Maria Edgeworth's *Castle Rackrent* (1800). She may, even more probably, have known the work of her fellow-Borderer William Carleton (1794/98-1869), whose 'Poor Scholar' and other works place so much faith on a landlord's potential for distributing happy endings in heaping handfuls.[38] (On the other hand she probably did not know the grim revelation of a kindly Catholic landlord's destruction by his own benevolence in Anthony Trollope's very well informed *The Macdermots of Ballycloran*, 1847.)[39] She shares with Catholic peasant folk tradition the theme of confiscation, but in terms of a landlord's abrogation of existing tenant rights, not of denial of the land titles of new or alien rulers. On the other hand, the idea of good versus bad landlords, middlemen and agents without questioning their rights as foreigners to own the land may be found in many Gaelic poems of very bitter protest (Richard Barrett's 'Eoghan Cóir' or Séan Clárach Mac Dómhnaill's 'Ar bhás Shéamais Dawson').[40] Charles Kickham's landlord family in his poem 'Myles O'Hea' are Protestant but beloved when not evicting voters for Catholic Emancipation.[41] The readiness to recruit God and Hell is as forceful on the part of Browne (many of whose works were for the Religious Tract Society) as for Mac Dómhnaill, although she refrains from his descriptions of the infernal torments awaiting the villain in the life to come. Self-respect seems a stronger theme in the Protestant peasant tradition via her hands.

Like many other good, neglected writers, Frances Browne had enormous if largely unacknowledged influence. A powerful case may be made for her decisive effect on Charles Kingsley, Frances Hodgson Burnett, Oscar Wilde and a chain of others including Enid Blyton. Burnett's *Little Lord Fauntleroy* (1886) is saturated within the theme of good landlordism emerging from bad and it, also, with American concomitants, makes everything of the importance of self-respect. But it's Big-House perspective, where Browne (a postmaster's child of improvident wealthy ancestors) is not (if here the grand-daughter who elicits the chair-stories does it in a castle, it is very much as the poor despised intruder). Kingsley's most notable debt (one he obviously holds in common with Wilde) is a delighted response to the coda of *Granny's Wonderful Chair* epigraphed above: the fairy-story as symbolic rejection of the materialist, Philistine, industrialising society ('some think it was the din of factories that frightened them'). Wilde takes up the 'hum of the schools' as inimical to fairy-stories when 'The Happy Prince' begins with the Mathematical Master reproving the Charity Children for seeing angels in their dreams: and *Granny's Wonderful Chair* tells 'The story of Childe Charity'.[42]

Charity carries an interesting transethnic resonance in Browne: the merman in 'Sour and Civil', the next story, tells Civil:

> ... make up your mind which of the maidens you will marry, for the third has no portion at all, because she is not my daughter; but only, as you may see, a poor silly girl taken into my family for charity.

The dowerless foster-daughter duly proves to be a victim of terrestrial as well as maritime snobbery, as explained by her real mother:

> Listen to my story. I was the widow of a great lord in the heart of the east country. He left me a fair castle, and an only daughter, who was the joy of my heart. Her name was Faith Feignless; but, while she was yet a child, a great fortune-teller told me that my daughter would marry a fisherman. I thought this would be a great disgrace to my noble family, and, therefore, sent my daughter with her nurse in a good ship...

Browne seems to have reflected not High Anglicanism (though she wrote a pleased poem on St Mungo and his Cathedral surviving in Glasgow despite Reformation zeal) but Evangelicalism, which assumed social equality with Catholics once they had become Protestants. Thus her *The Dangerous Guest* posits horror at a Jacobite victory in 1745 (James 'was then in Rome and much occupied with works of penance for an ill-spent youth, and with plans for the conversion of England to the Romish faith, when he should be restored to the throne of his ancestors, and was little expecting to retain to the last his ancient title of the Old Pretender'), but rejoices in the shelter given a gallant officer (who has rescued a Quaker family from his own brutal Highland soldier 'stayed by a blow with the flat of a sword laid across his shoulder'). The Jacobite duly forgets all about his aristocratic family and becomes a Quaker: so we need be in no doubt as to the desirability of *any* Protestantism over Popery. But the theme of welcome to the outcast is vital and so, too, is the principle of escaping from vendetta. Indeed, *The Orphans of Elfholm* makes a great point of the superior intelligence as well as charity of children reluctantly driven apart by the absurd feud of their authoritarian adult quasi-parents.[43]

And on one point Frances Browne was much less blind than her fellow-Protestants. Whereas Protestant poets from Samuel Ferguson to William Butler Yeats voided their rheum on O'Connell's name, very much in the way that white Southerners would scorn what they termed an 'uppity nigger', she singled out for respect at least one quality popularly associated with his name: the courage to brave public opinion in refusing challenge to a duel. It forms the background to her 'Found in the Far North', a Scandinavian story climaxing in Iceland. (Scandic settings had a natural attraction for certain Ulster writers; Alice Milligan and her brother used the Icelandic sagas for their story *Sons of the Sea Kings*, 1914.) The same story makes some perceptive dissections of Scandinavian embarrassment at having to adapt the Icelandic male habit of kissing other men. She certainly gave the Religious Tracts Society their money's worth. And she needs make no apologies when placed alongside other nineteenth-century fairy-tale tellers, not even her revered Hans Andersen. Her folklore base, her faith, and her proximity to pagan survivals, no less than her judicious use of hard social criticism, put her firmly among the classics. Ernest Rhys made *Granny's Wonderful Chair* one of the first titles For Young People in Dent's Everyman's Library, preceded only by Andersen, Hawthorne's *Wonder Book*, Lamb's *Tales from Shakespeare*, Grimm, *Tom Brown's Schooldays*, and *Robinson Crusoe*.[44]

Browne's work made its effect by simplicity interspersed with ironic little moralities much on the side of poor children listening ('"Not I, indeed!" said the spiteful fairy. "Her old skinflint of a father cut down the cedar which I loved best in the whole forest, and made a chest of it to hold his money in ..."'). And the cult of the ideal landlord, however illusory in the realm of human nature and economic facts, pushed environmentalism firmly on her agenda: even excessive tree-cutting for the poor is punished, with what the story implies should be seen as excessive brutality. Many of these themes, in more disparate form, arise in the work of William Allingham (1824-89), a milestone figure between Ferguson and Yeats, but also between the Border and London. His Ballyshannon, 30-odd miles south-west of her Stranorlar, had its imagination as fully peopled with fairies, and Allingham no less than Browne adapted them for British Victorian conventions. Yet both of them noted the malice of fairy interference with children, if not to the extent of victimising the ugly child as a changeling as the folk culture of their native Donegal might do. (Were any ugly or deformed children thrust on fires in the conviction that they were changelings whose true form revealed itself over flame? It is horribly likely.)[45] Allingham's most famous lines, opening and closing 'The Fairies', start as an adult-infant scare bedtime story (although handsomely told as though the adult is the more disrupted):

> Up the airy mountain,
>   Down the rushy glen,
> We daren't go a-hunting
>   For fear of little men;
> Wee folk, good folk,
>   Trooping all together;
> Green jacket, red cap,
>   And white owl's feather.

Alice Milligan (1866-1953) may have had this in mind in her 'When I was a Little Girl', where it is shown that the Fenians have supplanted the Fairies as a source of fear. (It is perhaps as well that this connection was not made to some of the more formidable American Fenians, where the word 'fairy' had taken a more sexual connotation by the 1890s. And many, including John Devoy, were bachelors.) Milligan's appeal to child rebellion in the context of sectarian and national rebellion lay scores of miles east of Ballyshannon, in Omagh, Co Tyrone, but the changeling principle is an eerie constant:[46]

> To hear of a night in March
> And loyal folk waiting
> To see a great army of men
> Come devastating -
>
> An army of papists grim,
> With a green flag o'er them,
> Red-coats and black police
> Flying before them.
>
> But God (Who our nurse declared
> Guards British dominions)
> Sent down a deep fall of snow
> And scattered the Fenians.
>
> 'But somewhere they're lurking yet,
> Maybe they're near us',
> Four little hearts pit-a-pat
> Thought 'can they hear us?'
>
> Then the wind-shaken pane
> Sounded like drumming;
> 'Oh!' they cried, 'tuck us in,

The Fenians are coming!' ...

But one little rebel there,
Watching all with laughter,
Thought 'When the Fenians come
I'll rise and go after'.

Wished she had been a boy
And a good deal older -
Able to walk for miles
With a gun on her shoulder;

Able to lift aloft
That Green Flag o'er them
(Red Coats and black police
Flying before them);

And, as she dropped asleep,
Was wondering whether
God, if they prayed to Him,
Would give fine weather.

Whatever about the weather, it is fine poetry. But in the context of Allingham's antecedent poem, it is alarming enough:

They stole little Bridget
          For seven years long;
When she came down again
          Her friends were all gone.
They took her lightly back
          Between the night and morrow,
They thought that she was fast asleep,
          But she was dead with sorrow.
They have kept her ever since,
          Deep within the lake,
On a bed of flag-leaves,
          Watching till she wake.

When we are children we will often be on the enemy's side at story-time: we will be pirates or fairies or Fenians, or at least want to be, however temporarily, on the side of the pirates or fairies or Fenians.[47] For that matter, Allingham's *Laurence Bloomfield in Ireland* (1864), his major poem, begins by showing his landlord hero in his teenage rebel phase. But then he reverts, indeed over-reverts, to the conventions of social order (for a time). Similarly, Irish folklore almost invariably turned on the sojourner being rescued from the fairies however voluntary the sojourn among them. Alice Milligan's little masterpiece may not consciously follow Allingham more than in colour kaleidoscope, child alliance, and fears half-ludicrous, half-perilous: but Milligan's own fate lived out that of little Bridget. She went on to found *The Shan Van Vocht* which printed James Connolly's first major Irish publication, 'Erin's Hope', in November 1896, wrote for Arthur Griffith's *Sinn Fein*, and was saluted by Thomas MacDonagh in the *Irish Review*, September-November 1914:

> Alice Milligan, Ulster Protestant, Gaelic Leaguer, Fenian, friend of all Ireland, lover of Gaelic Catholic as of her own kith, strong in faith and in hope and in charity, clear of eye and of voice, single-minded, high, inspired and inspiring, humorous and solemn, taking praise and encouragement and blame and rebuff as they come, without thought of herself, with thought always of Ireland's cause - Alice Milligan is the most Irish of living Irish poets, and therefore the best.

Less than eighteen months later MacDonagh, possibly the most challenging Irish literary critic of his time, was dead for his part in the Easter Rising, and Connolly followed him also by firing-squad nine days later (3-12 May 1916).

> Miss Milligan wrote no poetry during the 'Black and Tan' period, 1920-21, and very little after the shock of the Civil war of 1922-23, during which 'Till Ferdia Came' was written. She was then fifty-seven years of age; historic Ulster had been dismembered by the British, and the black cloud of Partition hung over her native Tyrone.

Thus the venerable Henry Mangan in a view from Dublin. He was a gallant old man, but although a fine historian, he was here speaking the orthodox Dublinspeak of his day.[48]

'Historic Ulster' was 'dismembered' in response to the dramatic wishes of the people whence Milligan came, and the act was undertaken largely to the indifference of the Dublin Sinn Féin whose civil conflict took place not over the North but over the oath to George V. What left Alice Milligan's Muse dead of sorrow was the action of the fairies/Fenians she had followed, much more than those of her friends who were indeed all gone from her native Tyrone or from the Belfast where she launched her literary nationalist career. Her final, bitter lament in civil war actually recalls some of the rhymes of 'When I was a Little Girl' and itself implies Ireland - and she - had never grown up until now (fifty-seven is not so old):

> And in these days of blood and tears
> The words re-echo in my ears,
> As many a comrade yields his life
> To former friend in desperate strife;
> I think of Collins in the West,
> The life blood clotted on his breast:
> And like enough the hand that slew him
> Not long before pledged fealty to him,
> With many another fighting man
> Linked to the cause Republican;
> And when through Dublin's street they bore him,
> Draping the flag of honour o'er him,
> We mourned to think of other days:
> His fearless feats, his merry ways.
> 'Death was a jest, the fight a game
> Till to the ford Ferdia came.'
>
> My grief for Childers, Boland too,
> And, oh, unconquered Cathal Brugha,
> When reeling through the lurid flame
> Still armed, defiant still you came
> To fall where oft your speech had rung
> In accents of our native tongue;
> You shed your blood on Dublin street
> Where oft, towards festive hall your feet
> Had walked in happy company
> With lads, who lived this sight to see.
> A foreign mandate forced the game
> Against Cuchulainn, Ferdia came.

In content it is all too credibly the end of the road which began with 'When I was a Little Girl', in style it seems hardly from the same hand. The enchantment was dying, the unravelling of the poetic genius the symbol of that death. It has the melancholy distinction of being perhaps the only notable lament in verse for both sides of the Civil War until Brendan Behan wrote his 'The Laughing Boy' as an IRA tribute to Collins.[49]

Milligan's last known poem before 'Till Ferdia Came' made much of St Bridget's Day: that was coincidence. But however forgotten Allingham may be, his 'The Fairies' was one of the best-known poems in Ireland up to the death of Alice Milligan. Written in 1849, it not only preceded the Fenians, but also the part-Fenian Land League, who (unlike the Fenians) ensured that landlords in some instances 'daren't go a-hunting for fear of little men'. It probably does reflect the old traditions of agrarian agitation and underground conspiracy, where miscreants threatening the power of the landlords might well disguise themselves as supernatural beings. No doubt that was not in Allingham's conscious mind: but it could offer an image on Consciousness's Border. And he himself remained a Border man, establishing an Irish frontier in the minds of Carlyle and Tennyson or improving on the ones he found. 'I love Ireland,' John Hewitt quotes him, 'were she only not Catholic, but would she be Ireland otherwise?' His body was cremated at Woking and his ashes buried in Ballyshannon: presumably its local Catholics of the time would have disapproved even more of the act, than of the place, of cremation.[50]

Laurence Bloomfield in Ireland, said Hewitt, is 'the finest large-scale political poem in our literature'. At times it suggests *Castle Rackrent* rewritten by Dryden, Pope and Byron. In particular, the galaxy of landlords with which it opens are stars every one, beginning with an avuncular discourse to young Bloomfield:

> The Laws were for the Higher Classes made,
> But while the lower gratefully obey'd
> To patronize them you had his consent,
> Promote their comfort, to a safe extent,
> And teach them - just enough and not too much;
> Most careful lest with impious hand you touch
> Order and grade as plann'd by Providence,
> An apophthegm, no doubt, of weighty sense;
> Had he but ask'd, is prejudice of mine
> A perfect measure of the Will Divine?
> Or by how much per annum is one given
> A seat as privy-councillor in Heaven?
> ...
> [Sir Ulick]
>
> He sometimes took a well-meant scheme in hand
> Which must be done exactly as he plann'd;
> His judgement feeble, and his self-will strong,
> He had his way, and that was mostly wrong.
> ...
> [Lord Crashton]
>
> Great owner here, in England greater still.
> As poor folk say, 'The world's divided ill'.
> On every pleasure men can buy with gold
> He surfeited, and now, diseased and old,
> He lives abroad; a firm in Molesworth Street
> Doing what their attorneyship thinks meet.
> The rule of seventy properties have they.
> Wide waves the meadow on a summer day,

Far spread the sheep across the swelling hill,
And horns and hooves the daisied pasture fill;
A stout and high enclosure girdles all,
Built up with stones from many a cottage wall;
And, thanks to Phinn and Wedgely's thrifty pains,
Not one unsightly ruin there remains.
Phinn comes half-yearly, sometimes with a friend,
Who writes to *Mail* or *Warder* to commend
These vast improvements, and bestows the term
Of 'Ireland's benefactors' on the firm,
A well-earned title, in the firm's own mind.
Twice only in the memory of mankind
Lord Crashton's proud and noble self appear'd;
Up-river, last time, in his yacht he steer'd,
With Maltese valet and Parisian cook,
And one on whom askance the gentry look,
Although a pretty, well-dress'd demoiselle -
Not Lady Crashton, who as gossips tell,
Goes her own wicked way. They stopp'd a week:
Then, with gay ribbons fluttering from the peak,
And snowy skirts spread wide, on either hand
The Aphrodite curtsied to the land,
And glided off. My Lord, with gouty legs,
Drinks Baden-Baden water, and life's dregs,
With cynic's jest inlays his black despair
And curses all things from his easy chair.

...

[Tom]

Tom is a staunch good Protestant by creed,
But half a Mormon judged by act and deed;
A dozen wives he has, but underhand,
Sub rosa, not confess'd you understand,
And this makes all the difference, of course,
His pretty little babes, except perforce,
He never knows, and never wants to know,
Yet clippings of his purse must that way go.

...

[Finlay]

Finlay, next Landlord (I'll abridge the tale),
Prince of Glenawn, a low and fertile vale,
No fool by birth, but hard, and praised for wise
The more he learn'd all softness to despise,
Married a shrew for money, louts begot,
Debased his wishes to a vulgar lot,

To pence and pounds coin'd all his mother-wit,
And ossified his nature bit by bit.
A dull, cold home, devoid of every grace,
Distrust and dread in each dependant's face,
Bullocks and turnips, mighty sacks of grain,
Plethoric purse, impoverish'd heart and brain -
Such Finlay's life; and when that life shall end,
He'll die as no man's debtor, no man's friend.
Who duns? - who loves him? - he can pay his way;
'A hard but honest man', as people say.

...

[Isaac Brown]

Pass on to Isaac Brown, a man elect,
Wesleyan stout, our wealthiest of his sect;
Who bought and still buys land, none quite sees how,
Whilst all his shrewdness and success allow.
On Crashton's mortgage he has money lent,
He takes a quiet bill at ten per cent,
The local public business much he sways,
He's learned in every neighbour's means and ways,
For comfort cares, for fashion not a whit,
Nor if the gentry to their ranks admit.
All preachers love him; he can best afford
The unctuous converse and the unctuous board;
Ev'n the poor nag, slow-rattling up the road
In ancient rusty gig a pious load,
Wags his weak tail, and strikes a brisker trot,
Approaching Brownstown, Isaac's pleasant lot.
For though at Poor House Board was never known
A flintier Guardian-angel than good Brown,
As each old hag and shivering child can tell, -
Go dine with Isaac, and he feeds you well.

And hear him pray, with fiercely close-shut eyes!
Gentle at first the measured accents rise,
But soon he waxes loud, and storms the skies.
Deep is the chest, and powerful bass the voice,
The language of a true celestial choice;
Handorgan-wise the holy phrases ground
Go turning and returning round and round;
The sing-song duly runs from low to high;
The choruss'd groans at intervals reply;
Till after forty minutes' sweat and din,
Leaving perhaps too little prayer within,
Dear Brother Brown, athletic babe of grace,

Resumes his bench, and wipes his reeking face.

...

[O'Hara]

One other landlord to conclude our list:
O'Hara - *The* O'Hara, some insist -
Of princely Irish race, which sounds full well.
But what an Irish prince was, who can tell? ...

The poem's quality is a reproach for its neglect, but its content has more to tell of the land question than almost any prose. These are the realities of the great agrarian revolt of the 1870s, dissolving much religious sectarian hostility on the Ulster borders until Gladstone's Land Act of 1881 gave Ulster what was still a Unionist answer to agrarian crisis, while Parnellism polarised politics in Ulster for the future. The inter-faith agrarian co-operation also owed much to under-representation of Catholics and over-representation of Pro-testants up to the Third Reform act, enacted in 1884 and effective in the General Election of 1885. But in addition there was a huge increase in the adult male vote, from 18 per cent in 1881 to 64 per cent in 1885.[51] Allingham's portraits convey the anger in the Protestant community stemming far back: revealingly it is from a figure on the class frontier himself, an officer in the customs in Donegal (in the initial instance), son of a merchant shipowner and bank manager, even a landowner in a small way. So Allingham, whose ancestors had been settlers under Elizabeth, had a paper-thin credential in landed society, but by occupation viewed it as an implicated out-sider. His ultimate solution was always going to prefer the humane landlord, he viewed agrarian secret societies with fear and loathing without denying the strength and substance of their bases, but his portrait of an eviction in *Laurence Bloomfield* was as bitter and as horror-stricken as any in the literature. It didn't prevent his having a sense of humour, as at dinner with Tennyson on 19 September 1880 in Land League times (his *Diary* as published tells us):[52]

T.:   A Russian noble, who spoke English well, said one morning to an English guest, 'I've shot two peasants this morning.' - 'Pardon me, you mean pheasants.' 'No, indeed, two men - they were insolent and I shot them.'
A.:   In Ireland it's the other way.
T.:   Couldn't they blow up that horrible island with dynamite and carry it off in pieces - a long way off?
A.:   Why did the English go there?

...

A.:   This last phase of discontent is perhaps the worst - flavoured with Americanism and general irreverence; but what

> I would have done long ago I would try still - encourage
> peasant proprietorship to the utmost possible.
> Hallam [T's son]: Get rid of all the landlords and give the land
> to the people?
> A.:   Not at all. There are many good Irish landlords, and
> they usually get on well with their tenants. The peasant
> proprietors would have to be made gradually, and on business
> principles.

Parnell was half-American, and Irish-America was then establishing
him in morale, finance and style (his grandfather was a War hero of
1812 against the British, of Ulster origin): he made rude remarks
when in the USA about Queen Victoria's parsimony during the
Famine. He spoke to and for a new constituency there. Allingham's
perception is partly that of a Donegal man of recent English domi-
cile, but it helps us see the alien element perceived among Ulster
Protestants in the new Catholic agrarian protest. So the Border
established itself in the mid-1880s when Catholics became the male
voter majority in western Ulster, when Catholic protest became more
Americanised, streamlined, republican, when the land agitation after
1882 was sidelined by Catholics towards Home Rule. The great new
voting mass, both Catholic and Protestant, enfranchised in 1884,
makes that Reform act much more 'the leap in the dark' for Ulster
than anything that happened in 1867 (the Second Reform Act year)
when British politics adopted the term. But however dark the night,
the dog that was not barking in 1884 is one which had been very
noisy and much deplored by Protestants in the 1850s and 1860s, the
Catholic clergy. The clerics were easing themselves into Parnell's
organisation, with his warm encouragement, especially from 1882:
but many had been very hostile to him up to then. Parnell ostenta-
tiously encouraged Protestant candidates in Ulster, and the future
rabid clericalist manipulator Tim Healy won hundreds of Protestant
votes in Londonderry South during the General Election of 1885
when he topped the poll, apparently because there the Catholic
priests were much less evident in Parnellite ranks. Once Gladstone
took up Home Rule as premier, the seat went Unionist and so
remained (electing a Catholic Unionist in 1918). Protestants would
have seen Catholic Bishops as closing ranks with a view to
controlling a new Home Rule state, a view determined for the
frontier by the Belfast Riots of summer 1886: core-periphery influence was very much a two-way traffic, and at points when the
crisis was perceived in the metropolis of London, the Ulster
metropolis of Belfast was the beacon to be watched on the Protestant
frontier. When not in crisis, the frontier preferred to express its
contempt for Belfast even when in the process of emigrating to it.[53]

IV

But if the land question in the 1870s made for frequent unity of purpose across the sectarian divide, and threw up various local heroes against party orthodoxies (J W Ellison Macartney, the tenant right rebel Conservative in Tyrone in 1873-74, Tim Healy in Monaghan in 1883, at that point winning Protestant support for having so ably improved the Land Act of 1881 which his party was principally known for opposing), the land war of 1880-82 showed features of its own also polarising the communities. In September 1880, the ordeal of Captain Boycott and the use of his name to baptise ostracism as a land war weapon had Ulster links: his agency for Lord Erne, and his ultimate recourse to Orange mercenary harvesters from Fermanagh, where Lord Erne owned 31,389 out of his total 40,365 acres.[54] There was nothing new to Ulster about such situations in theory: exclusive dealing was frequently practised by the religious sects or on simple private vendetta. Allingham sardonically noted the tradition of Orange eviction:[55]

> Six big-boned labourers, clad in common frieze,
> Walk in the midst, the Sheriff's staunch allies;
> Six crowbar men, from distant county brought, -
> Orange, and glorying in their work, 'tis thought,
> But wrongly, - churls of Catholics are they,
> And merely hired at half a crown a day.

So the polarisation could be more apparent than real, and co-operation could cross sectarian lines albeit in less elevating ways than sentiment would sanction. But the formalisation of the Boycott ultimately hardened sectarian tensions in very ugly ways. Shan F Bullock testifies to that.

Bullock was born John William (1865-1935), taking the name by which he was later universally known from William Carleton's *Traits and Stories of the Irish Peasantry* (1830-44) where the wedding of Shan Fadh (Long John) is told: it is a remarkable tribute to Carleton's permanence and Bullock's sense of their tradition-leaping and proximity of place (Carleton in the Clogher Valley moving south and east, Bullock in South Fermanagh looking west and south). It is possible to argue that Carleton, the Protestant convert from Catholicism, offered a counterpart to Bullock's own sympathies towards the Catholic community, but in both cases reservations must be allowed for, and they are not the same reservations. Bullock was the eldest son of the Earl Erne's steward, and in *After Sixty Years* (1931) he recalls the third Earl (1802-85) with even more terror than his own father who beat him so mercilessly and dominated a subservient brood, forced to call their parents 'Sir' and 'Ma'am' and leaving home as soon as possible. In fact the parental bullying sounds like a Border, Protestant variant of James Joyce's 'Counterparts', the loss of self-respect for the father in his job producing his denial of filial self-respect at home.[56] The steward's family was forced to treat Crom Castle,[57] held by the Crichtons since the Williamite wars at least (when they were Creightons):

> like so much holy ground, forbidden even to children: so that, as occasionally happened, my slipping through a gateway among the evergreens and flower beds to have a nearer look at the Castle was a dreadful adventure? Why did a few mortals need so huge a place to live in, all those bedrooms, scores of servants, a Frenchman to cook their food, horses and carriages galore, forty cows to give them milk and butter, yachts, steamers, even a grand pew all to themselves in church, with velvet cushions to sit on?
>
> Why did one shrink from meeting them, go sheepishly past with a pull at one's cap and never a word from them; and why were we all so terribly afraid when the old Earl came upon us at some mischief and lectured us from his pony chaise? He looked just like other folk, only better dressed and wore gloves, and he wasn't mean, and never complained about us to Father. Yet we trembled before him. Even Father called him *My lord* always and Mother would have to curtsy if she met him, we stood uncovered by the chaise, and I knew that when the tenants came to see him on business they had to wait on the terrace, bareheaded and perhaps in the rain whilst my lord questioned and answered them from his armchair inside the open window. It all seemed strange. God himself didn't seem to have more and want more than They did.

God gets a small 'h" for 'himself' in contrast to the Creightons' capitalised 'They'.

Bullock, anxious to be fair-minded, points out that deserving tenantry were permitted to betake themselves to the servants' quarters in quest of ale should the interview have gone well. The Earl could afford it, his income from his estates in Fermanagh, Donegal, Sligo and Mayo being £23,850 *per annum*. It was his son John Henry, the fourth Earl, who so graciously condescended to D'Arcy when Bishop of Clogher. John Henry's son died in the Great War before inheriting the earldom. The fifth Earl died of wounds received in the Second World War. They dominated their world in defence of their order, and they died for it. Their autocracy and courage interplayed to strengthen their model-roleing. Old Bullock was loud with opinions amenable to his master's, including the anti-urban. His sons were supposed to take to work on the Erne estate instead of seeking city jobs:[58]

> For the breed of clerks he had no better respect than for politicians of a certain colour, Orange drummers, Free trade, and those who lived in cities. Gladstone was a ruffian and ought to be hung.

The Free Trade vendetta arose from the collapse of Irish grain prices during the bad harvests and full-scale low-price American competition in 1877-81, part of the same tragedy that gave birth to the Land League. The antipathy to Orange drummers, however useful they might be at eviction-time, reflects the distaste of the Ulster aristocracy for what they regarded as a vulgar, brawling orgy, grossly caricaturing the Glorious Revolution of 1688 and the Protestant succession, institutions whose fruits were to be enjoyed rather than ensanguined. The exigencies of Gladstone's First Home Rule Bill obliged it to come suddenly to intimate terms with the Orangemen, but the days of iron paternal rule at home were largely an uneasy memory for the younger Bullock by 1886. They had involved a secret rebellion: if bullying exhibitionist heterosexual fathers produce homosexual sons, bullying Ulster Protestant fathers get ecumenical sons:[59]

> We little Protestants were, I suppose, always better clad and fed, certainly we had the rightful air of superiority becoming an ascendant class; this notwithstanding, it would be always the barefooted, ragged Catholic, with his hair in his cap and only a bit of oaten bread in his pocket, that I was drawn to for play or company. He was of another breed than ours, had softer ways and speech, better manner somehow, knew more about the country and its life and the things that mattered ... As mere humans they might be the inferiors of Sandy the Smith, Mr Greig the carpenter, Tom the keeper, old John who ferried us to church and school, of all Terry's print workers, and of our own fortunate selves even - inferior in point of strength, appearance, education, and the rest. Yet I preferred their company, and others also did. Why I did was hard to say, or why the impulse of preference continued, so that later on any attempt to portray them or their likes in a book would come easier and with kindlier effect than would the attempt at picturing their dominant fellows.
>
> They seemed more picturesque and homely and loveable, were less worldly and aggressive, had a sense of humour all their own, and a habit of kindness too; they had more stories and told them better, knew little yet had great

knowledge, were very poor and somehow rich. Perhaps, in a word, they charmed because they were real Irish. Much as I liked them it was plain, even to young eyes, that ourselves and the Others were people apart, different types, different ideals; perhaps they understood us, certainly a deal in them was outside our knowing.

All this may be gratifying enough, culminating as it does in a literary career whose frontier status was best known for its charity to the other side of that (sectarian, not geographical) border. As John Wilson Foster put it,

> His first and un-Protestant name, Shan, was self-bestowed and is a further indication that of all Ulster writers [save his master Carleton, Foster should add] Bullock perhaps comes closest to an intimate knowledge of both sects. Yet, Catholic characters also permitted him to exercise that democratic and para-doxically Protestant sympathy for the underdog that runs through his fiction.

But the underdog may be the victim of these gentle Catholics: again we are reminded of Joyce's 'Counterparts' - the victim may acquire a victim. Bullock's very first book of stories, *The Awkward Squads and Other Stories* (1893) includes a remorseless exposure of the cruelty of a boycott, 'A State Official', where an old man is hounded, ostracised, threatened, and ultimately driven mad for his refusal to join in such punishment of another. It is set, significantly, in Cavan, where Catholics were so much more numerous than in Fermanagh that Catholics even outnumbered Protestants on the 1881 electoral register:[60]

> '... The man betrayed the cause by takin' on an evicted woman's farm ...'
>
> 'The *cause*!' broke in Dan with a scornful laugh. 'Ye call it a cause to leave a man without a bite to eat, or a dud to wear, or a soul to cross swords with! D'ye call it a cause to let wee childher starve an' a woman to fret?'
>
> 'Ye may quit!' said the man abruptly. 'Say no more; ivery word takes ye deeper. Is that your answer?'
>
> ' ... Ye call it a *cause*. I say it's hellish persecution! The man has harmed no one, neither have his childher; he's only done what *you* think wrong. An' who are you, Micky Flynn, to judge another? I think he's done no harm, Micky; an' cause or no cause I'm goin' to think lek that.'

The story pulls no punches. Dan (it's a very Catholic, patriotically Catholic, name) breaks the boycott of the breaker of the taboo on tenancy of a farm whence a predecessor had been evicted. Parnell himself had called for such ostracism only days before Boycott's name began to win its immortality:[61]

> When a man takes a farm from which another has been evicted, you must show him on the roadside when you meet him, you must show him in the streets of the town, you must show him at the shop counter, you must show him in the fair and in the market-place, and even in the house of worship, by leaving him severely alone, by putting him into a moral Coventry, by isolating him from his kind as if he was a leper of old - you must show him your detestation of the crime he has committed, and you may depend upon it that there will be no man so full of avarice, so lost to shame, as to dare the public opinion of all right-thinking men and to transgress your unwritten code of laws.

Dan is a very sympathetic figure, but Dan implicitly dismisses the whole ethos of Parnell on the boycott, not to speak of Archbishop William Walsh's argument before the 'Parnellism and Crime' Special Commission in 1889 that boycotting helped to prevent crime rather than causing it, however much intimidation must be condemned.[62] Nor could Bullock be represented as special pleading from landlord perspective, as with Somerville and Ross in their *Naboth's Vineyard* (1889), or of ageing and disillusioned English former Hibernophilia, as with Anthony Trollope's posthumous *The Landleaguers* (1883). It is authoritative, and it is not partisan. But its ending is powerful in the extreme, especially from what Thomas Flanagan justly sums up as 'a very uneven writer':[63]

> Then a party of men, with blackened faces and carrying guns, visited him as he sat in his kitchen reading by candle light. They entered silently; and having surrounded him with a ring of threatening muzzles, one of their number, in forcible language, made clear to the trembling haggard old man the character and blackness of his offence and the swift punishment that would follow its repetition.
>
> Did he hear? shouted the man, and fired at the roof.
>
> Then, silently they went out, and left the old man to stagger to be with a great pain in his heart.
>
> The next morning another opened the post-bag; and now, people say that sometimes at night, if you lean over the wall, across the rotting flower-beds you will see a laughing,

muttering old man behind a closed window, hammering and reading away.

Sir Horace Plunkett, the great co-operative leader, strongly supported in his day by the Cavan-born Jesuit economist Tom Finlay, but defeated as Parliamentary candidate for Galway in 1901 by a Colonel in the Boer Army, had his own mixed feelings as to the Catholic Irish, but he may have spoken for Bullock as much as for himself in his prefatory lines to *After Sixty Years*:[64]

> he lifts the curtain for a moment on that mysterious underworld of Catholic and Celtic Ireland, that at once attracts and fearfully repels. *Odi et amo.*

Bullock's choice of Plunkett for his autobiography's introductory sponsor says a word on his limits as an ecumenist: it means he would not lightly surrender to Catholic nationalist shibboleths, for Plunkett, however enlightened, was a Unionist - albeit for a time a Free State Senator - and one burnt out of Ireland during the Civil War. But Protestant Ulster produced sympathisers for Parnell, some of whom became MPs under him. One, without reaching that height or depth, won the distinction in an admiring but satirical novel, of producing the most remarkable fictional sketch of Parnell the Parliamentarian from any source. *A Modern Daedalus* seems even by name to aspire to prototype status for James Joyce, who may well owe much to it. Its author, Dr Thomas Greer, died in 1895, three years after his quixotic attempt on North Londonderry in the Gladstonian Liberal interest, and ten after his novel, based on an old Derry folk legend. According to the story there was once a 'gommeral' named Hudy McGuiggan, who yearned to fly, made himself wings from goose-feathers, jumped off a high mountain and survived into venerable age. The Catholic O'Connellite Derry schoolteacher Hugh Harkin (1791-1854) who edited *The Lamp,* produced *The Quarterclift: or, the Adventures of Hudy McGuiggan* (1841?), a novel sold in shilling monthly parts. Greer was less frontier than his subject and subsequent safe seat, being born in Anahilt, Co Down, but he metaphorically spread his own wings in the less restrained landscape of Derry and Donegal. *A Modern Daedalus* ostensibly deals with a boy who learned to fly by watching the sea-birds: actually it uses the idea as a vehicle to discuss how politicians would react to the news of such a thing, uses the view from the air to describe evictions etc sympathetically towards the sufferers, defends agrarian activists even when physical force is involved, and gains independence for Ireland by means of an air-fleet. But the high point is the vision of Parnell in mid-career during the Commons debate on the flying boy:[65]

A sudden hush fell upon the chamber as it was perceived that the Irish leader was upon his legs. A bitter smile curled his lip as he looked around, his voice was quiet and incisive, and his manner in striking contrast to the heated declamation of the previous speaker [probably a caricature of Lord Randolph Churchill].

'If he were England's greatest enemy', he said, 'he could never desire to see a more pleasing spectacle than the House just then presented. The day had been one that would live in history, for it had seen the realisation of one of the oldest dreams of humanity. Some unknown man of genius - he knew not who or whence he was, but, like his hon. friend near him, he would be proud if it should appear he was an Irishman - had solved the problem of centuries, had given new powers to man, and had made that day an epoch in the history of the race. It was an occasion on which one would think that political strife might be forgotten, and men of all parties, and of all nations, unite in recognising a great advance in science and in civilisation, and in paying a tribute to the transcendent abilities which had made it possible. Such, one would think, would be the duty and the delight of the Representative Assembly of the British Empire on such an occasion. Could anything be more humiliating than the spectacle they actually presented? A great and powerful political party, thinking of nothing else than how they could further insult, and torture and goad to madness that unhappy country which their oppression had provoked into lamentable crime, and ready for that object to cast all truth, and candour, and justice to the winds! A Government bearded by their own followers, apologising with bated breath for the existence of the greatest inventor of modern ages, timidly explaining that they knew no harm of this man, that they had no evidence that he belonged to the hated and justly-suspected race! They did not know his name? Well, he could assure them that it would be known to posterity when many that he could mention should be quite forgotten. How unutterably paltry and contemptible the little tricks and dodges, the wily turns and subtle manoeuvres, in which the lives of parliamentary leaders were passed appeared when compared with the lofty themes which engaged the man of science in his unselfish and beneficent labours for mankind! The spectacle of a British Parliament listening with patience to a proposal that a great invention be suppressed unless its author would bind himself to their chariot wheels, and give up to party what was meant for mankind, was one of the most shameful that could be imagined; and England's bitterest foe could desire no greater triumph than it afforded. This the bulwark of Freedom, and the Mother of Representative Institutions! It represented England's selfishness and tyranny, and cynical disregard of all interests but her own. Let all the world look on, and realise what a blessing and what a privilege it was to live under a rule so beneficent, so unselfish, so tender of individual rights, so helpful to the general progress of mankind!'[66]

Greer can reflect the cutting edge of anti-landlord feeling neatly enough, as when he introduces 'a light dog-cart by the swiftest horse in the county, and driven by the smartest whip in Ulster - no other than "Tom Crawford", the sporting agent to Lord ---, known all over the county as the quickest shot, the keenest rider, the most merciless tyrant, and the jolliest good fellow to be found for fifty miles.'[67] And no doubt he enshrines much of the general trans-sectarian anger. But the intransigence of Parnell asserts another symbol. The Parnell of Irish literature is the sublime failure, in the phrase of another borderer-born, John Randolph Leslie, nephew of Lord Randolph, but convert to Home Rule and Roman Catholicism and enthusiastic if unsuccessful aspirant for Londonderry City in 1910 (twice) as Shane Leslie.[68] Leslie was born the year Greer published his book and came of age, the year John Synge, writing *The Playboy of the Western World* half looking back over his shoulder to the ghost of Parnell, testified to the Celtic imagination and its limits: indeed Leslie would write a fine piece of war propaganda, *The Celt and the World* (1917) for the conversion of Irish-America to the Allied case in World War I, arguing that the Teutonic element in the British make-up had oppressed Ireland while by opposing Germany the Irish would ensure the future lay with the Celt. This was no cul-de-sac eccentricity, but the heady result of lengthy discussions with the great historian Henry Adams, the young Scott Fitzgerald, and his fellow-Irishman, the British Ambassador to the USA, Sir Cecil Spring-Rice. To Leslie, as he put it in his shrewd, searching and sensitive anatomy of the pre-war United Kingdom, *The End of a Chapter,*

> 'If Parnell had remained chairman of the Irish party, Home Rule would probably have been passed in 1894, and England would not have been threatened by an Irish civil war twenty years later when she needed all her wits to face the menace of Germany.'[69]

But would success of that kind have attracted young Leslie to break with his ancestors and espouse Home Rule? Parnell could have used an earlier version, but as Greer demonstrates, it is the earlier Parnell, the figure of steel rather than the figure of soul, who transformed Ulster politics, as he had transformed British and Irish. The Parnell of steel had driven the Leslies from their hold on a parliamentary seat in the Monaghan of Castle Leslie since 1801 (apart from the 1830s). The Liberals swept the county in 1880 as the soft edge of land reform, driven forward by the hard core around Parnell, and after two defeats in the Conservative interest in 1885-86, Sir John Leslie gave up. The Parnell Shane Leslie's father knew was the Parnell who conquered with the fullest extent of Ulster Nationalist power, and ended any stake in Ulster public life for Shane himself save after surrender. Even then, he was allowed to seek Londonderry, a seat his successor candidate won: but Monaghan, now safe for Home Rule, was closed to him. His ancestors' beliefs were alive and well and in the custody of a soul far more romantic than Parnell's - Sir Edward Carson. It was because Shane Leslie and his like did not know Parnell that they could cast him as fount of liberal rebellion against the stifling orthodoxies of Protestant Ulster, much as young Irish Catholic intellectuals were finding Britain an arena if not a means of defying Irish Catholic clerical stiflement. Conor Cruise O'Brien would later speak of the 'Parnellism' of Sean O'Faolain: the Parnellism of Shane Leslie drew him towards the Catholic clerical autocracy against which his native-born fellow-Catholic intellectuals so often had to declare themselves independent in order to draw a breath.[70]

This brings us to the crucial point of the Border for Irish intellectuals: its offer of the Other. An intellectual by definition means independence of mind: it does not necessarily mean publication, however independent an action that has to be (until the new subjection to publisher, agent and market takes over the stifling process). We have to admit the self-contradictory truth that Protestants and Catholics could flourish without ever meeting one another, but this seems far more likely in cities and towns than on the rural frontier. Shan F Bullock looked back on a childhood whose 'atmosphere, generally, was English, tempered with gusts of Scotland, and subdued breath of mere Irish'. Yet his own preference for the Catholics brought him across the frontier, if not necessarily in all of his judgements. In particular he thought of - or imagined - the soft voices and gentle eyes of the Ulster Catholic girls, possibly with an unspoken notion that they might offer a warmer welcome to lads sex-starved by the punitive Protestant persuasion:[71]

> Protestants as a body stood for something tangible and not necessarily religious; Roman Catholics as a body stood for something else that perhaps was more religious, but almost of necessity was no less smirched with worldliness.

Similar sentiments might lead to a genetic crossing of the frontier, and its subsequent concealment: how many Ulster Protestants like Woodrow Wilson's paternal great-grandfather mysteriously vanish from genealogical tables?[72] Or, to put it less pleasantly, how many Catholic girls appealed to rather more animal instincts of Protestant boys in the manner of female slaves arousing the passions of masters by the rectitude of girls of their own ethnicity? The superior culture (materially speaking) officially defends its superiority by denying any crossing of the caste barriers, and hence conceals above all any sexual crossing. The more idiotic apologists for caste integrity deny any adulteration of the racial antecedents at any time, and are even prepared to argue for 500 years of radical homogeneity (regardless of the certainty that such isolation of a genetic strain would long since have resulted in congenital idiocy and physical, mental and moral degeneration of the most tragic kind: the Cruthin by now would be the Cretin). There is some blending of racial stocks, some effect of the evangelical movement in the early nineteenth century, some much smaller proselytism during the 1859 Revival. But the Revival's main effect was deeply to harden sectarian cleavage and hence butt-ress the myth of the non-mingling peoples. Clergy of all denomi-nations zealous to show the strength of the hold of their faith and their stewardship thereof, discouraged all mention in the community of persons defecting from Catholic to Protestant, or *vice versa*. Folksong is of another opinion: 'The Ould Orange Flute' assumes defection of Protestant man to Catholicism after marriage to Catholic woman as a natural course of events, and their subsequent migration from Dungannon to Connacht as equally natural. That the converse was also secretly feared as all too likely if publicly denied as in any degree likely, may be seen by the sanctions Catholic clergy invoked against even Catholic presence at a Protestant funeral service: yet they were ministering to a people who had held to their faith against all social and economic blandishments and threats when priests were in very rare supply. Modern converts would appear to be as much hidden history as Irish lesbians and gays, very deliberately hidden.

More material may be available on the allied question of anti-clericalism, but for various reasons it has received little study. In an intensely religious society, which Ulster certainly was by the late nineteenth to the mid-twentieth century, anti-clericalism may vary between absolute repudiation of the natal faith with fear and loathing expressed for its ministers, and full conformity to the practice of that faith with fear and loathing expressed for its ministers: in both instances a conviction that the anti-clerical would make a much better minister him/herself is likely. It often has political connotations, as we noted with what Cruise O'Brien called 'Parnellism', although the form dictated by actual excommunication such as was administered to the Fenians or the anti-Treaty IRA often simply went silent as to the clerics, often becoming much more vociferous in anti-clericalism after rejoining the church.[73] It may cast a very startling light on the conventional pattern of devout societies, and one much more realistic than the pious version in place for the edification of rival sects. For all of the airs intellectuals give themselves, most anti-clericalism probably arises from complaints about money, its use and its exaction, and hostility to a specific pastor may be unique in the lives of votaries' clerical diplomacy. Hangers-on such as wife, children, housekeeper, prominent laity, etc., are frequently the cause of anti-clericalism especially when the less-favoured in material or social status see clerical deference to the wealthy shopkeeper or to the squire and his relations. But for all of its want of written record, anti-clericalism, especially in Irish society where the sects are close in number as in central and west Ulster, may be a passion far beyond anything England knows. Scotland and Wales, on the other hand, may know Calvinist anti-clericalism with an intensity never fully equalled in Ulster, and a populist faith like Calvinism, or Irish Catholicism, will produce more anti-clericalism than a state church. The state church is simply hated as an institution by those opposed to its establishment.

A remarkable example of anti-clericalism on the Ulster Border arises in the case of the Rev Canon James McFadden (1842-1917), of Gweedore, Co Donegal, known to the Home Rulers as 'the fighting priest of Gweedore', and to Orange Unionists, especially to Colonel Edward Saunderson, MP, as 'that murderous ruffian McFadden'. McFadden, an agrarian agitator, was tried in October 1889 for the murder of Inspector Martin, killed when seeking to arrest the priest. McFadden pleaded guilty on a minor count and was released, and it seems certain he struck no blow against Martin although he had produced incendiary rhetoric before the event ('Will they dare to arrest me in Gweedore among my own people? ... It will take the whole British army to do it: there will be some blood spilt before they take me out of it ... I do not agree that the landlords are the only murderers: the police I regard as murderers, and they will have vengeance to fall on them in this world or the next'). But his fellow-prisoners suffered severe sentences, and McFadden was accused by the *Freeman's Journal* of saving his own skin at their expense. That produced anti-clericalism of one kind, offset by rhetoric of the 'patriot priest' variety. But he was also a severe ruler of his parish, abolishing crossroads dancing and merrymaking, keeping a hard hand on the teachers, and a firm eye on the financial fidelity of the flock. After his removal to Glenties he encountered the young Patrick MacGill (1891-1963) who left a searing indictment of his rapacity and tyranny in *Children of the Dead End* (1914) and *Glenmornan* (1918). The sectarian communities had their secrets, and what they said among themselves might differ very much from what was assumed of them by neighbours of a different faith. Where young MacGill spoke out, most would be silent, and hostility could thereby be all the more intense. The effect does seem to have assisted

MacGill in his agreeable relations with the Anglican Canon Dalton of Windsor and his pupil George V, among whom *Children of the Dead End* was written, but MacGill then married Cardinal Gibbons's niece, although not at the loss of his anti-clericalism.[74]

It may be difficult to detect anti-clericalism at work. John Bagnell Bury (1861-1927) was the Monaghan-born son of a Canon of Clogher, but agnosticised. He taught in Trinity College Dublin holding chairs of Modern History and Greek, whence he went to Cambridge as Professor of History. His Inaugural at Cambridge exhibited interests very different from what might be expected of a Protestant Clogher Canonry at that date:[75]

> ... there are few fields where more work is to be done or where labourers are more needed than the Celtic civilisation of Western Europe. In tracing from its origins the course of western history in the Middle Ages, we are pulled up on the threshold by the uncertainties and obscurities which brood over the Celtic world. And for the purpose of prosecuting that most difficult of all inquiries, the ethnical problem, the part played by race in the development of peoples and the effects of race blendings it must be remembered that the Celtic world commands one of the chief portals of ingress into that mysterious prae-Aryan foreworld, from which it may be that we modern Europeans have inherited far more than we dream. For pursuing these studies it is manifest that scholars in the British islands are in a particularly favourable position.

Bury followed this by *The Life of St Patrick and his Place in History* (1905), where he declared his independence of Trinity and the Clogher canonry even more drastically:

> For one whose interest in the subject is purely intellectual, it was a matter of unmixed indifference what answer might be found to any one of the vexed questions. I will not anticipate my conclusions here, but I may say that they tend to show that the Roman Catholic conception of St Patrick's work is, generally, nearer to historical fact than the views some anti-Papist devines.

That did not stop him from amiable cracks such as 'The Pope had not yet become the spiritual Caesar Augustus, as he is at the present day'. And when reviewing the evidence for St Patrick's connection with Clogher, he permitted himself a very tentative and guarded statement in its favour. But as he said, the ethnic problem and the effects of race blendings are very hard to determine: was his mother, the former Miss Rogers of Monaghan, a 'very clever woman and great reader', a descendant of Irish Gaelic MacRuadhri converts or was Celticism a rebellion against paternal orthodoxy, or both? Who can say?[76]

Conclusion

This essay is far too short. The subject, as even the above sketches must make clear, is capable of infinitely more complex and comprehensive treatment. We are seeking ideas of human encounter and understanding capable of setting themselves anywhere from one of native and settler as Yahoo and Houyhnhnm (in Swift's vision of how perceptions existed in his time) to one in which the other culture is accepted as the dissident's salvation (in Swift's vision of how perceptions existed in his time). *Gulliver's Travels* tells us the Irish natives were seen by their invaders as fouler and more reprehensible than any beast, and tells us that a frontier may mean cultural revulsion, and it may mean cultural submission, for Gulliver having defended his varying ideas of Englishness for three books wishes to abandon even his humanity in deference to the noble horses. The Border means exchange; the Border means enlightenment; the Border means entrenchment.

One conclusion at least should be clear. That the Irish Border long ante-dated Partition, and that it was firmly in existence a third of a century before Partition, should not have necessitated a restatement here, although no doubt every repetition helps in evangelising an unwanted truism. But what is new, I think, is my celebration of so many extraordinary intellects with Border origin or experience. We are so obsessed by our great names, and our great cities, that we ignore the harvest elsewhere. I have pursued them here for the historical evidence presented by facets of their careers, but taken together they compel so much respect for what they did, and warn us that the Border, so long deplored and defended with such aridity, was anything but a desert in itself.

The wider one casts one's net, the more one returns to William Carleton. Lucifer, Prometheus, Proteus, Odysseus, Aeneas, Faust, he stands gigantically between past and future, Catholic and Protestant, Gaelic and English, oral and written, source and novel, conservative and radical, priest and votary, Lugh and Luther, Colmcille and Calvin, Fionn Mac Cumhaill and Flann O'Brien,[77] folk and frontier, Border and boundary, cosmos and chaos. The very counts in past indictments against him testify to our debt: his apostacy, his uncertainty of loyalties, his changes of perspective, his varieties of audience, his shifting crusades, his grey areas between derivation and creation, his championship of and exploitation of and denunciation of and celebration of the plain people of Clogher valley and beyond. He is the Borderman *par excellence* in that he is on the inside looking out and on the outside looking in, the crude imposition of alien well-meaning evangelicalism reworked upon the complacency of a culture self-saved against all odds, the service of wants of misses and missionaries by premature naturalism only capable of being what it was. Innumerable voices speak in Carleton: he was the scientist setting up social history so compulsively as almost beyond his own operation, nearer to the world he describes than any of his Irish contemporaries and in these islands akin to Burns alone in being representative both in his origin and in his audience. He can recall Scott in his breadth of sympathies, and in his vicissitudes of empathies. He resembles Dickens in drawing the speech of a strange people from wounds in his past he will not let himself forget. He reaches out to the Wildes and the Yeatses, Synges and Joyces of the future. And in him is enshrined what the galaxy we have glimpsed shows in individual displays as component parts. If the Border is the great creative force of Irish literature and history it may justly claim to be, then Carleton is its midwife, but a midwife bringing himself to birth.[78]

But the dimensions of that Border would only be seen in full by grounding its study among the seventeenth-century Gaelic writers: Feardorcha Ó Mealláin, perhaps a Down man, perhaps a priest, making his verse plea that Cromwell's sentence of exile to Connacht prove as fruitful as the Israelites' flight from Egypt;[79] Sean Ó Colgáin from Donegal preserving the traditions of Irish saints and scholars among his Franciscan colleagues in Louvain;[80] Seamus Dall MacCuartha in Louth[81] making his blindness a transmission of love of Nature as rich, simple and varied as Frances Browne would later make hers at the opposite end of the geographical and sectarian Borders; Fermanagh's Cathal Buidhe Mac Giolla Ghunna lamenting the dead, parched yellow bittern whose thirst inspired an end to his own;[82] Aodh MacGabhráin from Cavan drawing on the local traditions of revelry under the old O'Rourke chieftains to inspire verse from Swift and establish his strongest known link to Gaelic mythology in which *Gulliver* is rooted;[83] and into the eighteenth century Art Mac Cumhaigh symbolising a Border between Ireland and Scotland in blending the usual Irish dream-vision of Ireland lamenting the Stuart defeats with the seduction and removal of the poet by the fairy as befell Thomas the Rhymer (and Fionn Mac Cumhaill's son Oisin or Ossian before him, be Ossian Irish or Scots) set in the personal background of his native Creggan graveyard in Armagh whose inhabitants only briefly dissuade him but among whom the fairy must promise to return his corpse.[84] Benign against them stands the great Protestant Bishop of Kilmore William Bedell, who struggled to have the Bible translated into Irish and died in the insurrection of 1641, mourned by the Catholic insurgents themselves, who fired a volley over his grave and said that if all had been like him, there had never been a rebellion, and whose disciple, the Gaelic-speaking convert Daniel Sheridan, aided in the translation, received ordination, and begat two sons to become Bishops (one to end as a Jacobite deprived of his see, one as secretary to James II, whose son would follow his Pupil Charles Edward to Moidart to launch the '45 (the Scottish Jacobite Rebellion of 1745), while the latter begat Swift's friend Thomas the schoolmaster, who begat Thomas the actor, who begat Richard Brinsley the playwright, who begat Tom the colonial treasurer at Cape of Good Hope, who begat Helen Selina the Countess of Dufferin whose songs included 'I'm Sitting on the Style, Mary', and her sister Caroline Norton the feminist and social reformer.[85]

Bedell's zeal for his vocation rather than his emoluments were matched on the Roman Catholic bench of Bishops (where there were no emoluments since no Catholic Bishops were permitted under the eighteenth-century penal laws) notably by Séamus Ó Gallchobhair of Raphoe, whose harried life did not prevent his preparation and publication of devout sermons in Irish-Gaelic explaining God's anger with the world for its murder of his son, and if this presumed many of his hearers in peril it must have assured them of utter damnation for their Protestant opponents: the brave Dominican had to take refuge in Lough Erne with its many islands at one point (Shan Bullock would know them well 150 years later) and his piety won the further support of James III, his exiled king, in whose gift Irish Bishoprics lay and who transferred him from Raphoe in 1737 to Kildare after twelve years. The sermons were reprinted several times in the next century-and-a-half.[86] Raphoe retained its high place as fount of catechetics in the Irish language with the slightly later appointment as its Dean of Andrew Donlevy, who published a bilingual catechism: its origin in many years of exile was evident in its vehement castigation of many sins its Irish readers and hearers would have been far too poor to commit. Bernard Callan returned to his native Monaghan as late eighteenth-century parish priest after education in Antwerp: he commissioned a prayer book in Irish. Unlike the rest of Ireland, the Border seems to have found men to face the linguistic crisis for Irish Protestantism and Catholicism.[87]

The links between religion and theatre, so well exhibited by the performance in pulpit of Calvinist preachers, and apparently supported by the ancestry of the playwright Richard Brinsley Sheridan and his father Thomas, were present also in young George Farquhar whose father was burnt out of his Rectory during the Jacobite wars while the boy aided in the defence of Enniskillen and the victory of the Boyne: but the first play for the future author of

The Beaux' Stratagem, Love in a Bottle, satirised the English readiness to assume all Irish as half-animals. Catholicism provided its counterpart for the stage with Charles Macklin, whose life spanned the eighteenth century give or take a few years, but whose origins were MacLaughlin of Donegal. The penal laws drove the Irish Catholics from the gentry and from public life, to which many responded by seeking financial careers with consequent denunciation from their persecutors of the kind Christians had been wont to hurl at the Jews they had driven into commerce by civil disabilities: Macklin, the leading actor of Irish-Catholic beginnings in his time, won his greatest celebrity as Shylock.[88] If he was the oldest Irishman of his time in the theatre, he just overlapped with the lifetime of the youngest, William Henry West Betty of Dromore; he began aged 12 in Belfast as Romeo (who was little more), added Prince Arthur in Dublin in 1803 - but then added Hamlet, Richard III and Macbeth for Cork and London. Pitt is said to have adjourned Parliament to see the Hamlet. A little older, Julia Betterton of Newry was forced to be infant prodigy of six on the stage. The Border liked extremes in its false appearances and politics of illusion. They were the achievements of a bolder rather than confident culture.[89]

Boldness rather than confidence also characterised the oscillation of freak local theatre into freak local politics. Henry Brooke of Rantavan, Co Cavan, was educated by Thomas Sheridan the schoolmaster, wrote vehemently on both sides of the Catholic question and produced plays among which *The Earl of Essex - a Tragedy* (1761), as performed under management of Thomas Sheridan the actor, reached its crisis when Elizabeth breaks with Essex over his treaty with Tyrone. His reply, that treaty was inevitable since he had been starved of funds and support, raised a question of the Border's politics to which the next generation's co-operation between Presbyterian and Catholic in the age of the American Revolution posed an answer.[90] But Presbyterianism was a majority faith only in Antrim, a plurality faith in Down, was second largest at one-third of total population in Londonderry, ran near equal to Church of Ireland in Tyrone, Monaghan and Donegal far below Catholics, and was practically non-existent in Cavan and Fermanagh. The Presbyterian split of the early nineteenth century between Henry Cooke, of Maghera, Londonderry, and Henry Montgomery, of Antrim, showed the frontiersmen the extremists for pan-Protestant co-operation against the Catholics, but the alternative frontier spirit showed itself when another theatrical figure emerged in the next generation from Dungiven, 11 miles west of Maghera, where John Mitchel was born to a Presbyterian minister in 1815. He was eight when he was transferred to Newry where he met his future brother-in-law 'Honest John' Martin. Thirty-two miles westward was Monaghan, where a year after Mitchel Charles Gavan Duffy was born. Between them, these three carried out the main brunt of the work in breaking O'Connell's consensus against physical force nationalism.[91] From that breach followed the Fenians, down to the Easter Rising of 1916, whither another route may be found via Tom Clarke, once resident in Dungannan.

The circle of politics, theatre, and religion on the Irish Border needs close scrutiny. In the end it set the match to the train of powder which destroyed the Union of Great Britain and Ireland while determining in what form would be created the Union of Great Britain and Northern Ireland.

And so, so far from the Irish Border having been imposed by the end of one Union and the creation of another, it was the Border itself which caused these things. But while we may cull its literature to our advantage in discovering how, that literature more specifically demands our study for its own sake. For culture must always be recognised as an end more than as a means of understanding.

Notes

1   I am deeply grateful to the organisers of the conference the proceedings of which are collected in this volume, notably the eternally patient and good-humoured Eberhard ('Paddy') Bort whose affection for the Irish people survives even their proverbial procrastination as represented by the present specimen. My thanks also to Professor Malcolm Anderson for his charm and humour encouraging Irish self-analysis over many years. The National Library of Scotland has as always been a womb with a view in which my pursuit of the pre-natal has received first-class obstetric advice and aid, above all from Mr Douglas Mathieson. Of the major sources for this paper, pride of place must be given to the *Dictionary of Ulster Biography* compiled by Kate Newman for the Ulster History Circle and published by the Institute of Irish Studies, Queen's University Belfast (hereinafter *DUB*: 1993). It outstrips all its rivals for comprehensiveness and establishes the possibility of a prosopographical history of Ulster (a few *lacunae* such as James Eadie Todd and Daniel Sheridan simply throw into sharp relief the general serviceability of the work). Other standard biographical sources employed are the *Dictionary of National Biography*, the *Dictionary of Irish Biography* (ed. Henry Boylan, Dublin: Gill and Macmillan, 1978), *The Dictionary of Irish Writers* (ed. Brian Cleeve, Cork: Mercier Press, 1967-71), the *Dictionary of Irish History 1800-1980* (eds. D J Hickey and J E Doherty, Dublin: Gill and Macmillan, 1980), the *Macmillan Dictionary of Irish Literature* (ed. Robert Hogan, London: Macmillan, 1980), *Ireland in Fiction* (ed. Stephen J Brown, S J, Shannon: Irish Academic Press, 1969), *Parliamentary Election Results in Ireland 1801-1922* (ed. B M Walker) - hereinafter respectively: *DNB, DIB, DIW, DIH, MDIL, IF, PERI.*

2   Ulrike Rausch, 'Transboundary Co-operation in Transatlantic Comparison: The Significance of the Boundary Concept', Paper

prepared for delivery at the Boundaries Conference at the Centre of Canadian Studies, University of Edinburgh, 3-5 May 1996, pp.4-5. (I am obliged to Frau Rausch for her courtesy in letting me have a copy of her paper.)

3   F J Turner, 'The Significance of the Frontier in American History', originally delivered at the American Association in its meeting at the Chicago World's Fair 1893 and subsequently reprinted frequently, notably in Turner's eponymous volume; See also Rory Fitzpatrick, *God's Frontiermen: The Scots-Irish Epic* (1989).

4   Owen Lattimore, 'The Significance of the Frontier in World History', in *Studies in Frontier History* (1962)

5   'Doire Colmcille', i.e. the oak grove of St Colmcille. Much local tradition involves Colmcille *aka* Columba either inaugurating or proscribing some pagan symbol (e.g. the Cursing Stone on Tory Island).

6   Not to speak of the day when the Roman came to Liffey or out to Tara strode, whatever the circumstances: the Roman invasion of Ireland and its unknown fate is surely the most entrancing of all of Ireland's frontiers.

7   I owe this reference, and so much else, to the late E R R Green, Director of the Institute of Irish Studies, Queen's University Belfast.

8   *Official Report. Debate on the Treaty Between Great Britain and Ireland Signed in London on the 6th December, 1921,* n.d., col.41.

9   D C Savage, 'The Origins of the Ulster Unionist Party, 1885-6', in *Irish Historical Studies,* Vol.XII (March 1961), pp.185-208.

10   Only two chapters survive, reprinted in *Nineteen Stories* (New York, 1949; I know of no English printing). Greene said he abandoned it (a) because *Brighton Rock* was more urgently trying to get itself written and (b) because the main character was too close to Anthony in *England Made Me.* Yet in some ways because the novel offers a frontier of the written and the unwritten and, Greene says, the known and the glimpsed, it has lessons for the study of frontier thought quite apart from Green's ideas in his completed narratives. A Catholic novelist should interest us in the unborn.

11   Dan Jacobson, 'Introduction' to Olive Schreiner, *The Story of an African Farm,* New York, 1971, p.7. The novel was published in 1883. Jacobson has impressively analysed the Old Testament in *The Stories and the Story.*

12   The fullest account of both Todd and his influence is in H A Cronne, T W Moody and D B Quinn, eds., *Studies in British and Irish History Presented to James Eadie Todd,* 1949.

13   Today 'The Young Historian' scheme offers the best example of school-university co-operation I have seen, deployed for all Northern Ireland schools for the study of Irish history.

14   It should be pointed out that the ridiculous idea of cultural, moral or spiritual superiority proving itself by capacity for slaughter of fellow-humans was used as a yardstick by a historian as influential (on Ulster folk) and intelligent as T B Macaulay in relation to the Jacobite wars.

15   The best account of the Londonderry Air appears under that heading in Percy A Scholes, ed., *The Oxford Companion to Music* ([1938], Oxford: Oxford University Press, 1978), p.580. Dr O'Regan's examination of the matter followed my private request of him, and I am much obliged to him for his courtesy and opinion.

16   Cecil Humphreys, *Hymns for Little Children,* 1848. See also *The Penguin Book of Hymns,* ed. Ian Bradley, 1990, Nos 8, 58, 66, 134, which omits this work but comments intelligently if not always accurately on its author; also *DUB, DNB.*

17 See also William Alexander, 'Preface' to Cecil Frances Alexander, *Poems*, 1896; also Eleanor Alexander, *Primate Alexander Archbishop of Armagh: A Memoir*, 1913. Cecil Alexander was dead when her husband was elected to Armagh.

18 Anglo-Catholics, like Roman Catholics, felt in some way obliged to defend the anti-Jewish record of the medieval Church; evangelicals giving close readings to the Old Testament acknowledged common ground with the Jews. I am grateful to Professor Alastair Fowler for stimulating discussion of this point.

19 Humphreys, *Hymns for Little Children*,

20 William Alexander, 'Preface', p.x, quoting William Verner, rector of Termonamongan, 1895.

21 The girl is usually alluded to as Lord Wicklow's daughter, but names and deaths do not correspond, so that a cousin or niece seems in question - or a natural daughter.

22 Cecil Alexander, *Poems*.

23 Alexander's successor as Archbishop of Armagh and Primate of All Ireland, John Baptist Crozier, had given strong support to the Unionists. But to have introduced him might have implied a subservience to the all-Ireland idea as opposed to Ulster resistance, or so it would appear. Belfast is in Down and Connor, whence the use of its local Bishop. Other magnates not present were advised to sign locally: The Duke of Abercorn, for instance, signed under an ancient oak tree in his estate at Baronscourt, possibly invoking a pre-Christian tradition, possibly not.

24 Charles Frederick D'Arcy, *The Adventures of a Bishop: A Phase of Irish Life: A Personal and Historical Narrative*, 1934. D'Arcy is an exhibitionist, but the book is vivid and engaging. See also A A Luce, *Charles Frederick D'Arcy 1859-1938*, 1938, for a dry view.

25 The goat may be found in the recorded folksong 'You get in the Order by riding the Goat'. For the Flute, see Colm Ó Lochlainn, coll. and ann., *Irish Street Ballads*, 1939, No.50, p.100.

26 *Ghost Stories of Antiquary*, 1903.

27 It was supposedly written by Thomas, Earl of Wharton, to the Irish air Protestants rendered as 'Lilliburlero'.

28 My data on MacDermott derive principally from the composite portrait from friends, acquaintances and his sisters Margaret and Rose, 'Sean MacDiarmada', on which I was so fortunate as to work with Aindreas O Gallchoir for his TV series *On Behalf of the Provisional Government* (Dublin: RTE, 1966). My debt to him is outstanding as is also what I owe to the late Desmond Ryan, Patrick Pearse's secretary and literary executor. Tom Clarke is a much more problematic figure, since very little evidence exists for the years in Dungannon which transformed him from the child of an apparently loyal British bombardier and Crimean War veteran into a devout IRA sympathiser shortly to embark on a dynamite campaign against the British civilian population among whom he was born. In his prison memoir, *Glimpses from an Irish Felon's Prison Life* (1922), a work of integrity for which it was praised above all other Fenian memoirs by the late Kingsley M Hancock, CBE, Superintendent of Prisons in Scotland, Clarke made a significant mention of Dungannon: 'Some time later they [the prison authorities] gave me an extraordinary book. I forget the title of it but it was one of the fiercest anti-Popery books I ever read, although I had read through some hot stuff of that kind in Ulster, where I was raised.' Louis N Le Roux, *Tom Clarke and the Irish Freedom Movement*, 1936, was described by Desmond Ryan (who translated his biography of Pearse) as very inaccurate and unreliable: it claims some data from Dungannon friends.

29 Desmond Ryan, 'Stephens, Devoy, Tom Clarke', in Conor Cruise O'Brien, ed., *The Shaping of Modern Ireland*, London: Routledge and Kegan Paul, 1959, p.37.

30 See the close of Yeats's play *The Death of Cuchulainn*, 1939; final poem.

31 Owen Dudley Edwards, *Macaulay*, London: Weidenfeld and Nicolson, 1988, pp.2-4 *et passim*.

32 Séamus Ó Duilearga, ed., *Irish Folk Tales: Collected by Jeremiah Curtin (1835-1906)*, 1956, pp.124-37 and 178-79, the version used here. I have compared a few of the other versions therein cited.

33 Cecil Alexander, *Poems*: 'The Legend of Stumpie's Brae'. 'This ballad embodies an actual legend attached to a lonely spot on the border of the county of Donegal. The *language* of the ballad is the peculiar semi-Scottish dialect spoken in the north of Ireland.'

34 Frances Browne, *Granny's Wonderful Chair*, (1857), introduced by Dollie Radford for Everyman's Library (1906) with (slightly inaccurate) bibliography.

35 Henry Glassie, *Passing the Time in Ballymenone*, 1982, p.507.

36 The variation in spelling of surname, 'e' being added after the first couple of books, seems the fruit of blindness rather than snobbery: the first works, romantic poems, are the more socially pretentious. She never read her own name written down. *DUB.*

37 Browne, *Granny's Wonderful Chair*, pp.14-15; 29; 49; 52; 172; 175. *The Nearest Neighbour*, pp.13; 24. The nearest neighbour is God.

38 I owe this phrase to P G Wodehouse, *Joy in the Morning*, 1947, p.5; a work written during the author's imprisonment by the Nazis.

39 See my introduction to the Trollope Society's text, 1991.

40 Padraig Ó Canainn, *Filidheacht na nGaedheal*, 1940, pp.173; 165-166.

41 I discuss this in Owen Dudley Edwards *et al.*, *Celtic Nationalism*, London: Routledge and Kegan Paul, 1968, pp.186-90.

42 Frances Hodgson Burnett produced a book owing so much to *Granny's Wonderful Chair* as to constitute a bad case of apparently unintentional plagiarism: she explained she had read the book as a child and forgotten its identity. The Kingsley evidence is internal: it may also explain why his *dea ex machina* is an Irishwoman despite his conventional good-natured contempt for the Irish expressed in the discursive passage when Tom finds the river. Wilde's debts receive an interesting further dimension when we consider his wife's *There Was Once: Grandma's Stories*, by Constance Mary Lloyd (1885).

43 Browne, 'To the Cathedral of Glasgow', in *Lyrics and Miscellaneous Poems*, 1948, pp.133-35. Browne, *The Dangerous Guest*, 1886, p.17 *et passim*. Browne, *The Orphans of Elfholm* (Magnet Stories, 1860; collected edition, 1864). It climaxes with two children clinging on to one another in a high flood in which the bridge on which they stand is gradually destroyed, a prospect even more terrible as conceived by a blind person. Blindness is yet a frontier which can more easily bypass certain others.

44 Cf. n.34 above.

45 Consider the Clonmel burning of a woman by her family in the 1890s, on such grounds.

46 Alice Milligan, *Poems*, selected and edited by Henry Mangan, 1954, pp.2-4. Several lexicographical authorities concur in the New York use of 'fairy' by 1895.

47 *DUB, MIDB.* John Hewitt, *The Poems of William Allingham*, Dublin: Dolmen Press, 1967, pp.17, 69-82, 24-26. William Allingham, *Laurence Bloomfield in Ireland*, 1869.

48 I recall Mangan in his 80s vigorously investigating the battlefield of Aughrim. Alice Milligan, *Poems*, p.xiv. He contributed impressive

essays to the Irish Literary Society, *Studies in Irish History*, ed. R Barry O'Brien, c.1904.

49   Milligan, *Poems*, pp.189-93. 'The Laughing Boy' first appeared in Behan's *New Statesman* review of Rex Taylor, *Michael Collins*, 1957, and was subsequently included in his *The Hostage* (London: Methuen, 1958) where it is sung.

50   John Hewitt, *Allingham*, p.18. How far did this reflect Hewitt's own view?

51   Brian M Walker, 'The Land Question and Elections in Ulster, 1868-86', in Samuel Clark and James S Donnelly, Jr, eds., *Irish Peasants: Violence and Political Unrest 1780-1914*, Manchester: Manchester University Press, 1983, pp.230-68; see also the essays by David W Miller ('The Armagh Troubles, 1784-95') and Paul Bew and Frank Wright ('The Agrarian Opposition in Ulster Politics, 1848-87') which precede it in that volume.

52   William Allingham, *A Diary 1824-1889*, ed. H Allingham and D Radford, [1907], 1985, pp.297-98.

53   Walker, 'Land Question', p.258. I am indebted to the late E R R Green for unprintable rural comments on Belfast. The non-Ulster counties stand in a similar if more subtle relationship to Dublin, envenomed sarcasm usually preferred.

54   George Edward Cokayne, *The Complete Peerage of England, scotland, Ireland, Great Britain and the United Kingdom, extant, extinct or dormant*, Vol.V, London: St Catherine's Press, 1959.

55   Hewitt, *Allingham*, pp.77-78.

56   Bullock, *After Sixty Years*, p.90.

57   A Catholic folklorist and poet from Cavan, Padraic Colum, made excellent use of the legendary Crom Duv in his epic reworking *The King of Ireland's Son* (1916). The Celtic thunder-god was Crom Cruach. It is agreeable to consider these as founders if not ancestors of the estate of Earls Erne. The change of name, if more inglorious in its attempt at self-aggrandisement, is interesting: an English spelling is discarded as insufficiently aristocratic, the Scots form being that of James II's Chancellor in the fifteenth century, Mary's Lord Advocate in the sixteenth, and an aristocratic assassin in the seventeenth, to say nothing of the mid-sixteenth-century polymath killed at 22 in a Mantuan brawl later termed 'the admirable Crichton'. The Ernes could not know that the spelling, and indeed the adjective, would be later best remembered for J M Barrie's super-butler who rose so high above his aristocratic employers. Bullock, *After Sixty Years*, pp.40-41.

58   *After Sixty Years*, p.90.

59   *Ibid.*, p.32.

60   Foster, in *MDIL*, pp.129-30. Bullock, *The Awkward Squads and Other Stories*, pp.157-58.

61   Quoted in Richard Barry O'Brien, *Life of Charles Stewart Parnell*, [1898] London: Smith, Elder & Co.,1910, pp.185-87.

62   John MacDonald, *The DAILY NEWS Diary of the Parnell Commission*, 1890, pp.228-30.

63   *TF*, pp.281, 296-97. Thomas Flanagan's comment was made to me when I asked his opinion of Bullock while writing this paper. Like all students of Carleton and of Irish historical novels, my gratitude to him is immense. See especially his *The Irish Novelists 1800-1850*, New York: Columbia University Press, 1959.

64   Plunkett, foreword to *After Sixty Years*, pp.vi-viii.

65   *IF*, pp.131; 119.

66 *A Modern Daedalus*, pp.102-105. It might seem to suggest a more literary Parnell than the conventional, but it is not inconsistent with his style. The hidden comparison of the Government to Pontius Pilate and the unknown inventor to Christ is highly characteristic, and the allusions to Homer's *Iliad* in the chariot-wheels and Goldsmith's lines on Burke, remind us that Parnell went to considerably greater lengths to get under the skin of the ruling elite, particularly Gladstone, than the mere necessities of a rebel stance might require for the benefit of the Irish-American press.

67 *Ibid.*, p.20.

68 *PERI*, pp.175,180,362.

69 Shane Leslie, *The End of a Chapter*, 1916, p.175.

70 *Maria Cross* (1952). I had the advantage of discussing his religious views with O'Faolain in 1970, in fact, the honour, because he asked my opinion on a theological point of personal importance to us. Leslie was to be victimised in the late 1920s when Cardinal Bourne joined an absurd government hue and cry about his novel *The Cantab* on absurd grounds of alleged obscenity, but this was English witch-hunting, not Irish, almost certainly started by Ernest Oldmeadow, the convert editor of the *Tablet* , who later tried to hound Evelyn Waugh out of the Roman Catholic church he had just joined, and who was afterwards Bourne's biographer.

71 Bullock, *After Sixty Years*, pp.vii; 31.

72 E R R Green, 'Woodrow Wilson and His Presbyterian Heritage', in *Essays in Scotch-Irish History*, 1969.

73 P S O'Hegarty left the Roman Catholic church and sent a message to a pursuant priest from his deathbed that he was too weak to be able to argue but he would make no return. But he supported the Treaty of 1921. His brother, who supported the IRA anti-Treaty war and was therefore excommunicated for it, returned, although he refused to be in his dead brother's house while General Mulcahy was in it and remained in the back garden until he had gone. The clerics are not always everyone's worst enemy.

74 *DIB* has a good, if not complete, account of McFadden. See also Edward Marjoribanks, *The Life of Lord Carson*, Vol.I , London: Victor Gollancz, 1932, pp.130-32,149,155. On MacGill, see *DIB*, *MDIL*, *DUB*. IF called *Children of the Dead End* 'unobjectionable' save for 'one unhappy jibe at the P.P.' but was hostile to *Glenmornan* (pp.188-89).

75 Bury, *Inaugural Lecture*, Cambridge: Cambridge University Press, 1903, p.38.

76 Bury, *The Life of St Patrick and his Place in History*, London: Macmillan, 1905, pp.vii, 221,309.

77 William Carleton, 'The Magic of Home - Fin McCoul, the Knockmanny Giant', from *Tales and Sketches Illustrating the Character, Usages, Sports and Pastimes of the Irish Peasantry*, 1845, reprinted in Tess Hurson, *Inside the Margins: A Carleton Reader*, 1992, pp.74-85. Significantly it is a feminist version.

78 The best introduction to Carleton are Flanagan (see n.63) and Benedict Kiely, *Poor Scholar: A Study of the Works and Days of William Carleton (1794-1869)*, London: Sheed and Ward, 1947. I must also indicate my gratitude to Kiely, *Modern Irish Fiction*, 1950, one of the most brilliant works of Irish literary criticism ever published.

79 Sean Ó Tuama and Thomas Kinsella, *An Duanaire 1600-1900: Poems of the Dispossessed*, Mountrath, Portlaoise: Dolmen Press, 1981, pp.102-09.

80 *DUB*.

81 *An Duanaire*, pp.128-32.

82 *Ibid.*, pp.132-35. Thomas MacDonagh's translation with variations is justly famous.

83 Vivian Mercier, *The Irish Comic Tradition*, London and New York: Oxford University Press, 1962, p.188.

84 *An Duanaire*, pp.176-81. For all of these poets, see the variant texts in Ó Canainn, *Filidheacht na nGaedheal*.

85 *DNB, DUB, DIB, MDIB*. I am much obliged to the Rev Professor Terence McCaughey's theologically profound and historically seminal O'Donnell Lecture on Bedell's Irish Bible delivered at Edinburgh University on 23 May 1996.

86 *DUB*. Ó Gallchobhair, *Sermons in Irish-Gaelic*, Dublin: M H Gill, 1877.

87 *DUB*.

88 Owen Dudley Edwards, 'The Stage Irishman', in Patrick O'Sullivan, ed., *The Irish World Wide: History, Heritage, Identity*, Vol.3, *The Creative Migrant*, London: Leicester University Press, 1994, pp.102-11; *DUB*.

89 *DNB; DUB*. The names are alternately found as 'Batty' and 'butterton'. Their obvious stage unworthiness raises the dreadful suspicion that they are the correct versions.

90 *DUB*. Brooke's daughter Charlotte (1740-93) as the compiler of *Reliques of Irish Poetry* (1789) is much more deserving of detailed study by the Irish historian than her father (who also fathered 21 other children).

91 For Mitchel, see his *Jail Journal*, 1982, with critical introduction by Thomas Flanagan. Gavan Duffy, *My Life in Two Hemispheres*, Vol.I, is informative on the social background in the early nineteenth-century rising Catholic world of Monaghan, and appealing, if probably improved for the edification of posterity. But Gavan Duffy is unusual as a liar: his lies are frequently self-belittlement in someone else's interest, a fault one would hardly ascribe to Mitchel. Martin, of course, was honest and therefore left no memoirs.

From *Partition* to *At the Black Pig's Dyke*: The Irish Border Play

Eberhard Bort

In spite of devastating and repeated acts of massacre, assassination and extirpation, the huge acts of faith which have marked the new relations between Palestinians and Israelis, Africans and Afrikaners, and the way in which walls have come down in Europe and iron curtains have opened, all this inspires a hope that new possibility can still open up in Ireland as well. The crux of that problem involves an ongoing partition of the island between British and Irish jurisdictions, and an equally persistent partition of the affections in Northern Ireland between the British and the Irish heritages, but surely every dweller in the country must hope that the governments involved in its governance can devise institutions which will allow that partition to become a bit more like the net on a tennis court, a demarcation allowing for agile give-and-take, for encounter and contending, prefiguring a future where the vitality that flowed in the beginning from those bracing words 'enemy' and 'allies' might finally derive from a less binary and altogether less binding vocabulary.

Seamus Heaney[1]

Survival in fact is about the connections between things.

Edward W Said[2]

Introduction

The Irish Borderlands are well represented in Irish literature, as one may have already glimpsed from the introductory pieces to this volume by Eugene McCabe and Shane Connaughton. All of Connaughton's and most of McCabe's work - notably the short story

Malcolm Anderson and Eberhard Bort (eds.), *The Irish Border: History, Politics, Culture*, Liverpool University Press 1998, 255-86

Cancer (in a collection of stories entitled *Heritage*, 1978) and the novel *Victims* (1976) and, in a historical perspective, *Death and Nightingales* (1992), a novel dealing with domestic violence against the backdrop of the age of Parnell - is set, to use a phrase from Connaughton's novel *The Run of the Country* (1991), in 'the tangled heart of Cavan, Monaghan and Fermanagh':[3]

> The land was impervious to maps. What appeared plain on paper was on the ground an orgy of political and geographical confusion. Cavan and Monaghan in the South were locked into Fermanagh in the North, like two dogs trying to cover the one hot bitch.[4]

Yet McCabe and Connaughton are not alone: Maurice Leitch's *Poor Lazarus* (1969), a fine novel, though sometimes criticised for its outspoken misogynist tendencies, is set on the pre-Troubles South Armagh borderlands, where Quigley, an Irish-Canadian recceing a television documentary on Ireland, gets hooked on Albert Yarr, a Protestant in predominantly Catholic South Armagh. Their first crossing of the Border goes unnoticed by Quigley:

> 'We *are* in the South.'
> 'But we didn't cross the frontier.'
> 'We did.'
> They looked at one another. Yarr was curious to see how he would react. At the time in Quigley's hired blue Anglia, directing him along the maze of by-roads between Ballyboe and Slaney, he hadn't given the Customs a thought. It was subconscious, because he would no more have dreamed of driving around by the long route - a good extra eight miles on the clock - along the approved road to the barrier than would have anyone else in the village. The Customs was only for strangers, greenhorns. A nuisance certainly - but only a nuisance to those who let it be.[5]

In the borderlands, we may gather from these novels and stories, politics and geography are intertwined. Mapping is difficult in the Drumlin belt that marks the historical and geographical boundary between Ulster and the other Irish provinces. Quigley is reminded to tread carefully and mind what he says in these environs:

> He edged forward on the seat and, touching him on the knee with a light fore-finger, confided, 'Watch what you say in front of this crowd about here. I know them. You don't.'
> 'You mean - about the frontier?'

'The Border, you mean. No, no. I didn't mean that in particular. Rule number one - eyes and ears open.[6]

Both Connaughton and Leitch describe smuggling as a way of life along the Border before the 'Troubles', 'nothing big; he was getting too old for panic - cigarette lighters, a case or two of matches, a dozen pounds of butter, the odd bottle of Power's Ten Year Old; it all depended on the economic see-saw which was very flighty these days.'[7] Or, in *The Run of the Country*:

> To live decent it was necessary to smuggle. Living well came with practice. In Prunty's house there was always chocolate, sweet cake, butter, and in the big kitchen bin, bottles of whiskey and razor blades. Blades fetched good money in Dublin. In the recess of the kitchen window sat a television.[8]

Colm Tóibín's *Walking Along the Border* (1987) opens on the same theme. Tóibín criss-crossed the Border from Lough Foyle to Carling-ford Lough, picking up the history, the politics and the gossip on both sides. Setting out from Derry towards Lifford, he muses:

> In half an hour I would be in the Republic of Ireland where the price of petrol would be much higher, where the price of drink would be a constant source of discussion and where just about everything else - new cars, hi-fi, televisions, videos - cost more than in the North ...
> I walked on towards the customs posts. The first one, which belonged to Her Majesty, was closed up. No one would dream of smuggling from the South into the North. The Irish customs official sat in the second hut, waving each car by. They were all locals, he said, he knew them; there was no point in stopping them, it only annoyed them. They were probably just driving over to get cheap petrol.[9]

'What will happen when the Border goes?', asks someone in Patrick Quigley's novel *Borderland* (1994), set in his native Monaghan Border area in the late 1950s. A neighbour answers, 'The end of the cheap butter.'[10] But the most striking notion we get from all these narratives is the fact that vast stretches of the 'green Border' seem unmarked, with a hint of being, like the Customs for Yarr, 'a nuisance for those who let it be':

> 'Where's the Border, Jimmy?'
> We were lying on the grass, ants crawling over the mossy stones beside us. He waved his stick at the tiny fields

folding into the distance, the blue hills merging into a wall around the sky.

     'It's out there somewhere.'

     'Is the army there?'

     'Oh yeah. Guns and tanks all over the place. They're dug into the sides of the hills.'

     I scanned the diminishing fields, looking for a wall across the land. From a story-book drawing I imagined watch-towers reflecting the sun, soldiers with strange weapons. An occasional hooded tree stood sentinel along the hedges. A dog's bark echoed in an enclosed farmyard. A motorcar droned along an invisible road.[11]

And, later in the book, there is a similar exchange:

     'But where is the Border?' she asked.

     'There are no traces of it here. No checkpoints or observation towers. Sometimes it's just a stream, sometimes just a hedge between fields.'[12]

Quigley's book, set during the 1950s IRA bombing campaign, already focuses on the darker aspects of the Border. Another Monaghan writer, Pat McCabe, tells of small-town life in the borderlands. *Carn* (1989), his novel about the shifting fortunes of a town 'half a mile from the Irish border,'[13] takes us, in its second chapter, back to the IRA Border Campaign, harks back to the Civil War of 1922, and pushes ahead to the Troubles after 1969. Benedict Kiely's early novel, *Land Without Stars* (1946), is set in the borderlands of Counties Tyrone and Donegal; the drama of his *Proxopera* (1979) is acted out at the Donegal-Derry Border, all in the short distance between 'the happiness of Donegal' and 'the haunted farmyard',[14] in which three IRA men hold a family hostage until the family's grandfather would deliver a bomb into town to blow up a local judge. A nightmare scenario, echoed in Seamus Heaney's 'The Flight Path':

     Enter this one I'd last met in a dream,

     More grimfaced now than in the dream itself

     When he'd flagged me down at the side of a mountain road,

     Come up and leant his elbow on the roof

     And explained through the open window of the car

     That all I'd have to do was drive a van

     Carefully in to the next customs post

     At Pettigo, switch off, get out as if

     I were on my way with dockets to the office -

     But then instead I'd walk ten yards more down

     Towards the main street and get in with - here

> Another schoolfriend's name, a wink and smile,
> I'd know him all right, he'd be in a Ford
> And I'd be home in three hours' time, as safe
> As houses...[15]

In Seamus Deane's novel *Reading in the Dark* (1996), an auto-biographical memoir of his childhood and adolescent days in Derry, of growing up against the backdrop of sectarianism and unravelling the family secret stemming from the period of the Civil War, is explicitly a novel 'about people in small places',[16] marginalised Border people. Deane, for instance, brilliantly evokes the puzzlement of crossing the Border into Donegal, physically so easy, and yet denoting a different world. In his novel, Seamus Heaney makes the briefest of appearances. Heaney, a classmate of Deane's, shares with Brian Friel this Border background.

'I was brought up in the North of Ireland,' John Montague has written:

> but in a country which should have belonged to the South, because Tyrone is largely Catholic, peopled by the descendants of the early Irish speaking inhabitants. So because of my ancestry, which includes persons, and illegal armies, I do feel that I am partly an Ulsterman, although I would never live there, to endure the brutal tensions fostered by partition.[17]

Yet he visits the Northern borderlands, and recently published a long poem, 'Border Sick-Call', dedicated to 'Seamus Montague, M.D., my brother, in memory of a journey in winter along the Fermanagh-Donegal border':[18]

> 'Border, did you say,
> How many miles to the border?
> Sure we don't know where it starts
> or ends up here, except we're lost
> unless the doctor or postman finds us.
>
> 'But we didn't always complain.
> Great hills for smuggling they were,
> I made a packet in the old days,
> when the big wars were rumbling on,
> before this auld religious thing came in.
>
> 'You could run a whole herd through
> between night and morning, and no one
> the wiser, bar the B-Specials,
> and we knew every mother's son

well enough to grease the palm,
quietlike, if you know what I mean.
Border be damned, it was a godsend.
Have you ever noticed, cows have no religion?"[19]

In *The Rough Field* (1972), Montague evokes his boyhood farm in Co Tyrone and creates a sense of borderland, weaving family memory and history into an intricate pattern. In the opening section, 'Home Again', his journey takes him from industrial - British - Belfast to rural Tyrone, full of resonances of its Gaelic past:

The whole landscape a manuscript
We had lost the skill to read
A part of our past disinherited.

But the 'green' Border, hardly discernible among the undulating hills, is only one side of the medal. Official Border posts, approved crossings, harassment, the presence of the Army, fortifications reminiscent of the Iron Curtain, are the complementary picture.

When Deeds and his (Catholic) cronies, in Eoin McNamee's *The Last of Deeds* (1989), head for a showdown with their Protestant counterpart Albert Glennon, this image of the fortified Border crosses their minds:

It was cold. We crossed the Esplanade. You could see the lights of Mill Street up ahead.

'Looks like a border,' Deeds said, pointing at the double row of streetlights. He was thinking that we were walking towards a border without passports, wondering if you could break out, climb the barbed wire, cross the brightly lit strip without stepping on the freshly dug patches that would conceal mines. Hoping that the guards were asleep in their watchtowers, or sitting in warm guardrooms passing around snapshots of their wives, children, sweethearts.[20]

Set in a Northern Irish coastal town, this passage in McNamee's novel points towards the presence of borders and border images within Northern Ireland, borders marking dividing lines between the communities - a theme we will come back to.

This short introductory survey, incomplete as it is (no mention of, say, John McGahern or Patrick Kavanagh), may suffice to illustrate that the development of and at the Border in the twentieth century is well-reflected in literature. One last example, Paul Muldoon's poem, 'The Boundary Commission', brings me, timewise and thematically, to the first instance of 'dramatic exposure' of the Border which I will mainly deal with in this chapter, by following the perceptions and understandings of the Border as expressed in a series of 'Border Plays':

The Boundary Commission

You remember that village where the border ran
Down the middle of the street,
With the butcher and baker in different states?
Today he remarked how a shower of rain

Had stopped so cleanly across Golightly's lane
It might have been a wall of glass
That had toppled over. He stood there, for ages,
To wonder which side, if any, he should be on.[21]

The Irish Border Play

'That village' could well have been D C Maher's 'Ballynadurgh' in his 'Farcical Skit' of 1916, *Partition*.[22] The situation here is even more ludicrous. Not just butcher and baker find themselves in different states; Andy Kelly's house in the centre of Ballynadurgh is divided by the 'Border Line of Eire and Northern Ireland',[23] as would be the case only a few years later in places like Pettigo. Yet Andy cunningly tries to make the best of it, owing money North and South. He *is* North or South as he pleases, depending on who is knocking at the door. But mostly he prefers to be neither nor - 'a Siamese twin', 'a sort of a two in wan',[24] particularly when it comes to sheriffs and bailiffs.

When the bailiffs from the North knock at the door, he firmly declares his loyalty to the Southern Free State and even shifts his belongings to the south of his chalk line - and vice versa, if the Free State authorities are after him! But what he does not reckon with is the combined force of law and order, Northern and Southern authorities working together to get at him. His last refuge is to frantically pile all his belongings on the chalk line; and we leave the scene with Northern and Southern bailiffs and policemen fighting over his furniture. The play ends, as '[t]the village cornet player is heard in the distance playing "A Nation Once Again"', with Andy's foreboding words: 'Begobs [sic] the Siamese twins will be kilt and buried in the wan coffin.'[25]

Maher himself seems to be absolutely unknown, apart from this little farce which predates the actual Partition of Ireland by six years. The 1975 imprint bears the note:

> When the play was written in 1916, the Author imagined the conditions that would prevail under the proposed Home Rule Act of 1920. This did not materialize but the conditions as envisaged did and remain so at present.[26]

Various traits in Maher's script seem noteworthy. There is, first, an overall feeling of incredulity about the workings of Partition, about the obvious ludicrousness of a wilfully drawn borderline, just as at the opening of Muldoon's poem. Second, Partition, as Ged Martin has shown in his contribution to this volume, was definitely on the table by 1916, reflecting in particular the debate in the wake of the Home Rule Bill of 1912 (Government of Ireland Act 1914), and already envisaging a post-war Bill (Government of Ireland Act 1920, which came into effect in British law in 1921) and Partitition. The time of writing and first production, half a year after the Easter Rising, has to be taken into account. It could be argued that the events in Dublin, as well as the Battle of the Somme a few months later, helped seal the prospect of Partition, and produced this curious combination of ridicule and anticipation, incrompehesion and foreboding in Maher's 'Skit'.

Furthermore, he seems to anticipate cross-Border collaboration of the authorities of state - the combined efforts of the bailiffs North and South - as well as, in the final scenes of mayhem, bloody conflict arising from Partition.

Yet, when Partition actually came, it seems not to have been the primary topic of debate and conflict. As Neil Jordan has pointed out recently, what struck him when researching his *Michael Collins* was that the fighting in the Civil War was about the oath of allegiance to the Crown rather than about Partition. Or, in the words of the historian Roy Foster:

> [The anti-Treaty side] repudiated the Treaty arrangement, not because it failed to deliver a United Ireland, but because it failed to deliver the 'Republic', that imaginary place wholly untainted by any association whatsoever with the British Crown.[27]

What does that mean in terms of the realisation of the Border in the 1920s?

'Many people at the time thought, ' wrote Liam de Paor, 'that the partition was a temporary expedient.'[28] And Hugh Kearney seconds:

The Treaty itself had been drawn up on the assumption that the partition of Ireland would not be permanent. It was perhaps not until 'Eire' adopted a neutral stance during the war of 1939-45 that attitudes finally hardened.[29]

Which nicely takes me to my second dramatic example, Paul Vincent Carroll's *The Devil Came from Dublin* (1946).[30] The play is set, mostly, in Stanislaus Brannigan's hotel lounge bar in the Southern Border town of Chuckeyhead, presumably not a million miles from Carroll's own birthplace, Dundalk. The action takes place during the 'Emergency' - as the Second World War was euphemistically called in the South. The landlord and publican, moreover, is the head of a lucrative smuggler's ring. Indeed, the whole community seems to thrive on smuggling. And, slightly altering Robert Burns, the 'Devil' coming from Dublin *is* the exciseman or, to give him proper title and name, the newly-appointed District Justice Udolphus McCluskey, equipped 'with very special powers, to reside in Chuckeyhead and relentlessly suppress all smuggling with all the rigours of the law.[31] Needless to say that hoodwinking him becomes the main task of the community.

The scene opens on the smugglers making ready for the trip across the Border, tying their parcels and writing their slips, exchanging in humorous banter:

> PETER. Ah, the same Border is the curse of the country. A
> bloody English crime.
> BARNEY. Well, will yous listen to what's talkin'! A man that
> put a hundred platinum watches in his grandmother's
> coffin and it crossing the Border.
> PETER. Will yous listen to Satan gettin' religious! A man that
> had to pretend to the Customs Officer that he was
> dumb, because his mouth was full of gold weddin'
> rings![32]

We get the impression of a roaring (illegal) trade. Cooked hams, cases of Scotch, lipsticks and perfumes and nylons - all to be wheeled up North in Mike MacNamara's lorry, let through by Customs Officer Ignatius Farrell who in turn receives 'his usual fifty pounds'.[33] The local Sergeant seems to be kept in a constant state of drunkenness in Brannigan's snug, 'a fair and dacent price for a blind eye'.[34] But just on the very night Mike MacNamara is supposed to deliver a major load of stuff across the Border, the law descends on Chuckeyhead: enter District Justice McCluskey. 'We might as well have no Border at all, ' muses a dispirited Barney, one of the older smugglers, 'for all the good it is to us now.'[35] Against rising despondency, Mike comes up with a strategy:

> MIKE. ...we've got to win this fellow over to be one of
>   ourselves. We've got to make him see that the Border -
> ALL (*raising their hats*). God bless it!
> MIKE. Amen! - is an English crime.
> ALL. Hear, hear! We're agin it to the death![36]

After having put half of the village's male smuggling population behind prison bars - thus effectively disrupting the economic basis of the place - and being pelted with ripe fruit by the wives and children of the jailed smugglers, McCluskey eventually discovers - nudged along by a few fortified 'tomato cocktails' and enchanted by the village redhead Rita - that he, too, is human after all. He is a forerunner, in this respect, to Sean O'Casey's Orange businessmen in *The Drums of Father Ned* (1958) who, also under the influence of alcoholic beverages, exclaims: 'To hell with partition!' Realising that Rita is in love with her 'hero' Mike MacNamara, McCluskey vanishes as surprisingly as he had turned up in the first place. Even if, in dramatic terms, rather unconvincingly, the old order is re-stored: Stanislaus, Mike and consorts can start to rebuild their cross-Border trade.

In *The Devil Came from Dublin*, the Border is depicted as an economic divide offering manifold prospects for enterprising folk, with agricultural and luxury goods scarce in the war-time North. Paul Vincent Carroll, although exposing the hypocrisy of condemning the Border and at the same time using it blatantly for profitable gain, takes a good-humoured look at the smuggling trade, interlaced with outbursts of more general anti-Dublin government feelings. This curious mix of anti-authoritarianism and general conservative out-look (annoyingly present in the authoritarian treatment of women in the play), is also observed by Patrick Quigley in *Borderland*, when he has his young revolutionary explain at the time of the IRA Border Campaign:

> 'The areas around the Border are the key to the revolution in this country. It is the crack that will open the crevices between the contradictions that are covered up by the media and political system. At the moment an armed campaign is underway to remove the Border. The people in the area have little respect for rules and authority. Am I correct?'
>   'Partly...'
>   'There is a long history of unlicensed economic activity in the area.'
>   'I don't un-'
>   'Smuggling. Another term for the same thing. There's a tradition of resistance to central authority. We should build on

that. Most left-wing people stay stuck in the cities and ignore
that potential resource.'
       'The people are very conservative in some ways. Many
are stubborn and don't take no discipline,' I reminded him.[37]

Any real political dimension is missing in Carroll's play. Not only is
there no presence of the IRA. One could argue that their campaign of
the 1930s had petered out. More important, the contradictions and
ambiguities in attitude and daily action with regard to the Border
remain unresolved. For smuggling and making a living, it is
regarded as a God-sent opportunity, as long as the central authorities
keep their fingers out of the game. That the Dublin government
sends a new District Judge to guard the Border might of course be
taken as a hardening attitude in official Ireland, as indicated by
Hugh Kearney. But still, the Border is 'an English crime', as Mike, the
lorry-driving smuggler, has it. And his final promise to his future
wife Rita is: 'I'll give you a son that will grow up like a lion, and he'll
abolish the Border!'[38] One thing the play makes pretty clear is that,
between Dundalk and Newry, it is not the 'other' that resides across
the Border, but countless relatives!
     The prevailing impression, however, is of the Border in the
middle of this century as an economic divide and opportunity. Thus
the play could be taken as an illustration of Liam de Paor's general
classification of borderlands:

> All border zones, everywhere, are potential areas of benefit to
> bandits, smugglers, guerrillas, 'special forces', and other
> practitioners of black arts and black economies. The Irish
> border zone, for a century and a half before it was given formal
> recognition through the partition, was already an area (not
> unlike the more formal Scottish Border of the Late Middle
> Ages) of outlawry and semi-legal activity. It is the zone where
> the overwhelming Catholic majority of most of Ireland shades
> into substantial Protestant numbers. It is the zone where, after
> partition, illegal economies flourished all the better for their
> situation in a minefield of religious and political bigotries.[39]

A darker version of the smuggling theme can, incidentally, be found
in Peter Ormrod's feature film *Eat the Peach* (1985), where a subplot
involves smuggling petrol from the North to the South. Here, against
the backdrop of the 'Troubles', the petrol, hidden under the disguise
of a hay wagon, is blown up by the Army.
     In Brendan Behan's *The Hostage* (1958) - admittedly a play set in
the northside of Dublin and thus not, in the stricter sense of the term,
a Border play - it is a member of the British Army, Leslie, who is
kidnapped by the IRA in Belfast and brought across the Border to

Dublin, in order to prevent one of theirs being hanged in Belfast the next morning. Yet, it is illuminating in the way the existence of the Border is implicit in the play, necessary for the development of the parallel fates of Leslie and the Belfast boy destined for the gallows - mirrored, as it were, at the Border.

The Hostage, written at the height of the IRA Border campaign by an ex-member of that organisation who had been in prison both in England and Ireland for his activities, is also noteworthy for its satirical treatment of the IRA. Pat, the landlord of the filthy brothel the IRA has chosen as a hide-out, declares the IRA to be 'as dead as the Charleston'.[40] This could be read as an ironic comment on the failure of the IRA to attract any substantial support for its Border campaign. It was also prophetic, as the IRA in the 1960s virtually ceased to exist - only to be revived in the pogrom atmosphere of 1969.

The irreverence of Behan's *Hostage* is matched by Spike Milligan's *Puckoon* (1963), a spoof for which Milligan seems to have borrowed some ideas from Alfred Hitchcock's *Trouble With Harry* (1955), as a corpse is being buried and frequently re-buried both sides of the Border. We seem nearly to have come full circle, back to the farcical spirit of *Partition*. The Border is again reduced to ridicule, can be made fun of.

This could, in a way, be reflecting the widespread belief in the first half of the 1960s that some kind of convergence between North and South was on the cards; that what was termed the Irish 'economic miracle' in the South, following the industrial policies of Sean Lemass and T K Whitacker after 1958, would bring economy and welfare in the South on a par with the North; the Border would lose its function as an economic divide and evaporate. This feeling of optimism, at the time of John F Kennedy's visit (1962), was boosted by the meetings between the Northern Prime Minister Terence O'Neill and the South's Taoiseach Sean Lemass, during which large-scale cross-Border co-operation was being discussed.[41] Everything seemed to point towards a development which would gradually make the Border as a dividing line obsolete. At long last, Michael Collins' s words of the early 1920s seemed to come true:

> A prosperous Ireland will mean a United Ireland. With equit-
> able taxation and flourishing trade our North-east countrymen
> will need no persuasion to come in and share in the healthy
> economic life of the country.[42]

Tim Pat Coogan, at the time, noticed 'a far better spirit of co-operation';[43] even in an unlikely source like the historian Michael Hurst's study of Maria Edgeworth,[44] this is expressed in an exemplary way in his 'Epilogue', which breathes the spirit of optimism and hope which, tragically, was already in the process of being blown to smithereens by the time the book was eventually published in 1969.

Yet, at the same time there appeared works transcending this (as the eruption of 1968/69 proved) superficial optimism, by addressing the underlying historical structures of Plantation, land ownership and religion in the Borderlands. In the words of Liam de Paor:

> The Border zone is ... an area of high stress in many other aspects. Much of the land among the drumlins is poor, and rural life is hard. The seventeenth-century Plantation left a settlement pattern in which, by and large, Protestants had the better land (mostly the valleys) and Catholics the poorer (mostly in the hills). Land-hunger, envy, bitter memories of real or imagined confiscations, evictions and expropriations long ago, begrudging and religious bigotry characterize parts of the area.[45]

Eugene McCabe, whose short story 'Cancer' belongs to the most impressive literary landmarks on the Border, started his career as a dramatist. His play, *King of the Castle* (1964), is set in Co Leitrim - mostly on Clonhaggard, a Leitrim farm - in the late 1950s. Sixty-nine-year-old Scober (the King) McAdam has married twenty-nine-year-old Tressa, but in three years the marriage has not yielded an heir. Teased by the other farmers, Scober tries to buy the services of a travelling thresherman to get his young wife pregnant.

Although the Border is not once mentioned in the play, we can here see the fate of the mountainy Border farmers. Moreover, Scober in his greed and industry has been successful. He has bought most of the heather fields on the mountain, and in Clonhaggard has taken over the local 'Big House':

> Hundreds of years - we've scraped those rocks - the graveyards full of McAdams - Tobins - Mullarkeys - lived and died - lek scarecrows. When I was a cub I could see this place - these windows lit up like a   ship. Now I look out of them.[46]

The 'King' represents the new Catholic landowning class which, particularly along the Border, has replaced the Anglo-Irish, Protestant ascendancy after independence. 'Taking the Border zone as a whole,' Liam de Paor explains:

> we are faced with a problem largely derived from the Plantation. Catholics form a narrow overall majority, in a crazy pattern of settlement by which Green and Orange are inextricably interlocked. They are interlocked too in a silent, straining struggle, each striving to dislodge the other. This is

largely a struggle over land, as it has been for two hundred years or more.[47]

What also emerges is that for the other mountain farmers who are hired by McAdam for the threshing not much has changed under the new rule. Scober's obsession with the land points towards the Bull McCabe in John B Keane's *The Field* of 1965, another dark tale which caused quite a stir in the 1960s, and to John McGahern's *The Power of Darkness* (1991).

In Stewart Parker's *Catchpenny Twist* (1977) - also, strictly speaking, not really a Border play - Martin and Roy, two Belfast teachers, recently sacked, feel the need to hotfoot it across the Border from Belfast to Dublin, after having committed the crime of writing ballads for both sides (and in consequence having received two ominous bullets with the mail). Their geographical move, first to Dublin, then to London, means also a border-crossing from traditional material into Pop music, which will eventually take them, and their singer-colleague Monagh, to the finals of an European Song Contest in Luxembourg where, after a disastrous performance, their past will eventually catch up with them at the airport in the form of a parcel bomb!

Set against the backdrop of the 'Troubles' - at that time nearly raging for a decade - *Catchpenny Twist* reminds us that hatred and feelings of revenge generated by the situation in the North do not stop at frontiers. Protestant Roy and Catholic Martyn come to symbolise the two communities of Northern Ireland. Physically crossing borders, trying to escape from the 'Troubles' by ignoring them, will not solve the problem.

Their move from Dublin to London is triggered off by further ominous warnings from Belfast, but also by the ignorance, if not hate, of Southerners towards the North, as exemplified by the owner of the nightclub in which Monagh sings:

> I'll tell you what I wish for you lot up North. I wish you'd get on with the bloody killing. Speed it up, hurry it along. Finish each other off, we'll be glad to see the end of you, Protestants and Catholics both, you'll be doing the world a service.[48]

This theme is further developed in Frank McGuinness's *Borderlands* (1984), in which four Derry youths, two Protestant, two Catholic, are - as their placard proclaims - 'marching to Dublin for the Third World'.[49] They cross the Border from Derry, and their banter is soon developing into a serious debate about otherness, different experiences, different backgrounds and traditions. What stops their 'Dancing in the Borderlands'[50] in its tracks is the ignorance they encounter as soon as they have crossed the Border.

In its frightened, fed-up form, this ignorance materialises in Vonie, the landowner, on whose meadow they have put up their tents for the first night in 'the Free State'.[51] Laser, one of the Catholic boys, banks on the proverbial 'Ireland of the Welcomes' and does not envisage any trouble south of the Border: 'They welcome strangers.'[52] A discussion about the Border ensues, as Rocky, the other Catholic boy, states:

> ROCKY: We're not strangers, Laser. We're still in our own
>   country. We don't recognise the border. We're Irish,
> FLUKE: Well, we do recognise the border. Once we cross it,
>   we're not in our own country. Whatever Irish we are,
>   we're not your Irish. We're in the borderlands, Scott
>   and myself.[53]

Yet their working out of what the Borderlands mean to them is interrupted by Vonie's appearance, evicting them from her private property. Her invective, based on Southern indifference, being thoroughly fed-up with the 'Troubles', echoes the prejudiced Dublin nightclub-owner in Stewart Parker's play:

> ... I'm sick and tired listening to your like whinging and whining whenever I switch on the television. I'm fed up hearing what you're going through. I'm sick of checkpoints and helicopters and army jeeps. It's been going on too long up there. One time you might have had my sympathy, but not anymore. Whatever you've got you've brought on yourselves. We've had enough of you. We're tired listening. We're tired of it all.[54]

In its state-authoritative form, the Southern attitude materialises in the Guard who is so brutish and ignorant that even Vonie soon regrets to have called him. The Guard orders them to leave: 'Just mosey on back across the border. We don't need your custom.'[55] When Vonie starts to have second thoughts about his bullying, he explains:

> You shift this type by one means only. When you order them out, you make sure they go ... Just clear them out. Hear no excuses. That's where the Brits made their first mistake. Giving them any sympathy. We won't make that mistake. They won't walk on us when they travel down here. That should prepare them for the day when they get their big wish. Are you all wee Provies, lads? Don't be. They don't look very far forward. They might be able to give us a hard time now. But they'll get a harder time when we have full rein in their united Ireland,

they might regret wanting that ... The silent majority is right behind us.

After that encounter, the boys are determined to turn round, even if Vonie now would let them camp on her land. Yet, their borderlands experience seems to have brought them closer together, seems to have created a new sense of solidarity. A TEAM production,[56] widely touring schools and youth venues and offering workshops, the play serves not only as a warning or a plea to people in the South to listen to people in the North, its themes revolve around images of identity, what it means to be Irish north and south of the Border. It ends optimistically, putting faith in the young generation's resolution to think for themselves, to talk and listen, and perhaps change.

Frank McGuinness, himself from Buncrana, near the Derry-Donegal Border, teaching in Maynooth and living in Dublin, should be the one to know what Southern prejudices are like. The Borderlands that formed him have also featured in *The Factory Girls* (1982), a play set in a Donegal shirt factory. By dramatising a women workers' strike, it highlights the problems of the textile industry, exacerbated in this case by the fact that Donegal is cut off by the Border from its neighbouring towns, particularly Derry.[57]

Like nearly everything that Shane Connaughton has written, his play *Lily* (1984) is set in the borderlands of Fermanagh, Monaghan and Cavan. And like most of his books, *Lily* has an autobiographical ring about it. It is set in an RUC station on the Border in Fermanagh, just as Connaughton himself grew up in Redhill in a Garda station, a stone's throw south of the Border in Cavan.

Lily, having fallen in love with Danny in Dublin, returns pregnant to the Borderlands. Her father meets her with utter incomprehension:

> I can't understand it! ... We arrested a Fenian last night in a farm yard. He was loaded. Right you bastard, don't move or you're dead! I wanted to kill him there and then. And I'm telling you I don't know what stopped me! But tell you this ... when I looked into his eyes and he looked into mine, I understood him better than I understand her!
>
> ...
>
> Goes away to the Free State and comes back loaded! ... Constable Agnew's daughter up the pole be a Catholic! It's the joke of the century round here.[58]

In his verdict, both the IRA man and his daughter are 'loaded', the paramilitary's gun as dangerous and outrageous as his daughter's pregnancy!

Smuggling illegal goods - from pigs to video tape recorders - and illegal cock-fighting preoccupy Lily's father, but the scene has changed since *The Devil Came from Dublin*: now there are, in Lily's words, '[g]reen, orange, red, white and blue lepracauns trying to kill each other.'[59] And her Northern suitor, Sammy, a Methodist preacher, has a bunch of cronies ready to give Danny a rough welcome - on the word of Lily's father. The play goes to the brink of destruction for the Agnew family, but eventually Sammy and Lily get away, and a faint hope remains that her father will accept his grandchild:

> LILY: Course you can. When it's born, it's a chance for us all to start clean and fresh again. Now isn't it?
> FATHER: Is it? Is it?
> LILY: What hope is there otherwise?[60]

Not much, anyway, if one were to go by one of the most impressive theatrical productions of the 1990s: *At the Black Pig's Dyke* by Vincent Woods, set at the very Black Pig's Dyke, marking the south-western Border between Ulster and Connacht. The play was first produced by Druid Theatre Company in Galway in 1992, followed by a nationwide tour and return visits to the Gate Theatre in Dublin. This 'truly superb and innovative piece of theatre'[61] tells a dark fable of love and hate on the Leitrim/Fermanagh border. Lizzie Flynn rejects 'one of her own' in favour of the Protestant shopkeeper Jack Boles, which sparks off a terrible 'chain of violence, murder and despair'.[62]

Most striking is the use of folk traditions in the play. In a bold move, 'reclaiming performance',[63] Woods demonstrates that theatrical performances can be rooted in folk traditions like the mummers, presenting us with a set of intriguingly sinister-looking 'Strawboys'. The play thus gains mythic quality, the violence becomes ritualistic, 'terrifying both in its intensiy and its inevitability.'[64] What makes the play gloomily pessimistic is that the second part, set a generation later, re-enacts the same bloody drama. There seems no escape, atavistically expounding the poet Carol Rumens's line, 'A border likes blood'.[65]

It is maybe no accident that the play appeared two years before the Cease-fires, at a time of disillusion about the Anglo-Irish Agreement of 1985 and frustration over the Brooke talks, a time of renewed terror in the aftermath of Loughgall and Gibraltar. It certainly marks the darkest and most pessimistic contribution offered by Irish dramatists on the Border theme - and yet it is exhilarating in its sheer energy and theatricality. Another example of a 1990s treatment of Border violence is Michael Harding's *Hubert Murray's Widow* which was presented at the Peacock Theatre in April 1993. With its dark shade of black humour, involving ghosts, terrorists and counter-terrorists, the play, set 'in a rural farmhouse, just inside Fermanagh',[66] revolves around a gun-smuggling plot across the Border to Cavan:

> ENDA: Tomorrow, Father Boyle, not only will you be
> honouring Hubert, but you'll also be presiding over
> twenty Kalashnikov rifles, which we urgently need to
> get across the border, and Hubert's coffin is about our
> only means of transport.[67]

Hubert Murray was ripped to pieces by a bomb; he either died 'in action', mishandling a bomb, or was killed by 'SAS units known to be active in the border area ... because he was a known Republican.'[68] Harding's play is a *danse macabre*, in which the two ghosts of Hugh Murray and of Gene, a young Protestant, are fighting over body and soul of Rhoda, Hubert Murray's widow. The backdrop of sectarianism is summed up by Gene: 'I understood that long time ago about Ulster. The problem has no solution. Violence is just a way of imposing order on the chaos.'[69]

In analysing the sectarian conflict in the borderlands as a conflict without a solution, or an ancient ritual, repeating itself generation after generation, both Michael Harding's and Vincent Woods' plays stand in a line - albeit at the pessimistic end of it - of dramatic exercises which have tried to get to the roots, the underlying structures, of the Irish conflict: Brian Friel's *Translations* (1980), Frank McGuinness's *Observe the Sons of Ulster Marching Towards the Somme* (1985), Stewart Parker's *Northern Star* (1984), and Friel's *Making History* (1988).

Brian Friel, of course, is a playwright from the Borderlands. Born in Omagh, Co Tyrone, he lives close to the Border on the Donegal side of the Foyle. Being located in the Republic - also known as The South - he actually looks south in the direction of Northern Ireland (or The North)! In a recent interview, Declan Kiberd quoted Friel as having said:

> My truest reality is not when I'm in the Republic and not when
> I'm in the North. It is the moment when I feel I'm crossing
> over. That is when I feel most alive, most myself.[70]

How Friel goes about boundaries is indicated most clearly in *The Freedom of the City* (1973) where three Catholic demonstrators cross the invisible border surrounding Derry's Guildhall, the symbol of Protestant/Unionist domination. Arguably, it is this violation of a sacred boundary which costs them their lives at the end. In his many plays, Friel may not have directly addressed the Border, as he avoids becoming too overtly political on stage, yet there is an underlying sense of the borderlands in many of his works, and ignoring the frontier of Partition in favour of an all-Ireland perspective is perhaps as political as dealing with the territorial and political dividing line. Quoting a Friel interview in the *Irish Times* (14 September 1982), Ulf Dantanus observed of Field Day, the company Friel co-founded in 1980 with, amongst others, Stephen Rea, Seamus Deane and Seamus Heaney, that it

> does not accept a simplified and entrenched North-South division because of 'the very fact that it's located in the North and has its reservations about it, and that it works in the South and has its reservations about it'... What Friel and Field Day are looking for is 'some kind of awareness, some kind of sense of the country, what this island is about, North and South, and what are our attitudes to it'.[71]

Field Day attempted to create a 'fifth province', transcending North and South, addressing 'the whole island culturally, if not politically.[72] Seamus Heaney saw himself and, by implication, Field Day, in the tradition of Louis MacNeice:

> ... he did not allow the border to enter into his subsequent imaginings: his sense of cultural diversity and historical consequence within the country never congealed into a red and green map ... and my suggestion was no more than another attempt to bring the frontiers of the country into alignment with the frontiers of writing, an attempt to sketch the shape of an integrated literary tradition.[73]

With plays like *Translations* (1980) and *Making History* (1988), Friel explored the crossroads in the shaping of Irish history and identity.

Another - less refined - attempt at showing the course of Irish history in the twentieth century, with Partition as the central event from which the 'Troubles' develop, is Bill Morrison's trilogy *A Love Song for Ulster* (1993). Here, in a slightly over-didactic script, Morrison uses the well-worn family metaphor ('1922-1936 The Marriage', '1939-1969 The Son', '1969-1993 The Daughter')[74] of living in a house divided by foreign (male) interference:

> SERGEANT: And where are you going?
> KATE: That's my mother over there. I want to go with her.
> SERGEANT: Sorry, the line's been drawn. You can't cross it.
> KATE: But I don't want to be here. I want to be with the rest.
> SERGEANT: You're left in the North. That's the way the line's
>   been drawn.
> KATE: Then redraw the bloody line.

SERGEANT: Sorry, love, I didn't make the rules.[75]

It is a big step from this undertaking to *A Night in November* by Belfast writer Marie Jones. This play opened to an enthusiastic response at the West Belfast Festival in 1994, just before the IRA cease-fire was called. In one of the most stunning one-man shows of recent years, it takes its cue from the last qualifying soccer match between the Republic of Ireland and Northern Ireland which was to secure the Southern team's participation in the 1994 World Cup finals in the USA.

This night in November 1993 becomes the point of departure for one man's journey, which will take him across several frontiers and change his outlook fundamentally. We take off with Protestant Kenneth Norman McCallister, from the dole office where he works and plays his discriminatory games with poor unemployed Catholics, through the haunting night at Windsor Park, with its sectarian excesses; we cross with him his first, and perhaps most mindboggling, frontier, the one between East and West Belfast, when he gives his boss, a Catholic, a lift - a truly unsettling experience! We see the alienation between him and his wife and their Protestant friends grow, all drawn against the backdrop of new developments in Northern Ireland, the Joint Declaration of December 1993, which his Unionist 'friends' and acquaintances seem to be determined to ignore.

Eventually he makes up his mind to cross that ultimate frontier between North and South and join with the droves of Irish fans to be whipped over to the States from Dublin Airport. He meets a Protestant from Dublin who seems to have no problem matching that fact to being an ardent Irish football supporter. Having no ticket for the first match, he witnesses the 1:0 victory against Italy in Eamon Doran's Bar in New York, and is swept out onto the street with the celebrating fans. It is here, at the climax of the celebration, that he learns of the terrible news from Northern Ireland. During the match, two gun-men had entered O'Toole's pub in Loughinisland, had produced rifles and riddled the place with bullets. Six people were killed, five were injured in this 'last mass slaughter of the Troubles'.[76] The effect is shattering, the contrast dramatically effective as in the best of O'Casey. Kenneth Norman McCallister's newly-found identity as an 'Irishman from Belfast'[77] is sealed by the shock of the revelation. Finally, he fully and explicitly renounces any tacit acceptance of Unionist/Loyalist political violence:

Come on in and have a drink Mick... I want you to drink with me, because tonight I can stand here and tell you that I am no part of the men who did that... I am not of them anymore... no, no-one can point the finger at Kenneth Norman McCallister and say, these people are part of you... tonight I absolve myself... I am free of them, Mick... I am free of it, I am a free man... I am a Protestant Man, I'm an Irish Man.[78]

This contrasts starkly with his definition of the Republic of Ireland as a foreign country, given at the beginning of the play when recounting an exchange in his former incarnation at the dole office where an applicant wants family income supplement but is put off by him till the next day:

> ... Sure I'm here now...
> So?
> So can I not see them people now...
> So am I...
> So are you what?
> Here now but I have to come back tomorrow don't I?
> Aye, but I won't be here... I have to go to Dublin.
> (*Writes*) Not available for work as out of the country.
> What... I'm only going to Dublin for the morning.
> You're out of the country.
> I'm going out on the eight o'clock and back on the 11 o'clock. I'm only taking my oul ma down to meet her sister who is meeting her at the station.
> You're out of the country.
> I'm not gettin' off the train I'll only be helping her onto the platform.
> The train will be in a foreign country and you will be on it and technically speaking you are not available for work as you are out of the country.
> Standing on a platform?
> A foreign country platform.[79]

By the end of the play, Kenneth Norman McCallister has travelled far. Little wonder that a play with a message like this, coming from a writer with a Protestant background, would be rewarded with standing ovations from a west Belfast and more than predominantly Catholic/nationalist audience. But the play has since successfully toured Ireland, and played to great acclaim in London and Glasgow, which should prove its appeal beyond any playing to the galleries.

Eoin McNamee's *The Last of Deeds* is no Border novella, but the passage quoted in the introduction to this essay indicates the presence of the Border image in Northern Irish society. Again, *A Night in November* may not be a Border play in the strictest sense of the word, but the theme of Border crossings is all-important in it. Thus it is in the tradition, but in its optimistic development also breaking with it, of other, darker, plays focusing on the crossing of internal boundaries. *Catchpenny Twist* has already been mentioned. The opening scene of Christina Reid's *Tea in a China Cup* (1983), highlighting the divisive borderlines extending to the cemeteries of Belfast, would also come to mind; or, starting its course in a cemetery, the late romance between a Catholic widow and a Protestant widower who have both lost children to sectarian violence, in Graham Reid's *Remembrance* (1984). This latter play is both an expression of the possibility of communication across the sectarian dividing line, and also an outcry against entrenched bitterness and blind hate, as this Indian summer relationship is ultimately frustrated by the younger generation not allowing their old folks to trespass into the territory of the 'other'.

Paul Muldoon's 'The Boundary Commission' led us into this survey of Border plays; it so happens that we may as well conclude it with Paul Muldoon. His *Six Honest Serving Men* (1995), set in a 'safe house', a house nearby, and a look-out post 'on the border of counties Armagh and Monaghan',[80] brings us back to the Borderlands proper. The house nearby is Kate's. She is the widow of 'Gilbey' Brian McInerney - 'The Chief' - who, as we learn early on, was assassinated and buried two weeks earlier:

> Himself and Clery had set out
> on another run of the mill
> run for the border ... He was killed
> when they stopped for a cup of tea
> in Omagh...[81]

Kate is under surveillance, surrounded by 'six honest serving men', six IRA activists who seem preoccupied employing the 'six honest serving men' of the song ('Their names are What and Why and When / and How and Where and Who') to make sense of the events a fortnight earlier and of what has happened since. Was the killing of The Chief an 'inside job', as McCabe insinuates?[82] How did Clery get away in Omagh? Did McCabe have 'the motive / to kill The Chief', as Ward suggests?[83] What has happened to 'Dumdum' Devine, 'Taco' Bell and Dessie Gillespie who have not been seen since The Chief was killed in Omagh? Were Clery and McGuffin really in Donegal at the time? What about the rivalry between Taggart and The Chief that Ward makes much of?[84] Has 'Shoshone' Taggart been 'turned' in the USA, where he was on a 'little shopping trip in Boston,' as McGuffin suspects?[85] And who of all of them had an affair with Kate?

> Suppose the men I took into my bed
> would take it then into their heads
> to give Gilbey the chop...[86]

Who of the six is Kate's mysterious visitor? Not McGuffin and Ward, as they observe the scene, not McAnespie and Clery who are still at the 'safe house'. Taggart or McCabe? Two pistol shots are heard.[87] Who has been killed? Certainly not Ward, as the play ends with his coming to Kate's house. McCabe returns to the 'safe house', and we leave that scene with him being tortured by Clery and McAnespie. No sign of Taggart and McGuffin. Were they shot by McCabe? Or by Ward? Did Kate have an affair with both Ward and Taggart, and why is she 'as if in shock',[88] when she sees Ward coming to the house?

Six Honest Serving Men is a cleverly, perhaps over-cleverly, written piece, intertwining nursery rhymes, music hall song and Yeats's 'Easter 1916' into a verbal fireworks. The urge is sometimes there to take recourse to one of Kate's inflight magazines, preferably the one advertising 'The Crosswords Puzzle Solver from Franklin',[89] to get all the clues and solve the riddle. Yet, perhaps that is, after all, not of paramount importance. What if the inflight magazine provides the cue - of a group of men in full flight (a 'flying column'!), encapsulated, as it were, out of touch with reality? Impersonalised voices bouncing off that capsule, making it impossible to personalise them; 'flying blind', and therefore doubly dangerous? We seem to get the image of a fraught IRA unit in the borderlands, rent by internal strife and divisions, faintly set against the backdrop of this unit's members and their irritated reactions to some of the new thinking within the republican movement. McAnespie has to reassure himself that the old values still count:

> When Michael Collins' time ran out at Béal
> na mBláth it should have meant the end of the line
> for the ballot-box, since the Armalite
> and the Armalite alone will hit
> the Brits where it hurts ...[90]

And Taggart has only a sneer for the Che Guevara adage that 'The terrorist of today is the statesman of tomorrow', here applied to McCabe - but which could also be seen as an echo of the aspirations of Gerry Adams and Martin McGuinness.[91]

Muldoon's verse play seems well within the tradition of the darker vision of circles of violence in the borderlands, characteristic in its pessimistic outlook for the majority of Border plays in the 1980s and 1990s - with the glorious exception of Marie Jones's *A Night in November*.

Conclusion

From *Partition* to *At the Black Pig's Dyke* and *Six Honest Serving Men* - we can follow in these plays the developments concerning the Border and its perception, from its conception and establishment to the coming to terms with the reality of the Border - perhaps only accepted by 1939, as Hugh Kearney indicated - and the establishment of the Border as both an economic and a political divide, connected with smuggling, checkpoints and bombing campaigns.

There can be distinguished two co-existing and conflicting images of the Border: one deeply pessimistic, a dark view of generations of conflict about land, of bitter feuds, of a never-ending circle of violence, as in Vincent Woods; the other expressing hope and the belief that people are fed up with it and want to create a more positive future, as embodied in Marie Jones's Kenneth Norman McCallister. But is it that simple? The more pessimistic view seems to transcend the reality of the frontier of Partition and take the boundary between the provinces as its reference point.

Does the Border delineate 'A Place Apart'? Or is it an artificial line drawn by an imperial power? Both Patrick Quigley and Shane Connaughton seem to tend towards the latter:

> 'You feel free of the world and its rules here.' She pulled a blade of grass across her tongue. 'You can see things as they really are. Just like the old Border they make so much fuss over. Up here you can see it doesn't exist. It's all in people's minds.'[92]

> The cobweb-coloured Finn divided the North from the South. But the country on each side showed as little difference as the two sides of your face. The country was one. It was the people who were divided.[93]

On the other hand, Ulster has always been, in the phrase of Dervla Murphy's influential book, 'A Place Apart'; and Liam de Paor assists: 'Ulster is different ... This was so before Partition; indeed, to some extent, it was true before the Plantation.'[94]

That second line would refer to the Border between the historic Ulster and the other Irish provinces, not the Border of the six counties - which divides Ulster. Let us not forget: the great Border to cross, from Cromwell to the Irish Renaissance, was the Shannon: Hell or Connaught, into the West, or even, as in Synge's case, to the Aran Islands. Here, beyond this Border, was the 'real Ireland', Celtic, peasant, rural, poor, as opposed to the anglicised 'West Brit' Pale.

The Border play does perhaps not amount to a sub-genre of Irish drama, perhaps it is no more than an extended footnote of Irish literature and drama. Perhaps, it might be argued, border crossings of a different kind, of the mind, of borders within north or south are ultimately of greater importance (East/West Belfast, Bogside/ Waterside, Dublin North and South, town and country), as shown in the examples by Friel, Parker, Jones, and both Christina and Graham Reid. Internal divisions and boundaries, as in Marie Jones's *A Night in November*, remind us of the lines in Louis MacNeice's famous poem, 'Carrickfergus':

> The Norman walled this town against the country
>   To stop his ears to the yelping of his slave...
>
> I was the rector's son, born to the anglican order,
>   Banned for ever from the candles of the Irish poor...[95]

Yet there remains the physical fact of the Border, and its importance for all kinds of activities. Not least for IRA activities: the 'safe house' in Paul Muldoon's play (close to the Border, convenient to get away into the Republic); or, as in M S Power's novel *Lonely The Man Without Heroes* (1986), where the IRA's Chief of Staff resides in Clones, just across the Border; and to Clones are brought both Sergeant Barton for questioning and Colonel Sharman, the IRA hostage. Another meeting place in the novel is 'Clancy's Pub':

> ... a small, crumbling, ramshackle affair with a thatched roof and two weed-ridden hanging baskets by the door, but it was strategically situated, close to the border, and approachable only by a narrow dirt track which was clearly visible from the windows.[96]

Irish writers throughout this century have written about the Border itself, and of the mentalities responsible for it or, indeed, bred by it. They have written about the divisions within society, about the boundaries between the 'us' and the 'others', geographically - town and country, east and west Belfast - as well as socially.

Shifting the political debate away from the territorial notion of the Border to the 'two traditions' and questions of identity puts the spotlight on these internal dividing lines. Many of the writers have themselves crossed these boundaries, or attempted imaginary border-crossings, as when playwright John Boyd (*The Flats*, 1971), a writer with a Protestant working-class background, depicts convincingly the beleaguered state of a Catholic family in the Divis flats of Belfast at the beginning of the 'Troubles', or when Frank McGuinness, with his Donegal-Catholic background, becomes the chronicler of the identity-forging Unionist/Loyalist First World War experience at the Somme (in *Observe the Sons of Ulster Marching Towards the Somme*, 1985) or when Marie Jones celebrates the resilience of Catholic working-class women in west Belfast in Charabanc's *Somewhere Over the Balcony* (1987).[97] Questioning cultural boundaries, making connections, and thinking the 'other', are subversive long-term projects, directed against what Carlo Gébler observed in his notebook during the marching season: '... two cultures shouting through their emblems vociferously at one another and yet not having the slightest interest in communicating.'[98] This found such explicit expression in the words of a school headmaster that his phrase gave Gébler the title of his book:

> 'There's a glass curtain here,' he [the Headmaster] said. 'When you first arrive, you can't see it, and many people who live here can't see it either, or won't. But it's here all right, separating the two commu-nities, only you don't find out about it until you walk into it - bang! - and break your nose.'[99]

Yet, after having lived for a year in Enniskillen, Gébler ends his book meditating on his experience in the old Catholic graveyard of Enniskillen, finding it

> a good place to consider the myth that here there are two monolithic communities, Protestant and Catholic, and that they have stared angrily at each other down the centuries. The evidence on the graveyard disproves that. Enniskillen - until comparatively recent times anyway - was an island town, and on such places people intermingle. That was how one got Catholic and Protestant Carsons.[100]

Relations along the Border have undergone many shifts and changes since Partition. In many places, they have particularly soured after 1969. William Trevor's story 'The Distant Past' is a perfect illustration. The Middletons of Carraveagh, a declining Protestant 'Big House', have long been seen by the nearby townspeople as being a bit of an anachronism. But they are well-liked; their little spleens (such as driving around in their Ford Anglia 'with a small Union Jack popped up in the back win-dow' to mark the coronation of Queen Elizabeth II[101]) caused benevolent laughter. Yet, with the outbreak of the 'Troubles', things change:

> There were incidents in Fermanagh and Armagh, in border villages and towns ...
>
> The town's prosperity ebbed. The border was more than sixty miles away, but over that distance had spread some

wisps of the fog of war. As anger rose in the town at the loss of fortune so there rose also the kind of talk there had been in the distant past.[102]

'Slowly the change crept about,'[103] until the erstwhile foibles of the Middletons are no longer seen as merely laughing matters. 'Had they driven with a Union Jack now they would, astoundingly, have been shot.'[104] The hardening of a frontier mentality has hardly ever been described more meticulously than in Trevor's story. 'For fifty years,' the Middletons have to realise in their old age, 'they had experienced, after suspicion had seeped away, a tolerance that never again in the years that were left to them would they know.'[105] In a touching epitaph, William Trevor, a Catholic born in Cork, catches the sad fate of these Protestants stranded on the wrong side of the Border, caught up in a past that has caught up with them: 'Because of the distant past they would die friendless. It was worse than being murdered in their beds.'[106]

The same theme is touched upon in a little anecdotal story Carlo Gébler noted in his diary:

> A true story. In a little village on the Tyrone-Fermanagh border, there is only one Lambeg drum. When the Orangemen march on the Twelfth, they take it. When the St Patrick's parade comes round, the Nationalists have their turn with it.
>
> This is in the early 1960s. In 1969, as the Troubles gear up, the arrangement collapses, and each side organizes its own drum, full-time.[107]

Ireland is an island, but it is not an isolated case. Writing in what was Britain's closest and earliest colony, Ireland's writers reflect the ambiguous post-coloniality of Ireland.[108] In the wider context of looking at the state of Northern Ireland as 'unfinished business', as an at least semi-post-colonial situation, we might be reminded of what Edward Said remarked:

> As the struggle for independence produced new states and new boundaries, it also produced homeless wanderers, nomads, vagrants, unassimilated to the emergent structures of institutional power, rejected by the established order for their intransigence and obdurate rebelliousness. And in so far as these people exist between the old and the new, between the old empire and the new state, their condition articulates the tensions, irresolutions, and contradictions in the overlapping territories shown on the cultural map of imperialism.[109]

Overlapping cultural territories - that is not a bad description of the Irish Border. Yet, as long as writers engage in the process of imagining the 'other', there is hope that boundaries can be transformed into lines of communication and exchange. As Said concluded:

> ... just as human beings make their own history, they also make their own cultures and ethnic identities. No one can deny the persisting continuities of long traditions, sustained habitations, national languages, and cultural geographies, but there seems no reason except fear and prejudice to keep insisting on their separation and distinctiveness, as if that was all human life was about. Survival in fact is about the connections between things ... It is more rewarding - and more difficult - to think concretely and sympathetically, contrapunctally, about others than only about 'us'. But this also means not trying to rule others, not trying to classify them or put them in hierarchies, above all, not constantly reiterating how 'our' culture or country is number one (or *not* number one, for that matter).[110]

Edward Said's observations, translated into the Irish context, point towards a way in which Irish writers can be understood as supporting the transformation necessary for, to come back to Seamus Heaney's words, 'a future where the vitality that flowed in the beginning from those bracing words "enemy" and "allies" might finally derive from a less binary and altogether less binding vocabulary.'[111]

'The writer,' Joe McMinn wrote, 'is someone who puts words into our mouths, who invents an identity for us, who provides us with a role to imagine.'[112] This crucial role of the writer, in Ireland, and particularly in the North, is emphasised, finally, by Fintan O'Toole:

> Stories have a beginning, a middle, and an end. Facts like the ones the people of the North have had to live with for 25 years, have a beginning and a middle. The ending has to be supplied by the imagination.[113]

Notes

1   Seamus Heaney, *Crediting Poetry: The Nobel Lecture 1995*, Loughcrew, Oldcastle: Gallery Press, p.23.

2   Edward W Said, *Culture and Imperialism*, London: Vintage, 1994, p.408.

3   Shane Connaughton, *The Run of the Country*, Harmonsworth: Penguin, 1995, p.2.

4   *Ibid.*, p.4.

5   Maurice Leitch, *Poor Lazarus*, Belfast: Blackstaff, 1985, p.31.

6   *Ibid.*, p.32.

7   *Ibid.*, p.71

8   *The Run of the Country*, p.46.

9   Colm Tóibín, *Walking Along the Border*, London: Macdonald & Co (Queen Anne Press), 1987, pp.9-10.

10 Patrick Quigley, *Borderland*, Dingle: Brandon, 1994, p.14.

11 *Ibid.*, pp.14-15.

12 *Ibid.*, p.213.

13 Pat McCabe, *Carn*, London: Picador, 1993, p.11.

14 Benedict Kiely, *Proxopera*, Boston: Godine, 1987, p.49.

15 Seamus Heaney, 'The Flight Path', from the collection *The Spirit Level*, London: Faber and Faber, 1996, pp.24-25.

16 Seamus Deane, *Reading in the Dark*, London: Jonathan Cape, 1996, pp.209-11.

17 John Montague, 'A Good Year', in Lothar Fietz, Paul Hoffmann and Hans-Werner Ludwig (eds), *Regionalität und Internationalität in der zeitgenösischen Lyrik: Erträge des Siebten Blaubeurer Symposions*, Tübingen: Attempto, 1992, pp.191-94; p.191.

18 John Montague, 'Border Sick-Call', in *The Southern Review*, Vol.31, No.3 (Summer 1995): A Special Issue: Contemporary Irish Poetry and Criticism, pp.409-23; p.409.

19 *Ibid.*, pp.415-16.

20 Eoin McNamee, *The Last of Deeds*, Dublin: Raven Arts Press, 1989; Harmondsworth: Penguin, 1992, p.52.

21 Paul Muldoon, 'The Boundary Commission', from the collection *Why Brownlee Left*, London: Faber and Faber, 1980, p.15.

22 *Partition* was first produced on 15 November 1916 at the Abbey Theatre, Dublin. First published Dublin: James Duffy & Co, 1917; twice reprinted, 1951 and 1975. All subsequent quotations are from the 1975 Duffy imprint. I am grateful to Séamus de Búrca for supplying me with a copy of this play.

23 *Partition*, p.7.

24 *Ibid.*, p.17.

25 *Ibid.*, p.20.

26 *Ibid.*, p.6.

27 R F Foster, *Modern Ireland, 1600-1972*, p.507.

28 Liam de Paor, *Unfinished Business: Ireland Today and Tomorrow*, London: Hutchinson Radius, 1990, p.61.

29 Hugh Kearney, *The British Isles: A History of Four Nations*, Cambridge: Cambridge University Press, 1989; Canto, 1995, p.264.

30 Paul Vincent Carroll, *The Devil Came from Dublin: A Satirical Extravaganza in Three Acts*, in P V Carroll, *Irish Stories and Plays*, New York: Devin-Adair, 1958, pp.179-278.

31 *The Devil Came from Dublin*, p.190.

32 *Ibid.*, p.183.

33 *Ibid.*, p.185.

34 *Ibid.*, p.186.

35 *Ibid.*, p.195.

36 *Ibid.*, pp.196-97.

37 Quigley, *Borderland*, pp.210-11.

38 *The Devil Came from Dublin*, p.277.

39 Liam de Paor, *Unfinished Business*, p.67.

40 Brendan Behan, *The Hostage*, London: Methuen, 1958.

41 See *The Irish Times*, 2 January 1996.

42 Michael Collins, *The Path to Freedom*, quoted in Eamonn O'Neill, 'Irish revolutionary had a sharp eye for tax detail', in *Scotland on Sunday*, 17 November 1996.

43 Tim Pat Coogan, *Ireland Since the Rising*, London: Pall Mall Press, 1966, p.297.

44 'British power and southern realism have prevented substantial trouble arising out of partition.' '...religious bigotry seldom finds an outlet of sufficient importance for provoking any major or persistent crises.' Michael Hurst, *Maria Edgeworth and the Public Scene: Intellect, Fine Feeling, and Landlordism in the Age of Reform*, London: Macmillan, 1969, p.181.

45 Liam de Paor, *Unfinished Business*, p.68.

46 Eugene McCabe, *King of the Castle*, Loughcrew, Oldcastle: The Gallery Press, 1978, p.31.

47 Liam de Paor, *Unfinished Business*, p.69.

48 Stewart Parker, *Catchpenny Twist*, Loughcrew, Oldcastle: The Gallery Press, 1977, pp.25-26.

49 Frank McGuinness, *Borderlands*, in Martin Drury (ed), *Three Team Plays*, Dublin: Wolfhound, 1988, pp.150-91; p.158.

50 *Ibid.*, p.175.

51 *Ibid.*, p.155.

52 *Ibid.*, p.161.

53 *Ibid.*

54 *Ibid.*, p.175.

55 *Ibid.*, p.179.

56 TEAM is a Dublin-based theatre-in-education venture which celebrated its 25th anniversary in 1995.

57 See my 'Acts of Inclusion: The Theatre of Frank McGuinness', in E Bort (ed), *'Standing in their shifts itself...': Irish Drama from Farquhar to Friel*, Bremen: European Society for Irish Studies, 1993, pp.221-41.

58 Shane Connaughton, *Lily*, London: The Irish Company, 1987, pp.44-45.

59 *Ibid.*, p.7.

60 *Ibid.*, p.54.

61 Mary Hyland, 'At the Black Pig's Dyke', review in *In Dublin*, Vol.19, No.5 (2-15 March 1994), p.24.

62 *Ibid.*

63 See Anna McMullan, 'Reclaiming Performance: The Contemporary Irish Independent Theatre Sector', in Eberhard Bort (ed), *The State of Play: Irish Theatre in the 'Nineties*, Trier: Wissenschaftlicher Verlag Trier, 1996, pp. 29-38; pp.32-33.

64 Hyland, *loc. cit.*

65   Carol Rumens, *Best China Sky*, Newcastle: Bloodaxe, 1995.
66   Michael Harding, *Hubert Murray's Widow*, in Christopher Fitz-Simon and Sanford Sternlicht (eds), *New Plays from the Abbey Theatre, 1993-1995*, Syracuse, New York: Syracuse University Press, 1996, pp.3-69; p.4.
67   *Ibid.*, p.43.
68   *Ibid.*, p.9.
69   *Ibid.*, p.42.
70   'The Only Thing Keeping Ireland out of the Third World is the Weather: An Interview with Declan Kiberd on Field Day and his new book *Inventing Ireland*', in *Hard Times*, No.58 (Autumn/Winter 1996), pp.22-29; p.25.
71   Ulf Dantanus, *Brian Friel: A Study*, London: Faber and Faber, 1988, p.207.
72   *Ibid.*, p.209.
73   Seamus Heaney, 'Frontiers of Writing', in S Heaney, *The Redress of Poetry: Oxford Lectures*, London: Faber and Faber, 1995, pp.186-203; pp.198-99.
74   Bill Morrison, *A Love Song for Ulster: An Irish Trilogy*, London: Nick Hern Books, 1994, pp.ix-xi.
75   *Ibid.*, p.9.
76   Terry McLaughlin, 'RUC hold two brothers over pub massacre', in *The Sunday Independent*, 7 July 1996, p.3.
77   Marie Jones, *A Night in November*, Dublin: New Island Books, 1995, p.46.
78   *Ibid*, p.47.
79   *Ibid.*, pp.9-10.
80   Paul Muldoon, *Six Honest Serving Men*, Loughcrew, Oldcastle: Gallery Press, 1995, p.9.
81   *Ibid.*, p.14.
82   *Ibid.*, p.12.
83   *Ibid.*, p.46.
84   *Ibid.*, p.20.
85   *Ibid.*, p.18.
86   *Ibid.*, p.42.
87   *Ibid.*, p.47.
88   *Ibid.*, p.50.
89   *Ibid.*, p.30.
90   *Ibid.*, p.27.
91   *Ibid.*, p.46.
92   Quigley, *Borderland*, p.80.
93   Connaughton, *The Run of the Country*, p.53.
94   Liam de Paor, *Unfinished Business*, p.59.
95   Louis MacNeice, 'Carrickfergus', in W H Auden (ed), *Selected Poems of Louis MacNeice*, London: Faber and Faber, 1964, p.29.
96   M S Power, *Lonely The Man Without Heroes*, London: Abacus, 1987, p.105.
97   See my 'Staging the Troubles: Civil Conflict and Drama in Northern Ireland', in *Journal for the Study of British Cultures*, Vol.2, No.2 (1995), pp.141-60; especially pp.157-58.
98   Carlo Gébler, *The Glass Curtain: Inside an Ulster Community*, London: Hamish Hamilton, 1991, p.22.
99   *Ibid.*, p.54.
100 *Ibid.*, p.216.

101 William Trevor, 'The Distant Past', in W Trevor, *The Distant Past*, Dublin: Poolbeg, 1979; also reprinted in Michael Parker (ed), *The Hurt World: Short Stories of The Troubles*, Belfast: Blackstaff, 1995, pp.247-60; p.253.

102 *Ibid.*, pp.257-258.

103 *Ibid.*, p.258.

104 *Ibid.*

105 *Ibid.*, p.259.

106 *Ibid.*, p.260.

107 Carlo Gébler, *The Glass Curtain*, p.34.

108 In Frederic Jameson's famous phrase of Ireland being, in terms of colonialism, both 'lord and bondsman together.' F Jameson, 'Modernism and Imperialism', Field Day Pamphlet, in Seamus Deane (ed), *Ireland's Field Day*, London: Hutchinson, 1985.

109 Edward W Said, *Culture and Imperialism*, pp.402-03.

110 *Ibid.*, p.408.

111 Seamus Heaney, *Crediting Poetry*, p.23.

112 Joe McMinn, 'Language, Literature and Cultural Identity: Irish and Anglo-Irish', in Jean Lundy and Aodán Mac Póilin (eds), *Styles of Belonging: The Cultural Identities of Ulster*, Belfast: Lagan Press, 1992, pp.46-53; p.49.

113 Fintan O'Toole, 'The Facts of History', *The Irish Times* , February 1994, reprinted in O'Toole, *Black Hole, Green Card: The Disappearance of Ireland*, Dublin: New Island Books, 1994, pp.88-91; p.91.

Contributors

Malcolm Anderson	is Professor of Politics and Director of the International Social Sciences Institute at the University of Edinburgh.
Paul Arthur	is Professor of Politics at the University of Ulster.
Eberhard Bort	is a Research Fellow at the International Social Sciences Institute, University of Edinburgh.
Steve Bruce	is Professor of Sociology at the University of Aberdeen.
Shane Connaughton	is a novelist, dramatist, short story and screenwriter.
Owen Dudley Edwards	is Reader in History at the University of Edinburgh.
Ullrich Kockel	is a Lecturer in the Institute of Irish Studies at the University of Liverpool.
Ged Martin	is Director of the Centre of Canadian Studies at the University of Edinburgh.
Eugene McCabe	is a novelist, short story writer and dramatist.
Máiréad Nic Craith	is a Lecturer in the Institute of Irish Studies at the University of Liverpool.
Etain Tannam	is a Lecturer in Politics at University College Galway.
Ian S Wood	is a Lecturer in History at Napier University, Edinburgh.

Culture and Economy Research Unit

The Unit was founded in 1992, originally as Culture and Tourism Research Unit, to develop applied and comparative research in the field of regional development. It brings together staff and graduate students from different departments in the University of Liverpool, associated members from other universities as well as from organisations in the public, private and voluntary sectors, and, from 1996/97, visiting fellows. The Unit places special emphasis on regional culture, heritage and identity in the context of social and economic development and environmental issues.

MAIN RESEARCH AREAS

The work of the Unit concentrates on three key areas:

- critical analysis of the development experience in the island of Ireland, to assess implications for other European regions;
- critical analysis of the development experience in other parts of Europe, to assess implications for the island of Ireland; and
- the advancement of theoretical approaches integrating culture and economy, such as, for example, political ethnology, cultural ecology, or endogenous development.

Irish Local and Regional Development

The Unit has conducted research into problems of local and regional development in both parts of the island of Ireland, and on socio-economic aspects of Irish migration to mainland Europe. Topics have included the heritage industry, cultural impacts of immigration, and languages in Northern Ireland, and cultural links between Ireland and Scotland.

European Regional Development

The Unit collaborates closely with institutions and individuals in the regions themselves, and with inter-regional organisations such as the *European Centre for Traditional and Regional Cultures*. Members of the Unit have carried out research in Denmark, Estonia, Finland,

France, Germany, Greece, Poland, Portugal and Spain, as well as Britain. Topics have included cross-border co-operation, migration, political culture, language planning, and cultural tourism.

Theoretical Approaches

Theoretical studies by members of the Unit focus on the construction of integrated models of culture and economic development. The aim of the Unit's work is to advance the theory of endogenous development.

CONFERENCES AND RESEARCH SEMINARS

The Unit organises international conferences which provide a forum for inter-regional experience exchange, bringing together researchers and research users from different parts of Europe. Meetings have been held in Liverpool (1993, 1995), Maynooth/Ireland (1993), Tartu/ Estonia (1994), Budapest (1994), and Llangollen/Wales (1996). A seminar series, the *European Research Colloquium*, was launched in 1996/97. These seminars offer a platform for research carried out by staff, postgraduates, associated members and visiting scholars attached to the Unit, and for the discussion of work in progress at other departments of the University of Liverpool and elsewhere that is of relevance to our research programme.

FURTHER INFORMATION

The Unit has an office at 22 Oxford Street, Liverpool 7. Details of the Unit's work will be made available on the Internet at URL http://www.liv.ac.uk/~ctru/ceruinfo.html from summer 1998. For further information, please contact:

Dr Ullrich Kockel
Institute of Irish Studies, University of Liverpool
P.O.Box 147, Liverpool L69 3BX, England
Tel.: 0044-151-7943075 or 7943833
Fax.: 0044-151-794 3836
e-mail: u.kockel@liverpool.ac.uk